CONVERSATIONS WITH TEXAS WRITERS

Number 16

Jack and Doris Smothers Series in Texas History, Life, and Culture

Conversations with

Texas Writers

Edited by Frances Leonard and Ramona Cearley
for Humanities Texas

Photographs by Ramona Cearley

Introduction and Essays by Joe Holley

UNIVERSITY OF TEXAS PRESS ❧ AUSTIN

Publication of this work was made possible in part by
support from the J. E. Smothers, Sr., Memorial Foundation
and the National Endowment for the Humanities.

This book originated from an
exhibition organized by Humanities Texas.

Printed in the United States of America
First edition, 2005

Library of Congress Cataloging-in-Publication Data

Conversations with Texas writers / edited by Frances Leonard and
Ramona Cearley ; photographs by Ramona Cearley ; introduction
and essays by Joe Holley.
     p.   cm. — (Jack and Doris Smothers series in Texas history, life,
            and culture ; no. 16)
     Includes bibliographical references and index.
     ISBN 0-292-70614-6 (cloth : alk. paper)
     ISBN 0-292-70641-3 (pbk. : alk. paper)

1. American literature — Texas — History and criticism — Theory, etc.
2. Authors, American — 20th century — Interviews.   3. Authors,
American — 21st century — Interviews.   4. Authors, American — Homes
and haunts — Texas.   5. Texas — Intellectual life.   6. Texas — In literature.   7. Authorship.

I. Leonard, Frances McNeely, 1936–   II. Cearley, Ramona, 1956–
III. Holley, Joe.   IV. Series.

PS266.T4C66 2005
810.9'9764'80904 — dc22   2004011369

Contents

Preface

IN OBSERVANCE OF its thirtieth anniversary, Humanities Texas, formerly the Texas Council for the Humanities, is honored to present this volume of interviews with fifty Texas authors. These conversations document the breadth and vitality of current Texas writing while providing extraordinary reflections on writers' lives, choice of subjects, and connections to their real and imagined audiences. The interviews also reveal the influences that have shaped writers' careers, including a fascinating thread of literary inspiration that Texas writers such as J. Frank Dobie and Américo Paredes passed down to succeeding generations.

This book has its genesis in "Texas Writers," one of three humanities exhibitions devoted wholly or in part to Texas authors. Joe Holley's introductory essay was written to accompany the exhibition, and Ramona Cearley's compelling photographs, which depict the authors in their informal settings, were also prominent features of the exhibition.

The selection of writers originated with the exhibition but was not confined to it. Joe Holley and colleagues at the Texas Institute of Letters identified authors to represent the many varieties of literature favored by Texas readers. Our broad definition of "Texas writers" encompasses authors who were born in Texas, as well as those who have lived in Texas for a few years and have produced works during, or as a result of, their tenure in the state.

Any collection of this nature invites questions about the inclusion of some authors and the omission of others. While many fine writers escaped our grasp, usually because time schedules prevented their participation, others were inevitably overlooked. Even so, a remarkable number of the state's leading writers participated in this endeavor. If the present volume finds a receptive audience, a subsequent book will attempt to fill the gap and include an even broader representation of authors.

Texas writers are as varied as the state's landscape, and this volume offers an enchanting glimpse of the state's literary riches. These conversations between people who share a passion for the written word create a tapestry of literary influences—of bright threads that gleam in surprising places. Poet Edward Hirsch states that when he moved to Houston in 1986, he suffered a shock of transition that inspired his poems about Georgia O'Keeffe's coming to terms with the landscape of the Texas Panhandle. But, he observes, the Texas experience extends beyond the western; in its diversity and combination of cultures, Texas has become a radically American place. It is this radical new Texas with its new voices, as well as the traditional Texas of the twentieth century, that shapes this book.

—*Frances Leonard*

Acknowledgments

THE TEXAS WRITERS project is made possible through the strong support of many individuals. Our heartfelt thanks and appreciation to everyone, especially the writers whose voices we celebrate.

Texas Writing

Joe Holley

THE FIRST LITERARY work of merit in Texas was written in Spanish, by a Spaniard, before Texas even existed. *La Relación*, published in Spain in 1542, is a report to the Spanish king, Charles V, from Alvar Nuñez Cabeza de Vaca, whose eight-year-long, six-thousand-mile odyssey back and forth across Texas and the American Southwest is one of the most incredible adventures in recorded history.

La Relación is not only an invaluable guide to pre-European Texas, with acute descriptions of flora and fauna, landforms and tribal customs, but it is also a genuine work of literature. As literary critic Tom Pilkington and other scholars have pointed out, Cabeza de Vaca's report anticipates such genuinely American literary themes as the journey of discovery, both geographical and spiritual, the conflict between races, and a tendency toward the metaphysical. *"La Relación,"* Pilkington observes, "makes Cabeza de Vaca more than just a physical trailblazer; he was also a literary pioneer, and he deserves the distinction of being called Texas's first writer."[1]

Other early Spanish narratives have survived, but it would be a long, long time—nearly three hundred years, in fact—before written accounts of life in Texas began to appear on any kind of regular basis. The first book about Texas published in English appeared in 1833. It was Mary Austin Holley's *Texas: Observations, Historical, Geographical and Descriptive. In a Series of Letters, Written during a Visit to Austin's Colony with a view to a permanent Settlement in that Country, in the Autumn of 1831.*

Holley (1784–1846), a Connecticut native and Stephen F. Austin's cousin, first visited the Austin colony in October 1831, four years after the death of her husband, Horace Holley. Her book of letters, at once a traveler's guide, a personal memoir, and a history, was published in Baltimore. Holley made other visits to Texas, and in 1836 published *Texas*, the first known history of Texas written in English. She also gathered material for a biography of Stephen F. Austin but died of yellow fever before she could finish it.

Although Holley never lived in Texas for any length of time, she was an enthusiastic publicist for the Republic that her esteemed cousin helped create. Her books and her charming family letters are invaluable accounts of early Texas.

In 1857, Frederick Law Olmsted, the urban landscape architect who in later years created New York City's Central Park, also visited Texas and wrote about the experience. His *Journey through Texas* is a detailed and perceptive account of a trip that took him from Natchitoches, Louisiana, along the Old San Antonio Road, through the Texas Hill Country, down to the coastal prairie towns, through San Antonio, Eagle Pass, Houston, and Liberty.

In the years immediately following annexation, the most significant works dealing with Texas were nonfiction accounts of life on the frontier. They include Noah Smithwick's *The Evolution of a State; or Recollections of Old Texas Days* (1900) and *Early Times in Texas* (1892), John Crittenden Duval's account of his escape from the Goliad Massacre. Duval—the "Father of Texas Literature," according to J. Frank Dobie—also wrote *Adventures of Big Foot Wallace* (1872), a collection of tall tales, legends, and straight history.

Holley and other early Texas writers reported. As the generation of pioneers passed from the scene, however, writers began to recollect and reminisce, usually in memoirs or autobiographies. Fiction about Texas began to appear early in the nineteenth century, although according to literary critic Don Graham, "the first Texas novel, *L'Héroïne du Texas: ou, Voyage de madame * * * aux états-Unis et au Mexique,* 'by a Texian,' was published in Paris in French in 1819, but was not available in English until Donald Josep's translation of 1937." [2] The author is identified only by initials.

Toward the end of the century, a woman named Amelia Barr published several novels, although it is her autobiography, based on her experiences in Texas from 1856 to 1867, that is more valuable today. Published in 1913, *All the Days of My Life: An Autobiography. The Red Leaves of a Human Heart,* includes a lengthy section on life in late-nineteenth-century Austin.

One of the more notable turn-of-the-century works was *The Log of a Cowboy* (1903), by Andy Adams, a real-life cowboy turned writer. Adams, a Texas cowboy during the 1880s, wrote his account of an 1882 cattle drive from Brownsville to Montana to counter the romanticized version portrayed in Owen Wister's popular novel *The Virginian,* published the year before. Adams's book evokes the dust, smell, and loneliness that was the cowboy's lot.

William Sydney Porter (1862–1910), the best-known Texas-connected writer of the time, began publishing short stories in 1897, after leaving Texas and after serving a three-year sentence in a federal prison in Ohio. Adopting the pseudonym O. Henry, he moved to New York City, where he published more than three hundred stories, many based on his life in Texas from 1882 until 1896. When he died in 1910, he was arguably the best-known writer in America.

Despite the literary output over the years, the makings of a true Texas literary culture didn't begin to coalesce until the 1920s. The reasons are understandable. "A populace engaged in the rugged business of making homes for themselves in a hostile environment has little time to read or write even the most rudimentary things, much less poetry, fiction and philosophy," Tom Pilkington points out.[3]

The catalyst for the creation of a Texas literary culture was J. Frank Dobie, whose outsized personality and passion for Texas lore made him the dominant figure in the Texas Folklore Society, founded in 1909. The society not only preserved invaluable items from the Texas past, but it also provided a rich trove of material for Texas writers, including Dobie. His first book, *Vaquero of the Brush Country*, appeared in 1929; *Coronado's Children*, in many ways his best book, was published the next year.

Other members of the Texas Folklore Society who made significant contributions to Texas literature include John A. Lomax, who collected songs and ballads from cowboys and ranchers; Dorothy Scarborough, whose best-known novel, *The Wind*, depicts the harshness of life on the Texas frontier, particularly for women; and Ben K. Green, whose best-known book, *Horse Tradin'*, appeared in 1967.

Dobie is important to Texas literature not only because of his literary output — which fell out of favor with critics years ago — but also because he validated art, ideas, and literature for a culture still uneasy with such endeavors. "Mr. Texas" was a bridge connecting the old, rustic ways of life with the life of the mind. His influential bibliography, *A Guide to Life and Literature of the Southwest* (1943), provided something of a canon for the growing body of work that explored the region from a literary perspective.

Larry McMurtry once described most Texas writing before the 1930s as "pioneer architecture — literary sod houses, so to speak." Texas' most accomplished literary craftsman of the middle decades of the century left the state as soon as she could. Katherine Anne Porter (1890–1980) spent her formative years in Kyle, thirteen miles southwest of Austin, but she was always ambivalent about the state. Many of her stories draw on her early childhood years in Texas, but she rarely visited the state throughout her long life and refused membership in the Texas Institute of Letters when the organization was founded in 1936. In a long career that began in the 1920s and ended shortly before her death in 1980, Porter produced some of the finest stories in American literature and, with the possible exception of Larry McMurtry, remains the most acclaimed writer Texas has produced.

Other Texas writers also began to transcend the regional in the 1930s and 1940s.

Perhaps the most notable was George Sessions Perry, a native of Rockdale in Central Texas. *Hold Autumn in Your Hand* (1941), his novel about struggling sharecroppers on a blackland farm during the Great Depression, won both the Texas Institute of Letters Award and the National Book Award, the first Texas novel so honored.

In the immediate postwar years, three Texas writers drawing on the southern tradition in Texas literature produced significant work. William Goyen, William A. Owens, and William Humphrey, all three East Texas natives, produced novels, short stories, and memoirs that had more in common with the rural South of William Faulkner than with the cowboy and cattle country of J. Frank Dobie and other quintessential "Texas writers."

In the late 1950s, a writer who grew up in Fort Worth came back to Texas from sojourns in Spain and New York and took a canoe trip down a portion of the Brazos River. From that trip came John Graves' *Goodbye to a River* (1960), a masterful blend of local history, observations of the natural world, tidbits of Texas lore, and philosophical musings. *Goodbye to a River* still stands as a Texas classic.

The 1960s also marked the debut of the most prolific writer Texas has produced and arguably the most accomplished. Archer City native Larry McMurtry published his first novel, *Horseman, Pass By*, in 1961. In more than three dozen books of fiction and nonfiction since, McMurtry has explored the angst of adolescence, the state's uneasy transition from rural to urban, comedies of manners (Texas style), the weight of history, the burdens of age, the myth of the West, and numerous other themes that will provide dissertation fodder for years to come.

McMurtry's best-selling novel is the epic *Lonesome Dove* (1985), a sprawling work that drew on the old traditions of cattle drives and Texas Rangers and won for McMurtry the Pulitzer Prize. Ironically, McMurtry's paean to a roistering Texas past appeared not long after he published a salty essay in the *Texas Observer* that chided his fellow Texas writers for a lazy nostalgia that blinded them to the messy, complex urban life around them. McMurtry contended later that he wasn't writing off the rural past as a fit subject for Texas writers, only the gauzy, mythic past that bore little resemblance to reality.

Texas writers — novelists, poets, essayists, playwrights, and screenwriters — were moving from rural to urban, both literally and figuratively, even before McMurtry's 1981 essay. As Pilkington points out, most Texas writers today did not grow up in the country or in small towns. Cities are what they know, and increasingly, cities are what they write about.

In the last ten or fifteen years, Texas writers have spilled out of the easy confines that the label "Texas writer" suggests. Today, writers with Texas connections are producing screenplays in Hollywood. They're living and working in Montana, editing magazines in New York, anchoring a news show in Washington, D.C. They're teaching in university writing programs throughout the nation and in Texas, where they become a "Texas writer," at least for a while, despite their Brooklyn or Boston origins. They're writing in particular Texas places—Houston, Dallas, San Antonio, El Paso, and Austin, to be sure, as well as Archer City, Lubbock, and Lufkin—but they're also writing in that no-place called cyberspace.

"The material is here, and it has barely been touched," Larry McMurtry wrote in 1968, in an essay about Texas writers included in his book *In a Narrow Grave*. The material is still here, more than three decades later. At the beginning of a new century, it is being mined, skillfully, by an impressive number of writers—writers who, like Cabeza de Vaca in a time long past, have been marked, for good or ill, by this place called Texas.

1. Tom Pilkington, *State of Mind: Texas Literature and Culture* (College Station: Texas A&M Press, 1999), 14.

2. Don B. Graham, "Literature," in Ron Tyler et al., eds., *The New Handbook of Texas* (Austin: Texas State Historical Association, 1996), 4:218.

3. Pilkington, *State of Mind*, 8.

Wendy Barker

The painting Picnic Island *for me represents
so much that is possible.*

Wendy Barker

It was painted by my mother's first cousin, a man I called Uncle Dick and whom I adored. Uncle Dick would come visit and bring with him a life that I didn't know existed. I would feel as if a wind had come through. It was air. It was language. It connected to me in a way that brought me alive.

Interview by Julie Koppenheffer

Julie Koppenheffer: In your wonderful warm study, you have a painting above your desk. Can you tell us about its genesis?

Wendy Barker: I'm glad you noticed the painting. It is an important one to me. It was painted by my mother's first cousin, a man I always called Uncle Dick and whom I adored. I grew up for the most part in Tucson, Arizona, in a very repressed WASP home with a father who did not like loud talking and loud laughing. Uncle Dick would come visit and bring with him a life that I didn't know existed. Like my mother, he had left England. My mother came to the States in 1939 to marry my father. Uncle Dick had gone to Paris to study painting in the '30s. Then when the war was about to break out, he left Paris and took the long way around. He traveled east, got on a freighter, and eventually got to Los Angeles, hooked up with some artists and arrived in Mexico, where he lived for the rest of his life. He was a portrait painter and, I understand, quite a successful one. He painted portraits to support his real art.

Occasionally, he would come to Tucson and visit and just bring humor and vitality and a sense of another culture. I would feel as if a wind had come through. It was air. It was language. Of course, his British accent and his jokes all brought something to this dreary blue-collar neighborhood I grew up in. He connected to me in a way that brought me alive and in a way that I think no other relative really did. I should say that my father couldn't stand him. My father was a banker, very Presbyterian, if not in practice at least in outlook. My father did not like his visits, but I adored them.

After Daddy died, Mom and I began talking about Uncle Dick, and I suggested we go find him in Mexico. Mom had never been to Mexico, and so we went to Guadalajara to visit Uncle Dick, who was delighted to have us. We had a marvelous visit. I should have had a tape recorder then, listening to the two of them tell stories about growing up in the '30s in England and Europe. These stories I think are lost forever. But at any rate, at that time he was painting this painting. He called it *Picnic Island*, and my mother just amazed me by saying, "Dick, I want to buy this painting for Wendy. Wendy must have this painting." I was overwhelmed because the painting is very bright and vibrant, lots of things going on, and my mother's tastes run to things very quiet and subdued. She does not prefer bright colors. And in fact she had criticized the folk art that I enjoyed and had in my home. But it became clear to me that she understood something through this painting. It was very moving. She bought the painting, and the painting was shipped home. In fact, the poet Denise Levertov was visiting at home when the painting arrived. We went to the airport to pick it up and Denise helped to unpack the painting. She was very moved by it also. The sad part of the story is that Dick died within a year. But I was very, very happy that we got to see him that one last time.

Koppenheffer: Do you look at it as you are writing? Does it connect to something in you?

Barker: I don't look at it as I'm writing. In fact, if our house now were bigger I probably would not have it over my writing space because, as you can see, it's quite busy. I usually work, until the last couple of years, with a much more blank writing space around me. But I've gotten to love it there. I don't look at it as I'm writing, although I'm aware of it as I'm moving around the room not writing, doing things other than writing. I think the painting for me represents so much that is possible. It's like a carnival. With all of these animals, it's like a Noah's Ark. In a way, everything is coming to the Picnic Island. There's a poem, in fact, in *Way of Whiteness* that is really for Uncle Dick. There's a quote from him, "everyone is having a picnic." I think I'm misquoting my own poem, but the idea is that everything *is* a picnic. All of life is a picnic. It is little moments, little bits that you can enjoy even if it's just eating a bit of apple while sitting on a curb with a dog sitting next to you. It's what we've got, and it's a picnic. It is all part of the painting.

PICNIC MAKINGS

Fourth grade cafeteria lunches. If you brought your own you sat on the floor.

A sea of crowded children. I'd look inside
my paper bag for the cookies and sandwich:
cheese, or baloney, or peanut butter and
jelly on a good day. Sucking the last
bit of milk at the bottom of the carton.

When we dated, I would ask him, could we
stop to eat, and he would always say "Sure,
how about here," swing his bright white Healey
into the nearest drive-in. He'd always be ready
to eat, or cook, and even baked the first time
I stayed with him in his trailer. Made me
oatmeal raisin cookies, a double recipe.

In Guadalajara my uncle showed us around.
He knew just where to eat, knew the owners.
In the streets he cried, *Look, people*
are eating wherever they like, they simply
sit down on a curb with their lunch, eat
together right here in the square,
in Guadalajara it is always a picnic!

On the train we ate on the pull-down table,
I trimmed green onions with an army knife,
we shared a quiche we had bought in Chartres.
Cherries. We gathered the pits into a kleenex.
The train swayed from side to side, rocking,
we had the whole compartment to ourselves,
and finished two bottles of wine, easy.

South Padre Island, the end of August.
On the sand you hold a spoon to my mouth,
soft white ice cream on the spoon. I take
the cold in my mouth, hold it on my tongue

before I swallow. You put your spoon back
into the cup, offer again, Would you like
some more? Here. Have some more.

—"Picnic Makings," in *Way of Whiteness*
(San Antonio: Wings Press, 2000), 65–66.
Reprinted by permission of Wings Press.

Sarah Bird

I blithely wrote about seducing my parish priest, kidnapping my own child, shoplifting at Kmart, and stealing my mother-in-law's meat loaf recipe.

Sarah Bird

Well, maybe not the last one, but they all taught me the invaluable lessons of how to fill a page, how to write in a specific voice, for a specific audience, and how to deal with rejection.

Interview by Henry Mills

Henry Mills: Growing up as a member of a military family, you say that you had a less-than-conventional upbringing. How did that upbringing affect your development as a person, as a writer?

Sarah Bird: It made me an outsider twice-removed, once by temperament, then again by virtue of moving around so much and always being the "new girl." As I wrote in *The Yokota Officers Club*, there is this myth that being a military kid, moving so much, makes a child a social genius. From the brats I met when I toured after the book was published, I'd say that is true for natural extroverts. I was extremely shy, and moving sort of bumped me from shy to catatonic. The gift of being shy, though, is that you have these lifelong, ongoing discussions with the one person you can talk to, yourself. In my case, much of the internal soundtrack was snarky comments, so I had a lifetime of snappy patter built up by the time I started to write. In retrospect, it's no accident that I chose to study anthropology, journalism, and photography. Outsider 101!

The other half of the military question is the family. In my case, thank God, we weren't a standard GI— Government Issue — family. I doubt that many other families had *The Well of Loneliness, Tea and Sympathy,* and *Tobacco Road* along with the Harvard Classics on their bookshelves. The other great gift I got from my family was a sense of subversion and the belief that a person could say almost anything if they got a laugh saying it.

Mills: Describe the influence that reading had on you as you grew up. What books were important to you?

Bird: Books became the friends that I never had to leave behind. They were my comfort. No matter how tough things got as the "new girl," I only had to think of Eliza in *Uncle Tom's Cabin* jumping from ice floe to ice floe or Anne Frank writing in her diary or Dorothy tumbling through a cyclone to know that other girls had faced much worse than having no one to sit with in a school cafeteria. I cannot overstate how important it was that the books I read always, always, starred girls. In a world before Mia Hamm, where the heroes of all the baseball and basketball games we watched were boys, and where on an overseas military base the only people who had important jobs were men, books showed me worlds where the stories were about girls, where girls faced challenges and showed courage and character and, sometimes, triumphed: a world where girls were heroines.

My favorite was Dorothy of *The Wizard of Oz* [series]. Dorothy Gale should be made the patron saint of military children. In book after book, little Dorothy was uprooted from her home in Kansas and thrust into one strange world after another populated by strange characters.

Mills: How did you become a writer? Was writing something you planned for as a vocation?

Bird: Essentially, I backed into a writing career and was being paid as a writer far before I ever had the confidence or training to call myself a writer. I worked in France as an au pair when I was nineteen. Theoretically, I was there to learn French, but the only person in the entire country whose French was worse than mine was the three-month-old baby I was taking care of. Given *bébé*'s limited conversational abilities, I was not making any colossal strides in *le Français* so I started reading these photo romance magazines they have there so I could learn something besides *Où est la bibliothèque?* Anyway, it occurred to me, while reading how Babette loved Guillame but was married to Jean-Luc, that someone must have gotten paid to write these stories. When I returned *chez moi* I looked for a comparable market, which turned out to be pulp fiction.

As I read *True Confessions, Modern Love,* and *Bronze Thrills,* a thought popped into my head that hadn't popped in when I'd read *To Kill a Mockingbird* or *The Scarlet Letter,* and that thought was, "I can do this." Better yet, all the stories were anonymous, so I didn't have the enormous hurdle to leap that most beginning writers do, the crushing terror that this thing is going to be associated with you, will represent and define you. No, with absolutely no one looking over my shoulder, no one correcting so much as a comma, no one "workshopping" any of my "pieces," I blithely wrote about seducing my parish priest, kidnapping my own child, shoplifting at Kmart, and stealing my mother-in-law's meat loaf recipe. Well, maybe not the last one, but they all taught me the invaluable lessons of how to fill a blank page, how to write in a specific voice, for a specific audience, and how to deal with rejection.

In retrospect, it seems clear that I arranged my life so that I was always writing for the rent. This gave me the cover, the excuse and justification, to do what I didn't even have the nerve to admit to myself, that I wanted to write. I made my living for several years before I had the courage to come out and admit that, yes, I was a writer. There are two paths to making a living as a writer. The major one is teaching at a university; the other one is everything else. I'm on the everything else path, where you write whatever pays the rent—magazine articles, romances, mysteries, scripts—then steal time from that to write what's most meaningful to you. For me, that's the genre of midlist literary novels.

Mills: In looking at your novels, you've said you see your fiction as "more anthropological than psychological or sociological." Can you explain?

Bird: My books are more anthropological because I tend to fall in love with a world, with a culture, more than I do with a character. That's why I get excited about sharing that world, portraying that world, capturing that world, and then writing about a person operating in that world, how it affects that character and what happens.

Mills: Your work has been noted for its playful wit and wry sense of the absurd. Where do these come from?

Bird: Repression, probably. I would say that my basic orientation comes from repression, from growing up in a very regimented world and finding solace in the little subversive activities that we had [in our family]—humor, primary, foremost among the subversive activities—and the way we were allowed to communicate, could communicate. I would say that that is where they originally come from.

Mills: What led you into screenwriting? Can you tell us about particular successes? Failures? Interesting projects?

Bird: Like most of my career, I backed into this as well. I was halfway through *Boyfriend School* when I realized that I didn't know my male protagonist, Gus. I learn who my characters are by writing about them, and since his identity had to remain a secret because of a plot demand, I hadn't gotten to know him. Now, I could have rewritten the novel from his point of view, but that seemed like an awful lot of work. I'd seen a screenplay and remembered all those glorious chunks of empty, white space and decided that that was what I would do: write the story from his POV as a screenplay. Dialogue, a few stage directions. I find out who this guy is and I finish the novel. So I performed this writing exercise—*et voilà*—ended up with a screenplay. Not really knowing what one did with screenplays, I sent it to my literary agent in New York. She sent it to the Mafia, I mean CAA, Creative Artists Agency, and things began to happen.

Had this screenplay *not* been purchased and produced, I would have embarked upon a swanky film career since it attracted a lot of attention pretty much up until the moment it was made as a massively mediocre movie. That disillusionment, combined with the arrival of my son, sent me back to novels until a friend told me a fascinating story she'd uncovered about a black woman after the Civil War who disguised herself as a man and served two years in the Buffalo Soldiers. As many times as I tried to turn away from this woman, from this story— telling myself [and] my friend that I had never done anything historical, the story would be better served by a black writer, I didn't have the time—it pulled me back. Finally, almost as a way to exorcise this tale, I wrote it as screenplay. The general wisdom came back to me that there was no longer a "crossover" audience for a story like this. But that script did reignite my career in film, made me many friends in Hollywood, and got me many jobs.

It was during an unmedicated moment on the long hot drive to Harlingen, Texas, that we all, all us sibs, realized we hated our ultra-Hibernian Catholic names. No one else at our new schools would be named after saints famous for being enucleated or having their tongues plucked out with pliers. We wanted regular names. So, as Moe passed around the potty seat, we rechristened ourselves with the most normal, most American names we could each think of. The twins, Frances Xavier and Bryan Patrick, chose Buzz and Abner. Joseph Anthony, just three at the time, selected Bob, since it was not only a great name and easy to spell but also his favorite aquatic activity. No one wanted me to change Bernie. Mary Colleen, our youngest sister, declared that henceforth she would be known as Nancy, her book-loving soul released in ecstasy at the thought of sharing Nancy Drew's name.

"Nancy?" We'd all hooted in unison. We'd already given her the perfect name, Bosco, when she was two and loved Bosco Chocolate Syrup, and we weren't swapping it for some girl detective in a roadster.

—*The Yokota Officers Club*
(New York: Knopf, 2001), 5.

Jay Brandon

The most enjoyable part about writing is writing the lives that you haven't been able to live.

Jay Brandon

That's one of the great pleasures of writing for me. It's always been the peripheral character that I like best, some shopkeeper or hairstylist, for example. They don't know they are a minor character; for all they know, your main character is just passing through their lives.

Interview by Julie Koppenheffer

Julie Koppenheffer: You have a master's degree in writing from Johns Hopkins University as well as experience as an attorney with the district attorney's office in Bexar County and the Fourth Circuit Court of Appeals. How many novels have you written?

Jay Brandon: There are ten novels that have been published and one nonfiction book.

Koppenheffer: Among the books, do you have a special attachment to any character?

Brandon: It is never the main character who is my favorite. For me, the favorite character is usually the most bland, because that has to be the character who behaves sensibly and is pursuing some rational goal. It's always some peripheral character that I like best, some shopkeeper or hairstylist, for example, that a more central character has to go and ask some question of. You can use peripheral characters in that one scene, display all their tics, and indicate what's wrong with their day. They don't know they are a minor character; for all they know, your main character is just passing through their lives.

Those "minor" characters are the ones I really like and some of my books have gotten skewed because of that. I've introduced some minor character whom I ended up liking so much that I made them more of a major character. One of my favorites is in a novel called *Local Rules*. In that one I liked the two main characters, the lawyer and the court reporter. I liked them as a couple; I liked the relationship of the characters and that's usually the case. In *Angel of Death*, there is a character named Malachi Reese, who is the villain, and I liked him a lot. I was surprised when a couple of reviews described him as "pure evil," which I didn't feel at all. In fact I was sympathetic toward him.

Koppenheffer: Is there any character that is most like you?

Brandon: No. I really don't do that. I'm bored with myself. That's one of the motivations for writing. I don't think there is any of me in the characters. In one novel, *Fade the Heat*, the story was told by one character named Mark Blackwell. A lot of people think that that was my voice and thought I was like him, but in fact he's very different from me. In the first book I wrote about him, he was ten years older than I was, he'd been practicing law a lot longer than I had, he was very cynical about the system, which did reflect how I felt at the time, but his career had not been like mine, and his life had not been like mine. There really wasn't much of anything of me in him, except perhaps parts of the voice.

People always make the mistake that I must be writing about myself. For me the most enjoyable part about writing is writing the lives that you haven't been able to live. That's one of the great pleasures of writing for me. I imagine that acting is the same way in that it allows you to live other lives that you haven't lived.

Koppenheffer: You have another book scheduled for release. What is it about? How do you decide on the title?

Brandon: It starts off with a scene which two characters see from two different perspectives. They see the same scene as two absolutely different things; that's the mystery of this book. In this one they are witnesses to a killing or at least a death, but they see it in completely different ways. The whole book leads to an explanation of that. I have a great title, which I love, but I'm not sure it will work. I want to call it "Sliver Moon," which just reeks of atmosphere as far as I'm concerned, when the moon is a tiny slice like that. But I know that on a book jacket, people will look and think it says "Silver Moon," which sounds like a romance novel. [The book was published under the title *Sliver Moon* —Ed.]

Koppenheffer: Do you see the world in all its complexity in terms of how you define yourself as a novelist?

Brandon: It seems more and more complex the older you get, doesn't it? You run into people you knew from different contexts, and they are serving different functions in different parts of their lives. I think I do see complexity, as a writer. I've been writing since I was about ten years old, and this week I noticed that I would see something and turn it into a phrase, not into a scene. That's what I see when I'm writing; I see everything happening when I'm writing, and then I have to describe it for myself.

Koppenheffer: So you're condensing reality into a phrase?

Brandon: I guess so, or just trying to turn a phrase. I'm going to get to use some more of that soon because I'm to write a serialized novel for the newspaper, two installments a week. This will be a great outlet. I will be able to use all those phrases that come to me all day long, more than I do now. [The novel, *Grudge Match*, was published serially in the *San Antonio Express-News* and in 2004 also published by Forge Books (New York) — Ed.]

The court reporter looked him up and down again just as quickly but with a touch less scorn. Without an apology or an invitation, she turned and crossed the street. Jordan followed.

"I have never altered a record in my life," Laura Stefone said as he caught up.

"Then you have very selective hearing."

"Maybe you're just used to having transcripts cleaned up for you. Do the court reporters in San Antonio do that for prosecutors?"

"No." But the question set him thinking.

"Maybe you need an elocution class then."

"Perhaps," Jordan said distinctly, popping the t's, "you—could—suggest—a—teacher."

—*Local Rules*
(New York: Pocket Books, 1995), 84.

Bobby Byrd — Cinco Puntos Press

We call ourselves the house that La Llorona *built.*

Bobby Byrd

Storyteller Joe Hayes came up with the idea of doing a bilingual edition of La Llorona, the Weeping Woman. *That book is our best seller. It's a little* librito. *It's a six-dollar book. We sold almost seven thousand copies of that book, and it continues to sell.*

Interview by Teresa Taylor

Teresa Taylor: How did Cinco Puntos Press get started? What were your early years like?

Bobby Byrd: We got started because both my wife and I were technical writers, and we were desperately looking for some way to get out of the nine-to-five job and concentrate on our own writing. We had always been interested in language and knew a lot of writers who we felt, because they live in the Southwest, were not receiving the type of attention they should. We knew absolutely nothing about publishing, and every time we shoot ourselves in the foot, we learn something new not to do. One of them, sadly enough, is not to publish many books of poetry. I say sadly because I am a poet.

Taylor: Was that the first book that you published, a book of poems?

Byrd: The first book that we published was a book of poems by my friend Joseph Somoza, *Backyard Poems*. It was a little *librito*. The next two books that we published were important to us because they defined the way our press was going to develop. We published *Winners on the Pass Line*, by Dagoberto Gilb, who was at that time living in El Paso and had just won a big James D. Phelan award in California. He could not get it published, so we told him we would, and we did. That was the adult literary end of our publishing. The other book involves a very close friend Joe Hayes, a bilingual storyteller. Joe and I used to sit on the back porch and drink wine and talk about publishing, and he came up with the idea of doing a bilingual edition of *La Llorona, the Weeping Woman*. That book is our best seller of all time. It's a little *librito* also, thirty-two pages. It's a six-dollar book. We sold almost seven thousand copies of that book, and it continues to sell. We call ourselves the house that *La Llorona* built. And so those two books, *Winners on the Pass Line* and *La Llorona, the Weeping Woman*, signify the two branches of our press.

Taylor: One of the things I wonder as I look through your books is where do you find the incredible talent? The graphic artists are just amazing. The use of color is phenomenal. How have you gone about locating the talent you need to produce these books?

Byrd: We have always tried as much as we can to use artists and designers that live in El Paso. El Paso has an abundance of artists and a wonderful creative community. With one or two or three exceptions, all of our children's books have been illustrated by Paseños. Lee and I have been writers in the Southwest for thirty years. We've made a lot of contacts and friends, and we have a sense of mission. When we started, we were thinking of the American Southwest, but as we continued to publish, we realized we live in the U.S./Mexico border region. We did a book by Debbie Nathan, *Women and Other Aliens: Essays from the U.S./Mexico Border.* Working on that book with Debbie was an eye-opening experience because it made us realize the political sense of our press: We really are not of the American Southwest so much as of the U.S./Mexico border.

We did that book and later my daughter, Susannah Mississippi, and I edited the book called *The Late Great Mexican Border,* which is a collection of essays by people from Brownsville to San Diego and Tijuana. We felt that the border is presented stereotypically in both the United States and in Mexico. You have people viewing the border through the eyes of people from Mexico City or New York City, San Francisco or Austin, but not from the border itself. So we selected essays written by *fronterizos.* That book again opened doors into Mexico, and we started doing literature of Mexico.

Taylor: How do you see the border changing?

Byrd: Since we moved to El Paso in 1978, two important things have become apparent. First, the border has become more militarized because of the drug and immigration laws and because they've erected a fence through El Paso, Nogales, Tijuana, and all the border towns. The communities along the border, which had a symbiotic relationship, have been torn apart because of drug laws, immigration laws, fences, and phobias of the United States and of Mexico. NAFTA, of course, is a situation where everything can move north and south, except human beings and drugs. Right now helicopters are all over, flying over our houses. The border is becoming much more of a dividing line than it has ever been in the history of the United States or of Mexico.

Taylor: Money and the military can move, but human beings cannot. I am curious about your response after observing the "Texas Writers" exhibit, which presents El Paso as a literary region or perhaps a cultural region in Texas. In your observation, what is the uniqueness of the El Paso area?

Byrd: Paseños would say we don't really feel part of Texas, especially culturally and politically. You come to Austin and you see all the money spent on public works, and you go to El Paso and you see the lack of money spent on public works. You can see that El Paso and the border region have been the stepchild of Texas and of the United States for centuries now. El Paso does have a very vibrant literary and artistic community, separate from the rest of Texas. We try to make the point that though this separation may seem to be our weakness, it's a chief strength. So we emphasize the fact that we are in the U.S./Mexico border. That is a unique way of marketing Cinco Puntos Press.

   Taylor: The National Endowment for the Arts withdrew funding from one of the books that you published, *The Story of Colors*, and then fortunately the Lannan Foundation funded it. Tell us the story of how that happened and how that affected your press.

   Byrd: The thing with the NEA is sort of a comedy of errors, and it's the best thing that ever happened to us. We had the opportunity to do this book that was illustrated by an indigenous Mexican woman, Domitila Domínguez, and we jumped at the chance. It was a natural book for us to publish, because we do bilingual children's literature. This is a Mayan myth that is retold by Subcomandante Marcos. It is just a beautiful book with no political content. It is the story of colors, how colors came into the world and how each should have a place in the universe.

   It was during the funding cycle of the NEA, so I call up Cliff Becker at the National Endowment. We have these several books, and I said, "Actually, Cliff, the one that we would like the NEA to fund, because it's the most expensive, is *The Story of Colors/La historia de los colores*, but one of the problems is that it is by Subcomandante Marcos. Even though he has refused all copyright privileges, it's a story that he has told." He says, "Ah, don't worry. The NEA has this long tradition of funding translated works by Latin American writers. There is no problem whatsoever."

   So we get the galleys done, and we send them to all of the reviewers just as we do all of our books. One of the reviewers was Julia Preston, at the *New York Times* Mexico Bureau. She loved the book. She called me up and we had this long conversation. Being a mother, her first question was whether I could say this was a children's book. I said that [it] is what people call illustrated folktales. It's really not a children's book, but that is the category that bookstores put them in. Anyway, at the end of our long, interesting conversation, she says, "Don't you think it's weird that the NEA is funding a book written by a revolutionary opposing a country that the United States funds?" I said, "Not really." And I went through this whole thing that NEA has a long tradition funding translated works by Latin American authors, as opposed to U.S. authors, that have a long tradition of being politically motivated. She says, "Do you mind if I call the National Endowment?" I said, "No, be my guest," and I gave her the phone number.

Within two hours I had calls from several people, one being Cliff Becker. I said, "Cliff, I have been telling you about this for some time." He says, "But you did not tell me about Marcos." And I say, "Yes, the guy with the mask." "Oh, *that* Marcos!" About an hour later, a lady called me from the PR department of the NEA. I asked, "What is the problem?" and she said, in effect, "They are afraid that the right-wing newspapers will use this as an issue." I said, "That is absurd." She said, "We are sending our budget to the Congress." It was right at the budget cycle. She says, "Don't worry about it." But the next morning Cliff calls me and said, "The NEA has decided to rescind the grant for that book." I hit the ceiling, and I try to get in touch with the director of the NEA. He did not call me for a few hours, so I call Julia Preston of the *New York Times*. She said, "Bobby, I am sorry. I did not realize this was going to happen." She was really contrite about it. She called me back about an hour later and said, "Look, if you don't tell this to anybody, this will be on the front page of the *New York Times* tomorrow." Who can I call, El Paso? She got the exclusive. It was on the front page of the *New York Times*. At five o'clock in the morning people started calling. The first person to call was somebody from *Good Morning America*. We sold so many books.

Like I said at the beginning, this is the best thing that ever happened because we got all of that attention. It shows what the media can do. It's amazing to us, the power of the *New York Times*. The presence it has in the American consciousness. Part of it goes back to the monad, one-eyed media governing our lives, but in this instance it was very good for Cinco Puntos.

Taylor: How can a small independent press survive when publishing is increasingly centralized under a few corporations?

Byrd: Since the big presses are owned by even bigger companies, they only look at the bottom line. Because their expenses are so high, they can only take books that promise to sell a certain number of copies. The smaller niche books, which sell anywhere from two to twenty-five hundred to ten thousand copies, they won't touch. So those books are available to small presses. Now in small-press literature, a lot of those presses are nonprofit. Cinco Puntos is not a nonprofit; it's a for-profit organization. We have been lucky to have developed a niche in bilingual children's literature, because it's a huge growing population thirsty for things that deal with their culture and their ways of understanding. They really want these books. It was by chance that we fell into it, but that is our backbone.

Because the book industry is notoriously cyclical, a book of poems or a book of fiction has a very short life span. But children's books have a long life span if they are good. So our books continue to sell, and we are developing a long backlist. So to answer your question, a small press needs a backlist that sells, and that is not going to be poetry. It's not going to be fiction, unless it is a certain special fiction. It's going to be nonfiction. It's going to be children's books, or it's going to be certain elements that sell to a niche market.

Taylor: I'm sure you're aware that Arte Público, which publishes out of Houston, has a recovery project that is reconstructing Hispanic literary history in the United States. One of the things they validate is the importance of small presses in keeping that literary tradition alive. How do you see yourselves fitting into the history of press and publication, and where do you see that future going?

Byrd: I am of the opinion that in the next fifteen or twenty years all of the large presses are just going to collapse. They are going to fall back into smaller pieces because, with technology, that one-eyed way of looking at the world is not going to survive. One book that I think is particularly relevant is Dee Hock's *The Birth of the Chaordic Age*. He makes two points: to continue to exist, world civilization is in desperate need of new metaphors; and once it finds these new metaphors it can go about the business of *discovering*, not *building*, new institutions. He states that the old institutional metaphors have long lost their usefulness. Presses like Cinco Puntos, which seem to be at the edge of nowhere figuratively and literally, are really providing extremely valuable insights for this process of finding new metaphorical structures. We are multiculturalists, and we look elsewhere.

A wonderful example is our book *The Story of Colors* by Subcomandante Marcos. It's based on Mayan understanding. El Viejo Antonio shows Marcos how all the colors in the world have a reason for existence, and he uses a macaw bird as his metaphorical construct. Curiously enough, this story contains the exact opposite meaning of the Tower of Babel in the Bible.

Taylor: The NEA defunded *The Story of Colors* due to its connection with Subcommandante Marcos. Does that imply that cultural funding should be a component of U.S. foreign policy? What role do you see the small presses playing in our national culture and freedom of the press?

Byrd: U.S. culture generally considers art and literature an accessory to our political and societal apparatus. But what we are beginning to witness is that the arts are becoming a fundamental element of political debate. Artists of all varieties believe more and more strongly that our understanding needs to have a place at the table. So, small alternative presses are happy to provide our artists a forum.

Taylor: You said that you and your wife are both authors and that you started the press in order to have more time to write. How is that going?

Byrd: Alternative presses are like a tar baby. You know the story of a tar baby—where you kick it and your foot gets stuck—so it's really hard to break away from the press to do things. But the interesting thing about a small press is that it is a really intellectual activity, so it feeds a part of you. It's creative in nature, but it also gives you this energy to write more, although you don't have the time to write more. I think both of us are significant writers, and we need time to fulfill that need in ourselves. Lee has this wonderful book, *My Sister Disappears*, which received all sorts of awards. It's sort of like the Jane Bold books. She does not write a lot, but when she writes, it seems almost perfect. Cinco Puntos Press was able recently to buy a building. We want to make it possible for one of us to stay home in the morning so that we can write.

Taylor: How do you mix family with business? Your children are involved in the business and live in close proximity, and it seems that there are a lot of dynamics that would need to be managed.

Byrd: A lot of people, especially our friends, think it is sort of odd and peculiar and dangerous, and it is all of those things. But it is a long tradition in human history to have family businesses. There have always been family businesses. The corporate world that separates everybody is a recent development in human history. What we are doing is really rooted in human history.

But it is difficult. There are a lot of problems that come up because you don't want to step on somebody's toes. At the same time, it is very interesting. Having a family business makes it more mortal. It is quite capable of dying not only because of business factors but also because of family and cultural matters. Cinco Puntos, I will tell you, is always on the verge of failing. We have been in critical situations that we have been lucky to get out of. Cash flow is an incredible problem. For the first time, Lee and I are getting paid on a regular basis. Before we were always living on all sorts of odd incomes.

"THE HANDSOME STRANGER"

The dark stranger in the fancy Mexican hat
strolled like one of Diego Rivera's
héroes de la Revolución
on a Sunday afternoon in the Alameda
into my neighbor's backyard
where a pit bull was barking
and yelping away his sorrows.
The handsome stranger crossed himself
and spit into the afternoon dust.

An old-fashioned silvery gun
slipped into his strong right hand
like a six-petaled flower, blooming—
                              BANG
                    BANG
and the door slammed shut
on that poor dog's life.
Sure, the dog squirmed a bit
in its complete surprise,
blood leaking out of its
gigantic pit bull grin.
Speaking very slowly
so even I could understand
his sweet-smelling Spanish,
the man told me that nobody
should let a dog live like that,
chained up in the radiance
of a hot desert day,
no water, no food, nothing.
"I don't think the dog
even had a name," he said.
The handsome stranger scowled at me:
"Where in the hell have you been?
Can't you even love a dog?"
Then he walked away,
the barrel of his muscular
six-shooter smoking
hot creamy juices
like the sweet milk
from the Virgin's breast.

—"The Handsome Stranger," *The Price of Doing Business in
Mexico: And Other Poems* (El Paso: Cinco Puntos Press, 1998), 102–103.
Reprinted by permission of Cinco Puntos Press.

Lee Byrd — Cinco Puntos Press

I write so slowly that life could be a whirl,
and I just poke along at it.

Lee Byrd

I always kept journals. With the Dobie Paisano Fellowship, the first month I went back through fifteen years of journals and culled out the things that were important to stories I wanted to work on; then I separated them into topics. That was a nice way to enter into the fellowship, this wonderful muddling through my journals.

Interview by Teresa Taylor

Teresa Taylor: Your husband, Bobby, said that before founding Cinco Puntos Press you both were technical writers. So you made the great escape from a corporate environment to a creative and cultural environment of your own making. How did you accomplish that?

Lee Byrd: One of us has had to work outside the house for a long time, and at first it was Bobby and then it was me. I don't know if Bobby told you of the fire that our kids were in. Our boys were in a fire when they were four and seven. They were in Galveston for three months in the hospital. They were really badly burned. That snatched me totally out of our life and to this life at the hospital. Every month they had to go back for surgeries; then it became every year. I was emotionally drained by that, and he was simultaneously drained by tech writing. We switched. He started being at-home mom, and I became the tech writer. His boss let us do that. That was one of the transitions that we made.

Then he decided to stay home to run the business. For a long time when people thought of the business, they thought that it was Bobby's business. Even people that were close to us somehow had the sense that it was Bobby's business. But I saw it as both of ours, because even though I was working out of the house, I served the purpose of supporting it. It came as a surprise to me, when I finally started working at home, that people considered the business Bobby's. I was a little testy about that. It took me a while to figure out they just didn't know. Now people know that we run the business together.

Taylor: I've seen that happen with political activists, where to be successful you really need one person who is bringing in the income, but it's a collaboration between both people.

Byrd: People only see the out-front person. But there was some part of me that realized when it all happened that I felt really testy about it, and I was cranky and needed to set people straight. I was going through a period where I needed to get that clear. Now it is not an issue anymore.

Taylor: So how have you maintained your creative energy, especially through really hard times with your children being in the fire?

Byrd: I write so slowly that life could be a whirl, and I just poke along at it. It just takes me a long time to write. Actually the fire was and continues to be an inspiration to me. At first it was just the story itself. Then it was a metaphor of being burned and starting a new life — totally different than what you had to begin with. Being born, having another chance to have a life except in a very corrupted body or a body that people don't recognize as fresh and new, all those things. So I actually write about fire a lot. I am just so slow. I go through periods where I feel so active writing. Then things will get really busy, and I just stop writing.

Taylor: Bobby had suggested that the press feeds his creative impulse, but it sounds as though you allocate — that a certain amount of time goes to the family or to the press, and the creative part of yourself needs its own time separate from those.

Byrd: Yes, except when I do brochures or fliers, when working on books. That's all creative work, but it's not the type of work that interests me. My neighborhood is really interesting to me, and I write about my neighborhood and my neighbors. The children in the neighborhood are incredibly interesting to me, and I like to do stuff with them. Then this thing about fire, I just can't quite get the story to work. I compartmentalize a lot more. I used to feel that writing was something I had to do to prove myself, but now I don't feel that way.

Taylor: Do you do journal writing?

Byrd: Yes, I always have. Mostly it's prayers. I am a Bible reader; so I read the Bible and if things interest me or they strike me as they apply to my life, I make a note. But I always kept journals. With the Dobie Paisano Fellowship that was one of the wonderful things I got to do. The first month I went back through fifteen years of journals and culled out the things that were important to stories I wanted to work on; then I separated them into topics, like the neighborhood, or the fire, or my mother, or whatever I wanted to work on. That was a nice way to enter into the fellowship, which fortunately was six months. The first month was this wonderful sort of muddling through my journals.

Taylor: That does sound wonderful. I get the sense that your creativity comes from a strong interior sense of self. How do you balance that against your national presence as a well-respected press that on occasion receives national coverage?

Byrd: I think that Bobby is much more of a public figure, and he is very comfortable making public commentaries. I am much more of a Bible reader than I am a newspaper reader. I am generally out of it, in terms of news. Susie Byrd, our daughter, is a lot like Bobby, and politics interest her a lot. During *The Story of Colors* funding controversy, people would call up. I always was fearful that I would say something that would give a twist that wasn't true. I am much more private. You ask me what is going on in my neighborhood, and I can tell you. You ask them what is going on in the world, and they will tell you. I am just not that interested. But the neighborhood? I am interested.

Taylor: They probably don't know as much as you do about what is going on in the neighborhood either. It's a very different way of observing life.

Byrd: Susie was saying this morning, laughing, that it must be weird to wake up in the morning and sense that somebody from the neighborhood is sleeping in the alley drunk and to know that is true. And I know it is true, because I have been watching him for a couple of weeks. He has been on a really bad drunk. He is one of the really nice persons that I like a lot. I am concerned, but I am not concerned in the sense that I am going to change him. I am interested to see what his heart is doing, what is going on, how he is. It interests me, and I like that more than what is going on in the world.

Taylor: Artists can have that type of interest. They key into a particular aspect of life in its minuteness.

Byrd: It's like that a lot, although the other thing you asked me about is tech writing. My sister has schizophrenia, so I am in this national alliance for the mentally ill. I have been writing grants for them. Grant writing, when it comes together, oddly enough has this creative edge to it. I was totally surprised that would happen. But when a grant comes together, you know what your organization — which is twelve parents of real severely mentally ill people — can manage. It's pretty astounding. When it works, it serves some sweet need.

Taylor: As the nuts-and-bolts person at Cinco Puntos, what do you do?

Byrd: I do all the editing. I make sure that we do double edit checks, not just me. Because by the time I finish with the book, I've seen it too much to find any interest in it. I do the production. I work with the designer. I make sure we are on schedule.

Taylor: What are the special issues involved in publishing bilingual books?

Byrd: There are a lot of them. One of them particularly is that the illustrator we choose is someone who captures the culture. The books that Cinco Puntos does are not re-renderings of *Little Red Riding Hood* or *Hansel and Gretel*.

[Take] for instance a book like *Little Gold Star*, which is a Cinderella *cuento*, but it's a Cinderella *cuento* that originated in Spain and then came to northern New Mexico. We wanted an illustrator that would capture the culture of northern New Mexico.

And then there is the language. We have been criticized nationally for using Spanish that is very regional. So we go to New York, and we get a Spanish speaker that we know in New York to check our translation. Then we weigh her comments again. If everyone in Texas says *troca* instead of whatever it is in New York, we are going to pick the Texas word because we want to be regional, but we also want our books to be read in other parts of the country. There is delicate balancing with the Spanish language. The translation has to be right culturally. It has to be regional, but not too regional.

Taylor: Capturing the particular nuances of the language is an important part of preserving this culture.

Byrd: But we have to be really careful. The lady in New York from Scholastic Books, who is like the guru of Spanish language publishing, is always saying our books could sell a lot more. But it would not interest us; it would bore us. We really have to know that we love the books we are doing. We have to feel satisfied with the book. We just have to really love it and put our weight behind it.

It was right around that time, during the summer after the prom and during the beginning of the next school year when she went to high school, that the Emily we knew disappeared and another Emily came to take her place. This new Emily got bad grades and put on weight. She was moved down to all the lowest-level classes and was afraid to go to school. She would leave the house in the morning when all the rest of us went off too, but she would only go as far as Park Avenue and then she would turn and come back home, lying on her bed all day with the covers pulled over her head.

Ma in terror took her to doctors and psychiatrists to have her evaluated, but they had no answers, had no idea where the Most Popular Girl at Maplewood School had gone to. They gave her tests and asked her many questions and they told Ma that this new girl was very slow, with a very low IQ, and that she would probably never get out of high school and would almost certainly never hold a job. . . .

It wasn't anything at all that you could put your finger on, though Ma, even now, when she is eighty-three and Emily is nearly fifty, still studies where she can at last put the blame.

It was only that someone else had come to live where Emily once lived, a someone heavy and distracted, whose mind moved like lead, who could not remember, whose medium seemed to be no longer air, but water, and whose movements to displace that water took time and enormous and visible effort. That person took up residence where Emily had been, pressing her slowly out and away, and though we hoped always, whether out of love or hatred or frustration, that the Emily we knew—that lithe and freckled ballerina, that astonishing beauty in the white prom dress—would return, she never has.

—My Sister Disappears: Stories and a Novella
(Dallas: Southern Methodist University Press, 1993), 97–98.

Viola Canales

*These stories illustrate the power of using
the imagination to transform difficulties
into opportunities filled with hope
and enrichment and even magic.*

Viola Canales

Part of the Spanish culture revolves around the telling of stories. I had this wonderful grandmother with whom I grew up. She was full of stories. Conjuring her up in my stories somehow made her come alive for me.

Interview by Graham Stewart

Graham Stewart: Tell us about your collaboration with schools as part of the "New Voices of Texas Author Tour."

Viola Canales: The book tour had four Latino writers visit high schools in Austin, McAllen, and Dallas. The school that I visited in Austin was LBJ High School. I was very surprised when I received an e-mail from the LBJ librarian saying, "We're very excited that you are coming, but could you give your presentation in Spanish?" I was a little thrown because this was a high school. I e-mailed back saying that my book was in English, but that I'd love to talk in Spanish.

It brought me back to my experiences as a student, as a child. When I started first grade, I grew up with my *abuelita*, my grandmother, and we couldn't speak English at home. When I went to first grade during the early 1960s, we couldn't speak Spanish in the classroom, or even on the playground. I had a difficult time because my teacher did not know any Spanish. When I spoke to the students at LBJ High School, I told them that they were very, very lucky, for not only did they now have books such as *Orange Candy Slices* and books by Sandra Cisneros where they could learn about their culture, but they weren't being penalized for speaking Spanish anymore. This is wonderful, because part of the Spanish culture revolves around the telling of stories.

Stewart: Were you surprised by the class at all, or did you feel at home?

Canales: I felt very much at home because I could relate to these students. They asked me to focus on the story "The Feather," which is about an angel, and also on the stories regarding my grandmother. I used that to connect with them.

I had this wonderful grandmother with whom I grew up. As a child, I actually shared a bedroom with her. She was full of stories. She was an incredible storyteller, but she would also use stories to get me to do things. For example, when I was playing late with my dolls, she would say, "Viola, if you play with your dolls at night, they're going to come alive at twelve midnight and start dancing on your head." Of course, that did the trick.

We all have grandmothers, but in the Spanish culture, *abuelitas* are extremely important in the sense that they are the ones who create magic for their grandchildren. I saw the students light up because they all had *abuelitas*. They all connected to this. I was also fascinated by their questions regarding "The Feather." The story deals with the dream world, with the mysticism and spirituality that is very much alive in South Texas, and that I felt was very much alive in their lives.

In my book *Orange Candy Slices*, a lot of the stories deal with a child and his or her relationship with a grandmother or grandfather. Usually these figures also have a connection with a community and the spiritual world, because one thing that is true with Hispanic cultures is that the spiritual is as important and as real as the physical. One of the things about this book that helps people go into the Hispanic culture and see the richness of its traditions and rituals is that the stories are told through the eyes of a child, and readers learn and see along with the child.

In "The Feather," a little girl finds a feather that is about five feet tall. It has a streak of blue on it and she can't understand what it is or to whom it belongs. Her grandmother tells her to dream about it. Through the dream world, the little girl is able to piece it together, and she then gets a visit from this very interesting lady—an angel. A lot of people in Latin America do believe in angels. It's tapping into this mysticism. The students were able to respond to it.

Stewart: Do you think that this mysticism needs a larger place in American schools around this country, or do you think it reflects a regional aspect of culture that is only along the border of Mexico?

Canales: I think it's universal. In my story "The Virgin," a girl is required to go to a church in the town of San Juan. She doesn't want to go because she feels the mass lasts for ten hours. Her parents say that the church has a virgin who performs miracles, but in the eyes of the child, the virgin is just a stupid doll. She thinks her parents are crazy, superstitious. But when the girl gets to the church, she sees that people have hung many *milagros* on the virgin to show gratitude for answering their prayers, for healing them. In other words, the skeptical little girl is forced to grapple with evidence against her belief that the virgin is simply a doll. She also personally experiences something that opens her to the existence of the spiritual, the mystical.

Clearly, we all dream. We don't always talk about it, but we are a nation that has a strong interest and belief in God, in spirituality. It is very much a part of people's lives, but schools often don't acknowledge or recognize it. I come from a family that had home altars for relatives who had passed and a grandmother who talked to the Virgin of Guadalupe on a daily basis. When I went to first grade, I felt that I was going into a different world that did not allow for this other dimension. It *is* part of people's lives.

Stewart: One thing they try to teach in language arts is "critical thinking skills." It almost implies being critical of superstition, perhaps.

Canales: I had an interesting experience when I went to Harvard. I was taking a course on Spanish literature and we were assigned a short story about an angel in a chicken coop. In the middle of discussing this story, the professor stopped and said, "I can't understand this discussion because you all seem to be asking questions and carrying on as though you believe in angels. Hold on. How many of you believe in angels?" Many of the students raised their hands. The professor became annoyed and angry. This did not compute with how he wanted to see the world. He expected us to have already outgrown such beliefs in angels. Again, I think that this is a big and important part of people's lives.

I'll give you another example. My story "The Egg" deals with *curanderas*, healers. It is based on a true story that happened to me as a child: I came down with a severe eye infection. This also happens to the child in the story. The mother takes the child to doctor after doctor, but the child's condition only gets progressively worse. So the mother finally brings in a *curandera*, who comes bearing an egg. The child is frightened because her mother has brought this strange woman who moves this egg around her forehead in a figure eight. The *curandera* then breaks the egg into a cup and slides it under the girl's bed. The next day the little girl is completely cured, which is what actually happened to me. One can say, is this "other dimension" superstition, or just coincidence? It is a mystery. However, there is no mystery for me about this particular incident: it worked.

When talking to the class at LBJ High School, they seemed to come alive when we discussed "The Egg." This is a real part of their personal life experience too. They spend hours in the classroom, but they spend most of their time at home. There is no bridge. They feel as though they're in two worlds. Mysticism or spirituality or the imagination: many of the stories in *Orange Candy Slices* deal with the power of the imagination. It is a wonderful and powerful tool that can help people create and shape their own personal worlds, in ways that can work to empower them.

Stewart: A lot of your stories seem to have some initial mystery, for instance, why does the town worship the coffee maker? You want to get to the end of the story to find out why. Or, what's this egg supposed to do? The kids in the story, their voices are skeptical, and the stories seem to be lessons in suspending skepticism as a way of growing up. I liked that aspect of the book.

Canales: Yes. The story "The Woman with the Green Hair" illustrates this point. The story is about a woman who thinks she's very spiritually evolved. She can look at a person's hair and tell exactly what he or she was in a previous lifetime. You have at the time a mayor's race. She looks at the hair of one of the candidates and says, "You know, I wouldn't get so pompous because actually you were a cockroach in a previous life." His competitor tries to take advantage of this, but he then turns out to have been a bug himself. It gets to the point that the whole town turns paranoid and completely shuts down. The story ends with a poignant turn: it turns out this woman got all her power through the use of her imagination, for it's finally discovered that she was completely blind.

Stewart: So the town sort of indulged it, because being imaginative was part of their fabric.

Canales: I think that is the thrust of these twenty stories in *Orange Candy Slices*. My little niece has a nine-year-old friend who wants to grow up to be a mermaid. We all know that's not realistic. But it gives you an idea of how powerful the imagination and stories are. They help shape our dreams, worlds, lives — our future. These stories illustrate the power of using the imagination to transform difficulties, whether poverty or sickness or death or growing up, into opportunities filled with hope and engagement and even magic.

I came here to Austin to attend St. Stephen's Episcopal School on a scholarship. I've since graduated from Harvard College and Harvard Law School. I am thankful for getting a good education. But what I think is lacking in education, especially now that it's become so tracked and competitive, is support in helping students flourish through the growth of their own imaginations. The imagination is such a powerful tool. Feeding children's imaginations and helping them get in touch with their stories, their own personal power, will help carry them through their lives, especially through the difficult times, and will enrich their experiences too. For example, I started writing stories to conjure up my grandmother, who had died the summer I left to attend St. Stephen's. It was a difficult time for me since I was very attached to her. But conjuring her up in my stories somehow made her come alive for me. I would have dialogues with her through these stories. Several of the stories in *Orange Candy Slices* actually originated from these first writings.

Stewart: As a spokesperson for this point of view, I think you have some very interesting accomplishments in your background: working for the Clinton administration, serving in the army as an Air Defense Artillery officer, graduating from Harvard Law School. These seem like very hardheaded, practical achievements. I think it adds credibility to the fact that letting kids be imaginative isn't going to hurt them later. A person is not going to be a bad mathematician just because she makes believe that she is a mermaid as a little girl.

Canales: Yes, I was a captain in the military, and I headed up the Small Business Administration for the Southwest under Clinton. I was an attorney and all, but I think that my creative writing gave me balance. On a day-to-day basis, I was dealing with other people's problems when I was a lawyer, or helping entrepreneurs when I was with the SBA, or leading soldiers when I was in the military. But I always kept a journal, and I always wrote. It helped me function better in the so-called "hard core" world because I had this outlet. I think that's quite valuable.

Recently I went through a difficult period when my father died. I was very close to him, and he died unexpectedly. After turning to my personal connection to God and the Bible, I re-read *Don Quixote* and *One Hundred Years of Solitude* by Gabriel García Márquez. I realized and personally experienced the deep, healing power of literature.

Stewart: Are you focused primarily as a writer right now, or are you still balancing the two?

Canales: After the Clinton administration, I decided to take some time to focus on my writing. I'm now doing readings and touring for my first book, *Orange Candy Slices and Other Secret Tales*, and have since finished a second book, *The Tequila Worm.*

I need this strangeness to stop. I need things to be normal once more. Pain is normal; an orbiting egg is not. My mother as my mother is normal; my mother as a wizard's assistant is not. I wonder how prayer seems normal with a church, but seems bizarre with an egg. An egg is to be cooked and eaten with salt. It's okay if eyes burn.

The egg stops. The humming stops, too. The egg then quickly departs from my head like a small white ghost.

I hear the egg. It is cracked and then poured into the cup. The cup is placed under the bed, directly under my head.

The next morning, I quickly open my eyes. The pain has vanished. There is no blur. I run and tell my mother. She runs to my bedroom and pulls the cup from under my bed. The orange round yolk is streaked with a blurry white cloud. My mother says it's the sign of the curse; I say nothing.

—"The Egg," *Orange Candy Slices and Other Secret Tales*
(Houston: Piñata Books, Arte Público, 2001), 33.

Gary Cartwright

---

*Even if we don't write about Texas, we feel Texas.
We feel the heritage of Texas.*

Gary Cartwright

My generation of writers is the first about which we could really say that Texas has a breed of writers. We all stayed in Texas, grew up in Texas, started our professional careers in Texas, and wrote about Texas because it was unexplored.

Interview by Teresa Taylor

Teresa Taylor: Is there something that Texas writers share, no matter what genre they're working in?

Gary Cartwright: Texas is a very special place, and we share that. My generation of writers is the first about which we could really say that Texas has a breed of writers. Katherine Anne Porter was from Texas, but left Texas and pretty much denounced it. Then there were historians and folklorists—Webb, Dobie, and Bedichek. But the first generation of writers—guys who made their living doing nothing but writing—[comprises] people my age: Bud Shrake, Dan Jenkins, Larry King, Larry McMurtry, Bill Brammer, who's dead now but was one of the first great Texas writers, and many, many more. We all stayed in Texas, grew up in Texas, started our professional careers in Texas, and wrote about Texas because it was unexplored. *Texas Monthly* started in 1973, and that gave us an outlet, both to make a living and to concentrate on Texas. Even if we don't write about Texas, we feel Texas; we feel the heritage of Texas.

Taylor: Is there something about Austin in particular that sets it apart?

Cartwright: Austin is very special and has been for a long time. The trouble was, back in the late '60s when I first came to Austin, you couldn't make a living here unless you were a university professor, or a politician, or a state worker. There were no jobs. So being a writer was a unique situation. I had a background in newspapers, but when I started freelancing, I could literally live any place I wanted to, any place that had an airport, or was close to an airport. I picked Austin because it was beautiful. Austin has always been, at least in my mind, the cultural center of Texas. The university is here. It's more liberal than the other cities in Texas, and it's a place that writers and artists and musicians have been drawn to.

Taylor: How have the political and social events of the 1960s informed your passion for writing?

Cartwright: Well, the '60s for me was a defining decade for a lot of reasons. I wrote in *Turn Out the Lights* about the influence of the Kennedy assassination in 1963; it's just one of those earthshaking things that changed everything forever. My whole world changed then. Maybe we're going through the same thing again now, with the September 11 terrorist attack. I'd started working for newspapers in 1956 and by the early '60s I was getting burned out. The '60s were also when so many people became disenchanted with this country. Vietnam was boiling up, demonstrations in the streets, blacks were rioting in the big cities. It was a time like no other time in American history, at least in the twentieth century. The '60s certainly defined me.

Taylor: From your stories I get a sense that you want to be involved in what the comedian Flip Wilson called the "Church of What's Happening Now." How has engagement with other people and with events affected your life? Is this something you could give up, or does it have to be part of your passion for living?

Cartwright: Well, journalism means that you're involved on a daily basis, almost an hourly basis, with crime and with corruption, with people experiencing life-changing events. It's exciting! My first job with the newspaper was as a night police reporter for the *Fort Worth Star-Telegram*, and I'd never been around that sort of thing. The thrill of the chase was exhilarating; particularly when you're twenty years old, you love it. I still get a big thrill out of the chase, being there and doing things firsthand. Some of the most successful stories that I've written have been things that I participated in on the ground.

The story that I did about the last of the big ranches in the Trans-Pecos — I went on a roundup with them. I rode a horse, which I actually don't do, but I got right in with the cowboys. Slept in a tent, ate from the chuck wagon. So I had a real feeling for what their life was about and why they loved it so much. Some of the personalities I've written about, I felt on a visceral level who they were and what they went through. That was my thing even when I was writing fiction. I fell back on my journalistic background. Find out all you can about a thing, get as close as you can to the subject, then back off and write what you want to write. In fiction, of course, it can take you far away from the subject, but you still have the original subject, the original feeling of the moment: how it smelled, how people reacted, the quick changes of life.

Taylor: What have you learned about human nature?

Cartwright: I don't know what I've learned about human nature. There are certain things I've become more cynical about because I know that people lie. I've learned that we're all terribly mortal, and that life is short. We need to live it as best we can, live in the moment-to-moment reality.

Taylor: Are you particularly interested in human memory and how it re-constitutes itself over time to fit circumstances?

Cartwright: Yes. One of the stories that I did involved a lot of research on human memory. It was a story about the Fran and Dan Childcare Center, and Fran and Dan being arrested for abusing children. It quickly got into allegations of satanic abuse. There were all these people who had recovered memories, generally of something sexual that had happened to them when they were quite young. At some point in their adult life, through therapy, they recovered — or claimed to have recovered — a memory of something. What I discovered in reading and talking to these people, investigating their stories, is that memory is not like a tape recorder; it's not something that you replay and it comes back to you as a whole piece of truth. It fragments its perception, its illusions. It is tainted not only by a great lapse in time, but also by everything else that has happened to you, so it's quite selective and quite unreliable.

In the case of Fran and Dan, they are two people who are in prison right now who "didn't do it," and I know they didn't do it. The district attorney probably realizes they didn't do it but can't admit the mistake. That has been one of the toughest cases I've ever covered. I still get letters from Fran and Dan in their separate prisons, fairly uneducated people who still can't understand what happened to them. I can and do understand what happened to them but am powerless to change it. They are two innocent people doing forty years in prison.

Taylor: Do you understand that kind of hysteria, that came out of nowhere but fed on itself and became a witch hunt? What explains that?

Cartwright: Yes, exactly, it became a witch hunt. What was happening during this time, too, was that prosecutors were realizing that there were more cases of child abuse than they had thought, and they became overly sensitive and erred on the other side. Anytime someone came in and registered a complaint of child abuse, they went after it like World War III, whereas in the previous decade, they had sloughed these cases off. Something else happened: therapists who were not medically qualified — mostly they had degrees in social science — set up therapist shops and began to concentrate on recovered memory. When someone would come in with a problem, such as alcoholism, depression, bad dreams, children acting out, behavioral problems, they began to diagnose it as a result of satanic ritual abuse.

There was a small group of therapists here in Austin connected to a statewide group that was in turn connected to a national group, and they would trade these taped cases. A famous case at the time was the McMartin case in Marin County in California, where a group of people who ran a child care center were accused of witchcraft, outlandish things, just crazy, crazy things — burying children alive, digging up corpses and sawing off arms and legs of corpses, making the children eat dead flesh. Things that common sense tells you didn't happen. Some investigation proved how absurd it is and also how it gets out of hand, much as the witch trials in Salem did, because leaders of the community were standing up proclaiming that there are witches among us and that there's evil among us.

Taylor: Do you think for that kind of hysteria to happen it requires a person in a position of authority to be the genesis for it?

Cartwright: I think it's absolutely necessary, because generally people on their own are not going to get on this sort of crusade unless they've got some kind of reaffirmation from someone they trust, from a minister, a psychologist, psychiatrist, or from the media. People like Rush Limbaugh have influenced people who are otherwise fairly sane and rational to be crazy, because they come up with these mad conspiratorial theories, and they've got a voice that's heard by thousands, sometimes millions, of people, and they represent authority to these people. There's always a group of people who are willing to believe anything, who are so unsatisfied with their lives and so apprehensive about things they can't understand, that if someone can come up with a simple explanation like "that's Satan's fault" or "it's Bill Clinton's fault," they will believe that. They take comfort in that, and they lose all sense of reason and fall into cults.

Taylor: So if there's so much potential there for damage, how do you reconcile that against free speech?

Cartwright: That's a constant problem. It seems to me that the best defense is not to censor but to make sure the voice of reason gets out. Explain the truth to people and I think the truth will out, but you're always going to have the voice of dissent in this country, and sometimes the voice of dissent is also going to be the voice of the loon. You just have to let the truth find its way to the top.

Taylor: You make a reference in one of your essays to your ability to write in the field. What role does emotion play when you're writing?

Cartwright: It's very tricky. Just as people suppress unpleasant memories and unpleasant feelings, writers tend to do that too. You tend to look for the easy avenue, but you also learn that you're successful when you really expose yourself not only to the reader but also to yourself. You keep rewriting, you keep digging, and you learn that ugly truth about yourself that you didn't expect and you wish you didn't know. But you do know, and you feel an urge, if it's pertinent to what you're writing — you feel an urge to let the readers know this too. It's part of being a writer. It's something that you learn over time at some cost and something you recognize that you try to avoid, but then realize "I've got to admit the truth. This is how I felt. This is what really happened." So you know you just have to make those things work for you.

———————

For more than an hour I sat there, astride an exceptionally gentle horse named Preacher, studying the spectacular terrain. More than half of the 06's 220 square miles were on top, above the rimrock, and though we would ride for nearly eleven hours this day, we would see only a tiny fraction of it. Nobody, including Mr. Kokernot himself, had ever seen all of it. Barney Nelson told me that she and Joel celebrated Thanksgiving every year by taking their provisions by pack horse and riding "as far as we can," to a pasture they'd never seen before. Sitting alone up there, I got a sense of why they loved it so desperately and an insight into the meaning of a quote I'd underlined in one of Barney's newspaper articles: "I am glad I shall never be young without wild country to be young in. Of what avail are forty freedoms without a blank spot on the map." . . .

The herd spread out now into a long oval, with a point man out front, eight riders at the flanks, and the others riding drag, picking up strays and laggards. The horses were almost as expert as the riders. When a slobbering, mud-caked old bull at the rear of the herd turned back uphill, my horse, Preacher, wheeled around, and before I knew what had happened I had caught the bull—or rather, my horse did—and directed him back to the main body of herd. I looked at Chris Lacy, hoping my grin wasn't as foolish as it felt.

"Let's take 'em all the way to Abilene!" I shouted.

"If you're sure there's a railroad," the 06 boss shouted back, grinning at my attempt at cowboy humor.

—*Turn Out the Lights: Chronicles of Texas during the 80s and 90s*
(Austin: University of Texas Press, 2000), 227.

Paul Christensen

We should go out like prophets into the wilderness
and preach this gospel of belonging and
deep-rootedness.

Paul Christensen

I sat down and began to write. What I was really looking back on was twenty-five years of being in Texas. I take the reader through the process of what it is to come into this land and be altered by it and develop a very strong attraction to it.

_____

Interview by Ramona Cearley

Ramona Cearley: What is the journey that inspired your highly acclaimed book *West of the American Dream: An Encounter with Texas?*

Paul Christensen: Many years ago I had a radio show in College Station called "Poetry Southwest," which broadcast to the Brazos Valley, and I brought in poets from all over the country and the state. It was for a time syndicated to twelve or thirteen stations. In the process, Lloyd Lyman, who was the director of the Texas A&M Press at that time, suggested that I compile some of these interviews and poetry readings and put them into a book. I said I would. Only about thirteen years went by. Then another director of the press, Noel Parsons, who is now at Texas Tech University Press in Lubbock, said, "I'd like to do that book. I do have a very long memory." I said, "Oh, dear, and I have a short conscience." So I sat down and began to write.

What I was really looking back on was twenty-five years of being in Texas. I'm a Pennsylvanian. I'm a Yankee. I had to think about why I came into the state and what it did to me when I entered it. How did I change? Where are my bearings now? Am I a Texan? Am I still a greenhorn? Am I still a foreigner? A lot of poets have called me "an émigré." There's a special kind of wink of the eye when they say that, I believe, and I said the book should be a baptism of sorts. I take the reader through the process of what it is to come into this land and be altered by it and develop a very strong attraction to it. To feel that your imagination has grown another lobe, another way of seeing now that I'm out here in the Southwest. So that's what I do in this book.

I detail all the poets I've ever known. I analyze their poetry and parse it down to its real ingredients. I give a history of the women writers of Texas. Women invented poetry in Texas. Did you know that? Oh, it's a wonderful story. They came in. They were more educated than the men. They said, "No, this is not going to do. We're not going to shoot up everyone on Main Street. We're going to write 'em up on side streets." The reading clubs and the writing clubs laid down a strong feminist consciousness and developed some marvelous writers who spoke of the land as an extension of themselves. They were offended by the slaughter of the bison and the deracination of the native people. They had a tremendous identification with the local flora and fauna. There are many wonderful poets who came out of the 1900s who are now unsung. That's part of the story.

Then I talked about the Vietnam generation of the '60s and '70s and how they threw off their attitudes of estrangement from the land and began to identify themselves very much as the women had done earlier. It brought about a mini-Renaissance. I remember I was beating my tub all over the state saying, "The Renaissance is here! The Renaissance is here!" Now they describe me as the man who cried wolf. It never happened. It came close. It came very, very close. We have seen presses come and go. We've seen some of them flower in beautiful ways and then fold up when the economy got a little scrawny.

We're seemingly in one of those troughs right now, but actually there's a rebirth. There are a half-dozen projects afoot right now aimed at producing new anthologies of Texas writers. I'm participating in a kind of rebirth right now talking to you. So I would say that *West of the American Dream* has those qualities in it. It's a memoir: a historical and critical memoir that uses me as the focus for everything that happened around me in terms of literature and ways of life. I shock a lot of readers by having two chapters in this book where I just wander around in thrift shops and all-night supermarkets and look at the underclass and see how they live, and sympathize with, and talk about the old country and rural ways. Somebody said, "What does that have to do with poetry?" I said, "That is the poetry, if it's any good." I mean, if we're any good. That is the poetry. So in essence that is what the book is about.

Cearley: Thank you for such an in-depth view. You describe yourself as an immigrant. Give us a sense of where you grew up.

Christensen: It's just a tremendous question. But you really don't know what you've asked. You've opened up Pandora's box. I was born in Pennsylvania. I was born in war, and I'll probably die in war. As soon as I was born, my mother whisked me off to New Orleans to the French Quarter. I lived on the corner of Bourbon and Barracks streets in my mother's original house. That's where I learned to walk. My uncle played with Louis Prima in a very good jazz band on Bourbon Street. I remember when he'd bring out his instruments, and he'd play

Dixieland to us. I'd be plunking at the piano at the age of one and a half making more noise than music but having fun.

I went back to Philadelphia and then moved to Virginia. That's where my father joined the Foreign Service. Very shortly after that I was whisked away to Beirut, Lebanon, where I grew up in my teen years. I came back for a year to Virginia; then went immediately to the Philippines, to boarding school in a mountainous village, which is where I first fell in love with someone. It was a very trying and glorious experience. I got kicked out of school because I was caught smoking. It was at the end of the semester, so it didn't matter. I went back to live with my family in a big old planter's villa in Saigon. This was in 1959, and so I lived there for about a year and a half and went through the various attempts to overthrow the government. Then I came back and finished high school in Virginia, went to William and Mary, then to the University of Pennsylvania for my Ph.D. The job that was offered to me was by Texas A&M. So I came here in 1974 and began teaching.

About ten or twelve years went by, and I started traveling again. I began to teach in Europe and in the Far East. When I came back I had a Fulbright to a little town in southern Austria. I also went to teach in Oslo, Norway, for the purpose of discovering my father's roots; he is Norwegian by descent. Then I started living in Provence part of the year and ultimately bought a house there in an old village. Now I'm about five months out of the year in southern France and seven months in Texas. Where I live in France would fool any Texan into thinking he was in the Hill Country — the same limestone, the same kind of crumbly houses. It looks just like being out there in the hills outside of Austin.

Cearley: You're right; I didn't know the expanse of your travel, especially beginning at such an early age. In terms of your writing encounters, who influenced you most?

Christensen: When I was in Pennsylvania I discovered the poet Charles Olson, a very sophisticated and worldly man who decided that poetry should be rooted in a place that you know and perhaps has shaped you. He spent the better part of his life writing about Gloucester. And Gloucester becomes a history of the world; that is, the local becomes the universal. I was thrilled that he could do that, and I remember sitting at a round table with a bunch of overly educated intellectuals like myself one night late. The wine bottle was empty, so I knew I was going to be eloquent. I said we shouldn't just all hang around the Northeast. We should go out like prophets into the wilderness and preach this gospel of belonging and deep-rootedness. They all laughed and said, "Well, that'll be the day." And lo and behold, I get this job offer to come out to a place called College Station, which didn't sound very promising to me. But I did accept the position.

A friend called me a year later and said, "Are you going to be true to your word? Are you going to sink some roots and do what you have to do, as we remembered your wonderful speech?" I said, "Well, I'm caught. I am truly caught." That was the major influence in my life as far as telling me "don't turn your back." Don't be the typical out-of-towner who just wants to commute back and forth to the supermarket and the job and then leave the state completely unexplored. I couldn't do that.

Another of the great influences on my life was Ezra Pound. He gives a global view, a deep and broad view of history and how we got to the twentieth century. Everything I write is tinged by, goaded by, the desire to expand the vision, because Ezra Pound is in my past and in my conscience. There are some wonderful poets from the San Francisco Renaissance. Poets whose names are not all household words, but they are extraordinarily important to me. I love them very much. There are some New England writers I've been deeply affected by, perhaps especially Robert Creeley, Paul Blackburn and, among the women, Lorine Niedecker is very dear to me. I'm a close friend and sidekick of Dianne Wakoski.

If I have a muse, an angel that tells me how to write, it's D. H. Lawrence when I write prose. Despite a lot of problems and limitations, he's a bloody genius. I sometimes just fall over as I did when I was in Taos. I asked rather timidly, "Which house did he stay in with Frieda?" And the women pointed over there, and I went and shot a whole roll of film as a way of mentally embracing the place. My camera was in my hands, you might say trying to open doors and see clearly what that place was really like because he did a beautiful job. He left and went to Mexico City and stayed in a place called the Monte Carlo Hotel. I slept in the room where he wrote *Mornings in Mexico,* and it was a good feeling. It was a very good vibe. I enjoyed myself immensely there.

Cearley: Among your many poetry projects, you've been featured in *Texas Nafas,* a video documentary program featuring poetry on community television based in Austin, Texas. Describe your involvement and a context for the program.

Christensen: First, Farid Mohammadi, founder and director of *Texas Nafas,* is a good friend of mine. He's a taxi driver and a very private man. He's an Iranian, and while I've lived in the Middle East and have many friends in that area, I doubt that we would have said a word to each other passing on the street. Except I was put in touch with him, and the description was, "this man loves poetry." It did not come by happenstance that I remember that Iran is probably the place where writing was invented. So I figure he has roots. He might know what he's talking about. The traditions of marvelous poetry go back twenty-five hundred years, and so when I met this man, who's a dynamo, he exploded with joy and enthusiasm and said, "So you're going to help me spread poetry to the United States?" I said, "I am now!"

I felt I'd been deputized by the sheriff of the world. We were going to ride roughshod on the public and get them to read poetry. I was very excited. *Nafas* is a Farsi word that means "breath" or "spirit." It's wonderful that we would bring in that old, old word and circulate it through the Southwest. I feel very strongly that Farid is on to something. He put poet John Herndon and me in front of the camera, and we did twelve or thirteen episodes of a poetry journal where we talk about individual poets each time for a half-hour. It was a wonderful verbal ping-pong between the two of us. We knew we had done a good job when we could see Farid in the background skipping around, hopping and clapping with joy that we had said something that made sense to him. I've had nothing but good vibrations from this whole experience.

We're also going to be doing a documentary in three or four countries of the Mediterranean, talking about the origins of love poetry. Of course, Farid wants to throw in his country too. So we may go to Tehran. I can't wait to do this because this is the world of Dante, this is the world of the troubadour poets. It will bring me to Sicily, where my roots are on my mother's side, and bring us all the way down into Spain. We're very excited about this. It's very small but very promising.

Cearley: Earlier, you spoke about a rebirth or reawakening of poetry and literature. In a larger, social context, where are we now?

Christensen: I believe we are in the last stages of a materialist, obsessive fever. I'll give you an illustration of this. The other day I was in Houston at the Town and Country Mall celebrating Texas Authors' Month. There were three audience areas for prose, nonfiction prose, and poetry. There were about sixty to eighty chairs in each of these areas. All the publishers were there with their books, and the authors were willing to sign their books. I counted four people in the audience, two of which were going to be readers. And this is in a city of four million people. But it was entertaining, and I was enjoying myself listening to the reading.

As one of the poets was reading, there walked through an average-looking family, a couple of youngsters maybe ten, thirteen years of age, and the parents in their forties. They were on their way to a store and came right into the midst of what appeared to be almost a spiritual gathering. The voice of the man who was reading was very sweet and alluring. There was a profound simplicity about his sentiments, his feelings. They were naked feelings, and it was very joyful and very positive.

These people looked as if they saw a dead person on a pavement. They shivered or pulled themselves back, maybe because they saw intimacy and were not prepared for it in such a place as a shopping mall. But on they trekked, and I saw them going into a candy shop. Now there's candy, and then there's food for the soul. They didn't know enough to stop and say, "Let's sit down and listen to this guy." No, it was a "let's go; let's get out of here." We have to be at the final stages of this kind of overconsumption. We're the most beleaguered consumers in the world. We're not prepared for any surprises. So I think one by one Americans are beginning to say, "Wait a minute. I don't know if I can keep doing what I'm doing. It's just not adding up anymore."

Fifty percent divorce rate in this country. Delinquency. Largest prison population in the world. We need to think about values that we can turn to. Americans are just beginning to turn around. The writers are here. They're doing their job. There's a new press, a new imprint called Harlem Moon; the African American middle class is devouring writing that is about themselves. Now they have a new, very bold trade imprint. I'm really excited to hear that. The same thing is happening with Arte Público Press in Houston, which is reaching across in our border countries and our southern towns. We're seeing something but whether it's permanent, I can't say. I hope it is.

How many others in America have bid farewell to friends and the familiar world and set off as we did, to parts unknown? . . . But I wasn't going only for a job. I had a theory that inland America possessed myths and secrets no regular history book or conventional poem had yet told about. I was going off as a kind of intellectual pioneer. For the past four years I had been studying poets who had looked for the myths of American life, in particular the poet Charles Olson, about whom I was writing a dissertation. It opened my eyes to the notion that land is not static or godless but an active ingredient in human identity, human consciousness. What Olson had discovered as myth in New England I wanted to find in Texas. That was my plan, my ambition—apart from teaching literature. I wanted to find the myths that created the sense of being Texan, and the assumptions that created a spirit of place called the Southwest.

—*West of the American Dream: An Encounter with Texas*
(College Station: Texas A&M University Press, 2001), 4–5.

J. California Cooper

*I write about things that I know can happen.
I know that most anything can happen.*

J. California Cooper

I'm fascinated by life. Not by anyone's life in particular, because they don't move fast enough for me. The story has to tell itself on its own terms.

Interview by Teresa Taylor

Teresa Taylor: You grew up in Marshall, Texas, is that right?

J. California Cooper: I grew up in Berkeley, but I spent a few years in Marshall, Texas, when the war started, 1941–1942, something like that.

Taylor: Then you came back to live in Marshall from 1987 to 1994, when you wrote several books of fiction. Have your experiences in Marshall influenced your writing?

Cooper: I don't think so, because I never write about anything that happened then. I write about things that I *know* can happen. As a Bible student, I know that most anything can happen. So, I like to write about life. I'm fascinated by life. Not by anyone's life in particular, because they don't move fast enough for me. If you're going to tell a story in seven pages, a person doesn't live that fast. The story has to tell itself on its own terms.

Taylor: I want to get back to the "seven pages" part, but first, are your characters drawn from people you've actually met or observed?

Cooper: Not ever. You observe things all through life without knowing you're observing. I am an observer. But I've never knowingly said, "Oh, I'll take some of this from him or some of that from her." These voices come in the rain. I hear them and it's their story.

Taylor: Do stories come to you very quickly and fully formed? Or do you work on them over a long period of time?

Cooper: Characters talk to me. As the person in my mind is telling the story to me, she can go from the beginning to the end. Some stories are written in twenty-four hours. Some take three days; some take three months. Depends on how often you can lure this person back. In Marshall, someone came to tell me this story. When she left, after about four pages, she didn't return for about three months. I was back in California, and some music happened to come by—which has a lot to do with my writing—and she flew right up with that music. Then I had to find that music to keep her talking. So that's the way: When it comes, you have to be ready.

Taylor: When you say that this person comes, do you feel a physical presence or do you hear a voice?

Cooper: It's a voice in your head. You can also see everything around them. It's just someone telling you a story. Did you play paper dolls when you were a little girl?

Taylor: Did I? No, I didn't.

Cooper: Okay, I played paper dolls until I was eighteen, hearing voices and things, not like hearing someone say "Heelllooooo" or anything like that. You just hear the story!

Taylor: Do you ever try to make it happen, like with music?

Cooper: I do. Music, the clouds, trees, anything. I fill myself up with as much beauty as possible. Because that's what I like, and I hope that's where they live. And when the right music comes out, they'll come out. If it hits the right spot, then they'll be ready to tell their story.

Taylor: What kind of music do you listen to?

Cooper: They like Rachmaninoff. They like Eric Satie. They like Bobby "Blue" Bland. They like Dinah Washington. But mostly they like music with no words. Words seem to interfere with their words. They also don't like tiddlywink music. I know Mozart is a genius, but they don't care for Mozart because it's like little doilies. But *powerful* music, Wagner! And then they don't like him because he seems to be off rhythm. But Rachmaninoff! Oh, they love him!

Taylor: Your stories are usually told through the voice of a narrator. Is this the voice that you are hearing?

Cooper: That's the one. That's why everyone says it's like sitting on a porch listening to a neighbor tell you a story. But that's because I *repeat* the story the same way I *heard* it. As they're talking, I'm saying it. Most people say, "I don't gossip, but I'm going to tell you a story about my neighbor across the street." That's how they talk.

Taylor: Are you actually physically speaking when you hear these stories or are you writing them?

Cooper: I talk to them, but I'm not doing the talking. I'm doing the listening. If I was doing the talking, I could write the story all by myself.

Taylor: When do you actually put the story to paper? Is it while they are telling you?

Cooper: Yes, because I write longhand first. They don't like anything mechanical. No computers. No typewriters. Nothing. They like everything natural. Down through the head, down through the arm.

Taylor: What about revision?

Cooper: All the stories I've ever done, there's been one draft, except the very last one. I've had editors that try to edit and change this and that. In one story there's an eagle. And they liked the eagle so much they said, "Let's have some more of the eagle." So I put in more eagle, and then they said, "There's too much eagle. This doesn't fit." Well, *no, it doesn't,* because *now it's me* and when she told it she said it exactly as it should have been. And if you mess with it, then it's not her story anymore. It makes some people think, "Oh, God, ghosts are talking to you." So I don't stay on this subject for long, because I can't tell it to anybody.

Taylor: Your comment about the seven-page story is interesting. When I first started reading your stories, I thought, "I've never read anything like this," but then they reminded me of the fairy tales I read as a child. The remarkable brevity of your stories, and how much gets communicated within a very short period of time. Can you comment on that?

Cooper: It's that the narrators are very good and they know their stories. When people say to me now, "Oh, you had to live this" or "You had to do this," they're blaming me for their lack of imagination. When you were reading fairy tales, had anyone ever really seen a diamond mountain or a gold apple? In fairy tales, you have an imagination! So when these people come, they're working with my imagination. Whatever they say happens, I just accept it.

Taylor: Your stories are very carefully crafted to deliver a message. Part of the message is about choices that people make and how you go about making a smart choice. Do you think about how to deliver a message without being too preachy or dogmatic about it?

Cooper: I just say what the narrator is saying to me. I have had a few fools that have talked to me, and I have finally written their story down. I've had some characters, and I would say to them, "Please, *please* don't do that," and they did it anyway, because it's their choice. I'm about choices, because that's what I see people making a mess of. And I see all the lies in the world that help them make these dumb choices. By "dumb" I use the word loosely, but they are empty choices. They are choices that lead nowhere that they want to go, because I do believe that everyone wants some satisfaction, wants to be loved, wants some happiness out of this life. In schools, if you are honest, study hard, try to remain a virgin, you're laughed at. You're not "one of the crowd." So this world is set up for you to make mistakes.

Taylor: Your first two stories in *The Future Has a Past,* "A Shooting Star" and "A Filet of Soul," are very interesting. The first one tells the story of a young woman who's clearly headed, by her own promiscuity, toward some form of destruction. And in that story the way that you depict her murder seems so over the top that I felt the story left room for a misogynous interpretation. The second story works at a much deeper psychological level. It's about a very secluded woman who has been terribly isolated from her community, and it's only through a desperate act on her part to engage herself with a man and push herself out into the world that she is finally able to find happiness. So these are very opposite takes on how a woman protects herself but also has the courage to be in the world and engage with other people. As a pair, the two stories are really quite interesting.

Cooper: Well, three things I'd like to say. Number one, about over the top, do you agree that there are people in life that go through that?

Taylor: There are plenty of men that would do violence against a woman, even kill her. The reason why I think that it might invite a misogynous interpretation is because there are not many men that would rape a dead body for five days.

Cooper: There *are* many men that like to rape dead bodies. Not rape them; just take them, and they usually take jobs in funeral homes.

Taylor: Okay, so tell me more.

Cooper: What's over the top? In this life, in which there are people like Dahmer who ate his people — where you have people doing all kinds of things for no good reason that we can see, nothing is over the top. What is over the top? What Hitler did? That's over the top, but it happened. I think Jack Kennedy was a relatively good man. He wasn't selfish. Why would you kill somebody that didn't mean you any harm? But this young lady went to bed with this man, and he couldn't make love to her unless she was dead. I bet that happens more than we think, because there are a lot of crazy people.

Now the second thing you said, what the first lady did, well, the first lady had her story. She was seeking love. She thought that all these boys loved her. And yet inside of her was really a core of sorrow. What I was trying to say at the end, when he made love to her for five days after she was dead: She was what she had made herself all her life, nothing but a vagina. And he still used it when she could no longer be there to say yea or nay. If you throw some slop in front of pigs, they all run to it. It doesn't mean they love you. It means they want what you are giving away. The second one, she had an entirely different life. Imagine being raised to think you're ugly?

Taylor: The second story is very powerful because of the way this woman is set up by a mother who is truly trying to protect her —

Cooper: Yes!

Taylor: — but doesn't understand the consequences. It's very painful.

Cooper: Life can change and be better. She was foolish.

Taylor: And that's something I find fascinating about your stories too. Some characters accept misery when life really doesn't have to be that way. Like this mother, who had a terrible experience concerning her prom, but she could have overcome that.

Cooper: No one told her. Plus they come in all colors, and they're all over the world. Not just in America, they're all over the world.

Taylor: Who do you mean by "they"?

Cooper: These girls. People like this; people that are isolated. Someone misled them. Changed their life by erroneous information. These people are all over the world. These people in my books are black because I'm black, but I don't write about one person. I write about every nationality under the sun.

Taylor: Well, that's interesting because there's not much description of cultural or economic or social background, which is a little bit disconcerting at first, but it also works at a psychological level because everything becomes so much more metaphorical.

Cooper: Right, and also more universal. Some of these people don't even tell me the name of the town they live in. I don't want them to. People say what year was it? What does it matter? The only thing that's changed in the world is the way we dress and the number of the year. Man and woman are still the same as they were when Adam and Eve were saying, "They made me do it. It's not my fault."

Taylor: Does this get us back to your reference to being a Bible student?

Cooper: No, it means that's where *my* wisdom comes from. This is how I know that when I'm talking about this girl, I'm talking about every girl that's like that.

Taylor: I usually look at the acknowledgments when I read someone's books. In your case, I saw the name of civil rights attorney William Kunstler. Is he someone that you knew?

Cooper: No. I choose people that to me are vulnerable. That's how Marilyn Monroe got in there. Different people that I have read or learned about through history. There's a certain vulnerability to the people that I fall in love with that gets into those pages. Lately, there are people who want to get in there. It annoys me no end. I don't like to be angry, so I'm wondering, why would you do this to me? If I want you, I will tell you.

Taylor: These are people that come to you as a voice?

Cooper: No, people in life that just want to find a way to get on the dedication page.

Taylor: Did you know that William Kunstler was also a poet?

Cooper: No, I didn't. If I did, I've forgotten it. But I could imagine it, because look where his heart is. To me it comes under the guise of love, whether you call it that or not.

Taylor: So let's talk about love. One kind of love is the kind that social activists have. To maintain a commitment to social justice takes a kind of love.

Cooper: Yes, it does. And it's social justice. It's *justice*. I'm this way about animals, people. That's why it's never good for me to be around very poor people. I'm poor, but a giver. When a giver is around a lot of takers, it's just too painful.

Taylor: Was there a time in your life when you had to learn how to protect yourself from the takers?

Cooper: My mother did that. She helped me all through my life growing up. But still, if you have a lot of love in you, you're vulnerable.

Taylor: Do you do journal writing?

Cooper: No. My life goes so fast and in so many different directions that by the time I'm going to sleep, I'm ready to dream. My life is one great big dream, except when I'm going to work.

Taylor: How does a private person manage to maintain a very public life?

Cooper: It's not very public. Only the books are. You cannot call me before two in the afternoon, because the mornings are my thinking hours. You cannot call me, say, after eight-thirty or nine in the evening, because that depends on who you are. You cannot come into my life whenever you get ready, because I don't know what you're bringing and I don't know what you're coming after. Now, when I do know, then you have certain license. We may just have a laugh, but in the meantime, I know what your intentions are. Those people that call and say, "Whachya doing?" No. Don't call me. That's how I keep my privacy, because I make dates with myself.

Some of the boy-men, after a few stolen drinks of somebody's cheap wine, hatched a trick-plan to send a fellow out to play a little joke on Sedalia and ask her to dance on the grass. One of the boys she had liked and stared at all the time while he was with other girls volunteered to go do it. I'm shamed not one of us girls spoke up to shame them from doing it, I guess we wanted to laugh too. Thought it was all in fun and I even thought she might like to dance at her prom even if it was outside on the grass. It must take common sense to be a decent person, cause none of us had any.

That boy, Wiley, went out there and a flustered, needy, pitiful Sedalia smiled up at him and when he held out his hand, she reached for it.

—"A Filet of Soul," *The Future Has a Past*
(New York: Anchor Books, 2001), 29.

Elizabeth Crook

You always have to know the places you're writing about. You have to have been there, and you have to have been there alone.

Elizabeth Crook

I spent a lot of time researching at the old mission, La Bahia. I knew all the facts, but what I needed were the feelings, the sentiments, that accompany the place. It is difficult to describe but there is something very magical about the area.

Interview by Ramona Cearley

Ramona Cearley: Let's begin with historical fiction, your genre of writing. Describe your process of writing a historical novel.

Elizabeth Crook: It's very much a slow process — a process of groping — and always a process of discovery, because the research is very exciting to me. Then I often have to turn back and cut out big chunks of material because I find that they're really irrelevant to the story that begins to develop. I'm not a writer that has a lot of vision in the beginning, so I don't know my characters very well when I start. The story often ends up being very different from what I planned. The thing I like about the history is the sense of a treasure hunt: you never know what piece of information you're going to find that will inform the story in some wonderful way. I like that history provides a backdrop. It's like having the stage already set for a story, and you have your touchstones there. All you have to do, rather than create the dramatic moments, is recognize them. You find them, you see them, and then you place your characters in them. So you have these guideposts along the way. When you are writing contemporary fiction you are completely on your own in a very wide and uncertain world.

Cearley: La Bahia, the Spanish mission in South Texas, is part of the story in *Promised Lands*. How is it significant in terms of establishing a sense of place?

Crook: You always have to know the places you're writing about. You have to have been there, and you have to have been there alone. I had spent a lot of time researching at the old mission, La Bahia. I knew all the facts, but what I needed was the feelings, the sentiments, that accompany the place. A man who worked there told me I could come one night and sit alone in the chapel. As it happened, I was on my way to Corpus Christi with my mother, so I asked if she could come along. She was also granted permission, after quite a bit of discussion, to go into the chapel with me. We stayed quite a while. It is such a mysterious place. The entire area of South Texas. The terrain. It is difficult to describe, but there is something very magical about the area — specifically about the presidio. We had an unusual experience there. I don't want to sound flaky, but it brought me alive to the past in a way that I would not have been had I not had the experience. It made me feel that the things that transpire in this world hang on somehow in an unfathomable way and that that is a wonderful thing. If you can capture it in any sense — even a fleeting moment of ascendance — then you've done something that's nice.

Cearley: That is beautifully said. Do you follow a similar pattern with your work in progress?

Crook: The difference between writing historical fiction and contemporary fiction has become very apparent to me recently because the book I'm working on now takes place, in part, in the past and in the present. I think I started it that way because I mistakenly believed that if I only placed part of it in the past I would only have to do half as much research, which did not turn out to be the case. This book in fact has been more than doubly hard to write because it involved developing two sets of characters, two different stories — integrating those stories in a way that's meaningful and relevant. And then cutting each one of them in half so that the book is a tenable length and making it fit into a whole. I have learned a lot. I've learned what is wonderful about writing historical fiction and what is difficult. The same with contemporary fiction.

Cearley: You spent part of your childhood in San Marcos, then lived in Washington, D.C., and later in Australia, where your father served as U.S. ambassador. What was your family's influence in terms of your writing?

Crook: The influence that my family had on my writing was primarily that my mother read to the three of us children every night for hours on end. We each had about an hour, so she was reading usually two to three hours a night, and we would all listen in on each other's stories with different levels of understanding. It was wonderful. It was a very bonding thing for the family and often a very cantankerous time, as you can imagine, but it formed all three of us in ways that have been meaningful in our lives. For me, it gave me a sense of language and story. My father was always quoting poetry and from that I got a sense of rhythm with the words.

Cearley: Jacqueline Kennedy Onassis was your editor for *The Raven's Bride* and *Promised Lands*, published by Doubleday. What was that experience like?

Crook: Yes. That actually was a big surprise. The manuscript had been through a number of rejections and had finally landed with Texas Monthly Press, which was going to publish it, and we already had galleys in print. We had book-signing parties scheduled. And then Texas Monthly Press was sold to Gulf Publishing in Houston, which publishes no fiction. So I was without a home at that point.

We started submissions again in New York, and I had already been down every road there was to go down in New York. Doubleday actually had had the manuscript several times before, under several different titles. Also my name had changed in the meantime, because I'd gotten a divorce. So I think it was probably unrecognizable. Jackie just really liked the book, and that's how it ended up with Doubleday. She called me and said she actually wanted it. I think, at this point, my feeling about that was, Why?

But she was lovely to work with and a wonderful, very maternal personality. She was very shy, and therefore made me feel comfortable with her. She was not at all intimidating and had a certain reticence about her that was nice and very genuine. I liked her and was very sorry to lose her. She died the day that I started my tour with *Promised Lands*, and that was a book she had spent a lot of time with. So it was a sad promotional period for the book.

Cearley: Tell us about your most recent writing project.

Crook: This book has been through so many different forms that it's even hard for me to talk about it. At this point I have no idea — it could either be very good or pitifully mediocre. I wouldn't be surprised either way. The difficult thing about writing is you never really know whether what you wrote is any good. It's not like a test where you make a ninety-five. You put it out there, and all these different factors influence how well it does — the jacket, the title, how much promotion the publishing company is willing to put behind it. So that in the end there's no final verdict, which is a little bit unsatisfying. But at the same time it's liberating when you're writing, because you know that if it isn't just top-notch nobody can ever prove that and hold it against you.

The reviews for *Promised Lands* were better than for *The Raven's Bride*, yet *Raven's Bride* sold better. It's a very mysterious process. I feel as if *Raven's Bride* was my first child that grew up to do all the right things, was socially adept, joined the Junior League, and was well liked, popular in school. *Promised Lands* was my more complicated, less easily understood middle child. I have no idea how this third child will come out.

Cearley: You took issue with the cover design of *Promised Lands*.

Crook: I'm still disgruntled about that cover. It's a big landscape with a large image of a horse head painted in the clouds. Everything is mostly purple. I'm not usually sensitive about gender issues, but I know Doubleday would never have put that cover on a man's book. They made it look like a romance, when it's a war story.

The first painting they did was even worse — it didn't resemble any place I'd written about. It certainly didn't look like South or East Texas during the rainy season, which is when most of the story happens. It looked more like Utah in a drought. There was a mountain range in the background and a Conestoga wagon the likes of which had never been to Texas at that time. And not one stick of timber or piece of grass in the whole painting. There was a cow skeleton beside a desolate trail, and some kind of bushes that looked like tumbleweeds. I sent the person who was in charge some pictures of Texas vegetation and suggested that the artist might use a little purple phlox for groundcover if he wanted to use purple, but otherwise might tone that down. I was told the artist had grown up in South Texas, which I doubted, so I said that if he could name the mountain range near Goliad, then he could keep the dead cow. Otherwise to give me some trees. He ended up adding a few trees and painting a treeline over the mountain range and taking the tarp off the wagon. He painted grass over the cow skeleton. But he kept the horse head in the sky. I've tried to quit apologizing for that cover. I guess it's like having a baby — you nurture it all you can before it's born, but then you just have to take what comes out.

Cearley: Do you already have another project in mind?

Crook: No, and I dread having an idea about another book. Once I have the idea, it's going to start nagging at me, and I want to enjoy the feeling of being finished for a while first. I only get that feeling about once every five or six years, and the rest of the time my mind is so cluttered with the research and the different drafts and the revisions I have to make, that I get too preoccupied.

I'm looking forward to going for a jog without a pencil and a piece of paper stuffed in my sock and driving carpool without having to pull over to make notes. I figure if I write about seven good books in my lifetime that'll be enough. I don't think I could do more than that. I have to go through too many drafts before it's any good or before I really define what the book is about. And I don't want to devote my entire life to writing — that would be a shame unless I were a finer and more solitary writer. I'd rather have family and friends around. After my first marriage I thought all I wanted was my books and my dishes and some place quiet so I could write. So I set things up that way. Of course I was on antidepressants within a month. So, no — no ideas presently, and no desire for any. I need a break.

Cearley: *Promised Lands* and *The Raven's Bride* have been reissued by

SMU Press as part of the Southwest Life and Letters series. Would you select a passage from *Promised Lands* that we may feature as an excerpt of your writing?

Crook: This scene from *Promised Lands* takes place at night. A family's raft has overturned while they are trying to cross the Trinity River and leave Texas in the panic that followed the fall of the Alamo. A young woman named Katie has managed to rescue her grandmother and swim with her through the current toward the shore and to grab hold of a tree limb. She is now exhausted and feels she can no longer keep hold of her grandmother.

She was unaware of anything but holding on. She held her grandmother by one hand and clutched the limber branch within the other, feeling the soft needled leaves inside her grip, the limb giving with the weight as if it would stretch out forever, all the length of that long river to the sea. The water was a force of evil with its awesome power. Katie sobbed aloud, "I can't, I can't," and felt the current stretch her arms, felt the bony grip of Grand's white hand between her fingers like the hand of death. Grand never looked at her. She never, ever did in that long time they clung there strung together like cut paper dolls with the water tugging them apart. Grand was looking at the moon. She fixed her eyes on the light between the spiny branches and she clung to Katie's hand.

Grand was still looking at the moon and gasping at the air when Katie's strength gave out, her fingers letting go, and Grand sank underneath the muddy surface with her face still turned up toward the light. Katie called and called, but she knew then, and always afterward believed, Grand never heard her calling.

And even while she clung there in the branches of the cypress tree and saw Grand fly away beneath the littered surface of the Trinity, Katie thought how horrible for Grand to know, the final human touch she ever had, was someone letting go.

—*Promised Lands: A Novel of Texas Rebellion*
(New York: Doubleday, 1994), 454–455.

Angela De Hoyos

---

*One of my earliest models was
Sor Juana Inés de la Cruz.*

Angela De Hoyos

When I was five years old, my mother read to me from the Spanish-speaking poets. Sor Juana Inés was one of them. I may have understood the poetry of Sor Juana Inés only halfway, but the poems being so musical and mystical, they never failed to mesmerize me on the spot.

Interview by Bryce Milligan

Bryce Milligan: Francisco Lomelí used an interesting phrase in discussing Marcella Aguilar-Henson's book *The Multifaceted Poetic World of Angela De Hoyos.* He said she uncovered some of your "poetic motives." What is it that makes you write? How do you think that your "poetic motives" have changed over the years?

Angela De Hoyos: All forms of social injustice, as far as the disadvantaged or disenfranchised are concerned, move me to respond, or at least to address those conditions which I feel need to be brought to the table. As to my poetic motives, they are essentially the same, but I have matured over the years and become more universal.

Milligan: I'd like to come back to the idea of maturing into universality, but let's stick with your early work for a bit. Professor Lomelí makes a point—in his discussion of Aguilar-Henson's book—that your work in particular, and bilingual literature in general, "demands of readers/critics a background encompassing at least two cultural currents to adequately unveil meaning and understand confluence." He does not specify that the two cultures be Mexican and Anglo, just that readers need to have a bicultural or multicultural background to understand this literature. How do you feel about that?

De Hoyos: As universal languages, both English and Spanish apparently go into more nooks and crannies than we ever imagined. I have had readers writing to me from Israel, Japan, Australia, France, Italy, The Netherlands, India, Germany, Russia, Brazil, and the like, expressing interest in my books. Of course, it could be that Spanish, being one of the Romance languages, is very much akin to the other Romance idioms. And if the authors "interweave" some English into the text, it should then help to define the idea expressed. That is, far enough so that the reader is able to grasp some sense and meaning of the matter.

Milligan: But is it enough for readers simply to "grasp some sense and meaning"? Poetry is so subtle. Describe your ideal reader, if you would.

De Hoyos: Yes, I do agree with Professor Lomelí that at least two cultural currents, English and Spanish, are necessary to understand Chicano literature. Of course, the ideal reader for my work would be one versed in related cultures, subcultures as well. For instance, there is Caló, a vernacular of the streets, the language of the barrio, and Tex-Mex, which uses *pochismos*, or corruptions of English words, to construct a Spanglish vocabulary. My work also incorporates phrases in Aztec-Nahuatl, the original language of the Azteca-Mexíca peoples, some phrases in Afro-American Black English dialects, and words sprinkled here and there from Italian, French, and other languages.

Milligan: Speaking of bilingual code switching, you began writing entirely in either Spanish or English. How and when did you decide to break the mold and begin to interweave the languages? There were few if any models for code switching when you began. Did you ever think about what you were doing in terms of theory?

De Hoyos: Honestly, I never got around to thinking in terms of theory. I was simply writing in English, in Spanish, letting the words fall at will, like a monologue — indulging myself. In other words, I was casually throwing caution to the winds because I was practically starving, literally itching to write creatively in my own native language, and therefore my readers/audience could-should-would disappear. But that was then. Nowadays, I carefully plan and intersperse my words, phrases, or even whole stanzas — whatever it takes to deliver a clear message, and this should involve translated footnotes.

As far as my poetic voice is concerned, I began writing entirely in English, influenced no doubt by the English-speaking world, scholastic and familial, around me. Although I grew up in a bilingual environment and talked bilingually, code switching with friends and family, my "poetic" voice was nonetheless initially born in English. But in the early '70s I began to realize that if I could speak bilingually, why not document it that way? It was almost like a dare, something forbidden, poems which I kept in the closet — these hybrid children, deviants from an acceptable norm. Then in the mid-1970s, I became involved in "La Causa" — *el movimiento Chicano* — and a whole new world of possible, valid expression was opened for me.

Milligan: In *Woman, Woman*, Nick Kanellos describes the book as focusing on a "leitmotif present in most of [your] works: that dynamic tension which both unites and separates male and female. . . . [T]hat tension is always erotically charged, always threatening to one sex or the other, always reverberating in the political." How conscious were you of shifting your political attention from the *movimiento Chicano* to the *movimiento feminista*? Or do you see it that way at all?

De Hoyos: The leitmotif of which Nick Kanellos speaks is true. It is the love-hate politics—the give-and-take rivalry that has existed between the sexes since Adam and Eve. By the way, I was never conscious of shifting my "political attention from the *movimiento Chicano* to the *movimiento feminista*." Actually, some of those poems—such as "Lesson in Semantics," "Words Unspoken," "You Will Grow Old"—were born in my teens, long before I had the nerve to call myself a "poet." So, the very idea of shifting my course in midstream would be, shall we say, strictly for the birds. As to my interweaving the languages, no, I do not always code switch as a way of expression. But when I do, maybe it's that I am trying to retain, as much as possible, the use of my motherland language, and because it falls in naturally. Theoretically, some Spanish words or phrases have no English equivalent—such as *piñata, ¡viva!, fiesta, nada, machismo, ¡bravo!*, etc. Therefore, the English version doesn't connote the vitality, the color, the passion, or the joy of the Spanish words necessary to accurately convey the idea.

Milligan: Political considerations have been a major influence on your writing for most of your life. When did you first become politically conscious? Do you remember your very first political poem?

De Hoyos: Come to think of it, there is, unconsciously, something of the radical "rabble rouser" within me. Juan Tejeda used to refer to me as the "fighting poet." The poem "To a Brown Spider" is probably my first attempt to verbalize my political concerns. One day, I was relaxing in my mother's backyard garden. I happened to glance up at a tree nearby, where a garden spider was quietly coming out of her web. And, suspended by her drag line, she then dropped straight down for about three feet, dangled there, seemingly helpless, as she was tossed to and fro in the breeze. All at once, she decided to climb back to safety. I thought of my people—nuestra Raza—their constant struggle just to survive. Of course the analogy did not escape me: "We too hang by a thread."

Milligan: Interesting. I never identified that particular "we" as specifically Raza. I took it as referring to the human condition. What was your poetry like before it became political?

De Hoyos: I wrote lyrics, ranging from those suitable for lovesick girls to poems with a philosophical bent—trying to understand the whys and wherefores of our human existence.

Milligan: Ah, there's that universality again. Who were your earliest models? What poets did you read as a child or young teen that first shaped your ideas about what poetry can be?

De Hoyos: One of my earliest models was Sor Juana Inés de la Cruz. As a young teen, I had a yen for the short, pithy poems of Emily Dickinson, whose terse style and dream images influenced me deeply. Later on, Carl Sandburg, Robert Frost, William Carlos Williams, Boris Pasternak, William Blake, and Walt Whitman, more than anything for the music, the cadence of his lines. Of course, the Spanish-speaking poets, the antipoetry of Nicanor Parra, Nicaragua; Rosario Castellanos, Mexico; Federico García Lorca, Spain; Alfonsina Storni, Argentina; Jaime Sabines, Mexico, to cite a few.

Milligan: Sor Juana seems to me to be a rather sophisticated discovery for a child. How did you come upon her work?

De Hoyos: When I was about five, six, seven years old, my mother used to read to me from the Spanish-speaking poets. Sor Juana Inés de la Cruz was one of them, as well as Amado Nervo, Rubén Darío, and others. I recall my mother saying that when she was about my same age, her *abuelita* used to read to her from Sor Juana Inés. True, I was probably ahead of my years, in which case my mom, being a doting mother, assumed that her daughter was somewhat precocious. I may have understood the poetry of Sor Juana Inés only halfway, but the poems being so musical and mystical, they never failed to mesmerize me on the spot.

Milligan: You had an experience in childhood that made you a very private person, yet you became a very public poet, especially in the middle 1970s when your first books were published. How difficult was that for you? How did it happen?

De Hoyos: I consider myself an ambivert. I love the quiet solitude necessary for creative production, and then again, in the proper *ambiente* — in the company of friends and relations — I can become a gregarious walking-talking performing machine. I think your present question refers to my hearing problem. It was a progressive condition, which affected both ears. A bone growth was obstructing the ear canal and keeping the sound waves from reaching the auditory nerve.

I clearly recall that when I attended my first Floricanto meeting at the Mexican American Cultural Center in 1976, here in San Antonio, I could hardly hear the people around me. Alurista asked me, "Can you read — would you like to read your poetry?" I could barely hear him. Then someone spoke directly into my ear, repeating his words to me. I remember stammering some strange words, so charged with emotion that I could hardly speak, "Well, yes, I do — I would like to read some of my poems," and then my voice trailed off. I was thinking, "What am

I saying, how can I possibly read my work when I can hardly hear my own voice?" Then, I did go on to read. My first public reading for *el movimiento* took place at Nuestra Señora de Guadalupe church. Rolando Hinojosa-Smith was there, Tomás Rivera, as well as Max Martinez, raúlrsalinas, Ricardo Sanchez, Cecilio Garcia-Camarillo, Reyes Cardenas, and many others. Later, thanks to ear surgery, my hearing improved. From this experience was born my unpublished poem "One-Act Play: A Poem."

Also in 1976, Dr. Rudy Anaya invited me to give a poetry reading at "Sol y Sangre," a Chicano poetry series at the University of New Mexico. This event was one of the most memorable for me. Of course, all of these events gave me a sense of belonging to something greater than myself.

Milligan: You've mentioned spending a lot of time in the public library as a child. Talk about that, if you will. What library did you like best and why? Was there a particular librarian who helped direct your reading or influenced you in some other regard?

De Hoyos: During my childhood, San Pedro Park was one of my favorite haunts. I grew up on San Antonio's west side, and San Pedro Park with its library was within walking distance of my home, so it was only natural for me to go there. Of course, one of my favorite pastimes was going to the library to read. I don't re-call the names of the librarians, but they were always ready to help me, encouraging me and guiding me in my choices of reading materials. I would like to add, from 1976 to the present many librarians, educators, and mentors, of whom you are not the least, have influenced my work.

Milligan: Speaking of reading, it was often pointed out during the movement, and well into the 1990s, that Chicano children never "saw themselves" in their textbooks. I think the changes that have occurred in this area are among the finest political achievements of the Chicano movement. Do you remember ever having one of those "lightbulb" moments when you realized that your textbooks were not addressed to you as a Mexican American? If so, how did that affect your life?

De Hoyos: The fact that Mexican Americans were nowhere visible in my textbooks was very disturbing to me. It made me feel as if I didn't belong, at least not as a first class citizen. What saddened me the most was that I had to turn to my parents to find out about Benito Juárez, or for that matter, about other important political figures of Mexico. Thanks to the Chicano movement, some of these wrongs have been righted and changes for the better are taking place more often. In the media, and elsewhere, more opportunities are available to us. For example, Richard Rodriguez appears frequently on the Jim Lehrer *NewsHour* (PBS) with his timely essays on diverse topics. Recently, on the same TV program, in a segment hosted by Ray Suarez, Martín Espada presented selections of some of his own poems. So I'd say we are definitely moving forward.

Milligan: You are also an artist. Did you draw as a child, or did this talent develop later? What, for you, is the connection between your artwork and your writing?

De Hoyos: When I was about four years old, I suffered serious burns on my throat and upper chest. I got too close to a space heater in my father's dry cleaning establishment. The short of it is, I had a long convalescence and somehow I taught myself to draw. I also began to put together childhood verses — a dog and a cat on my window sat — or jingles like that. I think the connection lies in the fact that I visualize my images before I write them down. This is, I am sure, a normal phenomenon for any creative artist.

Milligan: You met Moises (Sandy) Sandoval and founded M&A Editions. How did the press come about? Obviously, it responded to a very real need, but what was it about running a press that appealed to you personally?

De Hoyos: In 1976 Sandy, my business partner, and I founded M&A Editions. Around that time, we heard about Lorna Dee Cervantes and her heroic publishing efforts — chapbooks, handsome full-color posters — all produced on her own Mango Press. Of course Sandy was very impressed. And so, we founded M&A Editions because we too wanted to support *el movimiento*.

Milligan: You are a classic example of the prophet who is too little recognized in her own region. You've been published in a dozen or more languages, won international prizes, and who knows how many European and Latin American dissertations have focused on your work. Yet most professors of contemporary American literature in Texas would be stunned to know that such a poet lives in San Antonio, Tejas. Can you ruminate a bit on what it all means to be a poet, an activist?

De Hoyos: Thank you for considering me a "prophet." I am nowhere near filling the bill. But thanks! If my work can produce in others at least a hint of an emotional impact, then I consider myself redeemed. That is what poetry is supposed to do: shake you up until you feel all "electrified" inside.

ON THE UNACCEPTABLE
   for M. R.

Strip! Strip all things
down to the pure essentials
—you advised me—
or you will spend your life
eternally hiding
behind facades.

And yet
When I revealed
my pure
my beautiful
my essential and naked truth
everyone turned away.
No one understood.

—"On the Unacceptable," in Roberta Fernández, ed.,
In Other Words: Literature by Latinas of the United States
(Houston: Arte Público Press–University of Houston, 1994), 75.
Reprinted by permission of the publisher.

Mylène Dressler

I find writing extremely difficult. I write by inches.

Mylène Dressler

I had this naive idea that if you could finally hang to a place where most of the mundane burdens in your life are removed, writing would somehow become easier.

Interview by Graham Stewart

Graham Stewart: The Dobie Paisano Fellowship you've earned gives you beautiful surroundings and the freedom to focus exclusively on your writing. Tell us more of how you got here.

Mylène Dressler: I got here through a combination of luck and good timing. I had finished a fairly polished draft of my second novel, *The Deadwood Beetle*. It wasn't published yet. Of course, one of the things you're expected to do in applying for the fellowship is to submit a writing sample. So I was able to send the first section of the novel. In addition to that, the application requires that you answer two simple but important questions: the kind of work that you hope to accomplish here and how you think you would fare in this environment.

This is a place that is beautiful and inspiring, but it's vast. It is very large. The solitude is not extreme, but it is pronounced. The committee is interested in knowing how you would handle that, if you'd be at home here, if you'd feel comfortable, if you'd do good work. I was able to answer that question fairly honestly because I had done a couple of writing residencies, although nothing on the scale of this one. When I got the phone call, I was absolutely stunned, because a lot of people apply for this fellowship. It is one of the best fellowships, not just in Texas, but in the entire country: the beauty of the surroundings, the generosity of the fellowship, the extent of time one is allowed to stay here. The fellowship is open to a lot of people. Anyone who was born in Texas, anyone who has lived in Texas for a certain period of time, or anyone who has written extensively about Texas at some point in her or his career is eligible for this fellowship. So I really thought it was a long shot. I'm just delighted and amazed that I am here.

Stewart: Does your first book, *The Medusa Tree*, contain facts and stories involving Texas?

Dressler: Not at all. It was set on three different continents, but it managed somehow to neglect Texas. Like most first novels, it is semiautobiographical.

The narrator is a thinly disguised version of myself. I was drawing on experiences that I'd had in places where I had lived. I moved around quite a bit before I settled down here in Texas. *The Deadwood Beetle* also travels around quite a bit and doesn't settle in Texas. But the book that I'm working on now, as I said in my application, is set in the South, in Texas. So it was important to me to sink my roots here. The timing is just wonderful, to be able to come here and work on my third book, which *is* set in Texas. It just couldn't be better.

Stewart: As a fellow, do you have a quota that you have to meet in terms of your writing output?

Dressler: In fact, you are free to come here and do nothing but sit and read. There is no measurement. There is the idea that you will write—who wouldn't, given this opportunity? I'm sure every single writer who's come here has done well with her or his time. They do ask you to write a report and reflect on your time here, but the expectation is that you use the time as you see best.

Stewart: What were your expectations when you began the fellowship? Were they accurate?

Dressler: I came here with pretty naive expectations in spite of having written this thoughtful essay about how I believed I was prepared for the solitude and serenity. I had this naive idea that if you finally hang to a place where most of the mundane burdens in your life are removed, writing would somehow become easier. I find writing extremely difficult. I write by inches, and that has not changed since I've been here. What has happened is that the place has infected me in very unpredictable ways.

The first month that I was here, it was really exhilarating. The whole country is so beautiful and diverse. By the second month, I started to feel a bit overwhelmed. By that I mean, here I am working on a book set in Texas but not in this part of Texas. Yet this part of Texas is so powerful—and I don't just mean the physicality of this place but also the history in this part of Texas. This property, in particular, is so powerful that I could feel it begin to impinge on the work in ways that maybe were not appropriate. In the third month, which is where I am now, I feel an equilibrium. I don't mean this to sound negative, but it's a kind of pushing back against the property, the power and ambience here, inasmuch as it is claiming me.

Stewart: You have acres of rugged wilderness; I would imagine that would cause you to create austere characters.

Dressler: Exactly. Or birds start showing up in your book that perhaps don't belong there. Austerity is a perfect word for it. In the book I'm working on, although set in Texas, the environment is quite different from here, and the mood is different. The difference between the two is starting to serve me well now that I've figured out what is happening here.

Stewart: In your book *The Deadwood Beetle*, your main character is a feeble man who has had a few heart bypass operations. He finds it painful even taking a walk outside his apartment. Why did you choose a character with that many barriers? Was it a challenge to you?

Dressler: Absolutely. As I said a moment ago, my first novel was so close to me. I was writing about characters somewhat like myself, most of whom were women. When I finished that book, I was quite proud of it and I still am, but as a writer you want to challenge yourself. You want to grow and develop. With my second novel, I was very conscious that I needed to choose something radically different. Immediately I thought about gender distinction. What if I write about a male character and make him older? Even that decision was partly self-conscious; I have to say that my father had died a few years before I started writing this book. He died at a very young age, at fifty-five. It seems to me that it was psychically soothing, to contemplate spending some time with a character who was going to reach a greater age and face certain issues my father never got to deal with. Those two things probably spawned that idea of adopting the point of view of an elderly man. Once I got into the writing, it turned out to be a terrific challenge.

Stewart: So much of the book is inwardly focused. Tristan, the main character, is constantly thinking of how he is being perceived. He views himself as stoic, yet inwardly he's in complete turmoil.

Dressler: It's nice to hear you say that because I was thinking too about the challenge of writing about any character late in life and what I myself as a writer and human being believe is accomplishable at that point in life. I like what you're saying. That was the effect I was going for. He is outwardly somewhat passive. He is old for seventy. This man has been debilitated by his circumstances, not just by his physical inheritances, but by the tremendous weight of history that bears down upon him. He has this wonderful inner life, the life of the mind, which is wonderful for a first-person narrator. He is marvelously inconsistent, which makes him very real to me.

Stewart: Part of his temperament is created in childhood, which was very traumatic. You had some chapters in the book where he's recalling what it was like being a child in Holland. Did you do that because you wanted to describe the experience of war?

Dressler: This is a book about a very specific Dutch man's — or rather boy's — experience. He is the son of Nazi collaborators. That puts him in a very strange position, to say the least. On the one hand, it buys the family temporary illusory power, but they paid a heavy price for that. This is the recounting of a very specific character's experience of a very specific time.

Stewart: The repercussions of his father's decision turn out to be very profound and damaging.

Dressler: I was really interested in how the Nazi regime worked. How these ordinary people became part of this monstrous machine and how they felt, or did not feel, about their participation in that. As you can tell from this book, I was even more interested in repercussions on their children and their children's children. How these decisions reverberate throughout the generations. Whether or not, and to what extent, sins of parents are visible in children and what it takes to recover.

Stewart: I learned in the book that 70 percent of the original Jewish population in Holland was lost because of the Holocaust.

Dressler: Oh, even higher. Percentage-wise, the Dutch people suffered the highest Jewish mortality rate of any country. The Dutch have always been very bureaucratic. Always throughout their history, they have documented the lives of their citizens. So this innocent-seeming bureaucracy was in place when the Nazis came to power and co-opted it. That is a tremendous burden for the nation to carry.

Stewart: A review I read said the book is being translated into three languages, one of which is Dutch. Has that happened yet?

Dressler: I think it's in the works. Unfortunately, although I was born in Holland, I no longer read or speak the language, so I have no real involvement in the translation process. Fortunately, I have family and friends who are quite adept in Dutch, so I'll be relying on them to let me know how well the translation comes out. From what I can tell, there is an upsurge of these kinds of books in Holland, these kinds of reflections, a lot of conversation about what went on during the war, and what happened in that country. So the book is going to be inserted into an ongoing dialogue, and I'm interested in how it all plays out.

Stewart: There's a part in the book where Tristan goes back to see his dying mother. The country is completely changed. He describes it as being psychedelic. Have you gone back?

Dressler: I have, several times since we emigrated, and even now Holland is a startling place in its modernity, particularly in Rotterdam, which was almost completely leveled during the war. It had to be entirely rebuilt, and of course it was primarily rebuilt in the '50s, '60s, and '70s. So the buildings have this wonderful energy and exuberance and modernism to them. Very modern cities coexist alongside almost entirely preserved villages that are hundreds of years old. I don't find it confining in the way that Tristan did at all. It's a very interesting home-coming when I go there.

Stewart: Tristan's son, Christopher, is a religious zealot who is demand-ing an emotional output from his father. He accuses him of being emotionally ab-sent. That seems to be a strange juxtaposition. Tell us more about your different approach to this type of issue.

Dressler: I don't think I was so much aware of being different as I was try-ing to think about repercussions within the family and how decisions made in the not-so-distant past affect the generation ahead of it. Christopher is such a strange character. He seems illogical. Yet, as I think about him, he seems to be a logical extension of his family. Having come out of Nazi Holland, the father raises his son in a vacuum. The only framework that he provides is a scientific one, but the sci-entific model has its limitations. It is a very cold environment to grow up in. So it doesn't surprise me that this child of ineffectual parents, who were in turn chil-dren of ineffectual parents, would reach out in a very extreme way to understand the world. Readers don't like Christopher, but they understand him.

Stewart: There's a beetle on the cover design of the book. What made you decide on that?

Dressler: I didn't decide. This is one of the things that I love about being a writer. One of the things that I tried to do was find a connection with Tristan. I used to be an English professor, and I thought if I made him an academic at least I'd be able to explore some professional world that I knew. But I didn't want to make him an English professor. I wanted to explore some other venue. So I just began writing, describing the clutter in his office.

It seemed to me that this office was unlike any office I had ever seen. There were many small drawers for some reason. What do people collect in tiny drawers? And the image of insects flashed into my mind. Instantaneously, ab-solutely, this man is an entomologist. Almost at the same moment, I asked what kind of insect would he study? He would be studying something very armored and shielded. That's when the image of the beetle came to mind. I have fallen in love with those creatures. They carry such weight. They have such import in human culture. They have always symbolized rebirth and rediscovery. When I hit upon that, it was one of those truly glorious moments of the novel to stumble onto one of the core metaphors in the book.

I wandered around the city the next day. Rotterdam was almost unrecognizable. Gone were the vacant lots, the deep craters that had lin-

gered long after the bombings, the blackened facades of the old buildings. The sagging, horse-drawn carts filled with ash. The shells of the
burned-out churches, the piles of rubble standing on the corners. The city
was now modern. Sleek and psychedelic. . . . Here we had screamed at
gulls, and thrown coffee beans at them, and hidden behind barrels that
smelled of decaying fish. Here I had learned to doubt and admire my sister, both, the way all younger siblings do, watching the older one reach
farther and faster and more energetically. The memory of her bare, white,
golden-flecked arm hung in the air tracing a kind of script in front of me,
but the emotions it conjured were all contradictory, admiration and envy,
trust and fear, partner and competitor, love and hate.

—*The Deadwood Beetle* (New York: Penguin Putnam, 2001), 162.

Horton Foote

I don't know that we choose how we write.
I think it somehow chooses us.

Horton Foote

Essay by Joe Holley

"When I was a young boy, I used to take walks with my parents," Horton Foote told a class of aspiring dramatists a few years ago. "They would always point out the home of a distinguished gentleman, Mr. Armstrong. 'He got the call in the cotton fields of Mississippi,' Mother would say, 'to come to Texas to preach. Anybody can get the call.' At twelve, I got the call to be an actor. I don't know how it happened. Life's full of those kinds of mysteries. . . . Later I just stopped acting. I wanted to write. It was like when a butterfly leaves a cocoon. That's over."

Horton Foote was born in Wharton, Texas, in 1916, and his early years in that small southern town near the mouth of the Colorado River have nurtured a career as a playwright that's now six decades long. That career got its start when Foote, at the age of sixteen, left Wharton to study acting in Pasadena, California. From there he went to New York City to become an actor and writer. Over the years he has written plays for television, radio, film, and stage.

Although Foote is probably best known for his adaptation of Harper Lee's To Kill a Mockingbird and his original screenplay Tender Mercies, *both of which earned him Academy Awards, he has written some fifty plays. Most are set in fictional Harrison, Texas, which bears a notable resemblance to Wharton in the early decades of the century. Foote also has received an Indie Award for Best Writer for* The Trip to Bountiful *and a Pulitzer Prize for* The Young Man from Atlanta. In all of his writings, Foote explores what New York Times *drama critic Frank Rich termed "the unbearable turbulence beneath a tranquil surface."*

Foote lives in Wharton, in the bright canary-yellow house where he grew up. In 1999 he began publishing his memoirs and is now working on the third volume.

It's a very mysterious process, this finding what you want to write about and how it appears and how it urges you to finish it and to go through all the pain of finding it. But I think essentially I've always known that the search will always take me back here, to Wharton, Texas. I've just never had a desire to write about any place else.

Ramona Cearley: Much of your writing evokes a lyrical sense of place and strength of character. Where do your stories begin? How do you choose what to write about?

Horton Foote: I suppose it is oversimplification that you write about what you know. I've never really analyzed it. It's a very mysterious process, this finding what you want to write about and how it appears and how it urges you to finish it and to go through all the pain. But I think essentially I've always known that the search will always take me back here, to Wharton, Texas, at least for the place. I've just never had a desire to write about any place else. I've tried to write about New York, where I've spent a great deal of my time, and the work just doesn't have the same ring of authenticity as when I write about here. Of course I call my town Harrison, not Wharton. But you know it's based on my experiences here, things I've observed and grown up with.

Cearley: Is there a different sense of community between small-town Texas and places such as New York City?

Foote: That really doesn't interest me too much. I don't think of Wharton as a special place, because the things that happen here can happen in a big city. It's just that the sights and sounds are different. Maybe the physical things are different, but emotional life doesn't vary very much. Essentially, if you're dealing with human beings, as I try to do, you have to take a close consideration of the place and the particular influences.

For instance, I've only recently become aware of how much life here has been affected by the use of cotton-picking machines. Now I don't think anybody would say, "It's affected me." But in a peculiar way it's affected the whole area. It's affected the town visually because you no longer see the little houses out in the fields and people out there picking cotton. It's affected the town socially, especially on Saturdays; there's nobody in town anymore. It used to be so crowded. Subtle ways, they just creep up on you. All of a sudden you realize you are in a whole different era. You'll never go back to that again. Mechanization also has its great blessings because it was probably the least rewarding work in the world to sit in the hot sun and pick cotton. But there has been a change. So things like that creep into work, and after it's crept in, you analyze it and recognize that it is different.

You can find similar changes in a big city like New York. All of a sudden you look around and a building is gone. For instance, when I first went to New York, I often made my living running an elevator. Now, nobody runs elevators. You press a button and up you go and down you come. Those may seem far-fetched examples, but in a curious way they are examples of the kind of thing that is taking place all around, all the time.

Cearley: Is there a moment in your growing up that helped define you as a writer today?

Foote: I am working on the second volume of my memoirs. Scribner is publishing it, and I was just analyzing that very fact. In the preface I write about the time when I took a bus at seventeen to go to Pasadena to study acting. If I'd known then that I would end up being a playwright, I think that I'd have gotten off the bus and gone to college. I refused to go to college because I didn't think that would be good for an actor. Yet I am glad I didn't, because the unplanned things that I learned along the way before I began to write were very helpful. So it is very difficult to say.

I began writing almost casually. Agnes de Mille suggested I might think about writing a play; she had seen some improvisations I'd done. It began as casually as that. My second play — a full-length play — was written right in this living room. Then Brooks Atkinson, a well-known critic, saw it and liked it. My writing career began as simply as that. Then I had a lot of work to do, because I didn't know much about writing. I had a lot of humbling to do.

Cearley: What did that experience involve?

Foote: Well, it's not easy to learn in public. I had some reputation and I felt — and I think rightly so — the public was very demanding of me. It is trial and error. The key is not to get discouraged and not to let your ego get in the way. Being a theater writer is different than any other kind of writer. It is so public. Lord knows, everything funny reaches the public, but novels reach the public in a quieter way somehow. Another thing about theater writing is you need a vocabulary of the theater. As soon as you can get that, the better off you are. Therefore, I think being trained as an actor was very helpful to me.

Cearley: You chose from the beginning to write about the essence of life growing up in a small town?

Foote: I don't know that we choose how we write. I think it somehow chooses us. It's very mystical. At least I feel that's true about the writers I most admire.

Cearley: Who are some of the writers you admire?

Foote: Oh, I'd be here all day; there are too many people I love and admire. I go through phases. Right now, I'm very involved with an English writer named Henry Green, who's been dead many years. I read him long ago when I was a younger man. Recently I've been rediscovering him, and I am absolutely fascinated with him. I read him constantly. So in that sense, I'm an obsessive enthusiast. I get crushes, and I read and read and read. I think the writers I go back to all the time are Katherine Anne Porter and Reynolds Price and Flannery O'Connor. Eudora Welty. Willa Cather. Mark Twain. Faulkner. I suppose you might say those writers have been my influences in a sustained way. And then of course there are a number of playwrights, but I'm very eclectic. There is a writer who is not that well known, named William Maxwell, whom I think very highly of. Peter Taylor, who is a friend of mine, is a great, great writer. I'll get crushes on writers and just get obsessive about reading their work.

Cearley: In terms of your own writing, are there some stories that you favor above others?

Foote: I wouldn't dare; it's like saying who's my favorite child. They'd jump off the shelf and hit me. I think the thing you are working on at the present time is the one that gets the most attention.

Cearley: What qualities are important for a writer to develop?

Foote: The main thing about writing is perseverance. It's a job that you can easily be distracted from; there are a lot of temptations. When I was coming along, we didn't have the temptation of television. You could spend the rest of your life listening to that if you weren't careful. Writing is a lonely journey, and writers have to find their own way. That's the most important thing: to realize that your own voice is the most important gift you have.

Cearley: Explain what encompasses writing.

Foote: When I say writing, I don't mean taking a pencil to paper or going to the typewriter; I mean thinking about writing some part of every day. A lot of writing is thinking and meditating and not grabbing at the first idea that comes to you, but letting it take shape and form. You have to have trust in your talent, and nobody can give you that. Unfortunately, the world is very anxious to destroy that thing.

Cearley: How do you mean?

Foote: The world is very anxious to destroy that faith. I wish I could say definitely this is what you do, and then you do that, and you will be a great success. I don't think it is possible. You have to find your own way. I think you can early on look to writers that you feel compatible with and learn from. Don't be afraid of copying because actually you take what you need, then you soon begin to find your own voice.

Cearley: In terms of your career, what makes you the most proud?

Foote: I am quite proud that President Clinton gave me the National Medal of Arts in 2000 during ceremonies in Washington, D.C. I admire him. I was very happy to be there and very pleased that he selected me. There were two ceremonies at that time: the National Medal of Arts awards given to artists, writers, actors, theater people, and poets, and the National Humanities medals that were presented to scholars and writers. The reason the two events were at the same time was because of the campaign; Mrs. Clinton was running for the Senate. Having the two events together was very exciting. A lot of interesting people were there.

Cearley: That sounds wonderful. Since 1985 the National Medal of Arts has been given by the president of the United States to honor outstanding contributions in the arts. Congratulations to you, sir, as a recipient of the medal for your work as playwright and screenwriter.

Foote: Thank you.

Cearley: What brings you the most joy?

Foote: Just writing. I really do love to write. When I say write, again I don't mean paper and pencil. I mean thinking about writing. Reading other writers. Trying to find new projects. Then the actual process of writing, taking the pen—I don't use a typewriter, I use a pen—and a piece of paper and going to it. I feel very blessed that I like what I do so much.

The lady next to me called out to the lady across the aisle. "This boy," she said pointing to me, "is going to acting school. It's costing seven hundred and fifty dollars. Isn't that right, son?"

"Yes, ma'am," I said closing my eyes, hoping she would leave me alone, when the bus driver called out: "We're coming into Los Angeles."

I tried to look out the window again but it was pitch black outside now and I couldn't see anything but the lights of houses and cars. Then I could see streetlights and buildings and more cars and people on the sidewalks and the lady across the aisle said, "We're almost at the terminal now."

We rode on for another five or ten minutes and the bus pulled into the terminal, which was all lit up and seemed much larger than the Houston or Dallas bus terminals. The bus driver stopped the bus and called out, "Los Angeles!" and everyone began to get up from their seats. The lady next to me patted me on the arm as we started down the aisle and said, "Good luck to you, son," and I thanked her. I got off the bus and followed the people into the terminal. I saw Aunt Mag and Uncle Walt right away and they saw me. Aunt Mag hugged me and kissed me and Uncle Walt shook my hand as he said, "Welcome to California."

—*Beginnings: A Memoir* (New York: Scribner, 2001), 18–19.

Kinky Friedman

Fighting the good fight. That is what I believe.

Kinky Friedman

American society is pretty hung up about a lot of things. Americans get into a snit over minutiae that is not relevant. I am akin to people like Don Quixote. You ought to fight evil in the world. What I fight is bureaucracy, homogenization, sanitation, and all the chaining of America.

Interview by Susan Daniels

Susan Daniels: Your Jewish ancestry is very important to you. You refer to it throughout your writings. Are you a Jew with Texas influences or a Texan with Jewish influences?

Kinky Friedman: Probably a bastard child of twin cultures. Really the best thing about being Jewish is being on the outside looking in, the angle of observation.

Daniels: In terms of your writing, what formal writing courses did you receive?

Friedman: I was in Plan II [interdisciplinary honors program] at the University of Texas [Austin] but I had no clue as to what I was doing. It was a very liberal-arts program. In fact I graduated without a major.

Daniels: Do you have a favorite Texas author that you like to read?

Friedman: I read Sarah Bird. Lately I have started reading Sandra Brown. I may be the only man who reads Sandra Brown, but she is very funny. And she does have forty-nine *New York Times* best sellers, which says something. I am also reading *Woodcuts of Women* by Dagoberto Gilb, which I think is very good. I like Larry McMurtry's early stuff, *Leaving Cheyenne* and *Horseman, Pass By*, and I like Larry King's writing too.

Daniels: Do you see similarities between themes in Texas literature and the Greek and Roman stories that you studied at UT?

Friedman: I did come very close to majoring in classics, but I repressed almost all of that.

Daniels: You were once quoted as saying that you wanted to tone down your music to make it more commercial. Have you had to tone down your writing to make it more commercial?

Friedman: No, that has not been a problem. I like to write between the lines. I like to look deeply into myself, which some people confuse with self-absorption. But I believe that if you look deeply inside yourself, you will find everybody else.

Daniels: You once said, "I find fiction is a great place for truth telling." What truths do you tell in your books?

Friedman: I try to be as truthful as I can, without writing a tell-all book. Hopefully, there will be some commentary on the human condition. Certainly there is some unconscious commentary on America in my books, and that is why I have almost as many foreign translations as do people who have blockbuster Hollywood movies made out of their books. My books have been published in eighteen or nineteen foreign languages, just because somebody over there liked them. Ironically some of the biggest sales are in places like Germany where you would never imagine they would get it.

Daniels: Why do you think you are popular in countries such as Germany?

Friedman: The people who buy my books are westward leaning. If I were doing as well in America as I am in Germany right now, I would be Stephen King.

Daniels: You were a Peace Corps volunteer in Borneo. What about Borneo contributed to your creativity as a writer?

Friedman: Things move very slowly in Borneo. You can wait for days for a river launch to show up. So it lets things percolate. Also, I think you write from a distance very well.

Daniels: How did you select mysteries as a genre to work in?

Friedman: I like mysteries. They provide some kind of resolution, mysteries do. I find it very comforting to tie up things at the end. It gives me a kind of peace.

Daniels: Your work has been compared to Dashiell Hammett's.

Friedman: Hammett and [Raymond] Chandler were both very poetic in their own ways. They were better writers than they got credit for being. I think my writing is very close to early Kurt Vonnegut. Now, nobody but one man in Stockholm agrees with me on that, or at least has observed that.

Daniels: How did you develop your Kinkster character?

Friedman: It's just a reflection of myself in some bus station window in the rain in Nashville. It is not a contrived character. It is who I am pretty much. Well, the Kinkster is a little different than me, but not that much.

Daniels: What is your writing routine like?

Friedman: I have no real discipline whatsoever. I just have cleared the boards in my life. I am cautious about spending my life at book signings and literary functions. I am good at it: being at a Barnes and Noble and signing a lot of books and being gracious to people. I really don't think that is what Kafka would want. What would Kafka do? That is what I ask myself.

Daniels: He would transform himself into a bug.

Friedman: Right.

Daniels: Let's talk about point of view. How does working in the first person change the mystery, as opposed to having an omniscient narrator?

Friedman: I always write in the first person—with the exception of a couple of nonfiction works: *Kinky Friedman's Guide to Texas Etiquette* and *I Am the Lindbergh Baby*. For one thing, mystery writing, the kind I like anyway, is usually done in the first person. It also lets you play a little game with the reader. About midway through the book, the reader realizes that he is running ten steps ahead of the Kinkster, but the author is ten steps ahead of him. That would be ideal. That would be my little game.

The problem of the mystery genre is that most people do not take it seriously. I could be writing great literature. Some of it, I am sure, is great. It could be very poetic. And it would be lost like pearls in the snow. So that is the problem. When you write a novel like *Kill Two Birds and Get Stoned*, you have a chance people will accept it and say, "Hey, this is an important social document." That will never happen if I am writing a mystery series.

Daniels: Do you think people will be reading Kinky Friedman one hundred years from now?

Friedman: I think that there is a far better chance of that than there is of almost any of the mainstream writers. Dean Koontz recently was saying that he sold sixty million books a year and that Hemingway and Fitzgerald will disappear from college course requirements. My theory is just the opposite. I believe that Dean Koontz will disappear, and Hemingway and Fitzgerald will be around for a while. I certainly hope that Dean Koontz will disappear.

Daniels: Some of your writing and some of your comments are not considered politically correct. Why do you focus on sometimes-sensitive subjects?

Friedman: I write free form about what is going on in my life. American society is pretty hung up about a lot of things. If you get down to Australia you will see people who are a lot looser about things. Americans get into a snit over minutiae that is not relevant. I am akin to people like Don Quixote. You ought to fight evil in the world. What I fight is bureaucracy, homogenization, sanitation, and all the chaining of America.

Daniels: Do you think that you are jousting at windmills as Quixote did? Won't you ultimately be frustrated?

Friedman: Probably.

Daniels: Then why do it?

Friedman: Because it is fighting the good fight. That is what I believe. The flavor of what I am doing seeps through and sometimes the commentary does too. People remember the weirdest stuff that you think no one is going to get. Somebody will come up and say, "I loved that line in that book." There is a very good chance that my work will endure longer than the commercial best sellers. Who is to say?

Daniels: How do you know that you have achieved your goal when you select sensitive subjects?

Friedman: As an author you never do. What is a sensitive subject for some people is not a sensitive subject for others. For me, nothing is really a sensitive subject except maybe the death of my mother.

Daniels: How do your years spent on the road as a country-and-western star influence your ideas about celebrity?

Friedman: I have always wanted to be a bigger star than I was. I am having trouble with the idea that I have millions of fans around the world, and these days I do, because the books are turning people on to the music, and vice versa, but mostly the books. I was booked in Sydney, Australia, on a Monday night just to talk a bit, to answer questions, at this theater where they charged eight dollars. I thought we would have twelve people. There were hundreds. So that is a natural thing. No book publisher helped me with that. No record company promoted that.

Daniels: You don't have an ego, do you?

Friedman: I try to park my ego at the door if I can. I probably do, but as an author you are a step removed from the work. Now as a performer, the work is really you. A performer is only as good as his last show.

Daniels: Is not an author only as good as his last book?

Friedman: Yeah, but my books have a long shelf life. There will always be a handful of people doing better than you. If you want to count financially, my friend Sandy Brown is doing better. She gets all the money. I get all the glory. People always want what they don't have. I would like to have the money; she would like to have the glory.

Call Me Kinky.

It's not my true Christian name, of course, but then, I'm not a true Christian. If you don't believe me, maybe I can sell you the bridge of my nose. For, indeed, what true Christian, with Sunday-morning church bells ringing cacophonously all around him, would prefer sitting in a cold, drafty loft one floor below a lesbian dance class, puffing a cigar, sipping an espresso, and playing chess with a cat? It was a slow game, but I'd seen slower.

"Are you going to make a move," I said to the cat, "or are you just going to sit there?"

The cat, of course, said nothing. Nor did she deign to make a move. She was one of those maddening breed of finicky, meticulously conservative players who now and again cause you to want to reach across the table and yank their whiskers.

—*Blast from the Past*
(New York: Simon and Schuster, 1998), 19.

Laura Furman

When she read my memoir, she said,
"This is my life."

Laura Furman

I got a letter the other day from someone who had read Ordinary Paradise, *my memoir, who has a really different background. She's African American. She's seventy-five, and she's gone through a much more difficult time than I can imagine. When she read the memoir, she said, "This is my life." It was incredible to get that letter.*

Interview by Gary Kent

Gary Kent: Where are you from originally?

Laura Furman: I was born in Brooklyn Heights and grew up on the island of Manhattan. My parents moved there when I was about six. My father was a native New Yorker, and my mother was born in Pennsylvania and moved to Atlanta when she was just about pre-teen. So I grew up in the East; I grew up in New York mostly. And I moved to Texas in 1978 when I was about thirty-three.

Kent: That's a big move, New York to Texas. Had you been here before? Why did you move to Texas?

Furman: I had worked for seven years for Dominique de Menil in Houston. I was freelance in New York, but I'd come down to Houston enough times that I had really good friends there. Five years before I moved to Texas, I moved to a farmhouse in upstate New York. I spent five winters there, and it was enough. So I applied for teaching jobs. I'd had one story published in the *New Yorker*. I was really lucky and got a couple of job offers, but one was way up in the Adirondacks. The other one was in southern Mississippi, and I wasn't sure about that. Then I was hired by Tom Curtis, who was editing *Houston City Magazine*. I'd always made my living as a copy editor, as a book editor mostly, and he said, in May, "Well, if we're still in business in September, you can have a job." They were, and I moved to Houston and figured I'd stay until the summer. Thought I'd just get out of another winter. I've been in Texas ever since.

Kent: How long did you live in Houston?

Furman: I was there almost three years. I really loved it, and I still love it as a city.

Kent: When did you start writing? Were you in school?

Furman: I guess I always wrote. I wrote all through high school and in college. I was editor of the high school literary magazine. I took one writing course in college with Bernard Malamud, who was a wonderful writer. But something must have happened to me under his tutelage because I really froze up. So I traveled around and lived in the city. When I was about twenty-seven, I decided writing is what I really wanted to do. Then I set about figuring out how to write, because it was hard to sit down long enough to get anything done. That was the first struggle. In fact my friend, a painter to whom I dedicated *Drinking with the Cook*, said, "Just sit for fifteen minutes, and you don't have to work; just sit there. Then you can get up, but you can't get up before fifteen minutes." So I did that for about a week. And I just kept adding more time each day until pretty soon I could sit for longer. Since I was sitting in front of my typewriter anyway, I started writing. Then I worked my way up in stamina, so I was writing then.

Kent: When you write, are there special places or special times of day that are best for you for writing?

Furman: Sometimes it's whenever I can see fifteen minutes clear. That's during the term when I am teaching, but I like writing in the morning. I like waking up about a quarter 'til five and starting to write then. My family usually starts stirring around six-thirty or seven, and then they're gone by about eight.

Kent: Tell us about your family.

Furman: I'm married to Joel Warren Barna, who is the author of *The See-Through Years*. For eleven years he was editor of *Texas Architect* magazine, although he's not an architect; he was trained as a journalist. *See-Through Years* is a wonderful book about the recession in Texas and the relationship between design and the economy in Texas in the 1980s. Now he is development officer for the McDonald Observatory, so he works in the astronomy department at the University of Texas at Austin. Our son is talented and smart and beautiful, everything.

Kent: When a book or an article becomes real to me, it is because I identify with the people. I say, "I know that person" or "I know that situation," and that's really evident in your work. I think that I'm reading something very real. What triggers you to write? Where do your ideas come from?

Furman: First of all, thank you. That means a lot. I love it when people say that. I got a letter the other day from someone who had read *Ordinary Paradise*, my memoir, who has a really different background from mine. She is African American. She's seventy-five, and she's gone through a much more difficult time than I can imagine. When she read the memoir, she said, "This is my life. You said all the things that I've wanted to say; I feel like I've just grown up at seventy-five, and this is helping me." It was incredible to get that letter.

I think, though, I more often see form rather than people. For instance, there's a story in *Drinking with the Cook* called "The Woods," about a little boy who sees a man hanging in the woods, someone who has committed suicide, and nobody believes that he's actually seen this person. Everybody is very busy doing other things, wondering what his motivation might be in saying that. That actually happened to a friend of a neighbor, so I just started thinking about that. I started thinking not so much about the boy as about the woods and what it means—what these woods that I live in mean—because they're very carefully preserved in one way, and very foolishly preserved in another: there is so much cedar here. It is this human decision to keep things the way they were, or the way they are, which is an impossibility. During the latest drought it was terrifying to be here because if any of these cedar trees had caught on fire, we all would have been finished. They're pretty, but they also make us sick on an annual basis. And they're being preserved.

Kent: This is a gorgeous view outside your window. Cedar fever, does that afflict you at all?

Furman: No, I don't get it. In fact, nobody in my family gets it, but we get other things, and you can see the cedar going by as if it were smoke. Sometimes I've looked out at the valley and thought, "Uh-oh, something's on fire," but it's not; it's just pollen going by. But when I heard that story about the boy, it triggered my thinking about someone deciding to die, but deciding to die in the woods, and the way we try to preserve the woods, and the way also we try to cushion our children and keep them safe, and sometimes put them in peril as a result. So I just worked with that, and the story came out of that.

Kent: Do most of your stories come from real-life incidents that you've heard about or experienced? Or from your imagination directly?

Furman: The trigger is mostly things that I've experienced, although there is another story, "The Apprentice," that was triggered by a small biographical article about e. e. cummings and an affair that he had with the wife of a patron of the arts. I don't know what got me started on that, but I ended up writing a story about the daughter of an artist, someone unrecognized as his daughter, who goes to visit him. While she's there, she realizes that he is her father. That came out of an article I was reading, but most often my stories come out of something I've experienced or a friend has told me about.

Kent: You work in education. Does that conflict with your writing? Or is it part and parcel?

Furman: You know, it conflicts in a very basic, primitive, crude way—which is that it exhausts me, and it takes up my time. On the other hand, it pays me, which writing doesn't. And it's not all year round; it's thirty-two weeks. A lot of writers work every week, every day, so I feel I'm lucky in that way.

After eighteen years of teaching, I think I've gotten to the point where I've relaxed enough with it that I can learn things as I speak to the students. I'll realize, oh, I've learned this. I know this now. And in trying to instruct, I am forced to articulate things about writing that I never, never would have. Also I've been trying to not teach fiction because that really does interfere. I've been teaching essay and biography, and that's an incredible amount of fun.

Kent: How would fiction interfere? What does that mean?

Furman: When I'm writing fiction, I really like just thinking about *my* fiction. I don't even like reading much fiction. I read mystery stories when I'm writing fiction, and biography and essays. I'm also reading a hundred student stories a semester, if I get them to do three stories. I worked as an editor for so long that my approach to teaching is to go into the text and try to rewrite, to show them that these are moveable parts. You know that once you write something it is not stuck there. You can move it around. You change words. You can take out lines. So I get into the text very deeply in other people's writing. Once you've done that all day, it's really hard to sit down. So most of the time when I'm teaching, I'll try to work for an hour in the morning and then go off to school.

Kent: When you finish a page are you done with it, or do you polish page by page? Do you write and then come back to it later?

Furman: No, I usually work sentence by sentence. I can't go on until I can see the shape of the sentences. Then once I get to the end of a draft, I'll try to leave it alone, even if it's just for a day. Then I rewrite endlessly.

Kent: So you enjoy rewriting?

Furman: I love rewriting. It is such a relief from writing, and I can do that endlessly. I think that's one of the problems that I have with most of the writing classes that are taught. People usually do only one draft in a class or a workshop, and then they're reading finished stories; they don't learn that there are usually twenty-seven drafts in the middle, and that up to the last minute you're changing things. I mean some of my stories are at least fifteen years old, and with fresh editorial eyes, I was making changes on them.

Courses should be really long so that you can write a story, leave it alone for three weeks, then rewrite it. Then leave it alone. I try to do that with students to a degree, but they're under all kinds of pressures.

Kent: What is the basic advice you give to a student who says, "I want to be a writer?"

Furman: I guess if you want to be a writer you're already a reader. If you want to be a writer, and you're not reading, then you really should look elsewhere. In a way, if you want to be a writer, and you're not already writing, then what are you thinking about? Just get to it. There's no substitute for doing it.

Kent: The critics generally praise your work a lot. Are you affected by criticism? Does it help you, or do you even bother reading reviews of your work?

Furman: Oh, I read them. It's of course nice to be praised; everybody wants to be praised. It depends on who writes it, how seriously I'll take it, but if it is a writer or a critic I respect, I'm very pleased. I've gotten mediocre reviews, and I've gotten hostile reviews for *Ordinary Paradise*. Those reviews weren't mediocre; they were hostile. I think because it is memoir, they don't generally see it as a literary form. It wasn't so much that I was hurt as I was really shocked, partly because that had never happened before, and partly because it did feel personal. It didn't feel like it was about my writing. It felt like they were attacking me, and I think that's also the nature of memoir, that you kind of lay yourself out there.

Kent: Who are some of your favorite writers, people you really admire?

Furman: Let's see, Anthony Powell, who wrote *A Dance to the Music of Time*, whose name I know is pronounced "Pole," but I can't quite say it. I love Alice Munro. She's a really wonderful short story writer. Mavis Gallant. I think I've learned more from Mavis Gallant's short stories than from anyone because she really has stretched the form so far. And—I hope this doesn't sound pretentious—but I've learned a lot from Chekhov. I love Ivy Compton-Burnett. There's a mystery writer I really admire, Steven Dobbins, who's also a very well-known poet, and Raymond Chandler. I'm not the greatest plotter in the universe, and I've tried to learn from these folks.

Kent: What are some of the qualities you most admire in other people?

Furman: Generosity, loyalty, and intelligence. That's one of the things I love the most about my husband, that he's so smart and so funny, and he also knows when not to let you know how smart and funny he is.

Kent: What's in the future now?

Furman: I'm working on a novel called *The Right Age for a Widow* that's about a widow in upstate New York. After that I want to do a series of biographical essays about some writers who were friends in the '50s, and write stories. When I'm working on a novel I think, "If only I was writing stories and essays everything would be fine."

Kent: When you're writing a novel, do you write to a deadline, do you say, I've got to have this done by next spring?

Furman: No, I mean I'm a fool like everybody else. When I start a book I think I'll get this finished in a year. What's to stop me? Then it always takes me about seven years.

Kent: Oh, sure, the vagaries of life.

Furman: Things happen, and the book takes longer, and you can't force it. It is just impossible. I can't think any faster than I can think. I just had a couple of weeks where—well, actually this whole term from January until now—where I have not been able to write very much. I was working myself up to get unhappy about that. Then I woke up one morning and realized where I need to go in the next part of the book, and I wouldn't have known that if I hadn't had this break. So I am trying to just let it happen and not fight against it.

"I brought this," I said, and set the bottle on the table next to the jug. Acceptable wine may be found in jugs, but that jug wasn't one of them.

Geraldine gave the bottle her full attention.

"That didn't come from around here," she said.

"No. The moving van seemed so handy that I splurged and bought some cases."

"A woman after my own heart. The corkscrew's over there."

The elegance of her well-used utensils and hand-thrown pottery emerged, preening themselves next to the foreign bottle. I chose glasses with stems, poured a glass for her and a glass for me. Before I could drink, Geraldine raised her glass, proclaiming: "Welcome to the country."

Fun, I thought. I was new to living in the country and everyone seemed to be playing house.

The wine hit me hard, but was only a taste to Geraldine. She filled her glass and drank it down in a few swallows, then she sighed and refilled it. "It's really nice wine," she said. "I've forgotten. We drink anything." She turned to stir the pot.

—*Drinking with the Cook: Stories*
(Houston: Winedale Publishing, 2001), 4.

Dagoberto Gilb

I was always listening to stories.
That's what I love.

Dagoberto Gilb

Ordinary people are telling a story because they want someone to hear it. I like to hear them. I enjoy stories. I like people to tell me stories. I miss that.

Interview by Joe Holley

Joe Holley: Tell me about your origins—where you were born, where you grew up.

Dagoberto Gilb: I was born in Los Angeles. My mom was a Mexican. I've always been a little bit confused about where her family was from, but the cities talked about are Xalapa and Puebla, then Mexico City, where she was born. She came across when she was pretty young, about five or six. My dad grew up in East L.A., in Boyle Heights. He spoke Spanish.

Holley: But he wasn't Mexican?

Gilb: No, he was of German descent, although he didn't look so German. Everybody thought he was something not American. My mom grew up next door to where he worked for forty-five years, at an industrial laundry. Her mother lived in a little house next door to the laundry and was sort of the mistress to the owner. This laundry, the plant, washed and pressed things from hospitals and restaurants, sheets and tablecloths, things like that. The Playboy Club was a big, famous account. I started working there—my dad put me to work—when I was thirteen. They were divorced when I was very young, before I had consciousness, and I grew up with my mom. Neither of my parents is alive.

Holley: Where'd you go to college?

Gilb: UC–Santa Barbara. I transferred from junior colleges. I have a son at Stanford, so I joke with him, "Well, you got accepted at Stanford, but I got accepted to *many* junior colleges." I loved college. I loved everything. I loved every subject, but I ended up studying philosophy and religion.

Holley: So you really liked it?

Gilb: School was like a business to me. I took it extremely seriously. It was a struggle to get a B. I worked really hard. I wasn't smart, and I wanted to be smart. Instead of fighting, which is how I grew up, I wanted life to be about brains. I was just totally excited about that. The education world was this paradise. The problem I had was concentrating on one thing. I couldn't take a class that didn't excite me. I loved learning. I loved books. I loved books so much I stole them. I stole them all the time.

Holley: From stores, the library?

Gilb: No, not libraries, from bookstores. One of my worst experiences ever—I mean it really was a turning point—was that I would always steal my textbooks from this one bookstore. I got so casual about it, like when you're doing bad things you get so good at it, you stop thinking. I was a frantic reader, and I had to own them. Libraries didn't work, because I thought libraries were sacred. Besides, it had to be *my* book. I don't know what that's about, that you have to have that book and call it *yours*, even when there are a hundred thousand copies. That one book is your book, even though somebody could have scribbled in the margins. Anyway, I was stealing one this one time, and the man who owned the store—who had probably seen me a million times because I'd come in there every day for years—saw me doing it, and all he said was, "Leave, and don't come back." I was so humiliated.

Holley: Did that break you?

Gilb: Yeah, I really realized I had a problem. But you know, recently I met an interviewer on my last book tour, in Los Angeles, a pretty well-known interviewer, and the gossip about him is that his partner always has to save him from public scandal, because he steals books so often. And when I heard that, it occurred to me, "That's sweet!" I mean, of all the problems you can have, what a sweet one stealing *books* is. It made me feel much better about my bookstore history. I really didn't go after people's things. I went after books. What a good boy I was!

Holley: When did you sit down and write fiction?

Gilb: I was almost out of college. It didn't come to me quickly. I was in my later twenties.

Holley: You were still in college?

Gilb: I was just finishing. Really, I thought of writing as more of a practical thing. I talk too much, I had a thousand stories, and I'd been reading a lot. I didn't take any English classes. I'd failed it so many times. I couldn't write a paper. I couldn't write. I don't exaggerate; I didn't know how to write a composition. I had a lot of enthusiasm and teachers liked me, but I really made huge mistakes until I was a grad student. When I tutored a remedial English class, I learned how English worked. The woman who was running the class would teach me, the tutor, while she lectured, and for the first time in my life I knew what a period was, what a comma was, what a conjunction did, what a fragment was.

Holley: Was there a point where you began to read fiction for craft and construction?

Gilb: I don't think I was ever conscious of that until very recently. I knew, I guess instinctually, that you tried to write as well as you could. But I think once you really find your voice, the trick is, like Kerouac's "spontaneous bop prose," where you never look back, you're not supposed to edit yourself too much. Well, I think you have to lightly edit yourself as you're writing, not harming the natural music. I keep notebooks; that's my main occupation. Ninety percent of my writing is in a notebook.

Holley: How does the content of those notebooks find its way into stories?

Gilb: Most of my stuff comes from my own personal adventures. I've been around, like in my *Mickey Acuña* novel. I'd lived in the Y longer than I like to admit. I was bad off, and I couldn't figure out how the hell to get out.

Holley: And that was in El Paso?

Gilb: That was in the El Paso Y. I was stuck there. I had a master's degree in religion of all things — you know, a real valuable degree. I'd been doing construction for about a year by this time. As soon as I got out of college, I got a construction job in Santa Barbara. I'd saved some money. But when I'd come back to El Paso, after a car breakdown, I was destitute to the point that I met a girl who told me I could live in a Y. So I moved into the Y, and then I was really stuck. The Y finally hired me, very much like Mickey, and that helped for a while. Then finally I got another job. I moved out, and I lived in this funny place where the story "Hueco" takes place. I lived in this house where it was all blue. There wasn't a thing that wasn't all blue. Oh, my God, it was just the oddest place. As I was living there, I'd been working real hard, and I bought a '61 Chevy II. Four-door. It had been restored for the seller's daughter to go to college, and, of course, she wouldn't be caught dead in that car. Her dad had to dump it, and I was the dumpee. I was excited, because I thought it was a great car. So one day I go to the Y to play handball, and I come out and my car is stolen. All my belongings. Everything was in the trunk — tools, all my clothes. I went back to zero.

Holley: Were you still thinking of yourself as possibly a writer?

Gilb: At this point I was totally wanting to write.

Holley: Were you doing it?

Gilb: I was writing a novel. I'm in El Paso, and I'm working construction. I'd read in *Writer's Market* that a first book made fifteen thousand, so I told myself, "I can do that, I'll write a book every year. That's enough; it'll keep me going." I was confident. I was working on the campus at UTEP, doing a three-story add-on at the museum. And I decided — I've got maybe a hundred pages — to have somebody read it. I'd read in the paper that there was a writer at the university, Pat Carr, who had won a literary prize. So I go over to meet her and beg her to read mine. She was generous; she was very cool. She said come back at a certain time and we'd talk. I go back on a day we're pouring concrete. I'm in a tank-top shirt and the pour's just everywhere. I go to the meeting she's scheduled, and she says, "You have to go meet the chairman of the department. I have a job for you." I'm in my tank top with cement splattered all over me. I didn't want to go to school. I had no interest, but I said yes to some part-time work.

Raymond Carver was there then. Raymond Carver hadn't made *Newsweek* yet. He wasn't *Raymond Carver*; he was just Raymond Carver. I remember writing a note to him: "Dear Mr. Carver, as your colleague . . . how would you like to read a story and help me figure out what the hell I'm doing there?" Looking back, what an idiot I was. I didn't know. I didn't know there were living writers. I truly didn't have a concept that there were writers who were alive. I had read certain Chicano writers, but most of the writers I read were dead.

Holley: Did he read it?

Gilb: Yeah, he did, actually. He offered to get me into Iowa. I had no idea what Iowa was, and I did not want to go back to college. So anyway, I did in fact finish my novel during this time in El Paso.

Holley: *Mickey Acuña?*

Gilb: No, it's one you've never seen.

Holley: Will I ever see it?

Gilb: Probably not. It's pretty atrocious, though I didn't think so at the time. So I ended up in Los Angeles and joined the carpenters' union. Then for the next twelve years . . .

Holley: Twelve years?

Gilb: About seven years in L.A., then the back and forth from L.A. to El Paso.

Holley: Was there any teaching?

Gilb: No.

Holley: How did you write as a construction worker? Would you come home at night and write, or would you wait for a rainy day to get your writing done?

Gilb: I write every day in my journals. I have about six to seven thousand pages of notebooks to this day, which is major to my writing life. In my book *Gritos*, I included a little journal piece about winning my first literary prize. I write like that, but I could never write officially, that is, write fiction. I would always wait for a job to end, in whatever way it would end, and then I'd attack. I learned about short stories totally because of Ray Carver's rising fame. I learned that I could write short fiction and like it too.

Holley: Why short stories?

Gilb: Because he was publishing and getting a name for himself. And I thought, "Well, I can do that. They want working-class stories, I'll write working-class stories." Short fiction is, I think, closer to poetry than it is to the novel. It's tight. It's closer to images, to mythic tales. You don't have to be so "action" driven as you are with novels. You can, instead, work with mood and image and the words.

Holley: Did Carver show you they could sell, or that your life lent itself to the short form?

Gilb: I thought if I published a couple of short stories, this novel I had finished would sell. I figured I would get attention, and that it would prove that I could publish. And I would sell my novel. I didn't know that the novel wasn't good for about two years. Carver was starting to get big, you'd read about him in *Newsweek*, and I knew the guy, and I'm like, "No. His stories aren't about the working class, they're about graduate students." To me, it was really obvious. So I started writing stories about work, and I started cranking them out.

Holley: Did you worry about separating yourself from that working-class life, worry that your stories will dry up?

Gilb: I never thought about that. Although later, when I did get out of it, I did worry that I would turn into a professor — since I do that now! I still do, sort of vaguely, but I seem to have such torments that there's always something to write about. I wish it would slow down. I'm getting too old for my troubles. Early along, I am sure, I was the only high-rise construction worker in America publishing. I thought that was interesting. But you have to be a marketing person. You have to market yourself, and I didn't want to do that or know how to if I'd wanted.

Holley: So when did you sell your first story?

Gilb: My first story appeared in a Latino magazine out of Washington, D.C. It was kind of a funny story, called "El Fierro." Nobody's read it. I don't even know if I have a copy of it. It was a typewriter story. I have a lot of typewriter stories, and I've lost a lot of those. I feel bad about it, because I don't know where they are.

Holley: And you were paid?

Gilb: Yeah, they paid me pretty well. Then I had a story in a magazine in Las Cruces called *Puerto Del Sol*. Then *The Threepenny Review*, out of Berkeley, was the big, major breakthrough, because it's one of the top ten literary magazines in the country, maybe one of the best three now. Wendy Lesser, the editor, publishes really good work. She took a story, and my life altered. If she thinks it's good, it's good. She's hypercritical, really smart.

Holley: So you had this life, this construction work, this journal — many journals?

Gilb: And two sons.

Holley: And two kids and many ideas. How did you know when your writing was a story?

Gilb: I work from the end. When I know an end, I just have to figure out where it began.

Holley: You wouldn't start writing until you had the end?

Gilb: I have an end, I know what the end is. I may not have written it, but I know the image of the end. Later, when I get to write it, I refine the image in words.

Holley: A lot of your stories don't rely on some climactic end. It's more of a pause in the characters' lives.

Gilb: I'm hoping a question. I don't know where I get the idea that it's the end, but I'm usually clear about it. I know what it is. Maybe it's because I studied philosophy and religion, and my endings are at a different spot than people who studied literature.

Holley: Is the story that you sit down to write one that sort of causes an itch, or is it just a feeling that now is the time to write it?

Gilb: When I wrote short stories all the time, I'd make a list, and I'd work off that list. Now I resist writing short stories. When I used to do construction, I'd be so physically tired that sitting was a joy. I would love to be there in my little private space and not around people who are screaming and losing their jobs. The whole atmosphere of a job site is like a working-class war zone.

Holley: When you were on that construction site, were you working stories out in your head, or were they in the back of your mind?

Gilb: I was always writing something, trying to figure something out — or listening to stories. I miss that. I like to hear them. I enjoy stories. I like people to tell me stories. One of the things that I don't like now about this teaching business is that people are so "artistic" about stuff that it's like, "Are you telling me a story because you're pitching me something and I'm supposed to think you're talented?" Ordinary people are telling you a story not because they know who you are, but because they want someone to hear it, because they're obsessed or fascinated.

Holley: But when you're on the job, and you hear a story like that, you don't go home and transcribe? You somehow shape it?

Gilb: I reshape it. Absolutely. One, for instance, "Getting a Job in Dell City," is about a guy and this woman he loved and how he lost her. Well, that didn't happen in Dell City. It was from a guy at a job site in Los Angeles. But I had a job in Dell City, and I transposed a real lament of a man who lost the love of his life. He told me — over and over — because it was true, not because he wanted to show off with a "great" story. That's what I love. And I miss that.

Holley: So why don't you want to do short stories anymore?

Gilb: I love them, but they don't get enough respect, so I'm trying to do novels now. Novels sell. They say a book of short stories will sell four times less than a novel. They make movies from novels. It is finances. At some point, I want to liberate myself. I dream of having enough money so I can just write. At this point, I want that so much. I took this job because of a personal crisis and got through it; but now the whole country is having a personal crisis, so, I'm like, uh-oh, I better stay with this for a while. Even though I like my job, I don't see myself as a teacher. If I have to be a teacher, I often think, this is not what I would like to teach. I mean I should teach philosophy or a subject, not this craft biz.

Holley: So tell me about writing *Mickey Acuña*.

Gilb: It's an experimental novel, but I also thought it was commercial. I thought people would be interested, because how many people have written about living in a Y? I thought it a unique and strange story where I have personal experience — as a desk clerk. Everything I'm telling you I know firsthand — what it's like being a desk clerk, what it's like to live in one of those rooms. I naively, dumbly, thought it would be more commercially viable.

Holley: How did you know to write it that way, as opposed to writing a straight narrative story or a memoir?

Gilb: To tell you the truth, I have no idea. I don't have answers to why I write the way I write. One time I tried to write a Western, and it went weird.

Holley: When you began trying to write novels, did you have to teach yourself a different way of telling the story, in the sense that the arc is longer?

Gilb: See, this is the stuff that students ask me, and I have no answer. No, it's a story, it just happens to be longer. Now, it's true that I tend toward economy, and I like that, so I like the short fiction style.

Holley: Does the economy come in the early draft, or do you go back and figure it out?

Gilb: As I'm writing, I'm reducing, reducing. It took me a while, but I think what that is, is philosophy. Though I didn't read Kant, I read Plato and Lao Tzu. You can read a page of Plato or the Tao Te Ching, and that's going to take you a big day. I'm more involved in that kind of reading. I have a good friend, Francisco Goldman, and in our writing we're polar opposites. I might write a paragraph, and he'll write ten pages.

Holley: I'm interested in the arc — for lack of a better term — because I'm interested in how you keep the story going, how you keep it from being merely a series of episodes.

Gilb: My solution — I even wrote about this in my intro to *Gritos* — is that I go first-person stupid. Since I'm stupid, I let my characters be. You know, they can go wrong for long stretches. They're talking and telling a story the way they would tell a story. I try to capture a voice and let the story be told the way that voice would tell it. It doesn't mean it's right. There is no right.

Holley: Do you want to talk about what you're doing now?

Gilb: I guess it's safe enough — I always dread this. It's a novel set in Los Angeles. This boy's mother marries sort of a redneck named Cloid Longpre. His mother's Mexican, and Cloid starts out very happy because he has this pretty Mexican gal. I'm sure it'll be called a coming-of-age novel, although I really hate those labels.

Holley: Is it contemporary?

Gilb: I don't want it to be dated. I don't believe in time. I think it's a misconception, screws things up. But, yeah, there are, for instance, cars that are older. To me, it just so happens to be an older car; it's not what I care about, but I try to avoid too many references to a certain era of car. But, in fact, because I am who I am, and I'm the one writing, it comes from around the Watts Riots era. It's a little about the Watts Riots occurring a couple blocks away from this apartment complex where the characters live. It's about black people and various racisms and about being Mexican and Mexican American. About a boy living with this man who's into deer hunting.

Holley: Is this his dad?

Gilb: It's his stepdad. His mom abruptly marries and moves into this apartment complex with Cloid, whom he can't stand.

Holley: Did that name just come to you?

Gilb: I had a real stepdad, whose name I won't mention, who had one of those names. It was so country — so white country — and my friends would go, "Your mother married him?" The truth is, she was in a lot of trouble. She got married within a week, and in my own life, I was living with this man she married. It's a parallel story, though obviously my characters are exaggerated, are characters.

Mickey had become sure he was alive, body and mind. And he was sorry—because it wasn't fair. It wasn't Fuller's fault. Wasn't Omar's or Charles's. He'd say it wasn't his fault either, but that he felt like it was. If, or only if. But no, no, it was not intentional, that, he now knew, was not true. *Knew.*

"Say goodbye to Isabel for me," he told Butch as he opened the double doors. He shook his hand. "Well, nos vemos, take it easy."

"A dónde vas?" Butch asked.

The light outdoors was white, the air blue, the sun yellow. It was a warm day in the West. Mickey wanted to walk. "I'm thinking I'll go across and see if I can stay with Ema a few days. Then, well, who knows?"

Yards away from the clear doors of the YMCA, Mickey played more with the fit of his dark mirror glasses. He moved unsteadily for a few steps as he balanced the weight of the duffel bag to his back. He walked a few blocks and waited on a red light. He crossed on the green and headed south, the direction of downtown, or the border.

—*The Last Known Residence of Mickey Acuña*
(New York: Grove Press, 1994), 218.

William H. Goetzmann

I always thought of history as literature.

William H. Goetzmann

Adventure was not the be-all, end-all of my aim in recounting adventure. I think of these books as metaphors for the major categories of history of thought and science, and as I discovered in writing them, art.

Interview by Ramona Cearley

Ramona Cearley: Professor Goetzmann, in addition to recounting adventure, your books integrate the history of thought and science and art. Would you give us an example and set the stage for your writing?

William H. Goetzmann: My book *New Lands, New Men: Americans in the Second Great Age of Discovery* is about world exploration. It includes other explorers for comparison, such as Captain Cook and adventurers who claim to have discovered the Antarctic and the North Pole. But adventure was not the be-all, end-all of my aim in recounting adventure. Rather I had been teaching intellectual history and the history of science, so I think of these books as metaphors for the major categories of the history of thought and science and, as I discovered in writing them, art. I took great satisfaction in integrating the art — that is, the pictures — into the book as essential parts of the book rather than as decoration. That led to my creating a course, a television series called *The West of the Imagination*, and a book by the same name.

Cearley: That is a beautiful and rich study of "the West as people imagined it," which you coauthored with your son, William N. Goetzmann. You feature paintings, drawings, cartoons, and photographs of artists such as Catlin, Bodmer, Miller, Remington, among others. Describe your collaboration with your son and how the project came about.

Goetzmann: In exploring the American West, all of the American expeditions took artists with them, and later in the nineteenth century, they took along photographers. The artists drew the geological formations, the natural history of the West. One artist, John Mix Stanley, drew a huge herd of buffaloes going through North Dakota. If you look closely at the movie *Dances with Wolves*, when the Indians are looking at the buffalo herd, the ones in the back aren't moving. That picture was blown up to huge proportions as a backdrop.

I discovered that the federal government spent more on science and art between 1840 and 1860 than at any other time in American history; and that includes the New Deal and the present, in proportion, that is, to the federal budget. It was something close to 40 or 50 percent of the federal budget. So that suggests that the United States was not a backward country. It was much interested in science and art.

Photographers were very important because they had the means of taking more sharply imaged pictures of geological strata and geological formations. And so they became indispensable. Then with the railroads, photographers were all over, taking pictures of Chaco Canyon and Mesa Verde. So photography largely replaced the drawings. But I don't want to forget two of the absolutely greatest artists that America ever had — one of them was American — and that is George Catlin, who in 1832 journeyed up the Missouri when that was very dangerous, and painted the Indians up the Missouri in a great portfolio; and then the Swiss painter, Karl Bodmer, painted the greatest Indian pictures ever done. Even current Native American Indian artists today look at Bodmer's pictures as models for their paintings.

I teach a course that I designed called "The West of the Imagination," which tells the story of the West through the eyes of the artists, the photographers, cinematographers, and popular culture makers. I've done that now since 1984. The television series has been out since 1986. My son, who had been the director of the Museum of Western Art in Denver, helped me write the book because right in the middle of all this television stuff, running around, trying to teach, climbing on and off airplanes, I had a heart attack. He is the coauthor, and we got the book done in time for the opening of the television series. It was just wonderful working with him. He said, "If you don't like anything, cross it out." And now when I read over it again, I can't remember what he wrote and what I wrote. Now I've revised it and I want to get a new edition out with six new chapters and five extensive additions and a new introduction.

Cearley: Along similar lines, share with us some of the early explorers, artists, and scientists who helped define the Southwest and Texas in particular. For example, in what contexts did they influence our attitudes toward politics, conservation, and the environment?

Goetzmann: One of the really outstanding incidents was the relationship of exploration to politics. First was the discovery in 1823–24, in the winter, of the South Pass of the Rocky Mountains, which enabled fur trappers and wagon trains to cross over the Continental Divide and make their way to Oregon and California. Far more than the Lewis and Clark Expedition, this made California and

Oregon the targets for U.S. expansion. It was now feasible to get there. So when the news came back to St. Louis that they had discovered South Pass as a route through the Rockies—you could take wagons over—that really started the huge migration.

Another great one is Lt. William H. Emory's expedition during the U.S.-Mexican War in 1846, from Santa Fe to California. Emory's report declared that the Southwest was unfit for farming. Daniel Webster in the debates over the Compromise of 1850, knowing of Emory's report, declared that to talk about slavery in the Southwest was to talk about an imaginary Negro in an impossible place.

A third one that I think is terribly important is the exploration for the Pacific Railroad Survey. The U.S. Army Bureau of Explorations and Surveys, in 1853–54, sent out five expeditions transcontinentally to look for a railroad route across the mountains and deserts. These produced the first good scientific map of the West, but no feasible transcontinental railroad route. The expeditions also produced thousands of pictures, thousands and thousands of plant and animal specimens, and tons of rocks and fossils. And that, together with the great United States naval expedition, produced so many specimens that they had to build the Smithsonian Institution to house them all. The government reports ran about fourteen volumes, again profusely illustrated; and that, too, along with all the other military and naval expeditions, began the creation of the American scientific establishment.

Cearley: Backtracking a bit, speak to us about Cabeza de Vaca, the sixteenth-century explorer who traveled across Texas and the Southwest.

Goetzmann: The main problem with Cabeza de Vaca is they know where he started and they know where he ended up but they don't know very well what happened in between. There's been an ongoing debate for many years, since around 1919, about just where he went. So in that sense he's enigmatic. His *Relación* is one of the great travel accounts, but he doesn't locate the tribes that he visited with any kind of precision. Anthropologists have tried to figure out which ones were which, and of course he has different names than we have now. Some people think he went all the way up into New Mexico and then down to Sonora. Other people think he took the low route and went across somewhere near Rio Grande City, then across Mexico. But he remains an enigma. He was the first person to cross the continent in North America, so he's important. But where did he cross it? That's one of the things that leads a person to write about the history of exploration.

Cearley: How did your passion for history begin?

Goetzmann: It began by reading a lot of adventure books. I just read a lot as a child. My mother always said I always had my nose in a book, whereas I thought I was always playing sports. But anyway, I went to Yale, wanting to be a creative writer, and I didn't get into Robert Penn Warren's creative writing class. I moved into American studies, which is my degree, and ended up writing a history of the army's topographical engineer-explorers, which ended up being my first book, *Army Exploration in the American West, 1803–1863*. I always thought of history as literature as well, and people liked this manuscript before it was published. Alfred Knopf and a number of others made offers, but I had already given it to the Yale University Press. Then, great publisher that he was, Alfred Knopf offered me a very good contract to write a second book about all the explorations in the American West, which I did, and it won the Pulitzer Prize, among others. Some years later, after Alfred's death, I published *New Lands, New Men: America and the Second Great Age of Discovery* — a vast book that includes, besides the continental explorations, Americans exploring foreign lands and the marvelous work done by Americans on the oceans and the polar regions. The U.S. was the first nation to map the Antarctic and, landing on it, to prove it a continent. *New Lands, New Men* is my most intellectual yet exciting book. I like it the best of all my books.

Explorers and expeditions from all nations proliferated and bombarded the centers of learning with new discoveries almost daily. The constant flood of new specimens, new data, and new information eventually turned the static Newtonian worldview into an ever-changing, growing, cumulatively varied view of the world in which science itself and its basic categories were continually being redefined. It was also clear by the early eighteenth century, that science was rapidly emerging as a culture unto itself with its own language, institutions, symbols, and recognized practitioners, and, in contrast to the age of Columbus, its own nonreligious tests for truth.

—New Lands, New Men: America and
the Second Great Age of Discovery
(New York: Viking Penguin, 1986), 2–3.

John Graves

This land has been my subject matter.

John Graves

Essay by Joe Holley

"Most writers I really admire are word writers rather than idea writers," John Graves told an interviewer some years ago. "They may be idea writers too, but they are people who make music out of words, and who play with language and make it do things on its own." Graves had in mind such literary artists as Vladimir Nabokov and Anthony Burgess; he could have been alluding to a farmer in Somervell County, west of Fort Worth.

That farmer is John Graves, a country man who has spent a lifetime working the land, building and repairing things, and studying the ways of animals and of people. He also has crafted some of the most elegant prose ever produced by a Texas writer.

Graves, who was born in Fort Worth in 1920, left the state in 1942, when he enlisted in the Marines shortly after graduating from Rice University. He saw action in the Pacific and lost the sight in one eye. After the war, he earned his master's degree at Columbia University and lived off and on in New York City, New Mexico, Spain, and Mexico. He was writing all that time — his first published story was in the New Yorker — *but it wasn't until he came back to Texas to stay in the late 1950s that he truly found his voice. "I did an awful lot of apprentice work," he once said. "It took me a helluva long time to find out what I could do and what I couldn't do as a writer. In my case, 'til I was 36, 37, 38 — 'til I found that tone of voice with the river book."*

"The river book" is Goodbye to a River. *The book grew out of a leisurely canoe trip Graves, accompanied by a dog named Watty, took down the upper-middle Brazos River in 1957. Although based on a real trip — originally a* Sports Illustrated *assignment — the book is much more than a recital of facts and description.* Goodbye to a River *is Graves sifting through layers of time and place and memory. It is Graves in a slow, easy way telling old stories, resurrecting ghosts, ruminating. It is a masterpiece.*

Since Goodbye to a River, *Graves has written other books —* Hard Scrabble, From a Limestone Ledge, *and* Myself and Strangers: A Memoir of Apprenticeship — *along with countless articles for* Texas Monthly *and other publications and essay contributions to numerous books. In most of his work, he writes about country things, but as Larry McMurtry has pointed out, Graves is no "country ex-plainer." In McMurtry's words, "He seems more interested in increasing our store of mysteries than our store of knowledge. He loves the obscure, indeterminate nature of rural legend and likes nothing better than to retell stories the full truth of which can never be known. If nature continues to stimulate him, it may be because it too is elu-sive, feminine, never completely knowable."*

John Graves still lives at Hard Scrabble, his farm near Glen Rose. He is still hard at work farming and writing.

One thing that distinguishes me from the true naturalist is that I've never been able to look at land without thinking of the people who've been on it. It's fundamental to me. This land has been my subject matter.

Interview by Don Webb

Don Webb: You've been on a promotional tour recently with photographer Wyman Meinzer talking about your book *Texas Rivers*. Is there anything that people haven't asked you?

John Graves: I've been interviewed particularly of late because of the promotion going on with the *Texas Rivers* book, which features Wyman's beautiful photographs. The younger people who have interviewed me have not seemed to understand that my main impulse in terms of writing has been the language. I'm not an espouser of causes, by and large. I do have some causes, but I don't write much about that sort of thing. It's the aesthetics of the language that has interested me the most.

Webb: I know exactly what you mean.

Graves: There was a young lady here not long ago, a very nice person, but somewhere in journalism school she picked up the idea that you've got to stand for something, that you've got to have an activist streak. I don't.

Webb: Do you resent that we pigeonhole you as a nature writer?

Graves: No. It's been a little overdone. I've been referred to as a natural-ist and so on. I am just an amateur who is interested in natural things. I've been called the "Thoreau of Texas," but I'm not like Thoreau at all. He was a very pure person. I'm not a pure person. I never wanted to be in that sense.

Webb: In 1938, you're eighteen years old; you enroll in Rice University to become a petroleum engineer. What happened?

Graves: It was a short-lived ambition. Rice was small at that time. It's still small, but it was a much more intimate place then. Old Mr. McCann was the registrar. It was the height of the Depression, and everyone was thinking about a job. They interviewed everybody even as you were coming in. Mr. McCann asked me what I wanted to study, and I said petroleum engineering. He asked me about my interests and as I was talking, finally just broke in and said, "Son, you'd be a miserable engineer. Why don't you sign up for an academic course?" Which I did, and I've been glad ever since.

Webb: Your creative writing teacher at Rice was George Williams. He had many good students, including you, Larry McMurtry, and William Goyen. What was he like?

Graves: Oh, he was a very vital man. He was a strong influence on practically everyone who ever took one of his classes. It wasn't only writing classes. He taught literature and modern poetry. We all absorbed his [teaching], just ate it up. He was that kind of man. We were talking about purity a while ago. He was a very pure person. His values were very strong. They were liberal values. I used to argue with him some. I hurt his feelings one time. I remember one time in class, he was talking about our great debt to all the suffering and poverty-stricken people in the world. I said, "What debt? I don't owe anybody anything." It hurt his feelings badly. I finally had to think it over and apologize. I apologized quite sincerely. I didn't realize what he was talking about.

Webb: You said in *Self-Portrait, with Birds* that the war was looming pretty big in your consciousness while you were at Rice, and then later in the Marines. You saw action during the war. What did you take away from your wartime experience?

Graves: It's hard for me to say. I didn't last long in the actual fighting. I got zapped, sent to the hospital and then home. I had an incomplete feeling about the war, to be honest. I'd gotten all ready for it, got pretty good at what I did, which was artillery, and working with some very bright kids. But I didn't get to use it very long.

Webb: After the war, was Columbia where you received your master's in literature? Who are your favorite writers from that time? Who are your influences?

Graves: It's very hard to pin it down. Hemingway, of course. My whole generation grew up under his shadow. You couldn't get away from him. Ford Madox Ford. Nobody knows of him nowadays, but he's a very strong influence. Malcolm Lowry. Do you know who he is?

Webb: *Under the Volcano.*

Graves: Yes. And Faulkner, of course. I did my master's essay on Faulkner. The usual ones: Fitzgerald, Mark Twain, Shakespeare, Milton, the King James

Bible, Elizabethan poets, and people such as Yeats and Keats. All those were a strong part of it.

Webb: I would have guessed every one of them because there is so much lyricism in your writing. Your writing has this very beautiful approach to language.

Graves: I appreciate you saying so. As I stated a while ago, that is essentially what I am for: strong language. And I don't mean cuss words.

Webb: After Columbia, you taught for a while at the University of Texas at Austin. Your biographies say you were "disenchanted" with the academic world. What does that mean?

Graves: I taught there two or three years. At that time, junior instructors on college campuses, particularly in English, were a drag on the market. We got paid very poorly; we were overloaded with freshmen. I remember — probably wrongly — that I had five freshman classes there at one time, and every kid did a theme a week. You'd go around with your coat pockets stuffed full of those things and feeling guilty about it. Most of them didn't want to be there. I liked teaching, but only if the people wanted to be there. Anyhow, that and a failing marriage just did me in, and I bailed out.

Webb: Had you decided by then to be a writer? You'd already had a story in the *New Yorker*.

Graves: Yes, I had ambition by then.

Webb: When did you first decide you were going to write books?

Graves: In the 1950s, I was living in Spain, and I got the idea for a novel. It had the Texas background and the war. It was me, somewhat changed. I spent the better part of two years on it, and it turned out lousy. I probably could have gotten it published, but I wasn't satisfied with it. At that time I had to come back to Texas, and I'd gotten to fooling around on the Brazos River with all sorts of useful interests involving local history and nature. *Goodbye to a River* was the outgrowth of that, published in 1960. I published a good bit during that time, including some pretty fair short stories, but I was still struggling, still thrashing.

Webb: Your short stories are great. You received the O. Henry Award, among others.

Graves: Yes, I had three of them — two in the O. Henry *Prize Stories* and one in *Best American Short Stories*. I wrote some decent stories, but I wrote a lot of trash too, just to make a living. I did quite a bit of magazine article writing too, but it didn't come together for me until I got home.

Webb: Did home open up something for you?

Graves: It seemed to have done so, yes.

Webb: Why did you choose Glen Rose as the place to buy your ranch?

Graves: Like most Texans, I was always drawn toward the Hill Country. At the time, I was ready to get some land. My father was in very bad health, and my mother wasn't much better. So I didn't want to get too far away from them, and this was the closest thing to the Hill Country that was within reach.

Webb: When did you meet J. Frank Dobie?

Graves: When *Goodbye to a River* was in the process of publication. This is the sequence of events: I had an artist friend who was in the abstract expressionistic movement. He later switched to more realistic work and became one of the better western sculptors at a time when there was a real big market for it. Anyhow, he was being given a show in New York. He called Dobie and said, "Would you be interested in giving me a plug, an endorsement?" Dobie said, "I don't know; if you want to bring some of them down I'll look at them and tell you what I think." And when my friend Jackson showed up at the airport, I drove him down to Austin. I'd never met Dobie before. Mrs. Dobie met us at the door and said, "Now, I think thirty minutes would be about right." We said, "Fine." Well, we went in and liked the old man, and he liked us. We ended upstairs in his study, a bottle of Jack Daniel's, and three or four hours went by.

Anyhow, he not only gave Jackson the endorsement of his work, but he bought one of the pieces and Jackson gave him another one. Then Dobie gave us a bunch of his books. At some point that afternoon, Dobie said, "I know your name." I said, "I don't know why." In a little bit he said, "I know what it was, someone sent me a book manuscript of yours. I just don't have time for those things, and I haven't looked at it." I said, "I don't blame you, Mr. Dobie. I didn't tell them to send it to you." As we were leaving at the door downstairs, he leaned over, grinned, and said, "I'll read you now." And he did. When the book came out, he devoted one of his Sunday columns to it and gave it a big boost. I saw a lot of him during those four or five years. We were good friends. He died in '64.

Webb: *Goodbye to a River* certainly has a tremendous staying power.

Graves: It's been very well received and by the kind of people that I really like to have appreciate it. Knopf, in spite of all the changes in publishing, kept that thing in hardback for forty-two years, which is unusual to say the least. Then last year they put it into their own paperback series. It's had a very good career. I personally think that *Hard Scrabble*, which I just received as a new SMU issue in paperback, is as good as *Goodbye to a River*. It has found a much less responsive public because of its subject matter. There are not that many people interested in country places and such. It still looks good to me. I don't want to brag too much. Both of them could look better.

Webb: We stopped at the bookstore in Glen Rose as we were coming in, and Nancy Strickland, the owner, had many good things to say about you.

Graves: She's a nice ole gal. You know her daddy was in Bob Wills' band.

Webb: She told me that her daddy, Al Strickland, knew Bob Wills. You've written that one of the best things that people can get to know is what the land does to them and what they do to the land. What do you think the land here has done to you?

Graves: Worked the hell out of me. All my life I have been prone to passionate interests. It's important if you're a writer to have that old-fashioned interest turn into not just wasted time but writing. So in a simpleminded way, this land has been my subject matter. There was simply something in me that believed in the land, believed in our association with it, and believed we needed to know more about it. One thing that distinguishes me from the true naturalist is that I've never been able to look at land without thinking of the people who've been on it. It's fundamental to me.

Webb: Moving here was a major key to many things.

Graves: I realize that quite strongly.

By the time I pulled onto a sand bar below a narrow flat that lay between the river and a mountain, the wind on my neck carried flecks of cold rain. I set up the little tent under a twisted mesquite, threw my bed roll into it, chopped dead limbs into firewood, and finally carried up the other things from the boat—the map case and the shotgun and the rods and the food box, heavily full, and the cook box and the rucksack, all of them battered familiarly from other trips long before. With a juvenile shame from those days when we had tried to model ourselves on the old ones, going out only with a blanket, tarp, skillet, ax, twenty-two, jar of grease, and sack of cornmeal, I knew that I'd brought too much gear for one man. But it was November, and our stomachs had been tougher then, and anyhow the point was no longer to show one's hardihood. The point was to be there. . . .

The pup edged against me. He was a six-month-old dachshund and weighed about twelve pounds, and even after he was grown he wouldn't be a very practical dog, but he was company, too—more concrete, perhaps, than memories and feelings.

"Passenger, you watch," I told him. "It's going to be a good trip."

—*Goodbye to a River: A Narrative*
(New York: Knopf, 1960), 15–16.

James L. Haley

History is the single most important
thing that people can know.

James L. Haley

To me, everything that you believe in the world about everything that's important—what's right, what's moral, what's immoral—all of those personal decisions filter through what the individual knows about history—or doesn't.

Interview by Linda Evans

Linda Evans: What got you started in writing about history and, in particular, Texas history?

James L. Haley: I'm one of those kids that wanted to write since I was four or five years old. So from that standpoint, it's just in the genes, I guess. When I started writing history, it was really more a calculated decision than anything. To do anything in the way of social sciences, it's hard to get published unless you have a Ph.D. after your name. If you know your history, there's an "in" there. If you know the subject and you can write it well, you're going to get published. It's one of the best entry points for young writers. In fact, I started law school, not wanting to practice law, but knowing that they would remold my thinking process.

Evans: So you could think or write more coherently?

Haley: Yes, and I've stayed in history—though of course I also write fiction—because history is probably the single most important thing that people can know. When I was reading your material for this Texas Writers project, I was a little distressed that you have us divided up between intellectual historians and popular historians. I thought, "Well, now, maybe we ought to recalibrate this more in the way of, say, theoretical historians and applied historians."

Evans: Why would it be theoretical?

Haley: A theoretical historian would be somebody such as Walter Webb, who sat around thinking about what influence the Great Plains had on the western migration. On the applied side, you had J. Evetts Haley—no relation to me—who would go out and gather facts and write the stories about the people who were out there being influenced by the Great Plains. So today you have very good theoretical historians, such as William Goetzmann at UT-Austin. But to say that those of us who interpret or write stories for people to read are pop historians—that overstates the dichotomy between us. To me, everything that you believe in the world about everything that's important—what's right, what's wrong, what's moral, what's immoral, how should you live, vote, worship, raise your children—all of those personal decisions filter through what the individual knows about history—or doesn't. I can't count the number of people who have come up to me and said, "Nobody's ever explained history like that." There is an extent to which purely theoretical history has gone the way of classical music. It's being done mostly to annoy and outrage colleagues and win professional notice. It doesn't really matter whether anybody else understands it or can apply it.

Evans: That makes it rather exclusive, doesn't it?

Haley: Yes, it makes it rather exclusive. Theoretical history that people don't see or understand is like the tree crashing in the forest when there's nobody there to hear it. History is far too important a subject for everyday people to let it stay purely in that realm. So I hope your editor will find a more accurate way to describe us [laughing], instead of calling us intellectuals and populists!

Evans: Who gets to write history? What is it about you that can tell the story better than the next person, and is it the truth as *you* see it? Is it different for every teller?

Haley: Bill Brands raised that point: that his Benjamin Franklin is different from somebody else's Benjamin Franklin. I look at history as a wonderful kaleidoscope—that if you look at it this way, you will see Sam Houston my way, and if you turn it a quarter of a turn, all those little particles will fall in a different way and you will see Steve Hardin's Sam Houston or somebody else's Sam Houston.

Evans: You made a very good point at the Texas Book Festival, that you have to appeal to the reader. There has to be some kind of a narrative. You're telling a story through your own viewpoint. You're very meticulous in the way that you note your sources and help the reader by providing notes to the chapters.

Haley: It was either John Taliaferro or Bobby Bridger who raised the point that the history books that he respects most are really the dull ones. They've rigorously footnoted everything. But they're hard to read. And that was the style of Texas history before Fehrenbach wrote *Lone Star* in 1968. The big Texas histories were three-, four-, five-volume things that were very Edwardian in their prose, very leaden and almost unreadable. The trick is to get the facts right.

That's where the writer takes over because you've got to make the stuff, not just interesting, but compelling for somebody. My first interest in Sam Houston, aside from there being a hole in the literature—at the time I started he hadn't been written about in twenty years—was a very personal angle. I come from four generations of alcoholics. So when I look at Sam Houston, I don't see this Texas legend; I see a guy who accomplished all this stuff in the face of the bottle. How did he do that?

Evans: That is amazing. Most people I know who drink heavily do well to get to work in the morning, if they make it at all.

Haley: Right. And until he married Margaret in 1840, he was a far-gone alcoholic. He could lose whole months out of his life in fits of depression. So when I saw that human being, I wanted to know how he pulled himself out of the morass and got it together and became the Sam Houston that's in the books. Margaret had a lot to do with that.

Evans: I suppose you hear about great men and the women behind them.

Haley: When they married, she was twenty and he was forty-seven, or some such thing, and of course, that was scandal enough. He was this world-class alcoholic and roué and womanizer; he'd even lived with an Indian woman, and that was about as low as you could get. People asked Margaret at the time, "Why are you throwing yourself away on this rake?" Being Nancy Lea's daughter, she said, "One, I love him; two, I mean to reform him."

Evans: I think that's still going on today.

Haley: And she did. He fell off the wagon a few times, but he really pulled his act together, because in her own way she was no less a titan than he was. My entry point to Sam Houston wasn't so much the political figure as it was the human being. Of course, history in general and Texas history in particular has gone through quite an evolution in the last twenty years. We've gone from revisionism through political correctness through the new history, and now we're almost getting into a kind of historical deconstructionism.

Texas history was about heroes and patriots for a hundred and fifty years; in the last twenty years you would more often see Sam Houston painted as a cowardly, drunken, land-speculating, glory-grabbing, camp-following opportunist. Neither is really true, and I just wanted to get at the human being. In fact the manuscript was vetted by eight or ten professors to weed out errors. One of them was very irritated that I didn't spend more time on his political history. I spent an entire chapter on his first marriage and what might have gone wrong because that, to me, explains a lot about the man.

Evans: So, as a writer, you start out on something you're interested in and that's what drives it, not what you think someone else might want to know.

Haley: Bingo. When I was writing *The Buffalo War*, I was very young and very ambitious and very stupid. I asked my first editor at Doubleday, "How do you write a best seller?" He said, "Forget it. The biggest factors that go into making a best seller are so far beyond the writer's control that the most you can aspire to is to do a good book. If society helps you out, if the market helps you out, if prevailing winds help you out, all to the better; but you can't govern those." He used the example of Alex Haley—again, no relation, although I've signed copies of *Roots* before—

Evans: You have?

Haley: I have, indeed, yes! If *Roots* had come out five years earlier, it would have done no business. If it had come out five years later, it would have done no business. It happened to be the right book at the right time at the right stage of African American consciousness, when people were wanting to explore their heritage and where they came from. He just happened to hit the right time with that book. Of course it took him twelve years to write it, and he almost committed suicide twice over writing it. But just by the accident of the calendar, when it came out it created this national sensation; it hit that segment of the community at just the time when they needed to see what it had to say. So you can't try to write a bestseller. You do the best you can. If people notice, great.

Evans: It's interesting you bring up Alex Haley, because one of the things I've taken up over the years is researching my family, and particularly since I moved back to Texas, looking at my Texas family. Has that ever interested you?

Haley: I wish that I could say that it had, but the truth is that my mother was adopted by my Anglo grandparents from a Cherokee family in Oklahoma. I was born in Tulsa, which is so funny, because when you write Texas history—

Evans: Oh, my gosh! I have some Cherokee, too! Well, doesn't everybody.

Haley: Yeah, I was at the Western History Association Conference, and somebody was making jokes about people's Cherokee grandmothers. There's always somebody with a Cherokee grandmother. I have talked to probably every chapter of the Daughters of the Republic in the state, and just as sure as sunrise, somebody comes up and says, "Where you from?" And I say, "I live in Austin." "No, where you *from?*" "Uhh, I grew up in Fort Worth." "No, where were you born?" You know, like where are your people from. And I say "Tulsa." And it's like: "I thought so. I just don't know what you think you're doing writing Texas history when you weren't even born here."

Excuse the daylights out of me! But my mother was adopted from a Cherokee family, so I don't even know, to this good day, who my natural grandparents were. My father's side of the family was all either drunk or crazy, and I was hardly allowed to ever even see them. I was telling this to a friend of mine who is a psychologist. He said, "No wonder you're so interested in history, you don't have any!" I thought, "My God, he's right!" Which is probably a surprising answer to your question.

Evans: It's a wonderful answer and very surprising indeed. What do you do, Jim, when you're not writing? If you're writing history, that takes up a lot of your time. What do you do when you're not writing?

Haley: I play tennis when I can. I lived right by UT-Austin for many years; then I sold my house this past spring. I've been planning my escape back out into homeownership, probably outside the city. I love to garden, love to get my hands dirty. Usually I'll plot — that's more of a term where I think about the next book.

It's like a chess game. If you do whatever project lands in your lap, you can do creditable books but your career doesn't advance. You need to give some thought to what a book will do for you, which I've only just recently begun doing. Which is why at my age I'm a new discovery as a Texas writer after, what, twelve books? I haven't really promoted myself the way some of the headline writers have acquired the art of doing. To write good books is one effort, but to get out there and make sure people know what you're doing is quite a different effort.

It's a different set of skills entirely to be able to go out and give talks or be on panels and bring it off. Many, many years ago I was the board chairman of the Austin Writers' League, before it became the Writers' League of Texas, back when it had dozens of members instead of hundreds. We would get writers to come in and speak who were brilliant writers but, my heavens, they just died in front of an audience that was small and sympathetic. They just couldn't communicate orally, which is a completely different bunch of skills.

Evans: As an historian, an intellectual, a reporter of facts, a chronicler, you consider what you're doing an art.

James Haley: Absolutely. Biography, especially, is an art, because there are so many things that you can say about somebody. How do you convey an essence of somebody's career and character between the covers of one book? History is an art because of that sense of responsibility. Either you take five volumes and bore somebody to tears, or you find some way to get to them that will make a light go on in their heads. You can go see a play like *Greater Tuna* and see the essence of small-town rural Texas and just die laughing. But it's still so true that you could swear you've known all these people.

Evans: What is the best day you ever had?

Haley: Oh, my stars, since we're doing this in a literary context, when I was a sophomore at UT-Arlington, one of Texas' great folklorist-turned-historians, but who always remained a folklorist at heart, was William Owens. He was born in Pinhook, Texas, rose through the literary ranks. At the time he came through on his book-signing tour he was the dean emeritus of the creative writing school at Columbia—the absolute pinnacle of the profession. They had this big reception for him, and I worked in the library, so my job was to pick up the paper cups and plastic flatware as all the bigwigs left. I had written one magazine article and was working on my first book. My boss, who was running this whole show, said that he would introduce me to William Owens, which he did. Owens, at that time, was about seventy-two. We were supposed to run everybody out so he could take his nap before they took him back to the airport. He asked me, "Are you really serious about wanting to be a writer?" and, like Goofy, I was like "Uh, yes, sir!" He said, "Well, I tell you what, once this whole thing shuts down, let's get everybody out of here and we'll have a talk." I finished picking up the dirty dishes. He clicked the door shut and sat and told me about the writing business for thirty, forty minutes. Didn't take his nap. He said, "Your friends are going to outstrip you economically. They're going to have more money than you, but if you really feel called to be a writer you can't let anybody shame you out of it because they're better off than you. Now, you need to know this twenty years down the road, or you're going to be very disillusioned." I thought, "I can't ever do anything for him; why is he doing this for me?" But that's just the kind of man he was. I've been aware of that from that day to this.

If he hadn't sat me down and given me some handle on writing, not just as an art, but as a business and as a lifestyle, I don't know that I would have ever had the nerve to do it. He was responsible in a big way. For his eightieth birthday, one of his literary colleagues here in town, Dr. Elizabeth John, whom I had told this to, said they were having this big eightieth birthday celebration for William Owens in New York. They were having testimonials and would I write up my story? He probably didn't remember me from Adam, but at least I got a chance, years later, to tell him thank you. It was really meaningful to me.

Upon being introduced around, Houston mistook Nancy Lea's daughter, twenty-year-old Margaret, for his host's sister-in-law, Antoinette Bledsoe, and remarked to one of the guests, "If she were not already married I believe I would give that charming young lady a chance to say no."

Antoinette, who was younger than Margaret and fearful of her sister becoming an old maid, pulled Houston out of a conversation, interrupted her sister as she was passing a dish of strawberries, and introduced them. Margaret was a violet-eyed beauty with wavy brunette hair, accomplished, well connected, and deeply religious. Houston spent no longer explaining Texas' prospects to Lea, her son, and her son-in-law than it took to win their interest. Back at the party, he presented Margaret with a carnation plucked from the garden. She put it in her hair and they took a walk. Margaret imparted that she had seen him on the dock in New Orleans three years before; he pointed out a brilliant star and asked her whether that might be their star of destiny, and after he was gone, he hoped she would recall him and the Lone Star of Texas whenever she saw it. After the former president of Texas departed, Margaret was so overcome that she fled to her room and commenced writing poetry.

—*Sam Houston*
(Norman: University of Oklahoma Press, 2002), 211–212.

Stephen Harrigan

The Alamo as a subject chose me
when I was seven years old.

Stephen Harrigan

What animated my interest in the Alamo as a writer was the sense of a vanished world. It just would not let go of me. I finally realized that I had to probe into it in an imaginative way myself.

Interview by Ramona Cearley

Ramona Cearley: What were the beginnings of your writing life? Who were your early influences?

Stephen Harrigan: I started reading semi-seriously in high school. I'd read Hardy Boys and all those kinds of books before that. But it wasn't until high school that I started reading a mix of great literature and potboilers. I read a lot of Hemingway and Faulkner and then people like Leon Uris and James Michener. Kenneth Roberts was a big influence on me. He wrote a long series of historical novels set in the American Revolution. I just devoured anything over five hundred pages. I loved things that threw you back into a different time, the feeling that I was part of the experience.

Cearley: You engage in journalistic, fiction, and nonfiction writing. What are the similarities and differences in your writing experience as you work in these areas? What appeals to you most in each of these disciplines?

Harrigan: For me, journalism and various sorts of nonfiction writing have always been a means to an end. I've always thought of myself essentially as a novelist. And frankly, journalism is the way I made my living for a good part of the time that I tried to position myself as a novelist. But what I discovered along the way is that I could not have been a halfway decent novelist if it had not been for the demands of journalism. I learned how to shape a story from writing magazine articles. I learned how to gather information. I learned how not to be awed by the process of writing, just to get the thing done. It helped me a great deal in discovering the writer I wanted to be.

In many ways nonfiction and fiction are very similar. You still have to deal with a certain database of information and experience. You have to shape that knowledge into a compelling narrative story — or at least in the kind of writing I

* 141

do, that is the case. There are, of course, profound differences. A novel is fundamentally a work of the imagination. A magazine article or a nonfiction book is a work of fact. And you have to give yourself permission when you're writing a novel to depart as you need to from that information base. You have to rein your imagination in sometimes when you're writing nonfiction.

Cearley: We've read that you are a very disciplined writer. Describe your writing process and your typical writing day.

Harrigan: My typical working day is rather chaotic. I tend to work on more than one project at a time, sometimes three or four of them at various stages of completion or conception. So typically I work all day. I come out to my office behind the house at about eight or eight-thirty and check my e-mail. I have found that e-mail is a great procrastination device. The bulk of the morning is typically devoted to writing; it might be a book I'm working on, it might be a screenplay, or whatever has the most urgent deadline. In the afternoon I often read or do research for either that project or another one that's coming. At night after dinner, I'll try to work in another hour or two of pure writing.

Cearley: Several of your books, such as *Aransas, Jacob's Well,* and *A Natural State,* reflect on human relationships with the environment. In reference to *Water and Light: A Diver's Journey to a Coral Reef,* the *New York Times* praises your ability to explore the metaphysical and spiritual elements of nature. Describe the Texas landscape in your writing and a context in which people in your stories recognize an intimacy with the land.

Harrigan: Well, Texas is a difficult place in some ways to have an intimacy with the land. It's not always very welcoming, at least in terms of weather or pastoral landscapes, that kind of thing. It's heavily polluted in parts; it's heavily industrialized and urbanized. In some ways for me as a writer, or for anyone who has to wrangle with the Texas landscape, that's all to the good because that complexity, that kind of awkwardness can be very enriching and challenging. You have to put humans into that mix in Texas. You cannot think of Texas as a kind of laboratory-pure wilderness. Texas is a state that, for all its panoramic grandeur, still has a problem with making its landscape visible and accessible.

I just got back from San Diego, in Southern California, which is, of course, a heavily urbanized area, but within ten minutes or thirty minutes you can be in some national seashore, natural monument, some unbelievably striking headland or beach. You don't have that imposing and available scenery so much in Texas, particularly Central Texas, where I live. It's difficult to find those places. Here in Texas we don't have a tradition of public land. Land is owned by individuals, except for minuscule state parks and a few good-sized national parks. So in answer to your question, it's a very complex environment, and a somewhat corrupted one, which makes it that much more fascinating to write about.

Cearley: You explore another side of Texas in *The Gates of the Alamo*. Published to wide acclaim in 2000, it is a fictional story incorporating historical accounts. Why did you choose to write *The Gates of the Alamo*?

Harrigan: The Alamo as a subject chose me when I was seven years old. I was very susceptible to the popular culture and myth about the Alamo. That was the year that the Walt Disney movie *Davy Crockett, King of the Wild Frontier* came out, which kind of galvanized me, along with all the other kids in the country. What really animated my interest in the Alamo as a writer was the sense of a vanished world. I had been to the Alamo innumerable times growing up and as an adult, and it always seemed to me tantalizingly out of reach. What happened here? What was it like? Why are we so obsessed with this distant and rather minor event in history? I always thought of the Alamo as kind of a haunted house. It just would not let go of me. I finally realized that I had to probe into it in an imaginative way myself.

Cearley: Is there a screenplay in progress for the book?

Harrigan: For *The Gates of the Alamo*? Not at the moment. There's a lot of interest, but there are also a lot of other Alamo projects out there, so who knows what Alamo movie will eventually get made? I've been very careful about this myth. I've turned down a couple of production companies and producers because I just didn't think they would take the historical backdrop of the book seriously. I'm very persnickety about it being done right.

Cearley: You've indicated the importance of having the main characters in *The Gates of the Alamo* reflect the complexity of the story and, in essence, override the myths of the Alamo. Give us an example of what you mean by this statement.

Harrigan: The myth of the Alamo can be summed up as a triumphant Anglo moment in Texas history in which the forces of General Santa Anna were decisively defeated. Freedom was resoundingly won. But the reality is much more complex than that. The Alamo was a piece of a larger drama, a Mexican civil war. Texas was a part of Mexico. Mexicans were fighting against each other. It wasn't a simple question of good versus evil or tyranny versus freedom. Many of the Texas rebels had other agendas besides freedom, normal human agendas like making money and gaining political power.

I don't think the myth of the Alamo needs to be turned on its head, to say that all Texans were opportunistic and all Mexicans were high-minded. I'm very impatient with that kind of black-and-white thinking. But I did feel it was absolutely imperative to try to dramatize the story of the Alamo from every perspective that I could find. To that degree I've created characters who allow the reader to experience those different perspectives. I have Mexican characters. I have Anglo characters. I have a historical character named Joe who's a slave of Colonel Travis, the commander of the Alamo. And the black perspective is fascinating because the Mexicans were fighting against slavery. As much as the Texans were fighting for freedom, they were also fighting for the propagation of slavery.

The storm that Joe had seen on the horizon in the early hours of the morning veered off beyond the hills to the east, the sound of its thunder growing more and more muffled within the velvety gray clouds.

Joe went into the headquarters room to get some sleep, but found Travis in the midst of a cheerful burst of industry, sweeping the furniture clear of all the dirt that had fallen on it when the cannonball had slammed into the wall.

"You did a fine job shoring this place up, Joe," Travis said, "but I think more dirt is needed."

"What I need is some sleep."

"You had your chance. Don't think I didn't hear you prowling around in the middle of the night. Why you would want to waste an opportunity to sleep I have no idea, but now there is work to be done. Take the other end of this blanket."

Joe picked up the blanket and helped Travis snap it free of dust. Then he straightened up the rest of the room as best he could as Travis sat down to write more letters.

"I believe the tide is turning to our advantage, Joe," Travis said as he signed his name to the bottom of a page. "All we have to do is hold on for another few days, and we will have won a splendid victory here."

Joe mutely nodded his head and went on with his work while Travis took out the copybook in which he was writing his autobiography.

When he considered himself finished with his housekeeping, Joe lay down on his cot without asking for permission and went to sleep as he had so many nights before, listening to the sound of William Barret Travis's scratching pen.

—*The Gates of the Alamo*
(New York: Knopf, 2000), 417.

Jim Hightower

I really love to write.

Jim Hightower

I find it a joy, and because I am mostly a political, economic writer, there is no short-age of rich material. Whatever gets your blood boiling in the morning, you can actually do something about it.

Interview by Teresa Taylor

Teresa Taylor: When I walked in the room, there was a plethora of hand-written pages on your table with a very long and beautiful script. Tell me about the writing process. Do you do all of your work handwritten?

Jim Hightower: I do. I am a Luddite with the Web site. We are totally wired in terms of computer technology and all of that, but personally I am a hand writer. In fact, you can see my little finger won't go straight because I write with it tucked down under my hand, and so this pen is my printer and my notepad liter-ally is a notepad. It is how I am most comfortable. I love the feel of it. I feel my mind connected to what flows through my fingers more than I would typing.

Taylor: You feel your mind flowing through your fingers. Is this a physi-cal experience when you sit down to write?

Hightower: It's certainly a textural experience. The texture of the pen and the pad and then the text that comes out of that are very related. I am not a reclusive writer. I mostly write early in the mornings and mostly in coffee shops around town or on airplanes. When I am here in town, practically every morning I am at one of the many coffee shops that we have around here. I like the ambi-ence and being with folks, plus I get good coffee.

Taylor: That is a real Austin experience, especially in hot weather on a very languid day.

Hightower: And there are some wonderful places, some of the still funky, pure Austin joints like the Bouldin Creek Coffee House here on South First. They have a neon light that says CAFFEINE DEALER. They are just wonderful folks. I go from that to Mozart's on the Lake because the view is so remarkable and you can kind of lose yourself in denser mornings. Wherever I am it's a sense of being in Austin, being in a place. If I had to be alone and locked in a room, I would feel like I was being punished. So this is like getting a little reward even as I do my work.

Taylor: It sounds like a meditative or thoughtful process, as some writers use journal writing. Do you experience it in that way or is it entirely a political act?

Hightower: It's not a political act. Most of my writings are political, but it's a pleasurable act for me. I really love to write. I pick topics that keep me motivated. I just find it a joy, and because I am mostly a political, economic writer, there is no shortage of rich material. Whatever gets your blood boiling in the morning, you can actually do something about it.

Taylor: Jim, tell us where you grew up in Texas?

Hightower: I grew up in Denison, a family that came off tenant farms, small business people, and railroad workers. My parents both came off subsistence farms.

Taylor: Were there particular experiences you had there that raised your social awareness?

Hightower: Well, yes, beginning with the fact that there were no black people in schools, even though there were a lot of black people in town. That was number one. Number two, and in a way more fundamental, was the experience of growing up in my family and with families of the kids that I hung around with. We were mostly outsiders to the political and economic establishment, even in that little town, who largely felt politically, economically excluded by the powers that be.

In my own family's experience, my father would have to go hat in hand to the bankers to get the loan for the small business, would have to deal with the corporate powers as chain stores began to come in and dominate the market that he was operating in. Then seeing my farm relatives up against the same economic powers was a shaping populist experience, even though we did not know what to call it. Certainly we didn't know that it was called populism. But it was a reality that was experienced daily in people's lives: that a few had power and that they didn't. Or as the old Bob Wills tune "Take Me Back to Tulsa" has in that verse: "The little bee sucks the blossom but the big bee gets the honey. The little man picks the cotton but the big man gets the money." That was reality. That is how most folks I knew lived, and so that native populism was not academic. It wasn't even political. It was experienced life.

Taylor: Was this disparity in economic relationship and power something that was discussed around the dinner table, or at bars, or in the fields?

Hightower: A bit around the dinner table. But my parents weren't that politically active. They voted, they certainly knew what was going on; they read, they did talk some, but they didn't dwell on their problems. Mostly they were trying to make ends meet and keep their business going and their family ahead a little bit. Even though the economic disparity was a reality, the people I knew were optimists, and I think Texans generally are. It's born out of who we came from: people who were not only fleeing debt out of the tenant farm system in the South but also going for a new start. So that breeds a forward-looking person rather then somebody who wants to dwell in his or her own misery.

The real expressions were in the culture itself, as I say, through the music. Not only did I grow up with Bob Wills' music but also the pre-rock'n'roll rhythm and blues, which had plenty of songs about "the man" and what you're fighting against. Also in the churches—growing up in the little old Methodist church—it was quite common that the sermon would be taken from the scripture of Jesus the Rebel, and the likelihood of a rich man going to heaven being comparable to a camel going through the eye of a needle. So the God of Mammon was much talked about in the church.

I think the real development of my populist outlook came more around my father's Dr Pepper stand in Triangle News. He was a small businessman, as I said. He had a magazine wholesaling franchise for Denison and Sherman. He got the magazines from the publishers and put them in the grocery stores, drugstores, and what not. He and my mother ran what became the Main Street Newsstand, which not only sold magazines and sodas and candies but some school supplies and that sort of thing. It became a stopping point every morning for the other local merchants, delivery people, and regulars wandering around with nothing better to do. They would sit around and stand around shootin' the shit and solving all the world's problems of the day and playing off whatever was in the news. They had a very self-deprecating humor and a very strong antiestablishment take on things, sarcastic, irreverent. I grew up with that. That did more to shape me than any other educational experience about how the world works. It certainly has shaped my writing and my speaking and my work generally, because that is where I got the humorous outlook on things.

Taylor: You talked about the churches and the fact that black people apparently did not have access to the schools. Were there places in town, perhaps in the church, or other places where blacks and whites could meet and have common discussion?

Hightower: Not really. I'd like to say yes to that. Blacks and whites did come together in my father's store because we had magazines that appealed to everybody. But that was limited to using a commercial transaction to snatch a conversation, and it went by. During my time, and I graduated from high school in '61, there really was no communication. There was the black side of town, and certainly it was not an apartheid thing. People moved around, but they really didn't interact. That led to my rather rude awakening when I graduated in '61. A couple of months later I enrolled in what is now the University of North Texas and sat down in a government class next to a black guy from my hometown.

Taylor: You never met him before that point?

Hightower: No, I had not met him. What I think fueled the civil rights movement for whites of my ilk and my generation was the realization that essentially we had been lied to about who made up the world and why. So, there is nothing like a personal experience to agitate and activate somebody. That was certainly part of my motivation.

Taylor: I am going to use the term "class war" because you use it in at least one of your books. Do class war and class consciousness in Texas have aspects that are unique to this state's culture?

Hightower: Yes, I think that those who are not born privileged are born with an innate suspicion about the elites, the monied elites in our culture. Indeed, it was reflected in the founding of our state; it comes from founding folks who mostly were very low income, farmers and adventurers and a few criminals. The first Texas state constitution outlawed banks. You couldn't create one in Texas. To create a corporation, you had to get a two-thirds vote of both houses of the legislature. There were very strict rules on what that corporation could be, what it could do, how long it could exist. There was an antiestablishment skepticism about government power and about concentrated economic power.

Taylor: Our political system and the economy certainly are dominated by corporate power. Do you see that as such an inherent flaw in our political system that we might need substantial cultural and political change to address it? Or do you think that within our political framework and the constitution, we have the tools we need to create greater social justice?

Hightower: Well, this isn't just a state issue. To begin to get political democracy, we have to get the corrupting power of big money out of politics, because it means that politics goes with the money rather than with ideals or people or principles or need or anything else. This monetary distortion of our political process has resulted in a dangerous disconnect, because the vast majority of the people of Texas know they don't have money or power in the Texas Legislature, and not much in most cities. The first thing to be done is to have a system of publicly financing elections so that it's possible for officeholders, and maybe a whole party, to represent non-monied people, and so it's possible for regular people to run for office again. That is what a public financing system allows.

Taylor: Do you have any thoughts about if and how our system should be moved to a direct democracy?

Hightower: We are not even good yet at representational democracy. Direct democracy has increasing possibilities in our country because of rising education and technological possibilities, but we are not there. Right now it would be the noisiest, most technologically connected people that would be driving that democracy. There are also big issues about the increasing corporate control of the software and mechanisms within our computers and computer links that would be very dangerous. They are even dangerous with the electronic voting machines now, as to whether they can be manipulated and by whom. I think there are a lot of other reforms that have to come first.

Taylor: You mention proportional democracy. That seems like a system that would on occasion force coalition building among disparate interests.

Hightower: Our present system of winner-take-all is a skewed system in which even a majority of the people could have voted and still not [received] any of the decision-making authority. Under proportional representation, the Greens who got 20 percent [of the vote] would get 20 percent of the seats in the legislative body and the same with the Libertarians. So your vote would count even if you were not the majority, and it would count proportionally.

Taylor: Do you get a special charge when you are on the radio? Does it get your blood up?

Hightower: Yeah, that is performance art, doing the recordings, which I do here at the wonderful Production Block Studios. Joel Block and the wonderful people there have been Austin institutions for a long time, known internationally. Just another Austin treasure. I still get a big charge out of occasionally coming across a station as I am traveling around and hearing myself somewhere, but especially by people who profess to be touched by what I've written. That is reward enough, although I wouldn't give up the little money I make either.

Taylor: Andy Warhol once made the comment that he put on his Andy suit in reference to the difference between being his very introverted self and his extremely public lifestyle. Does it take a particular strategy or energy for you to maintain a very engaging public presence?

Hightower: Ah, yes, it does. I think it has to for everyone, because so much energy is required for essentially being on, even if you are not trying to formulate a persona, even if it's just you. If you meet that many strangers in your day, it taxes the old energy a good bit.

I approach it two ways. One is to be methodical. Typically on a trip, I have half a dozen things to do that day and night, so I want to see them in front of me as I head out. The second approach is to see what I can get out of this that makes it all worthwhile. Generally, more than half the time I get a good story from somebody or juiced by the experience. Or I find out something I otherwise would not have known or see something I otherwise would not have seen.

Taylor: I'm noticing quite a mix of office decor you have here, including a marvelous and mammoth-sized desk. It looks like an antique. Can you tell us about that?

Hightower: That is a post office desk out of the post office in La Grange, Texas, that I bought in 1982. It is a stand-up desk, and I do stand up a bit when I write, and as you can see it's an expansive desk. There is a lot of room to spread out and fling papers about, so I like that. It's sort of the aesthetic of writing, and it's important to me.

Taylor: There also appears to be an antique mirror, a mask that has horns, some artwork featuring a girl standing behind a bar, and then a black-and-white photograph. Who is the photographer, and is there a story with this photograph?

Hightower: There is a story in every photograph. That photograph is by Russell Lee, one of the great Texas photographers, great American photographers. A whole mystery is written in that one photograph. It's a guy sitting in front of an old icehouse with a big sign over him saying ICE and a big block of ice — this is in the old days of block ice — and he has an ice pick in his hand. It is just a spectacular photograph of what amounts to a regular working guy. So I like that, and I love art.

In my travels I go to art museums and experience them. I'm a fan of the Impressionists, Monet in particular, and Matisse and Picasso, but then I love the local artists and that is what the devil mask is. One of the great local artists made that, and of course I've got my old talk radio show sign here — The Hightower Radio Live from the Chat & Chew — and it is in neon with a flashing radio tower sign going off. I achieved two personal peaks in my career, one when I was able to have a neon sign — my name in neon — and the second when *Funny Times*, a periodical that collects great cartoons and funny writers, began to include me in their publication. So I can go to the grave happy, fulfilled.

Humor is so rare in politics these days that I've actually been asked by the *New York Times* where I come up with my stuff, like maybe I'd been sipping some well water no one else in politics knew about. No magic to it—in addition to being born full of bull, having a daddy named "High," and being a faithful reader of the comics and sports pages, I'm on the road and on talk radio a lot, constantly rubbing up against the

funny bones of hoi polloi. Like the elderly preacher—had to be eighty—who shuffled up to me after a talk I had given, patted my arm, and said in a confiding voice: "Some of these rich folks today seem to think everything belongs to them and they'll even get to take it with them when they die. But you know what, Mr. Hightower? You don't ever see a hearse pulling a U-Haul."

He smiled a big, gentle smile, like he knew he'd just put that line someplace where it wouldn't die. I've lost the preacher's name, but I've sure spread his jewel of a line all across America.

—There's Nothing in the Middle of the Road
but Yellow Stripes and Dead Armadillos
(New York: Harper Perennial, 1998), 260–261.

Rolando Hinojosa-Smith

Klail City is very important because it's given me my life's work, which is writing.

Rolando Hinojosa-Smith

Essay by Joe Holley

> *. . . Home to Texas, our Texas*
> *That slice of hell, heaven*
> *Purgatory and land of our Fathers*
>
> Rolando Hinojosa-Smith

Among the many writers who mine the same rich material that intrigued Américo Paredes are gifted poets, novelists, essayists, and short-story writers.

Outstanding, perhaps, among Paredes' heirs are two influential authors, both born in South Texas, both outstanding teachers and university administrators, both gifted writers and good friends.

One is the late Tomás Rivera, born in Crystal City in 1935, the son of migrant farmworkers. He earned his bachelor's degree in education at Southwest Texas State University (now Texas State University–San Marcos) in 1958 and a master's degree in educational administration in 1964. He received an M.A. and Ph.D. in romance languages and literature from the University of Oklahoma in 1969. Ten years later, he was appointed chancellor of the University of California at Riverside, the position he held at the time of his death in 1984.

Tomás Rivera's good friend Rolando Hinojosa-Smith was born in Mercedes in 1927, the son of an Anglo mother and a Latino father. A graduate of the University of Texas at Austin, Hinojosa-Smith was a high school teacher in Brownsville for four years and, after receiving his Ph.D. in Spanish literature in 1970 from the University of Illinois, became an assistant professor at Trinity University in San Antonio. He also has been chairman of the Department of Modern Languages at Texas A&I University (now Texas A&M University at Kingsville) and later vice president for academic affairs. Since 1981, he has been the Ellen St. Garwood Professor of Southwestern Literature at the University of Texas at Austin.

An immensely learned man, who leavens his learning with a quick wit and easygoing nature, Hinojosa-Smith has written poems, short stories, scholarly articles, essays, and novels. He is best known for his Klail City Death Trip series, a loosely linked collection of thirteen short novels, written in both English and Span-

ish and set in fictional Belken County in the Rio Grande Valley during the 1930s, 1940s, and 1950s. Most of the installments focus, however, on the Valley's border concerns, its close family ties, and its bicultural history.

No other Texas writer has attempted what Hinojosa-Smith is doing with his *Klail City Death Trip*. Characters appear in one novel and may reappear in another, the stories loop in and out and around each other, and incidents from one have consequences in later works. *Ask a Policeman*, for example, published in 1998, picks up a story first told ten years earlier in *Partners in Crime*. Hinojosa-Smith uses snippets of gossip, conversational fragments, offhand observations, multiple narrators, and both Spanish and English to continue what he calls his "ongoing conversation" about life in the Valley as he knows it.

Still living and writing in Austin, and still teaching at the University of Texas at Austin, Hinojosa-Smith lectures frequently at universities around the world. In fact, he may be better known in Europe and Latin America than he is in Texas.

I need a place. I need a base. I've always insisted on being true to a place, having a sense of the place. It's easy for me to write about home.

Interview by Gary Kent

Gary Kent: Share with us some of your early writing experiences while growing up in South Texas.

Rolando Hinojosa-Smith: We have a lovely program called "Creative Bits," which allows juniors and seniors to write and then, if selected, their work is bound and placed in the library. I discovered not too long ago that I had five pieces during my junior and senior year. They're still there in the library. I imagine that I sat in the same chairs that my two brothers and sisters did, it was that small a school. Being the youngest, unfortunately, the teachers already knew who I was, so I always had to be on my very best behavior and do the best I possibly could. But Mercedes was a nice town, agricultural, with a fine public library and outstanding high school library. Our board of education and city fathers provided good reading material for everyone.

Kent: Did you know you were going to continue on with writing in your life? Was this something you wanted to do or was this just a passing interest?

Hinojosa-Smith: Oh, no, I was very interested in writing. When one of the pieces won honorable mention, I think that clinched it. My grandmother and

my mother were both teachers, so that put me on the teaching road as well—genetics, I imagine. I figured I could wed teaching and writing, which is what I've done all my life.

Kent: What happened after Mercedes? Where did you go from there?

Hinojosa-Smith: I went into the service, and then after that I attended the University of Texas. After I graduated from UT, I worked for ten years before I returned to graduate school. And I read a lot, I read more than I ever wrote, and for those ten years I worked as a laborer for a chemical plant. I also taught high school a couple of times. I worked as an office manager and a sales manager. I think a liberal arts major can do anything. Eventually I became a civil servant, and that allowed me to earn more money than being a high school teacher, and I was on my way to graduate school. At the age of thirty-two, thirty-three, kind of late, but I went back.

Kent: You received your Ph.D. from the University of Illinois?

Hinojosa-Smith: University of Illinois in 1969, and some of the best times we've ever had, my wife and I, were when I was there.

Kent: What took you to Illinois?

Hinojosa-Smith: My baccalaureate is from UT, but my master's is from a very small New Mexican school called Highlands University, and the chair there was a U of I graduate, and he recommended me highly. He recommended good schools, but Illinois is where I wanted to go because I had studied the faculty and it was outstanding. Great time!

Kent: The Rio Grande Valley—it appears constantly in your work, and you must have a great love for it. What has changed about it, and why do you have this love for the Valley?

Hinojosa-Smith: Maybe because I was born there and our people came there with the first settlers around 1748 and 1749. Our names appear in the 1750 census, so I'm very close to it. I travel there a lot. I fly there and just have a good time. My relatives live there. And my friends are still in the Valley, up and down; they married and either moved away or stayed in Mercedes.

It has changed—the Valley has—as everything has changed. After the Depression, World War II came and that changed it, even changed the face of the little town. And of course our proximity to the border also involves many legal and undocumented workers who come there, so that has changed the face in some way. But around 1970 after I was already in the throes of writing the first two novels, I began to notice an economic change in the Valley. By 1980 it had accelerated. The Valley, which has a seaport with Brownsville, was mainly agricultural and small business and small manufacturing. A lot of money began to come in, but it was drug money, unfortunately. And it also involved some of the old families, as well as some of the new ones. That did not destroy my love for it, because I love the culture, the anthropology, the great folklore that the Valley has, and the great history.

But that change is why I wrote two of the detective stories. One was *Partners in Crime* in '85, and the other one was *Ask a Policeman*, which came out in '98. *Partners* involves drugs, and *Ask a Policeman* involves wholesale drugs and even fighting between the families for control of the drugs. All those changes gave me the idea to present that side as dark as it is, because it holds with the reality of the place.

Kent: You surely get the feeling, or at least I do in reading *Ask a Policeman*, that there is this tremendous web or thread between families, between cultures, between enterprises that sort of holds that entire region in its own special gauze.

Hinojosa-Smith: Oh, that's very well said, I couldn't improve on it. What the Valley shares — all the way up to, say, El Paso, which is nine hundred miles up river from Brownsville — is that we are tied to the border. We are tied psychologically, certainly historically — we share a lot of that. We are tied culturally and in many ways linguistically. Now the Mexican American population is in the majority, so that the political face has also changed. The intercourse between the northern and the southern bank is where it always has been, very closely tied to the economy, which we also share.

Kent: When you write, is there a special place you write, or a special time?

Hinojosa-Smith: Special place? I can write just about anywhere. If the airplanes aren't jumping up and down, I can write. I can also write in airports; I've written in almost any venue. If I'm at home of course I have a special place. As for the time, because I'm a full-time teacher and writer — and, of course, there's committee work — I write early in the morning. This morning I got up at four-thirty, and I wrote until six A.M., but ordinarily I'll get up at five, write for a couple of hours. If I have nothing to write, I don't feel nervous. I just pick up a book that I've been reading. Usually, like most writers, I read two or three books at the same time. Sometimes if I have time in the afternoon or the evenings, I will write then. If I'm really on a good drive, if I've got something to say in the work that I'm on — whether it is an essay or a short story or a novel — then I can just write any time. I take notes once in a while. I would sometimes speak into a little recorder which I have, but I don't want to rely on it that much. I want to rely on memory and then maybe on handwritten notes.

Kent: Why is Klail City so important to you?

Hinojosa-Smith: First of all, I didn't want to use my hometown because that ties down the writer. That ties down any writer, unless it's a large city, Madrid, New York, Paris. Then you can just situate it in the city and go into neighborhoods. But Klail City to me is very important because it allows me the freedom to write about a town in the Valley, any event, any historical moment as well, and the different ethnicities there. Very few Texas blacks appear — that is also a representation of the Valley, where they're not only a distinct minority, they're almost nonexistent. It is very important because it's given me my life's work, which is writing. I need a place. I need a base. I've always insisted on being true to the place, having a sense of the place, to convince the reader that whatever they're reading, this man who is writing knows what he's talking about. It's easy for me to write about home.

Kent: I certainly got that feeling when I read *Ask a Policeman*; it became very real to me, and I didn't consider it fiction from then on. The modus operandi of the policemen and their daily routine and how they interacted was so real that I thought, "Gee, this is taken right from the police blotter. Somehow he finagled his way into the back room and knows how they talk." But it was more than that. It was what they ate. I never got so hungry in my life! It was just a really pleasurable book to read. Back to this police authenticity, was your father a policeman?

Hinojosa-Smith: Yes, he was. It was a very small town, the town of Mercedes; I think there were two or three policemen in the entire town. And he worked nights; he preferred to work nights. But my experience regarding police and police routine and procedure has come through reading and some common sense. People say to do research; my research is reading and talking and listening to people. I've always found that to be very instructive for me. If it convinces the reader — and you were just very kind with all the things you just said; goodness, it was so affirmative! But that's what I want to do, convince the reader that the writer knows what he is talking about or presenting or showing, whether it's food or dress or motive, expression, just make it as realistic as possible. Not real but realistic.

Kent: Well, you certainly do that. I want to ask about *gente dura*, the tough guys.

Hinojosa-Smith: Yeah, those are the really tough guys! That's a term that I thought I invented, until I heard someone use it. So I said, well, it's one of those coincidences that writers are always coming up against. In fact I think I not only heard it, but I think I read it somewhere too, later on, after I'd finished writing and publishing *A Policeman*. I said, by gum, there it is again. Reality invading fiction or fiction invading reality.

Kent: In *Ask a Policeman*, the bad guys are referred to as *gente dura*.

Hinojosa-Smith: Those that deserve it. I think there are one or two characters that are surprised when Roston tells one of them that so-and-so thinks he's *gente dura*, and he says, "No, no I'm not. They are." And he's not being modest. It is recognition that he's limited in some way. Because the real *gente dura*, the real hard guys, they are. They're very professional, really cold-bloodedly professional, as if they're insensitive to everything. But I know that they are husbands; they're probably fathers as well. That's one thing, but business is business.

One of them is being asked, "After you shot those men at the parking lot, what happened to the kid?" A brother interrupts, "Oh, we killed him too." Just like that. I've heard people talk that way, and it is chilling. It is meant to be chilling. Unfeeling, unremorseful—this is just something that I did—as if they are completely divorced from everything else. You know family is one thing, but the job is another. It's a terrible indictment of the human psyche that it works that way.

Kent: I think this book *Ask a Policeman* comes closer to the daily routine of the homicide detectives and the police force, and how they work. There's nothing glamorous about what these fellows have to do.

Hinojosa-Smith: They go fishing, they go to the Gulf, they go boating, they go sailing. The reason murder is so interesting is that it doesn't happen every day, but when it does, it just catches their attention and forces them to focus on this. But they have a social life. They baptize kids. I want them to be ordinary human beings and this is their profession. They're good at it, and they respect each other. But they're not big heroes either.

Kent: Right, right, they're men doing their work. Are you free from the vagaries of criticism? Does that affect you any way, up or down, with your writing?

Hinojosa-Smith: When I first started, I was very anxious to see my name on the page. I remember the great Larry King, the Texas writer, the *real* Larry King, said that he wanted to see his name on every page when he bought his first book; well, I did too. I read that line and I said, "Yeah, I think he pegged me and everybody else." I don't read or try to read brief newspaper reviews; they're always on a timeline. They usually have to meet some deadline as well, and the number of words is restricted.

What I respect are long articles that take the critic, the reviewer, a year, maybe even more, to write it, hone it. Then he has to wait another year before it is published, so that that's a lot of stick-to-itiveness, and that demands respect. Added to which the literary critic signs his name, and he can't back down. Like the writer, I can't really go around saying, "Well, I really meant to say this." No, no, the book is published, that's it. So the critic is the same way.

In Spain this January a woman is defending her thesis on my work, and a year before that another young man published his thesis on my work. Now that I am bound to read because I want to see what they said. Prior to that, Joyce Glover Lee of this country published *Rolando Hinojosa-Smith and the American Dream*, and that's a book. So I wanted to read that as well, because their reputation is on the line, and it deserves serious attention. I will write these critics and say thank you, or I think you saw this very well, or I appreciate your pointing this out. Long articles and theses and books are very much appreciated, and they should be read, as I do, with great respect for their work. Not only for taking interest in my work but for how prescient they can be about future works, and some of them have been.

Don Aureliano Mora has moved to a shady part of the park; he's sitting in one of the six benches that are left now. Thinking, perhaps of Amador who died in Okinawa; on Serafin who left and never returned to Belken County: Serafin gave thirty years of his life to Inland Steel; in return, the company gave him a pension, and then, at his death, the Social Security Administration threw in a coffin; on the twins, Antonio and Julio who lived and worked and died; and surely, on Ambrosio, the Flower of the Flock, on whose behalf a *corrido,* a ballad, was written and sung, and for whom don Aureliano decided to rid Belken County of still another piece of cold hypocrisy that served as a slap in the face of the old man.

Once in a while, the old man gets up and walks to the east corner of the park. A smile. No; no more plaques; a clothing store now. (One mustn't stand in the way of progress.) The park, named for General Rufus T. Klail, has been subdivided and sold into lots; a mini mall, they call it, and this is where the Romans sell their wares and souls on a daily basis. What's left of the park is a strip of six benches and that's where the old man spends most of his days.

—*Klail City: A Novel*
(Houston: Arte Público, 1987), 39–40.

Edward Hirsch

Poetry is not a form of entertainment,
but a necessary form of spiritual knowledge.

Edward Hirsch

Poetry precedes prose in all cultures and all languages. There have been cultures with-out prose, but there has never been one without poetry. There is information that we get in poetry that we can't get elsewhere.

Interview by K Bradford

K Bradford: Why is poetry necessary?

Edward Hirsch: We need poetry for the same reason we need all kinds of art—that is to enlarge our sense of the world we live in. I've been in poetry so long, it's so much a part of my experience now, that it's hard for me to imagine my own life without it. There are all kinds of reasons that poetry is necessary. There are people that need their own experience delivered to themselves in words. In some way, your own experience is puzzling and bewildering to you until you can find out about yourself.

In the larger cultural perspective, there has never been a culture without poetry. Poetry precedes prose in all cultures and all languages. There have been cultures without prose, but there has never been one without poetry, which makes me think that poetry is not a form of entertainment, but a necessary form of spir-itual knowledge. There is a kind of information that we get in poetry that we can't get elsewhere. I believe that if we could get it elsewhere, we probably would. Get-ting the news through poetry is difficult, and it requires attention. It's necessary to pay attention because poetry carries a certain kind of cognitive, emotional, and spiritual information.

Bradford: Describe how the poet serves as a vehicle of our culture.

Hirsch: The poet carries certain kinds of cultural information. The poet is the keeper and the vehicle of the language in which he or she writes. In music you have the notes, in sculpture you have the materials, in poetry all you have are the vocal cords and the sounds of the words to carry all the information.

Bradford: How are we making poetry more present in the world?

Hirsch: There's been a tremendous difference in the place of poetry in the last ten years as far as I can see it. People read a poem and fall in love with po-etry. My book *How to Read a Poem: And Fall in Love with Poetry* is meant for both initiated and noninitiated readers. What I've discovered is that there is a tremendous number of people who were taught poetry badly. They felt excluded from poetry. Now that they've come to a certain age, they feel that there's something in poetry for them, but they don't quite know what it is. They are finding that the culture can't fulfill all of their needs. There's an increasing sense that popular culture cannot provide enough solace. It can provide plenty of entertainment and distraction, but it can't speak to something that is more secretive and personal and emotional in our natures. A large number of people have turned to poetry as a place where they might find out something about themselves. I feel part of my task has been to help show them the way.

Bradford: You were born in Chicago, lived in the North, and landed in Texas in 1985. How has Texas affected your writing?

Hirsch: I feel I live in a place that is radically American in its diversity and its range and its combination of cultures. That would have a great impact on me in any place I happen to be. I move comfortably in different kinds of ethnic groups and all kinds of urban experiences, which is an extraordinarily fortunate "post-contemporary" American experience. It's not traditionally a Texan experience, but this also exists as part of Texas. When I first came to Texas, I was so shocked that I wrote some poems about Georgia O'Keeffe when she first came here and of her experience coming to terms with the Texas landscape. Since so much of my own experience is mediated through art, I found a way of coming to terms with moving to this landscape through Georgia O'Keeffe's reckoning of vast empty spaces. I've written a lot about vast open spaces in the Midwest. I have the suspicion that what I've been doing is transposing the plains of Texas into the plains of the Midwest, because that is my imaginary homeland.

I remember growing up in Chicago when I first started reading poetry, how appalled I was that Chicago poetry was always characterized by Carl Sandburg. The city of the "big shoulders" and all of that hogwash. In my first writings I wanted to put in waitresses and factory workers and people that hadn't appeared in poetry before. But I also wanted to write about going to the Chicago Art Institute and seeing Paul Klee for the first time and Modigliani, and looking at those paintings which were my first experience of culture. I felt then at eighteen or nineteen, that if you wanted to describe a Chicago experience, it had to include that too. I guess that's how I feel about Texas too.

The extraordinary amount of so-called high culture that's here is very much a part of Texas too. When I think about what it means to live in Texas, I think about driving with Richard Howard to Austin and going into the Ransom Center and looking at manuscripts of Yeats and Thomas Hardy that don't exist any-

where else in the world. That's a Texas experience, but it's not what people traditionally think about. It's not Cormac McCarthy, and it's not Larry McMurtry, but
it's very much for me what it means to be here in Texas.

Bradford: What are the social and political forces shaping or being
shaped by poetry?

Hirsch: I think about the tremendous developments of feminism in the
'60s and '70s. I think about the importance of the work of Adrienne Rich in relation to that. It seems to me that Adrienne Rich gave a kind of poetic conscience
to what might otherwise be just an ideology. She gave a poetic care to what was a
large social movement and helped give it a language. So there's one aspect of poetry and activism. There's a strong tradition in America of poets involved in public affairs and using poetry on its behalf—the tremendous number of poems written about the Vietnam War.

Poetry gives us a kind of emotional data. Poetry offers us the experience
of what it felt like to be in a given place at a given time. What lasts in poetry is the
testimony of what it's like to be here. Newspapers give you the political data. Novels are terrific at giving us the social facts. Poetry is deepest and best at giving us
the emotional experience of what it felt like, because of the tremendous intensity
of the language and the rhythmic values attached to language; nothing can get
closer to what it feels like emotionally to be in a given place at a given time. I believe that in the deepest sense, poetry carries the record of what it felt like. My basic premise about poetry is that at the heart of lyric poetry in particular, is the idea
of death. We're going to die. What we experience is going to go away. Poetry needs
to intervene and speak back to death by leaving a record of what it felt like.

Bradford: Where does poetry occur?

Hirsch: You have to do the work. You can't go around waiting for inspiration. I couldn't write poems without my experiences. You need what happens to
you to happen to you. Whatever you go through becomes part of your experience,
and that becomes part of what might become your poetry. The thrilling moment
of writing poetry is when something takes over. When something happens in the
process of writing that hadn't been anticipated and planned for: in the process of
making, you also discover.

Bradford: You've said that poetry is dangerous. How so?

Hirsch: There's a lot in the culture that instinctively wants to repress certain kinds of information. No family wants their kids to go out and really say what
it's like. Society has a great investment in pretending that it's functional. Poetry
gets to that place where it feels uncomfortable and true, not because it's sensa-
tional, but because it's identifying something that is genuine. The reason it's dan-

gerous is that after a certain age, you don't need your parents to tell you not to do or say a certain thing. So successfully has culture worked on you, that you've internalized it. And so you have your parents inside of you. And there's plenty in you that says, "Don't say that. Don't tell the truth about what it feels like."

Poetry is most dangerous because of the way it can be turned against yourself, because of what it says about you in relationship to yourself. Poetry is an international enterprise. It belongs to all historical periods. Part of what I've tried to do is make known to people what exists in poetry in the history of the world — in oral poetries and written poetries and poetries from other cultures. So that what American poetry is can continue to expand and grow. So that it doesn't have to be dominated by its conventions.

I don't know how long I stood there on that rainy Saturday afternoon, lost in a book in a basement of my childhood house, in a cluttered Jewish cemetery on the south side of Chicago, in the middle of a field somewhere in Latvia, on an English moor. It would be years before I discovered I had been reading a lyric by Emily Brontë. I recognized the style as soon as I encountered "No Coward Soul Is Mine." I suppose that in some sense I never really shut that worn anthology of poetry again because it had opened up an unembarrassed space in me that would never be closed. I had stumbled into the sublime. I had been initiated into the poetry of awe.

—*How to Read a Poem: And Fall in Love with Poetry*
(New York: Harcourt, 2001), 63.

Robert E. Howard. Photograph courtesy of Robert E. Howard Properties.

---

*When in my dreams I fought the armored legions
of Rome, there sprang into my mind the picture
of a map, . . . the cryptic legend, "Picts and Scots."
And always the thought rose in my mind
to lend me new strength.*

Robert E. Howard

Essay by Joe Holley

The tiny West Texas community of Cross Plains may seem an unlikely place to nurture one of the most successful writers of science fiction this nation has ever produced, and yet on second thought, what better place could there be to encourage a writer of escapist fantasies? Robert Ervin Howard, creator of the world-renowned Conan the Barbarian, was born in 1906 in Peaster, a tiny hamlet some forty-five miles southwest of Fort Worth. His father, a country doctor, moved his family all over Texas for several years, before finally settling in Cross Plains, near Abilene, in 1919.

Howard began writing fantasy tales while still in high school, selling his first story, called "Spear and Fang," to Weird Tales, *a pulp magazine that helped launch the careers of Ray Bradbury, Robert Bloch, and the horror master H. P. Lovecraft. Howard continued writing as a student at Howard Payne College in Brownwood. He had enrolled at Howard Payne in 1926 to take bookkeeping courses, discouraged that many of his stories were being rejected.*

By 1930 Howard was a Weird Tales *regular, with stories about such recurring characters as Solomon Kane, the Puritan swordsman and redresser of wrongs; Kull, the Atlantean warrior who seized the throne of fabled Valusia in the precataclysmic age before the demise of Atlantis; and Bran Mak Morn, the Pictish chieftain who did battle with the encroaching legions in Britain. In addition to* Weird Tales, *Howard wrote for* Action Stories, Argosy, Fight Stories, Oriental Stories, Spicy Adventure, *and numerous other publications.*

Howard, who was still living with his parents in Cross Plains during the 1930s, introduced the muscle-bound character who would soon overshadow all his other fantasy heroes in the December 1932 issue of Weird Tales. *Conan the Cimmerian — thief, pirate, adventurer, and mercenary — lived in the Hyborean Age, a mythical period some twelve thousand years ago, between the sinking of Atlantis and the dawn of recorded history. During the next four years, seventeen Conan stories appeared in* Weird Tales, *some lengthy enough to require serialization.*

In June 1936 Howard's mother sank into a coma. When told that she would never recover, Howard shot himself in the head, dying eight hours later. His mother died thirty hours afterward.

It might be said that a good part of Robert's education was in poetry. His mother loved poetry and read to him a lot. Certainly his writing shows that he'd absorbed poetry into his bones.

Interview by Mark Finn

Editor's Note: Mark Finn speaks to Rusty Burke, foremost expert on the late Robert E. Howard.

Mark Finn: Let's start at the beginning. When and where was Robert E. Howard born?

Rusty Burke: He was born in Peaster, which he called a "fading little ex-cowtown," just a little north of Weatherford, Texas. He was born January 22, 1906, although the record of birth in Parker County says the 24th. It also got his middle name wrong, too, spelling it "Ervine" [instead of the correct "Ervin"]. Robert said his birthday was the 22nd, and other evidence points to that as the correct date.

Finn: As a doctor's son, did he receive any special education?

Burke: Not really. He attended public schools. When he completed the tenth grade, he had to go to Brownwood to continue high school, since Cross Plains' school didn't have an eleventh grade, which was required for college. After finishing high school though, Robert opted not to go to college. His only other education was courses in stenography and bookkeeping at the Howard Payne Academy in Brownwood. It might be said that a good part of Robert's education was in poetry. Apparently his mother loved poetry and read to him a lot. Certainly his writing shows that he'd absorbed poetry into his bones.

Finn: He showed an aptitude in school for writing, didn't he?

Burke: Yes. He won an essay medal during his last year of high school, and his first published stories were in the high school paper. In fact, since he won cash prizes for two of those stories, you could say it was his first paid writing. He sold "Spear and Fang," a caveman story, to *Weird Tales* in the fall of 1924, when he was eighteen. The story did not appear in the magazine until July of the following year.

Finn: Let's talk about what Howard wrote. He covered just about every aspect of the pulps, didn't he?

Burke: Well, not all, but quite a lot. He didn't do the "hero" pulps like *Doc Savage* or *The Shadow*. He didn't sell any air stories that we know about, but yes, he sold to a lot of different markets. In addition to *Weird Tales* and other horror or fantasy markets, he sold fight stories, Westerns, detective stories, "weird menace," historical adventure, what were called "oriental" stories or desert adventure, "spicy" stories—he definitely tried to "splash the field." He even wrote a great deal of excellent poetry, though it was published only in *Weird Tales* or small poetry magazines.

Finn: Did he have any early or notable successes?

Burke: His third story to appear in *Weird Tales* was given the cover, which was something of an honor. That one is an interesting story. "Wolfshead," which is a werewolf story, had been accepted by *Weird Tales* in October 1925. Just after Christmas, he learned it would be the cover story, and he was walking on clouds. Then just after New Year's, he got a telegram saying that the cover artist had not returned the manuscript for typesetting and it was feared lost; could he please send a carbon? Well, he hadn't made a carbon. He had to send the editor a telegram saying there wasn't a carbon, but that he was proceeding to rewrite the story from memory. Ultimately they found the manuscript, minus the first page, which they took from the rewrite. The story appeared in the April 1926 issue and was voted second place by the readers, after H. P. Lovecraft's "The Outsider." "Red Shadows," the first Solomon Kane story, was quite popular with the readers, and Howard finally won first place with "Skull-Face," a three-part serial in which he gave Sax Rohmer a run for his money. He also made a splash when he finally cracked the boxing-story market, selling stories pretty steadily to the Fiction House magazines.

Finn: Can you briefly run down some of Howard's more notable creations?

Burke: Well, of course, his best known are the fantasy heroes. Conan, a barbarian who wanders the lands of the Hyborean Age, supposedly an age of our own earth before the dawn of recorded history, is undoubtedly his most famous creation, having spawned countless imitations in most of the media. I think the Hyborean Age that he created for Conan is itself pretty fascinating, a land in which legend and myth and history can all intermingle. King Kull, an Atlantean barbarian who gains the throne of the most fabled kingdom of his day, is more quirkily philosophical than Conan, constantly musing on metaphysical questions, but the best Kull stories, such as "The Shadow Kingdom," are the equal of the Conan tales. Solomon Kane is a Puritan swashbuckler—Howard loved to shake up stereotypes. He knew that the swaggering Puritan adventurers of the Elizabethan Age were a long way from our picture of the New England colonists. Kane's best adventures are those in Africa in which he confronts the remnants of an ancient Atlantean colony, winged demons who are horrible descendants of the Harpies of Greek myth, a village of the undead, and other bizarre menaces. One of Howard's creations that I am most struck with is his "Picts," who are the oldest race in the world. They appear in the stories of Bran Mak Morn, their king who holds the Roman legions at bay in Caledonia, but also in the Kull and Conan stories, and a few that are set in other eras, both historical and legendary.

In addition to the fantasies for which he is best known, Howard wrote a number of very compelling horror stories, particularly those set in his native Southwest, in which he blended elements of the horror story and the Western. And two of Howard's most popular series during his lifetime are not especially well known today. These were the Sailor Steve Costigan stories that ran in *Fight Stories* and other boxing magazines, and the Breckinridge Elkins stories that ran in *Action Stories*.

Finn: How did Howard become involved in the Lovecraft Circle?

Burke: *Weird Tales* reprinted H. P. Lovecraft's story "The Rats in the Walls" in 1930. In it there is a bit at the end where the narrator begins relapsing into increasingly archaic speech as he goes mad, babbling in languages in reverse order of their historic primacy in Britain. One phrase is in Gaelic. Howard wrote a letter to the editor praising the story, but noting that, from the Gaelic phrase, Mr. Lovecraft must be an adherent of the theory that the Gaels preceded the Cymry in Britain. The editor passed the letter on to Lovecraft, who wrote Howard and admitted that he had simply lifted a seemingly apt phrase from the Irish writer Fiona McLeod, not suspecting that anyone would really notice.

The two began corresponding and continued to write really lengthy letters to each other until Howard's death in 1936. They discussed all manner of things, and the letters are fascinating reading. In an early letter, Howard rather timidly asked Lovecraft for some information about the myths of Cthulhu, Yog-Sothoth, etc., which had appeared in several different writers' work in *Weird Tales*. Howard thought his own education was somehow lacking, for he had never heard of these myths. Lovecraft told him, of course, that he had made them up, and that the reason they appeared in other writers' work was that he had revised those stories and stuck them in! He encouraged Howard to join in the fun. Howard did start writing some "Lovecraftian" type stories, some of which — like "The Black Stone" and "The Children of the Night" — are pretty good, but he ultimately realized this wasn't his natural style. It probably contributed a lot to the "cosmic horror" element that one finds in the Conan stories, though.

Finn: Let's talk about the creation of Conan the Cimmerian. When and how did that happen?

Burke: Howard claimed that Conan had "stalked full grown" into his mind when he was visiting the Rio Grande Valley in early 1932. He seems first to have written the poem "Cimmeria," then started on "The Phoenix on the Sword," the first Conan adventure. It's interesting that his first Conan story was a rewrite of an unsold King Kull story that had probably been sitting around for a couple of years. He went through a couple of drafts before he was ready to submit the story, and also wrote a shorter little tale called "The Frost-Giant's Daughter," which was a story of Conan's youth. He sent them both to *Weird Tales* and kept working on Conan.

Farnsworth Wright, the *Weird Tales* editor, sent the stories back, rejecting "The Frost-Giant's Daughter" outright but saying "The Phoenix on the Sword" had "points of real excellence" and asking for some revision, mainly tightening the beginning and end of the story. One thing Howard did that was a neat little riff was to create the "Nemedian Chronicles" that now opens the story, in order to get in some of the background for Conan's world from the parts Wright wanted cut. In the meantime, he'd also been writing other Conan stories, but he realized he needed some way to keep all this imaginary history he was creating straight. This is when he began "The Hyborean Age," a "pseudo-history" of this lost, pre-cataclysmic age of the earth. The terrific thing about the Hyborean Age was that it gave Howard all of history to play with without having to stick to known facts. He could have Conan running around with Cossacks, medieval knights, Elizabethan pirates, and American frontiersmen, all pretty thinly disguised, in this "age undreamed of." It's a neat concept, and it let him work directly with mythic, archetypal material without a lot of slavish attention to historical details.

Finn: Was Conan initially popular with the *Weird Tales* audience?

Burke: Oh, yes. Howard had already built up a pretty good reputation in the magazine, and Conan solidified his standing as one of the two or three most popular writers. In the readers' poll, "The Phoenix on the Sword" took second place for the December 1932 issue, and the next five Conan stories all took first place in the issues they appeared in.

Finn: All right, I want to talk about Howard as a Texas writer. Do you think that Texas, particularly living where he did, had an influence on his writing?

Burke: Texas was certainly a very strong element in Howard's writing. Some of his earliest attempts at fiction were either Westerns, or featured western characters, though all of this work was relatively minor. But I think that, even in his fantasy and horror, a lot of Texas comes in through Kull's and Conan's attitudes toward laws. The rights of individuals are, to my mind, reflective of that stubborn streak of southern independence that was particularly exacerbated in Texas by the years of Reconstruction. Authority that did not honor the rights of the individual and rules that did not make sense in light of conditions were simply not to be obeyed or trusted. There are some nice scenes when Conan or Kull confront the hereditary nobility and dress them down for exploiting the people: this is Howard's own populist beliefs coming through, beliefs he shared with a great many Texans of his day.

Many of his settings, too, I believe to be reflective of Texas. He wrote to a fan that his poem "Cimmeria," about Conan's homeland, was inspired by the Hill Country near Fredericksburg in winter. Conan himself was created, as I said, during a trip to the Valley. Howard said he was a mixture of a lot of types he had known, most notably oil field types like roustabouts and bullies, gamblers and lawmen, and so on. Howard had lived through some town-site oil booms and had seen the effects. He told Lovecraft that a boom would teach a kid pretty quick that life is a rotten business. The effect of those booms on Howard himself and on his work just cannot be overestimated.

Finn: At the end of his life, Howard was actually in a "Western phase," wasn't he? How does that compare to his earlier work?

Burke: Yes, Howard's work did seem to go through phases, and at the end he was devoting more and more of his time to Westerns. Of his straight Westerns, probably the best is the novel *The Vultures of Whapeton*, which compares quite favorably with his better fantasy work, although I have to admit that critical opinion of his straight Westerns is mixed. Count me among those who think Howard would have really made a mark with Westerns had he lived. He would have needed to find a sympathetic editor, though, who didn't think all endings needed to be happy. Howard's humorous Western stories of Breckinridge Elkins, Pike Bearfield, and others are rollicking tall tales, and the best are on a par with his fantasy; though because of the nature of this type of story, a sameness creeps in that makes it inadvisable to read more than one or two at a sitting.

The best of Howard's Western fiction was horror stories with a western setting, such as "The Horror from the Mound," about a rancher who gets a lot more than he bargained for when he goes digging into an old Indian mound; "The Man on the Ground," a marvelous psychological study of the hatreds that led to Texas feuds; and "The Dead Remember," a ghostly vengeance story told in the form of letters and depositions. Another indication of what Howard could have done with the Western, had he lived just a little longer, are the wonderful passages in his letters, particularly to Lovecraft, recounting tales of Billy the Kid, John Wesley Hardin, Big Foot Wallace, and others. In fact, given that hatred and feuds were among Howard's most powerful themes (witness the Conan story "Red Nails," some of the Oriental adventures such as "The Lion of Tiberias" and "Lord of Samarcand," the Turlogh O'Brien story "The Dark Man," and on and on), and given his apparent fascination with Billy the Kid and Hardin, I believe it is very likely he would eventually have turned his hand to stories of the Lincoln County War, the Sutton-Taylor feud, and others. It's a real shame he didn't live to try.

Finn: How did he die?

Burke: Howard took his own life on June 11, 1936, at the age of thirty. He had apparently contemplated it for some time, and some of his poetry seems to reflect suicidal ideas. When his mother sank into a terminal coma and it was clear she would no longer need him to care for her, he went to his car and shot himself.

I was an instinctive enemy of Rome; what more natural than that I should instinctively ally myself with her enemies, more especially as these enemies had successfully resisted all attempts at subjugation. When in my dreams—not daydreams, but actual dreams—I fought the armored legions of Rome, and reeled back gashed and defeated, there sprang into my mind—like an invasion from another, unborn world of the future—the picture of a map, spanned by the wide empire of Rome, and ever beyond the frontier, outside the lines of subjugation, the cryptic legend, "Picts and Scots." And always the thought rose in my mind to lend me new strength: among the Picts I could find refuge, safe from my foes, where I could lick my wounds and renew my strength for the wars.

—Robert E. Howard, "Foreword," *Bran Mak Morn*
(Riverdale, N.Y.: Baen Publishing Enterprise, 1996), 4–5.

Molly Ivins

Humor is the great cure for absolutely everything.

Molly Ivins

I'm greatly aided by the fact that I really don't have to be funny; it's all in the material. What could be funnier than Texas politics—except possibly national politics?

Interview by Graham Shelby

Graham Shelby: What is the difference between "liberal" and "progressive"?

Molly Ivins: I'm not sure there is one. It's almost a distinction without a difference. If someone wants to call me a liberal, that would be fine. Myself, I think I'm a left populist and somewhat libertarian as well. It used to be in the '60s, when people were far more political, if you didn't have at least two hyphens in your political affiliation, you were clearly nobody and hadn't thought about the matter at all. You had to be a Maoist-Menonist-Anarchist to even count. But I'm fine with "liberal." I think the demonization of that word is just silly. But "progressive" is more accurate, and in my case, "populist" is more accurate.

Shelby: How did growing up in East Texas inform your beliefs, for example, about racism?

Ivins: I think this is true of almost all southern liberals — that we started with a question of race. I grew up in East Texas before the civil rights movement. My family lived in the white part of town. I can remember once at the grocery store I went to drink out of the colored fountain, and my mother said, "Don't drink out of that fountain, dear." I said, "Why not?" She said, "It's dirty." Well, the white fountain had had little grubby kids with grubby hands and bubble gum crawling all over it all day, and it was clearly filthy, whereas the colored fountain, which nobody had used, was clearly clean; and in that terribly logical way that little children have, I remember thinking, you know they're lying about this. That is not an uncommon experience with southern liberals. When you figure out early that they're lying to you about race — as they certainly did — then you start to question everything else that's received wisdom.

Shelby: If that's the impetus for your political exploration, what led you to deal with politics through writing?

Ivins: I read a lot when I was a kid. I suspect that's how anybody ever learns to write: by reading a lot. I read really dreadful stuff. We're not talking high-grade junior intellectual here. I read entire shelves of novels by lady novelists with three names, like Frances Parkinson Keyes. They were historical romances, many of them set in the antebellum South. But I do think that being a reader opens your world. The only talent I had ever shown, besides basketball, was for writing. When I was a teenager I wanted to write the Great American Novel. By the time I started college, it occurred to me that there were lots of other people also planning to write the Great American Novel. That meant that some of us weren't going to make it. I knew I should find a way to make a living in case I turned out to be one of the people who were not going to write the Great American Novel. I naturally fell back into journalism. The only thing I could do was write, and the only interest I had besides literature was current affairs. I had been active in the civil rights movement even when I was in high school. So from civil rights I went naturally into the antiwar movement. But I always thought there was a difference.

One of my theories of the '60s, which was such a bad, ugly, angry, crowded time, is that generations were unnaturally foreshortened. Normally a generation is defined by sociologists as either a time span of twenty years, or people whose lives are most profoundly influenced by one single event, so one can speak of a Depression generation or World War II generation. What happened in the '60s was that generations became much smaller in terms of their cohort. If one went into the Peace Corps, was influenced by John Kennedy, or worked in the civil rights movement in the early '60s, one came out with a different kind of politics and a different attitude than people in the later '60s.

By 1968, the kids were saying, "Tune in, turn on, and drop out." That was really a generation who had no experience of the civil rights movement. Their first political involvement was the antiwar movement. Those years, I always say, conveyed two giant political lessons simultaneously. The civil rights movement is enough to persuade you to be permanently optimistic because, as anybody who grew up before the movement can tell you, we came a long way in a short time. The civil rights movement proved how much and how fast things can change. That makes me a permanent optimist and a great believer in small "d" democracy. The Feds on the whole were the good guys. State and local law enforcement in those days was really the enemy. So you did have a tendency to cheer when the Justice Department showed up. But the war taught the opposite lesson. It was the example of how bad government can be when it lies to you and commits you to a stupid war which is pointless and futile and kills lots and lots of good people. So the '60s to me was a double lesson about government. My original optimism and liberalism were counterbalanced by this enormous example of just how bad government can be when it goes on its own for dumb reasons.

Shelby: What do you see as your role in that as a writer?

Ivins: Initially I had grand ambitions. My great heroes of the era were George Orwell and I. F. Stone. They played major roles in their time. They were leading intellectuals; they took important stands on public issues, and they really made a difference. On the other hand, they had communism and fascism and colonialism and all sorts of wonderful stuff to work with, and all I ever had to work with was Lubbock. I have excuses.

Shelby: How have your ambitions as a political writer changed?

Ivins: Every now and again I think I can prevent a bad bill from getting through the legislature. That's the grand total of my ambitions. Maybe I'm aiming too low. I like to get people involved in the political dialogue, because it's fun and because they have a responsibility. It's great entertainment—politics.

Shelby: A lot of people have a hard time with politics.

Ivins: I think people are hungry—people are nearly desperate for somebody in public life who will just tell the truth without all this bull. It's the reason they responded immediately to Ross Perot, to John McCain. Of course when you know politics, you'll understand there are reasons why candidates stick to pabulum absolutely guaranteed to offend no one. In politics you need 51 percent to win. I frankly think that we could do with a lot more people who actually said what they thought and in rather forthright and plainspoken terms.

Shelby: Why do you think that people who speak forthrightly don't win?

Ivins: Because of the money, and here we get to the heart of what is wrong with American politics. We are about to lose representative democracy completely and become a corporate oligarchy. This is not news to anybody. It has been evident for a long time. It's not that people don't care about it; they do care, but they think there's nothing they can do about it. What you have to do is persuade them that it can be fixed. There are ways that we can keep big money from ruling in politics.

Shelby: What are the keys to deciphering politics?

Ivins: The system is disproportionately canted toward the people at the top. The defense for that is, "Well, they pay more in taxes." No, they don't; they're not paying taxes in proportion to the share of the country's wealth that they hold. The phenomenon of the rich getting richer and everybody else staying the same is well documented. It's one of the most troubling phenomena in our political life. When you bring it up, Republicans leap up and say you're fomenting class warfare. If giving a tax cut where 43 percent of the benefits go to the top 1 percent is not class warfare, I don't know what is.

Shelby: What are some of the things you do to make politics readable?

Ivins: Humor is the great cure for absolutely everything. And I'm greatly aided by the fact that I really don't have to be funny; it's all in the material. What could be funnier than Texas politics — except possibly national politics? I went to journalism school in the days when the theory was preached that journalists could make themselves perfectly objective; you could report just the facts, no opinion, and you reported in a pyramid style so the lead sentence had to contain all the answers to the questions Who, What, Where, When, and How. From there you went on to lesser details so that the story could be edited from the bottom up. And, of course, the result was simply deadly. You would get leads out of the Texas Legislature such as "House Bill 327 was passed out of subcommittee by a unanimous vote on Tuesday." Period. Paragraph. What they didn't say was that there had been a committee meeting hip-deep in double crosses and triple crosses and lobby pressure. One guy was under so much pressure he had to go for a walk before the vote. All kinds of signals were being passed, and this hilarious testimony came up. None of that gets in. All the color and flavor and juice and joy of daily life are simply drained out of what was presented as news. No wonder people thought it was boring.

There's no such thing as objectivity, because we all see the world from where we stand. I am fifty-six years old. White. Female. Have a college education. All of that influences and shapes the way I see the world. With the best will in the world, with the greatest empathy and the largest stretch of imagination, there's no way I'm going to be able to see the world the same way a fifteen-year-old high school dropout does. Or the same way a seventy-six-year-old Polish American plumber does. We all see the world from where we stand. There is no perfect, right way to see it. That is why when you are an observer, you have to recognize your own bias and allow for it. I always thought that it was fair enough to say to my readers in essence, Okay, here's who I am and here's how I see it, and you can take that with a grain of salt, or a pound of salt, depending on your preference.

I will tell you as somebody who does my best to approximate the truth that I find it useful to look regularly for information I don't agree with. If you are liberal, you should be reading conservative magazines; and if you're conservative, you should read at least one good liberal magazine. If you are interested in the arts, you should read science magazines. If you're an engineer, you should open yourself to the arts. The mind is a muscle, just like any other muscle. If you use it, it stays limber and strong and grows. If you don't use it, it will contract and become flaccid and finally atrophy. And there are quite a few people whose minds have atrophied.

Shelby: So why do journalists attempt to cover politics with an objective stance?

Ivins: Because they think that's the way you're supposed to do it. It's the process of getting the facts straight and letting the truth go hang itself. The classic example was during the McCarthy era when Senator Joseph McCarthy was covered in objective fashion by most newspaper reporters. So that you get a lead like "'There are 57 communists in the United States Department of State,' said Sen. Joseph McCarthy." The trouble was, it wasn't true. Very often when you get the facts straight, the truth can go hang itself. You see it all the time.

Shelby: What should be the goal of the journalist?

Ivins: Accuracy. Always accuracy. There's no excuse for getting a fact wrong. If the name is Smith, it should be spelled *Smith*. If it happens to be spelled *Smythe*, it's on your head to find that out. And fairness.

I must say there are an enormous number of people in journalism who are not journalists. That's one of the problems we have right now. I find it a very distressing contemporary trend that people who are presented as journalists, particularly as pundits, as talking heads on television, parts of the casts of talk shows, are not journalists at all. They've been plucked straight off the front lines of partisan political warfare, and they're there simply because they add heat rather than light. George Stephanopoulos would be an example. If you look at the Reagan administration, the following people have had nationally syndicated political columns: Kenneth Adelman, Richard Perle, Mona Charen, Caspar Weinberger, Edwin Meese, Pat Buchanan, Jeane Kirkpatrick, Henry Kissinger, Peggy Noonan, John McLaughlin, Linda Chavez, Ollie North, Gordon Liddy, Michael Reagan, Roger Ailes, Mary Matalin, William F. Buckley. These are people who have never covered an automobile accident. As one old friend of mine once said, "If you can't cover a five-car pileup on Route 128, you should not be covering the presidential campaign."

Going out to interview all five eyewitnesses to an automobile accident and then trying to write an accurate and coherent account of what happened gives you a certain respect for the complexity of truth. It gives you some understanding that a sense of certitude is one of the greatest of all enemies of truth. I find it very distressing that people are presented now as journalists who really are partisan political warriors. They are not capable of stepping back, of giving a historical comparison, of just being helpful to those who are confused by the eternal contending claims.

Shelby: Your health has been on the minds of many.

Ivins: I wasn't sure that the world was terribly anxious to hear about my health, but as it turned out, people were quite glad that I wrote about it. One reason, of course, to continue speaking about it is simply to say the obvious to women: "Go get the mammogram. Go get it done."

Shelby: How was it writing about yourself?

Ivins: Unpleasant, of course. I must say going through the illness didn't do a thing for me. I had initially hoped that by confronting my own mortality, as they say in self-help talk, I would become a deeper, more profound person and perhaps a great thinker and philosopher. Develop a deep spiritual life. Alas, no such thing occurred. I spent the entire nine months going, "I can't go on a spiritual journey; I'm constipated." It was about that level of unpleasantness. I do think that being sick makes you more selfish, focuses you more on yourself. What has been interesting is the experience of getting better. Getting better does in fact make a real difference in one's attitudes toward life, and particularly in terms of how I want to spend my time and what I think is worth getting upset about.

Finding Barbara Jordan in the directory of distinguished Americans is easy. She was always a First and an Only.

First Woman, only black; in the Texas Senate, in the Texas congressional delegation, from the entire South. She served on the Judiciary Committee during the decision on Richard Nixon's impeachment. Her great bass voice rolled forth: "My faith in the Con-sti-tu-tion is whole, it is com-plete, it is to-tal." She sounded like the Lord God Almighty, and her implacable legal logic caught the attention of the entire nation.

. . . As it happened, the night B.J. spoke to Congress in favor of impeaching Richard Nixon was also the last night of the Texas legislative session. Came B.J.'s turn to speak and everyone back in Austin—legislators, aides, janitors, maids—gathered around television sets to hear this black woman speak on national television. And they cheered for her as though they were watching the University of Texas pound hell out of Notre Dame in the Cotton Bowl.

—"She Sounded Like God,"
You Got to Dance with Them
What Brung You: Politics in the Clinton Years
(New York: Random House, 1998), 231–232.

Mary Karr

I grew up in what Molly Ivins called one
of the roughest, toughest places in the country:
southeast Texas in the Port Arthur area.

Mary Karr

It's home to one of the richest idioms. The vernacular there is poetry. There was a natural skepticism and a bemusement at the face of the world, a combative attitude that is an interesting ethos for an artist to have.

Interview by Teresa Taylor

Teresa Taylor: Do you believe that Texas culture and the physical environment have influenced your writing?

Mary Karr: I grew up in what Molly Ivins called one of the roughest, toughest places in the country, southeast Texas in the Port Arthur area. It's also home to one of the richest idioms. The vernacular there is poetry. It's living poetry. To say "It's raining like a cow pissin' on a flat rock" is to speak a line of poetry. It's metaphorical. It's crude. It describes a whole world that people really don't even write about.

Taylor: An absolutely wonderful line.

Karr: The language is poetic. My interest in language stems from that. There's also a great oral tradition where I grew up, a great tradition of storytelling. There was a natural skepticism and also a bemusement at the face of the world, a combative attitude that is an interesting ethos for an artist to have.

Taylor: People such as Janis Joplin, I believe, come from your part of Texas?

Karr: Janis Joplin comes from Port Arthur, Texas. I knew her brother.

Taylor: Did you have an interest in Janis Joplin?

Karr: Oh, yeah. I loved Janis Joplin. I was a huge fan of hers. I saw her at the 7-Eleven once. I rode to school with Michael Joplin for part of my senior year. So, yeah, I was and am a huge fan. My son's a big Janis Joplin fan. I'm also a Robert Rauschenberg fan. Rauschenberg was also from there. There's a great tradition of blues down there. I used to go hear blues all the time at little juke joints and roadhouses in East Texas and western Louisiana.

Taylor: I get the sense that some people have had to get away from Texas to realize their artistic selves. Have you felt that kind of push?

Karr: Certainly from where I lived. Nobody wants to live there. I basically have gone where they've given me jobs. And at the time I left Texas, you had to leave Texas — from where I lived — to be able buy books. There weren't any books there. I had to go to Houston to buy books. So in that sense, it was a necessity.

Taylor: In *The Liar's Club*, you talk a lot about your mother's artistic energy and much of the focus is on your mother. But at a very young age, you had your own creative and artistic energy. Do you remember your first experience writing?

Karr: I have an early journal. I always wrote. I never didn't write. I wrote poems. I learned to read when I was very young — like two and a half. I have a letter I wrote to my grandmother when I was three, about a guy in a car wreck. And I have a journal from 1965 — I was about ten — that says when I grow up, I will write half poetry and half autobiography. I don't even know where I had read an autobiography. I guess I had read the Helen Keller book. I read biographies of Lincoln and Madame Curie. *To Kill a Mockingbird* is written like an autobiography. But I was always interested in the first-person narrator, and I was always interested in the shape of a life.

Taylor: That's quite interesting. So at that early age you had an awareness of how incredible your life was.

Karr: I thought the people around me were incredible. Amazing. I also knew they were people who would not be celebrated or written about unless I did it. My mother took the *New Yorker* for years and used to get the *New York Sunday Times* about two weeks late from somebody who subscribed to it down there. You know, when you read things in the *New Yorker*, you notice that no one you know is in there. In 1965 or 1970, there is nobody who looks like Port Arthur, Texas. It was mostly John Cheever and John Updike and a very different cast of characters. I remember reading Maya Angelou's *I Know Why the Caged Bird Sings* when I was a junior in high school and thinking, oh, my God, you can write about these people. You can. You can write about the kind of people I see. Working people.

Taylor: The people you write about have tremendous strengths and flaws. Are there any particular boundaries that you observe when writing about people who could potentially be affected by your publications?

Karr: I always try to tell the truth. I always tell people in advance what I'm going to write about them or not and roughly what it will cover, and give them a chance to say don't do that. And nobody's ever said don't do that. In *Cherry*, my friend Meredith, who's dead now, had asked that I cut out some stuff about her mother until her mother was dead. I edited it so the next time they print it, it will be slightly different. But it would be minor to anybody else. I make up names for everybody. I had somebody ask me for a different name and give me a specific name. So I said that was fine.

Taylor: I'm impressed by how funny and how painful your writing is, especially *The Liar's Club*. There's a lot of honesty in that writing. Have you always had that honest sense about yourself and your family, or have you come to that through the writing process?

Karr: Well, I don't know. I've always seen writing as a way to tell the truth. Obviously, we don't always know what the truth is, but that's what I'm trying to do when I'm writing: Say the truest thing I know. It's what Hemingway always said, "Say the next true thing." You know, some people don't have that sense. Vivian Gornick has this book on writing memoirs, and she says, "Just make it up and see if it's true." I thought, goddamn! The idea that people in memoirs would make up shit and publish it when everybody they know is alive! You know what I mean? People accuse me, "Oh, that didn't happen" or "You made that up." Why would I make this up and then publish it?

Taylor: It would discredit the memoir.

Karr: Not only that. It would make me look like a fool when my mother and my sister and everybody I knew said that's horseshit.

Taylor: They'll be the ones doing the talk show circuit.

Karr: People do make up shit, but their family isn't as well armed as mine has traditionally been. They're not the kind of people you just make up shit about, because they would object.

Let me say one other thing about that. I've also always written out of love. I've never written to settle a score. People that write memoirs to settle scores ought to have great trepidation about their motives.

Taylor: It probably shows in their writing too.

Karr: That's what I think. People then mistrust them. In my book, even though my mother had a psychotic break, she was also smart and beautiful and funny, and a great mother in a million other ways. Obviously, I wouldn't have traded her for all the cookie-baking mothers.

Taylor: That's something that does come through strongly in *The Liar's Club*.

Karr: She was a great and interesting woman, and I'm privileged to have her as a mom.

Taylor: You communicate that, while at the same time talking about things that were pretty traumatic.

Karr: She was a pain in the ass.

Taylor: In one of your poems, "Incant Against Suicide," you say, "Empty yourself of self, then kneel down to listen." To me that sounds very much like Daoist philosophy. Do you have an interest in Asian philosophy?

Karr: No, I actually converted to Catholicism in 1996. So I'm a Roman Catholic. Probably not the pope's favorite Catholic, but there you go. It's also a tradition in Christian mysticism — that notion of stillness or truth coming in silence. My mother studied Buddhism when I was a kid. And I read more about it probably before I was twenty than a lot of people wind up doing. I'm interested in any kind of religion or philosophy. I figure everybody knows something that's true.

Taylor: Do you meditate?

Karr: Every day.

Taylor: Do you see that as a form of prayer?

Karr: No. I pray *and* meditate every day. I do a kind of centering prayer, which is pretty much about getting quiet, about emptying yourself. It's sort of mantra based. But I also do a kind of prayer. I did the spiritual exercises of Saint Ignatius, which are a series of meditation exercises that you learn when you become a Jesuit, of all things. So at night I tend to do an Ignatian-prayer exercise. I try to do an accounting of the day and ask guidance from the Holy Spirit in what I ought to be doing.

Taylor: Can you tell me more about the mantras?

Karr: Well, they vary. It's not so different from the Jesus prayer, the "Lord Jesus Christ have mercy on us." And there's a chaplet for mercy. I call it the chaplet for divine mercy, which is a prayer for mercy for the whole world. "Have mercy on us and on the whole world." So it's usually a mantra like that. Sometimes I just count my breaths up to ten and then do it over. If I feel like my head is really chattering at me, I don't need to be saying anything. Just get quiet.

Taylor: Do you have an interest in using art as a form of social or political activism?

Karr: Art is always a form of social or political activism. Art that is pedantic is boring. It's hard to do political art that isn't pathetically predictable. But look at the poems of Czeslaw Milosz. Look at the poems of Adam Zagajewski. Look at the poems of Lorca. When there's a revolution, they shoot the poets first. They really do. Stalin proved that. So whether they're from the left or the right — César Vallejo or Osip Mandelstam — those are great poets of political protest. Robert Hass, who was my teacher and poet laureate, is a great political poet. But he's rarely pedantic or predictable. His political poems are always very wild and surprising.

Taylor: In your poem "Dead Drunk (or the Monster-Maker at Work)," you make a direct challenge to the reader to consider how we might respond to a homeless man passed out in the snow. What do you think makes for effective social commentary that is not just dogmatic?

Karr: Just not being pedantic. Not being rhetorical. Not preaching to the choir. That's the thing about a lot of political poems; they're talking to people who agree with them. Hopefully with that poem, I was saying: People know the right response to someone who's homeless. I don't think it's giving 'em money. I think it's buying them something to eat. I think most people, if they stop and think about it, usually know what the right thing to do is; they just don't often do it. And that's myself included.

Taylor: Who is Tom in this poem?

Karr: He's this guy I knew.

Taylor: And he was a homeless person?

Karr: Actually, he'd been a lawyer.

Taylor: Wow.

Karr: He lost his hands and feet. He got drunk and passed out and lost his hands and feet in the snow.

Taylor: I guess I made an assumption, then, that he was homeless.

Karr: No, he was a Harvard lawyer.

Taylor: That's something for everyone to think about.

Karr: Well, it can happen to anybody that lives where it snows and you drink enough to pass out outside.

Taylor: In your essay "Against Decoration," you talk about the trend toward overly decorative but emotionally vapid poetry. Does the slam poetry scene have any appeal for you and have you participated in it?

Karr: My first teacher was a black poet named Etheridge Knight, who published his first book from prison and really started the poetry slam in 1974, back before the Nuyorican Café. I haven't really participated since, I would say, 1978. I am more interested in history than in the moment, and I am more interested in the page than in the performance. So I write to put something on the page that will endure, because I'm not always gonna be there to say it. I'm also really interested in hip-hop. I think it's like what jazz was. It's like the cutting edge of what people are doing with language and music right now. I love it.

Taylor: It's a real contrast to the formalism you were describing. And it has emotional conviction.

Karr: It always has emotional conviction. That's true. Sometimes at its worst, it can be predictable. But so can anything. It can be predictable in attitude, but so can anything. It's also getting more musical and less dogmatic, and that's interesting too.

Taylor: How do you manage to enjoy the mysteries of life without being done in by day-to-day domestic chores and professional chores?

Karr: I'm a single mom. I work full time, and I run a business, to the extent that my writing and my going around and talking to people is a business. I think that you have to be pretty disciplined about it. And for me again, I lead a pretty simple life. I live in a kind of small town. I get up every day, and I work a little bit and get my kid off to school. I try to go to the gym. I don't drink, don't smoke, don't gamble, don't chase guys who are going to be a lot of trouble. I figure if there's going to be a lot of trouble in a relationship, I ought to be the one causing it. You're right. It's a lot of work.

Taylor: A lot of repetitive work.

Karr: It's funny. When I go on the road, people imagine I'm having fun. I'm going and seeing all my friends. But I get up at five in the morning. I never eat outside my room. If it's someplace where I have a friend, I ask them to come up to my room or go to the gym with me. I need a structure. I'm on the National Book Award selection panel this year for nonfiction. It's a lot of reading. And I have students to supervise. I'm on thesis committees and dissertation committees. My son plays three sports, and I try to be at every game when I'm in town. Well, I missed two games last year.

Taylor: What's the secret to staying sane?

Karr: Oh, God. I don't know. I don't know anybody sane. I wish I knew. You let me know when somebody gives you the right answer to that. I was in therapy a lot in my twenties, and I think it was really money well spent. I wouldn't hesitate if I had a protracted depression to seek help and take any medication they had. I'm a big fan of the mental health profession. I think it has served me very well, and I did a lot of work in my twenties that has stood me in good stead.

Taylor: Do you have particular strategies for staying out of a depression?

Karr: I just work out all the time, and I eat pretty well. Drinking is a depressant drug. Given the fact that I haven't had a drink in thirteen years, it's not surprising that I haven't had a major depression since I quit drinking.

Taylor: Other people associate creativity with mental distress.

Karr: I don't get much done when I'm mentally distressed. I've been mentally distressed, and I've been not mentally distressed. I tend to work better when I'm not mentally distressed. All my best books were written when I was just working my ass off. And as you know, when you work your ass off, you don't have time to be mentally distressed. Nobody will stand for it. If you're a single mom and you're working full time, when do you get to be mentally distressed?

As the violin's body shudders with the tree's
      lost song, so my mother's soul longs
to rise from its fleshy husk. "I'm over this shit,"
      she says. Her gray eyes have sunk
to the sockets' hollows. (Beloved worlds)
      The concerto moans from the stereo,
and bare trees claw the sky. Surely hers was the first face
      I saw clear from the infant mist,
the whiskey timbre of her voice the first.
      My mouth was clamped to her breast.
Warm milk poured down my throat,
      and inside that lavender ether
I was a god afloat and barely came to sense
      an alternate god: Ma and ma and mama . . .

—"The Invention of God in a Mouthful of Milk," by Mary Karr,
from *Viper Rum* (New York: New Directions, 1998), 36.
Copyright © 1994, 1995, 1996, 1997, 1998 by Mary Karr.
Used by permission of New Directions Publishing Corporation.

Elmer Kelton

My father tried very hard to make a cowboy out of me. I was a pretty poor cowhand.

Elmer Kelton

Essay by Joe Holley

If John Graves is Texas's most accomplished pastoral essayist, Elmer Kelton is the state's foremost pastoral novelist. A native of Crane, in far West Texas, and the son of a cowboy, Kelton served in the military during World War II and afterward acquired a degree in journalism from the University of Texas at Austin. He was a farm and ranch reporter for the San Angelo Standard-Times *for fifteen years, editor of* Sheep and Goat Raisers *magazine for five years, and for twenty-two years an associate editor of* Livestock Weekly, *published in San Angelo. He retired from that position in 1992.*

As an agricultural journalist, Kelton paid close attention to the tales and stories and conversation he heard from farmers and ranchers across the state. He began writing fiction in his spare time and since 1955 has published more than thirty novels. Some are pulp Westerns, while others are serious works of art. Six of his novels — The Time It Never Rained, The Day the Cowboys Quit, Buffalo Wagons, Eyes of the Hawk, Slaughter, *and* The Far Canyon *— have won the Spur Award from Western Writers of America, while his novel* The Good Old Boys *was made into a television movie in 1995 for the TNT cable network. The movie featured Texas natives Tommy Lee Jones and Sissy Spacek. In 1977 Kelton received the Levi Strauss Golden Saddleman Award from Western Writers of America, Inc., for the contributions made by his work to the general body of Western literature. In 1990 he received the Distinguished Achievement Award from the Western Literature Association.*

Kelton has said that The Time It Never Rained *(1973) is his favorite of all the novels he's written, because "it was the most personal one I've ever done." The novel's main character is a West Texas rancher named Charlie Flagg, who is struggling to survive during the killing seven-year drought of the 1950s. "Part of the appeal of Charlie," the critic Tom Pilkington has written, "lies in the fact that he is an anachronism, one of the last survivors of a dying breed. He springs from an older, better time — a time when, it is widely thought, our forebears acted from a deep conviction that seems increasingly implausible in the gray, ambiguous morality of the modern world."*

The Wolf and the Buffalo *(1980), set on the dusty West Texas plains nearly a century before Charlie Flagg's time, illustrates Kelton's skill as a historical novel-*

ist. It is the story of a young Comanche warrior, Gray Horse Running, and a former slave named Gideon Ledbetter, a "buffalo soldier" in the post–Civil War army. The Indians called the black cavalrymen buffalo soldiers because their tightly twisted hair reminded them of the buffalo that roamed the plains. Typical of Kelton's "serious" novels, The Wolf and the Buffalo *is both a compelling tale and an honest, careful rendering of a particular time and place.*

Elmer Kelton continues to live and work in San Angelo.

I grew up on the Macaraw Ranch, east of Crane, Texas. My father tried very hard to make a cowboy out of me, but in my case it never seemed to work too well. I had more of a literary bent. I loved to read, and very early I began to write small stories— short stories, out of the things I liked to read.

Interview by Gary Kent

Gary Kent: You've been described, sir, as the South's greatest pastoral novelist. That work was grounded, was it not, in a long career of writing for agricultural journals and farming journals smack dab in the middle of the Texas Plains? Isn't that how you started?

Elmer Kelton: Basically. Although actually I had sold one short story to a pulp magazine before I was graduated from the University of Texas and got my first newspaper job. But I was an agricultural journalist for forty-two years until I retired about ten years ago from that line of work.

Kent: I want to get back to that in just a second. Would you, sir, tell us a little bit about your childhood?

Kelton: Well, I was born on a ranch in Andrews County, where my father was a working cowboy. When I was about three, we moved down to Crane, Texas, where my dad took another cowboy job and within a couple or three years was the ranch foreman. I grew up on that ranch — the Macaraw Ranch — east of Crane. My father tried very hard to make a cowboy out of me, as he had the three younger boys, my brothers, but in my case it just never seemed to work too well. I was always a pretty poor cowhand. I had more of a literary bent. I loved to read. And very early I began to try to write small stories — short stories, out of the things I liked to read.

Kent: When did you start reading? Were you a reader early on?

Kelton: Mother taught me to read when I was five, and so from that point on as soon as I was able to conquer a book, I tried it at least. I think I read just about all the books in our school library the first few years I was going to school. I read magazines pretty religiously, whatever came to hand and whatever subject matter came to hand. I just loved the whole idea of reading. It transported me to other worlds, other parts of this world.

Kent: Was there a movie theater in Crane?

Kelton: Yes, there was one theater. And I loved movies. I didn't get to go as much as I wanted because we lived nine miles from town. I was especially in love with Westerns, and to a lesser degree just about anything else, mysteries, musicals. As long as they were on the screen and they moved, I loved them.

Kent: Can you tell us, Mr. Kelton, who were some of your favorite writers back in those days — people that impressed or captured your mind?

Kelton: I know the first book I ever owned — I badgered my mother into buying a copy of it — was *Treasure Island* by Robert Louis Stevenson. I loved any kind of book about adventure, but I always gravitated back to Westerns. In the early years, I would say the three most important figures to me in the western literature field were J. Frank Dobie, the Texas folklorist; Will James, who wrote and illustrated these wonderful horse books like *Smoky*; and finally Zane Grey, who was a master of the action Western of that time. There were many, many others. A few of those I read in the pulp magazines, I later got to know — particularly people like S. Omar Barker, who was a presence in those days in stories and western poetry and who became a considerable influence to me as I began to write and sell stories myself.

Kent: Did you ever have occasion to meet Zane Grey?

Kelton: Oh, no, he was before my time. He died when I was still in high school. I did get to meet Luke Short (real name: Fred Glidden), who was one of the people I studied considerably when I first really got serious about trying to be published in the Western field. And some of the others, just to name a few, Peter Dawson, Frank Gruber, some of those who were pretty much masters of the pulp genre, Wayne Overholser. They all became friends of mine later when I joined the Western Writers of America. There were still quite a few of those old-time pulp professionals around in those days when I was kind of a beginning writer, although I had begun to amass a few credits — enough so that I more or less fit in the fringe of the group. And they were, most of them, very helpful to a young writer, which I've always appreciated.

Kent: You mentioned that you wrote your first story before you started writing for the farm journals and farm reporting.

Kelton: When I came back from World War II, I still had three semesters left at the university. I had gotten out of high school at just barely at sixteen, and so I put in two years at the university before I was old enough to be drafted for the military. So when I came back home I still had those three semesters to go, and by that time I decided to get serious and begin trying to sell stories. I'd been writing them for years, but I hadn't tried to sell any.

I would sit at night whenever I finished whatever lessons I had to do and pound out stories on a portable typewriter. I'd mail them off mainly to the Western pulp magazines. And they of course would come back with mostly printed rejection slips. But I began getting letters from one editor, even though she rejected the stories, who would explain what was wrong with them. This was a big help, and finally she bought one of my stories my last semester at the university. Now that was before I came out to San Angelo for my first newspaper job. So in a way, my fiction writing career came earlier than my journalism career.

But I'd have to say for at least the first twenty-five or thirty years, the journalism career pretty much bought the groceries and paid the bills. The fiction writing never paid that much until I'd been in it for a long time. It would have been terribly hard to have made a living from that alone. By having a regular job, regular income, I wasn't forced to sit down and write some things I might not have wanted to write because I needed the money. In a way, having a regular outside income was a liberating influence for me as a writer.

Kent: A lot of time people sort of scoff over things like the *Farm Journal* and farm and ranching journalism and reports. I know myself from having done a little bit of that work how important that journalism is to the people that live on ranches and farms.

Kelton: In a sense, I always looked at it as sort of a branch of the extension service. We were the ones who disseminated the information that researchers found. We served, in other words, an educational function. I always considered that important. Of course, part of that is the extreme importance of being accurate with it. But part of what I did all those years was report on research. There was some research being done in the agricultural field that's important to you if you like to eat. And I find most people are somewhat enthusiastic about that. Even beyond that, I did a lot of how-to features from the viewpoint of people who were doing it and doing it successfully: what they did, how they did it, why they did it that way. You know in this way we were helping spread the word.

Kent: Well, I was raised on a wee ranch in Walla Walla, and I remember how important it was to my father to hit that mailbox and get the latest *Farm Journal* or the different horse magazines and read those things. It was considered not only good reading about their peers but also great entertainment.

Kelton: Of course, too, there was a marketing function, price reporting, so that people knew more or less what the market was at a given time. They knew, within limits, what to expect when they sold their cattle or their sheep or their wool or their grain. It's highly important, especially in a day and time like this when the profit margins, if there are any in agriculture, are extremely thin. Very often the profit margin is on the negative side, so they need all the help and all the information they can get.

Kent: Many of your novels, *The Time It Never Rained*, *Buffalo Wagons*, and *The Day the Cowboys Quit*, among others, all won Spur Awards from the Western Writers of America. They're pretty clear on the theme you touched on then: the land is sovereign and freedom is precious. It was a tough go back then. Is that still so?

Kelton: It still is. We've unfortunately seen too many ranchers, too many farmers go out of business in this country because the profit margins just aren't there any more. The cost of production has risen so much more than the prices they receive for whatever they produce. It is tragic. It really is a heartbreaking thing to see ranches and farms that have been in the family for three or four generations lost.

Kent: Is that the future, then, Mr. Kelton? Is it going to all end up a corporate kind of farming, or will there always be a place for the small rancher? Is he on his way out?

Kelton: The small rancher and the small farmer by and large are people who have other income, usually another job in town, and can help subsidize the farm or ranch out of their other income. The people who are really hurting though, today, are the middle-size operators who have too much on their hands to handle an outside job, like a three- or four-hundred-cow operator. He has all the work he can handle right there at home. And yet it's not paying him. The small operator with thirty or forty cows can hold a job in town, come home and take care of his cows in the evening. And then the huge ranch operation, they have some economy of scale they can draw on which helps them maybe survive better than those who are caught in the middle ground. It's the middle ground ranchers that I've seen go out the most.

Kent: Your novel *The Good Old Boys* was made into a television movie in 1995 starring Tommy Lee Jones and Sissy Spacek in Texas.

Kelton: Right, and a lot of the supporting cast down the line were Texas people. We drew on the old local theater groups, and then Tommy Lee Jones pulled a lot of friends of his, acquaintances, into it. So it had a very strong Texas flavor.

Kent: That particular movie was nominated for and received a lot of awards, as did the actors that performed in it. What was that experience like? Was that your first experience with filming a movie based on your books?

Kelton: The first and only one I ever had made from one of my books. I had over the years any number of calls from Hollywood people expressing an interest in one book or another. Quite a few have taken options, but they've fallen through or the options are not renewed. Usually it comes down to money. They've got great ideas and great intentions, but they have no money. And you can't make a movie without that.

In the old days when everything was run by a few big studios, they had their own financing operations and so forth, and they bought their own pictures. Nowadays these movies are made by independents. They have to go out and raise the money wherever they can. So it's a tougher deal, and then when they go out to make the movie, it seems — at least from an outsider's viewpoint — mostly by committee. And when you get a large enough committee together, you can ruin mostly anything.

Kent: Yes, that is true. I'm afraid a lot of today's audience and a lot of today's readers aren't really aware of the Old West or country life unless they have access to writers like you and movies that are made — not only *The Good Old Boys* but movies like Clint Eastwood's *The Unforgiven* — that can build a great audience once every ten years for this kind of work.

Kelton: But we've not had that much exposure to Westerns, especially in film versions, over the last twenty or twenty-five years. They had their day in television in the '50s and '60s, and except for a few shows that went on and on, like *Gunsmoke* and *Bonanza*, pretty much faded out of the picture. We've not had any successful long-running Western series since, with a couple of exceptions. They very rarely make movie Westerns anymore. There have been spoofs and travesties on the Western. So we've raised a young generation that's not been exposed to it very much. We've also moved into a new century, and the nineteenth century, which is the basis for most of the Westerns, is now that much farther behind us, much farther from the present generation's experience.

Kent: You've said that your favorite work is *The Time It Never Rained.*

Kelton: I would have to say so. It was more personal to me because in a sense it was more of a reporting job than it was fiction, although I fictionalized the characters. Just about everything that happens in that book, it happened to people I knew about. Very little of the consequences of the drought in that book was not real to me; in other words, I'd seen it happen to someone.

Kent: What advice do you have for kids starting out writing today, other than things we've already touched on?

Kelton: I would say the first thing for a beginning writer or would-be writer to do is to be a reader. Read and read and read. Read in a wide variety of subject matter. Study people whose writing you like, try to analyze why you like it, what makes it work. When I was starting out, really getting serious about it, I would copy stories on the typewriter just to get a feel for the way the words flowed. I had a lot of really good teachers who were not aware of it, never met me. But that is a very important quality; if you don't like to read, you're not going to like to write. You can do a lot of self-education by reading and analyzing other people's work. After that, the most important thing is to sit down and write until the process becomes more or less second nature to you. If you get down to cases, there aren't too many full-time fiction writers in the country. A majority of the people writing fiction today have some other outside job like I did for all those years.

Kent: What's your next project? What are you working on now?

Kelton: I would like to do one more about Hewey Calloway; I just haven't come up with a complete story line yet. I have to go back to the character from *The Good Old Boys.* If I can get one more Hewey story — because I love Hewey — I feel like there's a little bit more to be said about him because he just represents all of my roots back to the time of my grandparents, the time of my father and mother. When I deal with Hewey, I just feel like I'm home.

Kent: We'll look forward to more of your work, sir.

Kelton: I hope there's a few more yet. I used to always have three or four book ideas working on in the future, you know, in my head. Nowadays I do well to juggle the one I'm actually writing. So I don't know how many more there'll actually be, but I plan to keep at it as long as — Hercule Poirot says, as long as the gray cells work.

Kent: Good for you. You're a treasure, and we appreciate it. We will be waiting for your work.

It crept up out of Mexico, touching first along the brackish Pecos and spreading then in all directions, a cancerous blight burning a scar upon the land.

Just another dry spell, men said at first. Ranchers watched waterholes recede to brown puddles of mud that their livestock would not touch. They watched the rank weeds shrivel as the west wind relentlessly sought them out and smothered them with its hot breath. They watched the grass slowly lose its green, then curl and fire up like dying cornstalks.

Farmers watched their cotton make an early bloom in its stunted top, produce a few half-hearted bolls and then wither.

Men grumbled, but you learned to live with the dry spells if you stayed in West Texas; there were more dry spells than wet ones. No one expected another drought like that of '33. And the really big dries like 1918 came once in a lifetime.

Why worry? they said. It would rain this fall. It always had. But it didn't. And many a boy would become a man before the land was green again.

—*The Time It Never Rained*
(New York: Doubleday, 1973), prologue, vii–viii.

Joe R. Lansdale

I write what I want to write. That's always been the key to whatever success I've had.

Joe R. Lansdale

I try not to fit into any category. I'm uncomfortable trying to force myself into a box.
Labels constrict your audience.

Interview by Rick Klaw

Rick Klaw: Your work has been called Texas gothic, gothic Texas fiction, mystery, suspense, crime, horror, Westerns, and damn near everything in between. How would you describe your work?

Joe R. Lansdale: I think of it as being Lansdale work. I try not to fit into any category. I'm uncomfortable trying to force myself into a box. I write what I want to write. Labels constrict your audience.

Klaw: One theme that is common to all your work is racism. Why is that?

Lansdale: I was born in 1951, and in the South there were a lot of Jim Crow laws. I grew up in East Texas, which is considered part of the South, unlike most of Texas, which is considered Southwest; so I saw examples of it. The separate water fountains for blacks, separate toilets, going around to the back of restaurants to get their food, theaters where they had to sit in the balcony, a general attitude that they were not as human as whites. I always felt uncomfortable with segregation and didn't understand exactly what it was about. It really struck me deeply. I think, too, that my mother was very progressive for her time; she planted that seed for me. All the things we take for granted now and are very common were at one time taboo socially — not just in the South, but across the United States. Perhaps racism struck me more deeply because we had more blacks, and there was this ill legacy of the Civil War. People were still fighting the Civil War when I was a kid. Even though it was over, they were still fighting it emotionally.

Klaw: Your work is filled with the mixture of violence and humor. Do you find these to be elements essential to your work and do you feel you always need the combination?

Lansdale: I don't think you always have to mix them, and I don't think I always have. It's more common in my work than not, because I saw a lot of violence when I was growing up. Not necessarily murderous violence, but in school

Gladewater was a tough town. But there was a lot of humor in the way people conducted themselves, and the way they saw things. That rubbed off on me a lot.

Everybody sees humor in violence, even those people who don't think they do. If you are watching Laurel and Hardy or any comedian, whoever it is on these old shows that we grew up on, people are falling off ladders and viewers are laughing. People have always laughed at those sorts of things. Sane people laugh when they realize that no one is actually hurt. It's nothing new. Humor and violence have always been intertwined. Robert Bloch probably had a big influence on me as a writer because he always recognized that.

Klaw: In your books, the violence is very realistic. Why do you make it that way?

Lansdale: Like I said, I've seen it. I've been involved in it, in the sense that I grew up with people that would fight at the drop of a hat over almost anything. I've been a martial artist all my life, and I've actually used it in self-defense. I've also made a point of not using it a few times when I could have. And though I'm not anxious to get involved in violence myself—I'm not very much a fan of violence—it intrigues me. It's so much a part of the human condition, even though some people try to deny it. Writing this kind of fiction allows you to tap into that and let off some of that steam.

Klaw: Your stories are steeped in Texas. Someone once said you're a writer that practically oozes Texas. Beside the fact that you grew up in Texas, is there another reason? There are plenty of writers that grew up here that don't have as much Texas flavor to their work.

Lansdale: First of all, as you said, growing up here. But I also believe that my parents were proud of being Texans. Their people actually come from somewhere else. But my father was a Texan. My mother was a Texan. Prior to that, we weren't generations of Texans. We epitomized what Texas represents, at least in that mythological sense, as being hardcore, independent people. My father was a person who could not read or write. Yet I think he was a vast success. He taught himself how to be a mechanic. My mother bought him a Model T and says, "Take this apart and put it back together until you can do it." And he did. That's how he learned to be a mechanic and, of course, continued to learn and update his knowledge. I look at my mother as coming from a somewhat better but still a poor situation. As a child I always loved mythology. Texas has its own mythology. It's bigger than life. My father was the kind of person that's a real, everyday, down-to-earth person, but was yet somehow bigger than life. He was what John Wayne thought he was.

Klaw: Which Texas writers have influenced your work?

Lansdale: Most of the writers that influenced me early on were not Texas writers particularly, but as I got into my teens, I discovered Robert E. Howard. I liked the fact that here was a guy who lived in a small Texas town, had a tremendous imagination, and made a living by his own wit—which is what appeals to me perhaps more than the literary side. You don't have some sonofabitch standing over you telling you what to do. I think that's exactly what Howard said, or something very close to that. I related to that too. I was always independent. I didn't want to work for someone else. Now everything's much more connected and it's different. But even when I was growing up, the idea of being interested in things like science fiction or the fantastic were almost considered—not *almost*, they were *definitely* considered to be weird, very weird.

Neal Barrett Jr. was another Texan with a big influence on me. His influence came later. We were kindred spirits in that we saw a goofiness to the world and we have this whole laconic voice most of the time. We're probably both influenced by people like Twain. Neal tends to be more on the lighter side. I tend to be more on the darker side, like Flannery O'Connor and people like that.

Klaw: Was your Edgar Award–winning novel *The Bottoms* based on an actual event?

Lansdale: Many of the events in the book were based on actual events. The story itself was of course concocted, but it was concocted from many stories that I actually heard. When I was growing up, my father was in his forties and my mother in her late thirties. I often heard stories from them and others, loosely about murders that had happened in the 1930s. People thought that there was somebody going around and killing hobos, for example. I remember that story. I don't remember all the details because I was young. But I remember a variety of stories like that from relatives and people who grew up at that time. I think those stuck with me. Many events that take place in the novel are based on events that I heard about or extrapolated from. So a certain amount of it is true in that sense, but the rest of it of course is fiction.

Klaw: This wouldn't be a Joe R. Lansdale interview if we didn't talk about Hap and Leonard to some degree because, of all your characters, they're probably the best known. They have been called some of the most unique characters in crime fiction. Hap is obviously you.

Lansdale: To a great extent, yeah. Leonard is made up of several people I know, both gay and straight. He's a combination of those. Hap and Leonard in many ways reflect both of my sides, because I've always found that the liberals consider me a conservative and the conservatives consider me a liberal. Somebody once said that I'm an Old Testament liberal, which I thought was one of the funniest and most accurate things I'd heard, even though I'm not by nature a religious person. However, the concept was just perfect. When they said that, I knew exactly what they meant. I also have a way of irritating either side, which gets me back to—what the hell was the question?

Klaw: The genesis of Leonard?

Lansdale: He's a combination of things. They're also *both* a combination of me. Hap, in personality and attitude and approach, is more similar to me. Maybe if I had been less ambitious and hadn't met my wife, I might have lived like he did. Not with all the adventures, of course.

Klaw: You once told me that you were surprised at how popular Hap and Leonard were with older women. Have you ever figured out why?

Lansdale: I have not. What's interesting is that it's not just older women now. The more the series has been around, the more women are responding to it. I only know that people have said that women will never like this because there are references that they may find offensive. And I think some have.

Klaw: There are references that we all find offensive.

Lansdale: That's part of the point. One thing that a lot of the readers never understand is that there are some people that are offensive just because they are writing offensively, and there are other people that are using offensiveness as a tool and sometimes just for the hell of it. Just for the shock of it. It's also because this is how a lot of the people that I know talk. This is how they really are. I'm trying to tap into that. A lot of guys have responded to that. They've said, "This is the way we really talk." The other part of it is that Hap does come across as a good man and he means well; he's honest and he's trying his best. People respond to that. They respond to that in Leonard too.

Klaw: Is there a future for Joe Lansdale in film?

Lansdale: I've always felt that there was. I've written four screenplays, all based on my work. All of which have been either optioned or sold. None of them has ever been filmed. However, I've had a number of other options, and among them was one called *Bubba Ho-Tep*, which was a novella I wrote, and it's been filmed. It stars Ossie Davis and Bruce Campbell and was directed by Don Coscarelli. It's one that I never thought would be filmed, it's so crazy. But when I viewed some of the filming, I was very pleased with what I saw, and I saw some of the editing and was impressed with that.

I had the feeling that it was going to be a good, fun, small-scale film that will appeal to those people that think of themselves as Lansdale fans. I've never liked to use the word "cult." I've never been very fond of that. The people who like my work and are very dedicated to it, many of them will respond to it. For the future, it's my intent to do some screenplay work again, to do more ambitious screenplay work, meaning not based on my novels, but original screenplays. Right now prose is more important to me.

Klaw: What's your favorite Joe Lansdale novel?

Lansdale: *The Bottoms* is my favorite because I felt like I got all of the themes that interested me in that novel, yet it was a novel that seemed to be more accessible to a larger group of readers without my gearing it to be that way. That's always been the key to whatever success I've had. That is, I've written the novel that I wanted to write for me — and let the audience follow if they wanted to. I'm happy for that reason. I also like *Mucho Mojo*. I like it because it's the best novel about my series characters, Hap and Leonard. It's one of the best novels I've ever written; it does what I want it to do more than most. I like *The Magic Wagon*. Those three novels are favorites of mine. If I had to pick a collection of stories, I would pick *High Cotton* because it's more representative of all my stories, the best of the best. That's the vain way of answering "which is your favorite novel," by giving you three novels and a short story.

Klaw: Well, I wouldn't expect anything else. What else would you recommend to readers?

Lansdale: I recommend reading the novels and short story collection I just said; they can go on from there. This is my sneaky way of getting that next novel in: *The Drive-In 3* is for people who want something really strange and outré. That is probably my most imaginative work.

Doc Stephenson, sucking from his flask, wobbled over to the body and looked down. He said, "Now that is one dead darkie."

The colored men who had toted the body out in the galvanized tub looked at the floor. Doc Stephenson punched the one on his right with his elbow, said, "Ain't it, boy?"

The man lifted his chin slightly, and without looking at Doc Stephenson directly, said, "Yas suh, she sho is."

It embarrassed me to see that colored man have to act like that. He was big and strong and could have pulled Doc Stephenson's head off.

But if he had, he would have been swinging from a limb before nightfall, and maybe his entire family, and any other colored who just happened to be in sight when the Klan came riding.

Stephenson knew that. White folks knew that. It gave them a lot of room.

—*The Bottoms*
(New York: Mysterious Press, 2000), 73–74.

David Lindsey

*One of the richest things you can do
as a writer is simply daydream.*

David Lindsey

Essay by Joe Holley

In the early 1970s, David Lindsey's job as editor at the University of Texas Press came to an end, and he resolved to be a writer—a mystery writer, in fact. On his first day as a writer, Lindsey rose and put on a tie as usual, walked downstairs to the type-writer installed under the staircase in the Austin home he and his wife, Joyce, shared with their two children, and commenced writing mysteries. Thirty years and thirteen novels later, Lindsey is the preeminent mystery writer in Texas, among a large and talented group.

Lindsey's early novels, beginning with A Cold Mind *(1983), are set in Houston and feature a highly educated, independently wealthy police detective named Stuart Haydon. Haydon, who drives a Jaguar, wears tasteful, expensive suits and lives with his wife in a beautiful River Oaks home. Haydon also knows the seamy side of Houston, a "city of dreadful night," and he's not afraid to get his hands—and his well-tailored suits—dirty as he solves crimes that baffle run-of-the-mill police types. Later Lindsey crime novels, all extensively researched and smoothly plotted, are set in Mexico, Guatemala, Russia, and Italy.*

A writer's life—and his life with his characters—is a far more involved thing than simply sitting at the desk. You live with those people all the time and you daydream about them. I don't feel I can begin writing until I know the subject so well I can sit down and write like I'm one of the participants.

Interview by Teresa Taylor

Teresa Taylor: What makes you a Texas writer?

David Lindsey: I was born on the border. Grew up there for six or eight years and then moved to the oil fields and ranches of West Texas. I have always lived in Texas, so I guess I have to be a Texas writer.

Taylor: Do you feel that there are regional similarities among Texas authors, even those working in different genre?

Lindsey: Probably. I think one of the things that influences me the most throughout all of my novels is a Mexican influence.

Taylor: How does this affect you personally?

Lindsey: Early on I attached a really romantic feel to Mexico. We would go to a town called Rio Grande City. I remember courtyards, banana trees, palms, parrots, and people who dressed differently and looked different, were graceful, and behaved in a manner that I just found attractive. That has always stayed with me.

Taylor: Have you traveled much in Central America?

Lindsey: One of my novels called *Body of Truth* was set in Guatemala. So I spent a lot of time down there doing research both in the city and in the jungles.

Taylor: On your Web site you refer to human rights activities in support of Guatemala. What were your activities and how long were you involved? Does this predate your *Body of Truth* novel?

Lindsey: Yes, it's the reason *Body of Truth* was written. For years I belonged to an organization called the Guatemalan Human Rights Commission. I would receive a bimonthly update of all the *desaparecidos*. It would be a printed-out list of all the people who had disappeared in the previous two weeks. It would be page after page. It would do the same for the bodies that had been found. Sometimes if you kept up closely, you would find the disappearances and the bodies matching. The novel was deliberately written to bring attention to the plight of the *desaparecidos* and Guatemala.

Taylor: Did you have concerns for your safety while doing research in Guatemala?

Lindsey: That actually is the only time I have been afraid for my life. I was spending a lot of time going around to the morgues in Guatemala City. I was monitoring the bodies coming through the morgues. The morgues kept *Libros de los Muertos,* a compilation of photographs of all the bodies they had found in the last twenty-four hours. When a family loses someone, they will go to the morgue and see what bodies have turned up since their family member was missing.

It was clear from the photographs that many of them had been executed. Some had their throats cut. Some had bullet wounds in their heads. The wound was clear, and it was visible that they had been executed — in what is called extra-judicial execution — they didn't go through the judiciary process. But under the picture it would have *borracho,* which means drunkard. Authorities simply didn't care at all about the dichotomy between what was apparent in the photograph and what the words under the photograph said. After I had done that for a number of trips I began to feel I was being followed.

Taylor: Did that fear work its way into your writing?

Lindsey: It certainly did. The fear was palpable. I saw things and reported them to embassy officials, and then things began to change and happen. I saw things alter in my routines. I just got scared and finally quit going down there.

Taylor: So when you're afraid and you're also committed to a project, how do you negotiate your way through that fear?

Lindsey: Probably differently at different stages in my life. When I first began doing research into homicide, I wasn't ever really in danger. The danger is all over with. In Guatemala it was very different because the disappearances were still happening. It was probably foolish for me to be doing what I was doing. When I began to realize that it had gone so far it was foolhardy, then I left.

Taylor: When you're writing about violence and crimes—when you're considering how to portray characters or the crime scene or the nature of the crime—are there any ethical considerations that come into play?

Lindsey: Ethical considerations? No. As a novelist, the only ethical decision I made regarding depicting violence and its victims was very early on when I was doing research. I decided I would never write about something I actually saw or someone I actually met or describe a situation I heard about from the homicide detectives. I would never pilfer reality. Everything I did was parallel to reality, but not a part of reality. One of the reasons was that I knew if I began writing about things the detectives were telling me, they would quit. So I made sure that they never read about anything they were telling me in any of my novels. Once they realized I wasn't going to do that, after a couple of books, a lot more doors opened for me. As far as ethical decisions, when you are a novelist, simply being true to the truth of what you are trying to translate is the greatest ethical decision that you have to make.

Taylor: Some teachers of writing would say that part of the writing process is to immerse yourself in the work and perhaps into a particular character—become that character. Does this play a role in your writing experience?

Lindsey: Yes. For me, that's what it's all about. When I began doing research for writing mystery stories, I took voluminous notes and carried a camera with me and took pictures of places. I was afraid of forgetting. When I do research, every one of my senses comes into play. This became very emphatic when I went to my first homicide scene. Prior to that, I was afraid I'd forget something about the scene. But in fact, it would be difficult to forget anything about the scene, because a homicide scene is one of the strangest things you'll ever see.

Nothing can prepare you for the reality of a homicide scene. It's got a smell. It's got a taste. It has a tactile element to it. There's this creepy seventh sense about it that is simply inexplicable. Everybody reacts to it differently. Then you react to the fact that the men and the women doing the investigating have gone past that and have a different reaction to it. I don't feel that I can begin writing until I don't have to use notes, until I know the subject so well I can sit down and write like I'm one of the participants. If I have to use notes, I haven't done enough research.

Taylor: How do you gain the trust of people that you need to get information from?

Lindsey: That takes time. And also people have a visceral reaction to you. They either trust you or they don't trust you. It comes from the sincerity of your desire to do the right thing by the subject you're dealing with.

Taylor: When you are writing, do your characters walk around with you during the day?

Lindsey: One of the richest things you can do as a writer is simply daydream. All of that feeds into your psyche when you sit down and start working. A writer's life—and his life with his characters—is a far more involved thing than simply sitting at the desk. You live with those people all the time, and you daydream about them.

Taylor: When you are writing about characters that are disturbing individuals, how does that affect you?

Lindsey: Well, it is stressful. The novel that was really disturbing for me and finally changed my writing was *Mercy*. To do the research that I did and to think about it in detail for the length of time it took to write the book was really disturbing. It affected my personal life, my family life, everything. That's why that was the last book like that I wrote. I didn't continue to write about serial or psychosexual murder. It was a deliberate walk-away. It was shortly after that book that I quit going to homicide scenes as a matter of routine. I did go straight from that novel into Guatemala, which was a disturbing experience of a vastly different kind. Then after that, I turned to completely different novels.

Taylor: Was there any element of purging yourself when you went from *Mercy* to Guatemala? The violence in Guatemala is very real, while *Mercy* was an exercise in imagining violence.

Lindsey: That's exactly what I did. After *Mercy* I thought, I am going to do something just dramatically different. It may not seem to people that it is dramatically different to go from psychological violence to real, brutal, physical violence, but it was, because it helped me explore different parts of my psyche. I've learned over the years that there is no simple violence, that it's all very complex. And the relationship between sexuality and violence is so tightly connected, even when you think it isn't, that I tried desperately to move away from that kind of violence and to the institutional violence down in Guatemala, where it was violence by routine rather than violence by peculiarity. There was a culture of violence down there that was state supported. I had to look at it in a different way than the violence of a disturbed individual.

Taylor: So how do you maintain a creative flow? Are you pulling from your subconscious? Do you have routines or techniques to keep that flow strong?

Lindsey: One of the things that happened to me when I began writing novels is that I quit reading fiction. I feel it is not a deviation from my profession to read ancient history, or theology, or books about art, because all of this is part of the same human soul. If I only wrote about intelligence and spy work, and only read about it, I feel I would lose some dimension of my humanity. I need to read about all of these other things to keep my characters human. Otherwise, they would cease to be multidimensional.

Taylor: Do your dreams play a role in your writing?

Lindsey: No, not really. Although when I get stumped in a story, I deliberately go to bed thinking about it so that I will lose consciousness thinking about it and, oddly, that often results in solutions.

Haydon remembered every detail of the morgue. It wasn't a place you were likely to forget. It was, of course, like so many other buildings in Central America, of cinder-block construction. And stucco. Though the law provided that unidentified bodies could be held up to several weeks, pending identification, in actual practice the lack of refrigeration necessitated that bodies be autopsied as soon as possible and buried within twenty-four hours. Naturally, sometimes schedules could not be kept and bodies lay in the holding rooms until they began to smell. This happened so often, in fact, that there was a permanent smell of death about the place. In the rainy season it smelled so strongly of mildew and death you could actually detect the reek of the building before you got to it.

—*Body of Truth*
(New York: Bantam, 1993), 103.

Arturo Longoria

Listen to the soft cooings of mourning doves.
That's the most beautiful sound in nature.

Arturo Longoria

I'll watch the sun go down beyond the mountains in Mexico, and the monte *will be absolutely still. The mesquites become like old men with their hands raised toward the heavens. This is where I feel the most like me. Calm and spiritually whole.*

Interview by Graham Stewart

Editor's Note: Arturo Longoria's books *Adios to the Brushlands* (1997) and *Keepers of the Wilderness* (2000) are intimate tours through the landscapes of South Texas and northern Mexico. The following interview takes place on his leased property in Starr County, Texas, just north of Rio Grande City. Graham Stewart and Longoria spent an afternoon there roaming the land lined with dozens of rare indigenous herbs and cacti.

Arturo Longoria: All these plants are native with the exception of several grasses. Most of the nonnative grasses were planted by cattle ranchers decades ago. Unfortunately, the nonnative grasses have become pervasive. My neighbor to the east cleared the brush off his land. Within a couple of months his field will have returned to the semidesert he created. That's the mind-set: clear everything and plant grass. That is one reason I wrote *Adios to the Brushlands.* People came in and cleared the *monte* with impunity. In deep South Texas, 98 percent of the native habitat has been destroyed.

Graham Stewart: We saw so many different types of plants in the twenty square feet that we just walked through.

Longoria: The brushlands of South Texas and northern Mexico are a diverse habitat — one of the most diverse in North America. The curious thing is that most people don't see the diversity. They say things like, "It's nothing but stickers and spines." They don't allow themselves the opportunity to really look and experience the brush. This is croton. Locals call it *salvia.* Some people use it to treat bronchitis. See that cactus over there? It's called *pitaya.* My grandfather and I would make forays into the brush looking for *pitaya* fruit — called Mexican strawberry by some. You shave off the dried spines on the fruit and then peel back the skin and eat the pulp. Quite delicious. My *papagrande* was the consummate ethnobotanist, though he was never formally educated in that field. He grew up in a world where people learned which native plants could be eaten and which had medicinal values. He taught me a lot of what he knew. Look, there's a pencil cactus. They're hard to spot unless they're flowering.

Stewart: It camouflages itself with the branches. It's a really thin, branching cactus that we're looking at.

Longoria: The cactus on the ground below the pencil cactus is called devil's cactus. It's related to *nopal* and *tasajillo*. This here is *Krameria*. Deer like to snack on it. There's *chaparro prieto* over there. It's very common. *Chaparro prieto* means "dark wood." My father tells me that people used to take the bark, boil it, and use the liquid to treat diabetes.

Stewart: What's that plant right there? You see it in all the old Western movies.

Longoria: That's *pita* or Spanish dagger. The Indians took the tips of the leaves and used them as needles. They'd pull the tip back and the fibrous leaf would provide a long thread.

A walk around this place is a little more than four miles. I like to come out here at daybreak or a few hours before sunset and hike the perimeter. Sometimes I'll see coyotes or bobcats or javelina crossing in front of me. I often sit within the *ramaderos*—which are tracks of thick brush that follow underground watercourses—and listen to the soft cooings of mourning doves or white-tipped doves. That's the most beautiful sound in nature. I'll watch the sun go down beyond the mountains in Mexico, and the *monte* will become absolutely still. The mesquites become like old men with their hands raised toward the heavens. It brings tears to your eyes. If I had my druthers, I'd be out here all the time. This is where I feel the most like me. Calm and spiritually whole.

Stewart: I see you brought a canteen of drinking water.

Longoria: It's the wise thing to do. Never go out into the *monte* without water. In fact, this is one of the canteens I carried on that trip into Mexico that spawned the book *Keepers of the Wilderness*.

I used that trip as a metaphor for the way we treat the earth. I camped along a river for a little more than a week. In the course of that stay I realized things about myself, about human behavior, and especially about the ethic that drives us. Or I should say, that is the driving force in our modern world. From the side of that mountain, I could see in the distance where massive logging operations were under way. Later on I met some people who were living in the forest not far from where I was camped. I stayed with them a couple of days.

It's funny how those sorts of experiences can act as a catalyst for enlightenment. When I got back to Texas I began work on *Keepers*, which itself became a journey to understand why we act the way we do toward nature and what can be done to reconnect us to the natural world. Our teachings of ecology and conservation biology and other related fields as a way of creating a oneness with nature have proved futile because science doesn't promote the system of values we must embrace if we are to connect subjectively to the earth.

Stewart: You also made that point in *Adios to the Brushlands*, toward the end of the book.

Longoria: That's exactly right. In the last chapter of *Adios to the Brushlands* I write about that subjective connection with nature that must occur if we are going to alter our land ethic. *Keepers of the Wilderness* takes it a lot further.

Stewart: I thought it was a provocative statement: that technical knowledge about the environment is not enough to make us, as a culture, begin to respect it.

Longoria: What I'm saying is that technical or scientific knowledge will not alter one's perspective toward nature if the underlying ethic or worldview is rapacious. To become truly connected to nature one must acquire a subjective union with it—and that's not what science preaches. Subjectivity is an anathema to science.

High game-proof fences are becoming the norm in much of Texas. Besides the fact that they are an eyesore, we're learning that they fragment habitat. They kill birds that fly into them, and it seems they've become a contributing factor in other states for the proliferation of diseases like Chronic Wasting Disease. But beyond those negatives, they are nothing more than traps. It's the ultimate canned hunt. It doesn't matter if it's ten thousand acres enclosed within a high fence; the bottom line is that animals don't have free range. They're trapped. It's unethical. Where's the challenge, the honor?

Stewart: Did you bring a gun today?

Longoria: I brought a twenty-two. I don't shoot rattlesnakes anymore. I love snakes. But I carry a gun when I'm woods roaming. It's prudent. In fact, an ideal vacation for me would be to spend my days looking at the scenery, brush, mountains, and streams. And at night go out with a flashlight looking at reptiles— or maybe just watching clouds glide across the moon. I should tell you, and it's important to make clear: I'm not a biologist. I consider myself nothing more than a woods roamer and a scribbler. If I'm feeling really good about things I might venture calling myself a writer. So I guess I'm just a woods roamer who loves to write—or on better days, a writer who loves the woods.

Stewart: You teach *something* related to biology.

Longoria: Environmental studies. But most of my adult life has been spent as a journalist and magazine writer. Now I tell people I'm semiretired, and what that means is that I can finally concentrate on the types of writing that suit me.

Stewart: You were one of the first reporters to cover the issue of water pollution in the Rio Grande.

Longoria: I was the first reporter to cover water issues in deep South Texas. Having lived here I've developed a great love for the Rio Grande. When I was a kid I'd go fishing with my grandfather and uncle. My late uncle Bill Valverde holds the state and national record for the alligator gar. He caught it with a bait-casting rod and reel. My son Ethan is an avid fisherman. He says he wants to top his great uncle's catch.

Anyway, I'd spent some time with the U.S. Customs Service and the Border Patrol, working along the river on different stories, and during that time I'd noticed how poor the water quality seemed to be. A hydrologist from Houston was doing work on the Rio Grande with another scientist, from El Paso. This was back in the mid-1980s. Their data showed that the sixteen [Texas] counties lining the Rio Grande from El Paso to Brownsville had the highest incidence of liver and pancreatic cancer in the United States. The number of cases was so high that it resembled a Third World disease. There are too many people concentrated on both sides of the river. There's also a mind-set here that promotes unrestrained growth and development, a blind adherence to neoclassic economic theory, where no consideration is given to natural resources. As I wrote in an essay in *Borderlands: Texas Poetry Review*, the Rio Grande was once a raging serpent that's become nothing more than a sluggish worm. It rarely flows into the Gulf of Mexico, so clogged and channeled and dammed it's become.

We've experienced exponential human population growth both on the U.S. and Mexican side of the Rio Grande — a lot of it because of the tremendous expansion of the assembly plants called *maquiladoras*. There are thousands of *maquiladoras* now. In order to keep labor costs low, they encouraged an influx of people, a diaspora of sorts, from southern Mexico and even Central America into northern Mexico. There was no forethought, no vision, no one to contemplate what could happen. On the contrary, the predominate thinking was for unbridled growth.

Stewart: How do you rate the wilderness preserves that are in this region?

Longoria: The only truly viable wildlife refuge in deep South Texas is Laguna Atascosa. It's large and round and fits nearly all the criteria for a healthy refuge. There are other places like Santa Ana Refuge and a couple of state parks, but those are all small and severely impacted by growth all around them — as in Bentsen State Park. Or they've experienced outright exploitation and ruin like Falcon State Park, which is blanketed by drilling rigs and surrounded by obnoxious refineries.

There's the sinuous Lower Rio Grande Valley Wildlife Refuge, which borders most of the Rio Grande from its mouth to Falcon Dam. But it suffers from what biologists call extreme "edge effect." In some places it's not more than a hundred yards wide, and so it's accessible to predation, poaching, human infringement, trash dumping, etc., and it has no "core" area to speak of. The ribbon of the refuge that lines the Rio Grande is highly fragmented by roads, easements, highways, and towns. It's also impacted by pollution from Mexico. And though it was a brilliant idea to establish refuges in deep South Texas, the concept of placing a sanctuary along the Rio Grande was myopic at best. It's not a corridor, and much of it is still occupied by agricultural interests.

Stewart: The majority of Texans dwell in cities and don't commune with nature that often.

Longoria: Texas has very little public land, and most people in Texas have little access to unmanicured or wild land. For the most part, and despite what Hollywood might portray, Texans are urbanites with very little access to nature.

Stewart: There's *so much land* that we could be exploring, bonding with, as you've been able to do. But we don't.

Longoria: In my writings and talks I pressured the U.S. Fish and Wildlife Service to open up that ribbon of land they call a refuge—which is probably the best purpose it can serve—for bird watching and things like that. For many years the refuge along the Rio Grande was off bounds to anyone but Fish and Wildlife personnel, the Border Patrol, Tick Riders, customs agents, Army Special Forces teams, and of course illegal aliens and drug smugglers. I told Fish and Wildlife officials that they should create a stewardship program that would allow people other than government bureaucrats to bond with the land. My original idea was to give the little hamlets and towns that border the refuge a concession that they would manage. Finally—at least to a point—the Fish and Wildlife Service acquiesced and developed a land steward program.

Ideally, the Fish and Wildlife Service should have purchased some of the huge ranches that went up for sale on the northern and western boundaries of the Rio Grande Valley. These forty-to-sixty-thousand-acre ranches could have been purchased for less than what the Feds paid for land bordering the river. The big ranches would have had little edge effect, and they would have contained major core areas that protect species from the ills I mentioned earlier. Unfortunately, the people who came up with the idea for a refuge system in the Valley had not adequately studied the historical, political, social, environmental, and cultural dynamics of the region.

Had they bothered to inquire, they would've seen that placing a refuge along the Rio Grande was not a wise move. Who knows, maybe the Feds can be persuaded to buy the next big ranch that comes up for sale north of the Valley.

Stewart: In your writing, I like how you describe people interacting with nature, urbanites who don't know how to keep their steps quiet in the woods, or who wouldn't know a rattlesnake if it fell in their lap. As a person who lives in a city, I find these descriptions fascinating.

Longoria: We were taught about the woods as we grew up. One of the most important lessons was on being quiet. Being quiet was more than just not making noise. It was also being quiet in your mannerisms and what you wore. My grandfather and uncles weren't happy if we went into the woods dressed in bright red or yellow or anything that was loud and out of character with the *monte*. They insisted on earth tones. And you never spoke out loud in the brush. Not ever. You were very careful about how you stepped. When you came into the brush there was almost a reverence about it. When you enter the woods you become the deer, the coyote, the bobcat.

In *Adios to the Brushlands*, I write about an incident I witnessed in Big Bend National Park. I was at the ranger station in the Chisos Basin. A female ranger walked in and said to another ranger, "I just had this guy brag to me that he did this six-hour trail in less than four hours." The other ranger said, "You should've asked him, 'What was the point?'" And yet I see this often with people who come from the city. They never connect. They travel through the *monte* as if lost to its treasures, and then they're gone.

I hiked in the woods once with a fellow who was a jogger. He complained because I stopped and examined every track or bird that I saw. He became so exasperated that he finally said, "Must you look at everything? Can't you just hike?" But for him a hike through the woods was akin to a horse wearing blinders. His intentions were simply to get from one place to another and nothing more. He might as well have stayed home and worked out on a treadmill.

I leased [this] piece of property mainly for woods roaming and birding. In my life I caught the tail end of the great river forests. I remember ebony and cedar elm trees that stood fifty feet high and had trunks that took several grown men to reach around. Nearly all of those great trees have died. The unique conditions and settings that once existed along the Rio Grande, whether they contained Montezuma bald cypress or great copses of ebony and cedar elm, have all but disappeared.

One afternoon in the fall of 1973 I stood atop a small hill between Rio Grande City and La Gloria and watched four bulldozers desecrating the earth. They worked relentlessly, columns of charcoal exhaust puffing from their noisy diesel engines. Into the night—floodlights illuminating their paths—they laid waste the life that had grown free for countless millennia. At last, overwhelmed by emotion, I wept in the darkness.

I spent the night on that hill. In the wee morning hours, deer fleeing for their lives ran past me. And, a group of perhaps twenty javelina wandered by looking confused and disoriented. When the first meager shades of tarnished yellow sunrise surfaced behind me, I looked on in horror at what had occurred during the night. It was as if a great monster had erased the landscape. What had been was now gone. Only blistered earth remained. *Glory hallelujah to man and his machines . . .*

—*Adios to the Brushlands*
(College Station: Texas A&M University Press, 1997), 39.

Phillip Lopate

I had a fantasy that if I left New York City,
I'd find a Texas gal and get married.

Phillip Lopate

I was offered a job by Cynthia MacDonald, who was organizing the creative writing program at the University of Houston. So I came down to Houston. I didn't come with the expectation that it would be New York. I was looking for something else. I found something else, a community of like-minded souls.

Interview by Ramona Cearley

Ramona Cearley: We've been discussing your essay "Heroic Age of Moviegoing." Share with us how your passion for film informs your writing.

Phillip Lopate: Oh, it gave me a way to organize a visual world and to understand that no matter what was happening to the characters, there was always a consolation of the surround. A long shot, that's the equivalent of the perspective or wisdom for me. Most artists have another art that they get interested in. For me, my primary art is literature, and film became another way for me to think about aesthetic problems. Often we're less tolerant of people in our own art but more tolerant of people in another. I mean, I have friends who are photographers and they are very critical of other photographers but very open to writing. I may be impatient with certain books, but I can always give an hour and a half to almost any movie.

Cearley: How did you fall in love with literature? What were your beginnings?

Lopate: I think it started with the fact that my father wrote poetry and loved to read. He was a factory worker who read people like Eugene O'Neill, Faulkner, Dostoyevsky, and Kafka. He would come home and read and pass his books on to us. By the sixth grade I quickly became the class poet, the one who had to write all those poems about Thanksgiving turkey and Christmas. So I had a knack for language inherited from my father and a love of reading. I came from a large family. Reading was one of the main ways that you could withdraw legitimately. When everybody was trying to get under your skin, you could pick up a book and people would leave you alone. So for me the love of literature came from reading. First came reading, then writing.

Cearley: Often in her writing workshops, acclaimed poet Naomi Shihab Nye enters the room holding your books in the air and shouting, "One must read

Phillip Lopate! One must read Phillip Lopate!" From that resounding endorsement, what is your definition of the personal essay?

Lopate: Well, first I'd just like to thank Naomi for being such a supporter and fan over the years, as I am of her work. I think the personal essay is a conversation between the writer and the reader. You have the feeling that the writer is not holding back but is giving you something intimate. It doesn't have to be a confessional, although it can be a confessional. It can just be a confession of one's own sensibilities, for instance, or the track of one's thoughts. In any case, it's not formal. It's more informal, and there's a kind of game involved with, let's say, disclosure and reticence. You can never say everything. Montaigne, the greatest essayist, said, "I tell people some things to get them off the track of others."

So I think the main way to teach the personal essay is to put students in touch with the tradition, to read other personal essays, understand this has been going on for a while. And if they like it, then they'll want to do it themselves. There are certain classic topics in personal essays, so you start to write about friendships, for instance, or manners, or aspects of daily life. You discover that somebody's been there before. It's helpful. You talk to your predecessors as well as to a reader.

Cearley: You've written that in order for a place to have a soul it has to have a visible witness to a past. How did you come to adopt Houston, Texas, and what did that mean to you?

Lopate: I had been teaching little kids for about twelve years and had become a kind of expert in that field, working with them in creative subjects such as writing and filmmaking. We did radio with them; we did comic books. All under the auspices of Teachers and Writers Collaborative, an organization that sent writers and artists into the schools. It was wonderful work. However, it was very poorly paid work. I had done pretty much everything that I could think of in the way of experimentation and was ready for something new. I'd also been a bachelor for quite a while, and I had a fantasy that if I left New York City, I'd find a Texas gal and get married.

I was offered a job by Cynthia MacDonald, who was organizing the creative writing program at the University of Houston. I went down there and interviewed for it, liked what I saw, and they offered me the job. I was the first fiction writer, the first prose writer, down there. The program was started by Cynthia MacDonald and Stanley Plumly. They hired me, and then they hired Donald Barthelme. And quickly the program took off.

I wanted to experience another kind of city. Certainly Houston was a kind of spatially spread-out city, a car-oriented city, and a city with many wonderful amenities and opportunities, but you kind of had to dig for them. They weren't all out there very clearly the way they were in New York. So I came down to Houston. I didn't come with the expectation that it would be New York. I was looking for something else. I found something else, mainly a community of like-minded souls. When you come to a place like Houston or Texas in general, from somewhere else, especially the Northeast, you come with so many fantasies and stupid generalities. I was expecting a world of shotguns and pickup trucks. Somewhat to my dismay I fell into a community of intellectuals, who read books, went to movies, loved classical music, and did not carry around shotguns.

Cearley: Lorenzo Thomas was a colleague of yours at the University of Houston during your residence there. Did you share similar experiences?

Lopate: Lorenzo was a link with my old life. He had connections to the New York school of poetry. I quickly looked him up, and we became friends. Lorenzo took me around to some of the clubs. Zydeco was really interesting to me because it was this meeting of jazz and country music. I was a big jazz fan, as is Lorenzo. And I was a big blues fan. Houston was the home of Lightnin' Hopkins and the whole blues tradition, as we know from Juneteenth. But the zydeco was something new for me. It was really more Louisiana than Texas. I liked that haunting sound. Years later I went to Buenos Aires in Argentina and found the same feeling for the tango.

Cearley: What other experiences in Houston are especially memorable for you, that may have provided a context for your writing?

Lopate: I was fortunate enough to fall into a community of architects and architectural critics, mainly people who wrote for *Cite* magazine for instance. Some were teaching at the University of Houston, some were teaching at Rice. They helped educate me to the issues of urban fabric in a place like Houston. And in a way, this really improved my understanding of New York because it was another way of looking at situations. Often it was the same issues, issues of public space, issues of trying to keep some sort of pedestrian thing going or mixed use. These people operated as a kind of conscience for Houston's built environment, you might say. People like Stephen Fox and Drexel Turner and some of the architects there, Bill Stern, so it seemed to me that the architecture and visual arts community was very vibrant in Houston, more so than the literary community.

In the literary community, every writer was a kind of big fish in a small pond. I was happy for the opportunity to participate so totally in the life of the writing community. I myself was receiving more stimulation from the visual arts community. I've always had a love of the visual arts. There was always so much interest in the '80s. There was a feeling in Houston of real civic-mindedness, I thought. I was recently in Honolulu, and it seemed to me Honolulu was like Houston but without the philanthropic spirit. The wealthy people were not stepping forward to improve it the way they were in Houston. In Houston they're always thinking about tree planting along main street, how to make Hermann Park more user-friendly. So for me it was a real experience in another kind of urbanism.

Cearley: What are your connections to Texas today?

Lopate: Mainly through friendships. I don't have any institutional affiliation, but I see people when they come to New York and every once in a while I go there and give a reading or something like that. I have a lot of fond feelings about Texas, and I don't allow anybody to say anything mean about it in my presence.

Cearley: Your cat, which has not left your side, listened patiently throughout our visit. Would you read to us a passage from *Bachelorhood*, perhaps something cats may enjoy?

Lopate: Gladly.

After so many years of living alone, I broke down and got a cat. I really didn't want a cat. Once I was in Jungian therapy and the therapist said to me, "You should get a cat." He was a very decent man, I gained a lot from him, I listened respectfully to everything he said, except when he gave me practical advice like this. "You should try it. You'll learn interesting things about yourself. . . ." And then he slid away into his mysterious smile. One might almost say, a Cheshire cat smile.

You can't imagine how many people have been offering me their superfluous kittens over the years. Why was everyone so eager to give me a cat? I saw them all smiling, rubbing their hands: "Ah, he'll get a cat, very good, it's a good sign, means he's settling down."

By what Darwinian logic was I supposed to graduate from one to the other? Maybe I was to start with a cat, then go to a sheep dog, next a pony, then a monkey, then an ape, then finally a Wife. It was far more likely that, if I got a cat, I would stop there.

—*Bachelorhood: Tales of the Metropolis*
(Boston: Little, Brown, 1981), 47.

James Magnuson

---

*It is incredible every year to see people come
in here totally jazzed up about what is possible.*

James Magnuson

James Michener was very generous with his program. Because of what he has given, we are able to bring in all these wonderful writers. I admit to being inspired. It always gives me the juice.

Interview by Bruce Snider

Bruce Snider: Although you have been primarily a novelist for the past few years, you actually started out as a playwright.

James Magnuson: That is right. When I was young I wanted to be a writer, and it did not matter what form. I was writing stories. I was writing novels. I was writing plays. The first bit of attention I had, I was living in New York. I was twenty-three years old and wrote a one-act play called "No Snakes in This Grass." It was set in the Garden of Eden. Adam gets a black Eve. It was a little parable about thirty-five minutes long. It was done in Harlem, and then it was done all over the country. So I really began with plays, and I did a long list of plays in New York early on. In the meanwhile, at night I was writing novels, and nobody was buying. So it was really the theater that shaped me more than anything, particularly in those early years.

Snider: A lot of aspiring writers today go through writing programs.

Magnuson: I think there might have been two or three writing programs in the whole country during my early writing years. And it did not seem as if that was the way to go. I always intended to be a writer. I got a master's degree in English literature. When I came to New York, I was working for the welfare department and writing in the Columbia University library. It was great in a way to write without anybody knowing about it. Maybe I am wrong, but I imagine that a writers' program would have taken the juice out of me.

Snider: I think it does sometimes to some people. So how long was it, then, that you wrote plays?

Magnuson: From the time I was twenty-two until I got a grant and went to Princeton, when I was twenty-eight. I wrote and produced eight plays in four years there. Then I wrote another play that was in *Playwright Horizons* in 1975. I somehow always thought that I was going to be able to write a novel a year and a play a year — so young and full of delusions. At that point, I was really on my own in trying to support myself. So desperation had me writing novels to get from one advance to the next.

Snider: Having started as a playwright, do you feel that you took something from those experiences into writing novels?

Magnuson: Oh, I know I did. It is a certain dramatic sense of structure, for better or for worse. You could argue that all my novels have a fairly dramatic organization and seem to be written in scenes. They tend to have a fairly compulsive narrative line. I spend much time trying to figure out how to ratchet up the tension in the little scenes. It is something I do almost involuntarily.

Snider: For a time you also worked in screenwriting for television.

Magnuson: That was later, after I had come to Texas in 1991 or 1992. A friend who was executive producer of a show in Hollywood had me come out. I had a very good time. The stuff was basically dreck, but it was fun to do. It was like swimming in water. It was so easy.

Snider: So do you think you took anything from that into the more serious work?

Magnuson: I suppose that I did. Part of it was writing under pressure, writing against deadlines and figuring that you could hammer out a solution. You are forced outside your own consciousness. You are forced to create voices for characters other than yourself, which may be one thing that I do better than others.

Snider: In your novel *Windfall*, I see that there are certain cinematic qualities.

Magnuson: Yes, I tend to approach things visually, which is odd, because plays are not visual. The other thing that I do is see details. My instinct would always be to write poetry. My sentences are so short that I just hold details to such vividness.

Snider: In what sense do you mean plays are not visual?

Magnuson: They are the spoken word, really. You do have to be able to conceptualize and choreograph. Novels are so often out in the natural world. It is what the major characters see, but I do keep close tabs on character.

Snider: What do you mean by close tabs?

Magnuson: You always know where they are. How they get in and out of a room. Where they are going, and who is crossing to a table — all the small changes of writing.

Snider: Now is that something you do when you are working on a play?

Magnuson: I did it in plays, and by the time I got to novels, it had become instinctive.

Snider: I would think from writing books, teleplays, and plays that you get a pretty sound sense of structure.

Magnuson: They are different forms. Television is very precise. It is four acts, and each act is twelve minutes long. They are all two-minute scenes. There is an "A" story and a "B" story that you keep alternating. You always end an act on the "A" story. So it is almost, not being pretentious, a sonnet. A given. Very restricted. Rigid.

Snider: In terms of your novels, what are the challenges of writing something with a complicated plot, as opposed to something that is character-driven?

Magnuson: The books are not very elaborate in terms of plot. They may seem that way, for example, because you have taken an ordinary man and put him in extraordinary circumstances. This assistant professor of English finds a cooler of fifty-dollar bills under an abandoned feed store. What does he do? In one sense, it is very simple: just follow the consequences of his actions. In certain ways that is an uncomplicated plot; even though it does speed along, it has a compulsive element to it. Those books that are in a sense closer to thrillers are about moral choice. They have a parable-like quality to them.

Snider: About money?

Magnuson: Or greed. *Ghost Dancing*, which was set in New Mexico, was about a film director who has made his reputation on a series of very violent antiheroic films. He has lost his son, who disappeared at the height of the antiwar movement. Twenty years later the film director thinks his son may be alive, and he begins to search for him. So that is an examination of his own character. The meaning of his own life. His own career. The way he failed this relationship. It is about fathers and sons. Does that make sense?

Snider: Certainly, and that is one of the things that is interesting about the kind of books you write. To just call them thrillers is probably to minimize them.

Magnuson: Some people compare certain of the books to Hitchcock. That seems to me to be worthy. They are dramatic, written in a spare style. They are suspenseful. They do try to examine moral issues. The last couple of them ended pretty darkly. There is little redemptive tone in them.

Snider: In terms of the way you conceive these books, do you usually start with character or an event?

Magnuson: Each is very different. *Windfall* was set up so simply. We have the assistant professor finding the money, and it occurred to me that he did not know what to do with it. He would be stuck. He had a wonderful problem. That is all I needed. Once I started to write, I took it step by step. With *Ghost Dancing*, I had a heck of a time trying to figure out how to plot that book. It had to do with finding his son. It was like putting a mosaic together, putting together the past.

Snider: How long does it take you to complete a novel like *Windfall*, for example?

Magnuson: That was fast for a variety of reasons. That was just a couple of years. When I was young and did not have to work, it would take me essentially two to three years. Now that I have a serious job, it has taken me longer. With *Ghost Dancing* it was ten years before I did the next one. A decade slipped by. My goal, now that I have hit sixty, is to publish three books in the next decade.

Snider: Ambitious.

Magnuson: I am going to be more disciplined. I am not going to do foolish things.

Snider: You are returning to your youth.

Magnuson: That is right.

Snider: To return to *Windfall*, is it the first of your novels to be set in Austin or Texas?

Magnuson: I grew up in Wisconsin. Lived in New York. I always loved the American West. It has been really important to me. Three of my novels before I ever came here were set in the West: two in New Mexico and one in Wyoming. I was always scooting up there. I love the mountains. I love the American Indians' story. And cowboys. I did not feel that I had the right to write about Texas for a while. It takes a while for it to enter into your imagination.

Snider: When did you come to Texas?

Magnuson: I came in 1985 but did not write anything about Texas for twelve or thirteen years. I had written one novel that did not quite work, and I said the next time I am going to write about what I know, something really close to home. So I never had to go much further than the Dobie Paisano Ranch to do research. It was everything I could see or reach within about twenty minutes. It was wonderful to do that.

Snider: So was there a challenge to suddenly be looking at something so much closer to you?

Magnuson: In a way, I loved it. You could see where I tweaked various people. That was fun. And there are little observations about everything from the boom to Westlake Hills to South Austin. It felt very comfortable to me.

Snider: What kind of response did you get from Texans and Austinites?

Magnuson: Texans were great, and Austinites were wonderful about it. I felt that every book group in this town was reading it. The other thing that was funny: I went to the Texas Book Festival, and people kept coming up to me saying, "Oh, I love your book. Come meet these people. We loved your book because you put our restaurant in it." Three different chefs said that.

Snider: You see, there are some perks about writing where you live. Do you feel Texas has influenced your work or the shape of your work in ways other than geography?

Magnuson: The other thing that has affected me is to become part of this Texas writing community. My best writing friends are Texans. Steve Harrigan is a good friend to whom I show my work. He shows his work to me. There is a wonderful writer named Naomi Shihab Nye who comes to teach here. They have affected me in important ways.

Snider: It is probably important for a writer to have that kind of community.

Magnuson: Exactly. I have probably split my life between Wisconsin for twenty years, New York for twenty years, and Texas for what will be twenty years in a minute. So it really has been an important part of my life. Like many people, I was an outsider.

Snider: Right, but you are a true Austinite.

Magnuson: I love this city, and Texas is endlessly interesting to me. I must say another thing that I love about teaching undergraduates here is that you get people from all over the state. You realize how diverse they are. You get kids from Fort Stockton writing real Western stories. You get East Texas, which is Deep South. You get stories from the border. You get suburban Dallas shopping stories. You get everything.

Snider: As the director of the Michener Center for Writers at the University of Texas, there would have to be all kinds of influences that you receive from students and visiting writers working in poetry, playwriting, and screenwriting.

Magnuson: It does influence me. I try to shove it away for the first part of the day, so I can keep some focus on my interior life. I try to keep my mornings free. The other thing, though, is that Michener was very generous with his program. Because of what he has given, we are able to bring in all these wonderful writers. I admit to being inspired. It always gives me the juice.

Snider: Right, and what about these up-and-coming writers that you work with all the time?

Magnuson: It is incredible every year to see people come in here totally jazzed up about what is possible. They work so hard; I can't let down my guard.

Snider: It keeps you young.

Magnuson: That is right.

Snider: Is there anything you can tell us about the novel you are working on?

Magnuson: This belies everything I have just said about Texas. This is set in Wisconsin in the winter. It has a thriller structure, but it is also a psychological novel about a man who loses his daughter. It is about the nature of grief, the way we all experience it. It is a very different examination of the past.

The lid was taped shut, but the tape was old and dry. He sliced through it quickly with a fingernail. Pickles, he thought, it's probably nothing but old jam jars. But his hands were trembling as if he were an eleven-year-old boy.

He opened the lid. The cooler was filled to the top with stacks of fifty-dollar bills. He took a quick involuntary breath. The bills were in two rows, eight stacks per row, and the cooler itself was maybe a foot high. Each stack was wrapped in its own individual wrapper and taped shut.

He grabbed the corner of a second cooler, spun it toward himself, then slid it down the rough dirt slope. His eyes stung from the mold and the dust. He opened the second cooler. It too was filled with fifties.

He knew it had to be dirty money. Either that or it was counterfeit; he wasn't an idiot. He knew he should leave, but he couldn't. It was the most extraordinary moment of his life and he wanted to savor it.

—Windfall
(New York: Villard Books, 1999), 11.

Larry McMurtry

I don't think about being a writer in Texas at all.

Larry McMurtry

Essay by Joe Holley

The most prominent, the most prolific, and occasionally the most provocative Texas writer is Larry McMurtry. Born in Wichita Falls in 1936, McMurtry grew up near Archer City, a tiny town thirty miles to the south. The McMurtrys were a ranching family, and McMurtry himself—despite a yen for writing rather than riding and despite living in Washington, D.C., for many years—has never lost his attraction to the land where he grew up. "It's still such a strong landscape for me," he told a New York Times reporter in 1998. "I can't escape it in my fiction. I can work away from it, but I always start here. And whatever place I'm writing about, I'm still describing this same hill."

After graduating from Archer City High School, McMurtry briefly attended Rice University, then transferred to North Texas State University (now the University of North Texas), where he received a degree in English. He returned to Rice in 1958, where he received his M.A. in English in 1960. That same year, he won a Wallace Stegner Fellowship to Stanford University and in 1961 published his first novel, Horseman, Pass By. The novel became the movie Hud, starring Paul Newman, Patricia Neal, and Melvyn Douglas. McMurtry's second novel, Leaving Cheyenne, came out in 1963 and was made into a movie called Loving Molly.

His next novel, The Last Picture Show (1966), not only became a movie—directed by Peter Bogdanovich and starring Cybill Shepherd and Timothy Bottoms—but it also established McMurtry as an insightful interpreter of the mythic West and its passing. He has explored variations on that theme throughout his long career, but after The Last Picture Show he began paying more attention to urban Texas. The characters in Moving On (1970), All My Friends Are Going to Be Strangers (1972), and Terms of Endearment (1975) have only a vague and distant connection to the romantic, mythic Texas of cowboys and ranches and wide-open spaces.

In 1981 McMurtry published an essay in the Texas Observer in which he chided his fellow Texas writers for failing to break out of a "country-and-western" genre and for ignoring the rich and complex subject matter of urban Texas. The state's literature, he wrote in the essay—titled "Ever a Bridegroom"—was "disgracefully insular and uninformed" at a time when its cities were developing the "dense, intricate social networks" that sustain serious writers.

Not long after "Ever a Bridegroom" prompted angry letters to the editor, thoughtful essays in response, and soul-searching seminars on the state of Texas literature, McMurtry produced Lonesome Dove (1985), an 843-page epic Western that at first glance seemed to be precisely the kind of book he had been attacking. McMurtry tried to explain that he never said the frontier West wasn't worth writing about; it was the mythic, romanticized West that he felt had been mined out. Indeed, he considered Lonesome Dove an anti-Western.

Since Lonesome Dove, which won the Pulitzer Prize for fiction in 1985, McMurtry has produced sixteen novels, a biography of Crazy Horse, and five books of essays and reflections, including Walter Benjamin at the Dairy Queen: Reflections at Sixty and Beyond. He also has moved back to Archer City, where he presides over what he expects will be the world's largest used-book store, an American version of Hay-on-Wye, the legendary British book town that draws visitors from all over the world.

In an early book of essays titled In a Narrow Grave (1968), McMurtry described growing up in a bookless town in a bookless part of the state. With Booked Up, his bookstore in Archer City, McMurtry is working to make sure that small-town youngsters in his part of Texas will never again be so deprived. "I still believe that books are the fuel of genius," he writes in Walter Benjamin at the Dairy Queen. "Leaving a million or so in Archer City is as good a legacy as I can think of for that region and indeed for the West."

I think about being a writer where my books are, which is here. Or where my book town is, which is here, but Texas itself doesn't have anything to do with why I write. It never did.

Interview by Ric Williams

Ric Williams: In the course of the last five weeks, I've read twelve of your works.

Larry McMurtry: I have to tell you that I have almost no memory of my works and almost no interest in them. I can only remember the last two or three; beyond that they are like something that happened to somebody else. I wrote *Horseman, Pass By* over forty years ago, and I haven't read it in over forty years, so it's just the vaguest of memories for me.

Williams: The archetypal nature of these characters struck me as I was reading, how they represent certain energies, and you put them into different scenarios.

McMurtry: Actually, my favorite characters are my domestic characters, not my Western characters at all. In *Terms of Endearment*, Emma is my favorite of all my characters, one that I have been occupied with the longest, nearly ten years. She was in and out of several books.

Williams: Yes, she was the star.

McMurtry: She was in and out of them for quite a while, as in *Moving On, All My Friends, Terms of Endearment.*

Williams: What is she like in *Moving On?*

McMurtry: She's a tangential character. She and her husband are best friends, the young couple who are in graduate school.

Williams: That's what I like about your writing, the archetypal aspect.

McMurtry: Well, that's not archetypal; that's a novel of manners type, it seems to me. I've done that a lot. It's fun to take a minor character in one book and give him or her a major role in another.

Williams: In the Greek plays, often one character would play a minor role in one story, then a major role in another story. This play against the history of myth and the myth of history seems to be something that you do.

McMurtry: Early on, only a little bit in the Westerns, very lightly; it's not the main drift of my fiction at all. In fact it's been imposed on my work to some extent. I didn't think that way about *Lonesome Dove* when I was writing it. *Lonesome Dove* grew out of a screenplay. Because of job and work, the movie didn't get made for various reasons. The process of not getting made occupied about twelve years. So during that time, I considered how it might be a novel rather than a movie. I wrote it as a movie for three actors: John Wayne, Jimmy Stewart, and Henry Fonda. It was conceived and written with Peter Bogdanovich between *What's Up, Doc?* and *Paper Moon.* I mean that's when we were working on it, when *Paper Moon* was going on. Then John Wayne died and it ceased to be viable in the way that we had initially conceived it. We could have made it with Gregory Peck or Burt Lancaster or somebody like that. Peter lost out on the project, and it sat around for twelve years. In the meantime, I wrote several other books. In fact, I stopped working on *Lonesome Dove* twice and wrote *Cadillac Jack* and *Desert Rose* during those times. I finally went back and finished it. It was touch and go because I had lost interest in it a couple of times. The problem with a long book is that you can satisfy yourself before you end any story.

Williams: Yes, I've heard that.

McMurtry: So you write five hundred pages, and you've really satisfied yourself with these characters. You don't want to keep them moving up the trail. It had no title for a long time; the screenplay was called *Streets of Laredo*. If I hadn't found the title, I don't think I would have finished that book. I was driving back from a restaurant in Hondo, Texas, just west of Denton, not far from the airport. I saw a church bus sitting on the side of the road that said "Lonesome Dove Baptist Church," and that's where I got my title. There is a Lonesome Dove Cemetery. It's just a church and a cemetery. I've never been there, but it's right at the north end of the runway. If I hadn't gotten a title that really pleased me, who knows if I would have finished that book.

Williams: Oftentimes in your novels, little things play havoc with your characters as well. It changes their direction.

McMurtry: That's the fun of being a novelist. You're going to get surprises, but it's just a process of discovery. If you knew the story before you started, you wouldn't be interested in telling it, although I usually know the ending before I start. I usually recognize some scene that is forming in my mind. It is a terminal or climactic scene, like the picture show closing. These two boys make up on the last night. That's the end of the story. It doesn't give me the story; it gives me something to work toward. In most cases, I've started with the ending and spun back and arbitrarily written in that direction. And in most cases I've gotten exactly the ending that I've started out with. Now in the case of the recent tetralogy, that story doesn't resolve itself until maybe twenty-five to thirty pages from the end of the book. I really didn't know where we were gonna stop.

Williams: Which character told you what to do?

McMurtry: I'm not going to tell you that. I don't want to give it away.

Williams: But a character tells you?

McMurtry: A character came in, but she came in only forty pages from the end of the tetralogy. She made it possible. But I didn't anticipate that, even in fifty pages, even ten pages back. It just popped in.

Williams: We so dearly love your characters. In *Somebody's Darling* you apologize at the beginning almost as if you had lost touch with her for too long, like an old friend.

McMurtry: Well, I had. You're absolutely right about that. I still think that's my worst book. I think this happens to most writers who write very prolifically. You really want to write another book about Joe, but then something comes up. Then by the time you get to where you do write another book about Joe, you're not as interested as you were five years ago. Something somehow has slipped past you. Some people like *Somebody's Darling*, and I like it a little bit. I don't think I knew enough about Hollywood at that time to write the kind of book that

I can and may write today. I used the technique of three different voices, and I'm not sure whether that book should have been told in a single voice. That's the thing that I question most when I look back at *Somebody's Darling*. Did those voices work or should I have used one voice? Maybe Joe Percy the screenwriter, the narrator's voice, might have been better.

Williams: Yes.

McMurtry: It's really only failures that linger in the mind, something that nags at you. Books which, in my own opinion, don't quite work, those are the ones you meditate about.

Williams: But *Lonesome Dove* did work.

McMurtry: Well, now, I don't know. I passed right on from *Lonesome Dove* without a break. I was doing a lot of screenwriting. I really don't remember finishing it. It never came back into my life; it still hasn't. I've never seen the miniseries of *Lonesome Dove*. I had no involvement with it. I was out of the country when it came out. It must have worked at one level. As I said in my introduction to the anniversary edition, it's kind of the "*Gone with the Wind* of the West." But that's an opinion based on years and years ago.

Williams: Did you enjoy *Gone with the Wind*?

McMurtry: Yeah, I think that's the limitation of *Lonesome Dove*. It's a good read, like I think *Gone with the Wind* is a good read.

Williams: You said that your work was set in your domestics and your Westerns; are you working on a domestic now?

McMurtry: I have two domestics to write, but right at the moment, I'm doing a nonfiction book about massacres in the American West. That will probably occupy me for about a year; then I'm going to write another Hollywood novel. I'm not going to get around to it until Simon and Schuster finishes publishing the tetralogy in the spring of 2005. There's no reason for me to get into a sweat over what the next novel is. I mean, they don't even want to see it until 2005. So I'm writing a book about massacres, and that's what I'm focused on right now.

Williams: So what you write, is it all driven by the publishing world?

McMurtry: It's driven by a need for money, of course.

Williams: I mean, you're Larry McMurtry.

McMurtry: They won't publish but one novel a year. They'll publish a novel and a nonfiction book in the same year, nine months apart. There are only two real seasons in American publishing. They've got the tetralogy, so that's slotted in the May spot for the next few years. So, to write a novel that wouldn't conceivably be published until the spring of 2006 doesn't make any sense. I might as well write some nonfiction. There's some screenwriting if I can get it.

Williams: Do the characters ever call you from one place or the other?

McMurtry: No, until I start there are no characters.

Williams: I mean, some of the recurring characters, like Emma?

McMurtry: No, Emma's dead. She's not coming back. I don't think I will write a third Harmony book. I wrote the second one, and I like it. I'm not going to let it bother me.

Williams: Are characters like that calling you from someplace?

McMurtry: They don't call me until there's a reasonable slot to put them in. I'm not called to write; I'm only called when I need the money.

Williams: Oh, really?

McMurtry: I'm not compelled to write. I'm not compelled to write fiction. I would love to be able to stop writing fiction. If I could afford it, it would be over. I'd be through.

Williams: Why? What has changed?

McMurtry: I don't think you're as good when you're old. I've said this many times in print: the novel is the middle-age genre. Very few people have written really good novels when they are young, and few people have written really good novels when they are old. You just tail off, and lose a certain level of concentration. Your imaginative energy begins to lag. I feel like I'm repeating myself, and most writers do repeat themselves. They keep writing novels well into their seventies and eighties and end up repeating themselves for the most part, the same themes, the same folks. I don't want to do that.

Williams: But there's a crystallization that can occur sometimes with that.

McMurtry: Very rarely, it's very rare to find. You can say that Saul Bellow's last book is a good book; I mean it's okay. But it's not the Saul Bellow of *Augie March* or *Herzog*. You know it's not. You lose a certain kind of imaginative vitality. I've been preaching that for years. I firmly believe it. I know that there are times when I have really felt that I am flogging myself with a story. I'm committed to it. I've got to do it. It's not a joy; it's just a job.

Williams: What was your first screenplay?

McMurtry: The first screenplay was made from a chapter of a book by Paul Wellman, a story about outlaws along the Natchez Trace before the Civil War, *A Spawn of Evil.*

Williams: *A Spawn of Evil?*

McMurtry: That's the name of the book; it has twelve different outlaws in it. The script that I did was on the man who tried to organize the slave rebellion, and they caught him and executed him.

Williams: So this is a real person, it's historical.

McMurtry: It's a real person.

Williams: What's the name of the movie?

McMurtry: Oh, it was never a movie. They own the book. It's called *Spawn of Evil.*

Williams: It sounds like a horror film. Are you happy with your movies that have been produced, *The Evening Star,* for example?

McMurtry: I had a heart attack in the middle of *The Evening Star.* I finished it, and I have no memory of it. I have no memory of the next three or four because I had heart surgery. I picked up *The Late Child* the other day and I had absolutely zero memory. It was like a book I had never seen, or thought of, or heard of.

Williams: Did the heart attack occur about the time Aurora's did in *The Evening Star?*

McMurtry: 'Bout half way. I finished the book, and then I had heart surgery. I mean, I didn't have a very bad heart attack at that time. I had surgery; then I had a trauma for the next five years, and I don't remember. The books I wrote then came to me as if they were faxed from afar, so I have no memory of them. I have more memory of, say, *Streets of Laredo* and *Dead Man's Walk* because of course we produced them and were involved with the filmmakers for a couple of years. So I know more of what's in them than I do some of the others. I have no memory of those books at all.

Williams: Would you talk about your ambivalence about Texas?

McMurtry: I don't think I have any ambivalence about Texas, that's one thing I don't feel wishy-washy about.

Williams: Yet you're still here in Texas.

McMurtry: I'm here because I have a book town, a really good book town, and that's a large part of my life. If I want Booked Up to function at the level that it can, then I gotta be around. I have twenty-six thousand books at my house, and when I am writing nonfiction as I am now, it's much better that I am here. I will have fifteen or twenty books out on my table that have some reference to one another. If I were thousands of miles away it would be much harder to put those chapters together. That's why I came back; in a way I had to straighten out Booked Up. I had five nonfiction books to write, and it's much better for me to be here than to be anywhere else. I need my books. I don't think about being a writer in Texas at all. I think about being a writer where my books are, which is here. Or where my bookstore is, which is here; but Texas itself doesn't have anything to do with why I write. It never did.

Williams: In 1968, you wrote about your family.

McMurtry: You saw that picture on the desk. It's my family reunion. It's my family's first reunion, in 1919. I gave a speech at the opening of a public library about two or three years ago. I passed within a mile of where that was taken. I made a speech in a place where they had once been, probably close to eighty McMurtrys. Not a single soul remembered any of them. They were as gone as if they've never been. My own uncle, that I'm named for, was killed not three blocks from where I made that speech. My father picked him up and took him to the hospital. One person vaguely remembers his widow, and that's all. They were such a strong clan; they were all over the Panhandle: Silverton, Pampa, Clarendon, Amarillo, Dalhart, Muleshoe. They're all gone. There's no memory of them at all.

She pushed the dirty dishes out of the way and sat down by the window where she had sat the night before to listen to the rain. For weapons she had coffee and cigarettes, the want ads and the crossword puzzle, and even her old shabby copy of *Wuthering Heights*. The book was one of her unfailing comforts in life, but for once it failed her. She couldn't lose herself in it, and all it did was remind her of what she already knew too well: that in her life nothing that total would ever be at stake. No one would ever think she was that crucial—not truly or absolutely, not life or death, commit or die. . . .

Emma stared at the want ads, quivering slightly. She had stopped feeling angry at Flap; what she could not stop feeling was disappointed. Life had far too little of *Wuthering Heights*. Now carelessly, now meticulously, she peeled an orange, but it lay on the table uneaten until the late afternoon.

—*Terms of Endearment*
(New York: Simon and Schuster, 1975, 1989), 44–45.

Pat Mora

Language nurtures me, and it also frees me.

Pat Mora

*When I graduated from eighth grade my parents gave me a typewriter and this
beautiful box of stationery. After people went home I sat and wrote all of these
rhyming saint poems. When* Aunt Carmen's Book of Practical Saints *came out, I
could see that that was a full circle.*

Interview by Liz Gold

Liz Gold: Tell us about your childhood.

Pat Mora: I was born and spent most of my life in El Paso and was
blessed with a wonderful family—a really devoted mother and father. My father
was an optician. He worked incredibly long hours to support four children. My
maternal grandmother lived with us part of the time, and a maternal great aunt.
So he really did work a lot, and my mom helped him. Each one gave me different
gifts; as I said in *House of Houses,* "I am both my mother and my father's daughter." My father and I were the punctual ones; my mother was always late. My father had an incredible heart. He'll be dead ten years next year and I will mourn
him my whole life—a really, really great man. My mom I have described as bilingually fierce. She was the first in her family to speak English, the child of two very
quiet parents. I dealt with part of her story in the children's book *The Rainbow
Tulip.* She was always this wild extrovert—loved school, loved being on stage,
loved being in speech contests when she was in high school. Then, due to the Depression, she was not able to go on to college. All the capacity was there.

Gold: And your grandparents came across from Mexico?

Mora: All at the time of the Mexican Revolution. My dad, also. He was
a little guy when he came over.

Gold: Those were certainly turbulent times.

Mora: Turbulent times, and it just shows that some of us have never had
to face those kinds of uprootings from place, from a way of life. We don't know
what that is like to have that sort of survival instinct.

Gold: That's so true. Your descriptions of your childhood made me, coming from a middle-class Anglo family, feel like I had sensory deprivation. It's really

amazing how you use all the senses in your writing. How do you do that, how do you get there?

Mora: Well, it's a very kind thing for you to notice, and it's a very kind thing for you to say. To some extent, it is unconscious, and I am very interested in the mystery of writing. On the other hand, there is part of me that delights in sensory experience and that wants to put the reader there. It's been a great compliment when people will say, "I felt like I was part of your family." I want them to feel that.

Gold: You mentioned earlier that your relationship to your family seems different from what we've seen with a lot of Anglo-American writers. Would you talk about your relationship to your family and how that comes through in your work?

Mora: I would shudder at the thought that people would perceive it as nostalgia or some kind of burnishing of the truth or removing the rough edges. I tried in *House* to suggest that of course there were tensions. Every family has tensions. My parents could not have been more different: physically, my mother's about five-two, my father was six feet tall. As I said, a totally different sense of time: my mother could easily be an hour late, my father was always pacing five minutes ahead. Different psychologically. My mother is very assertive. My father was a big, imposing man, but he was more likely to be quiet. Since I'm the first of four, I probably, early on, had a lot of private time with them. Every family has tensions, but I am aware that one of the gifts that life has given me is my family. That beginning was, for me, solid ground.

Gold: You've written, "We do not travel alone, our people burn deep within us." Would you say more about that?

Mora: When I wrote that line, I was thinking a lot about first-generation college students, figuratively, on University Avenue, although they may be literally on University Avenue. One of my personal interests is how literature can help us all feel less alienated in this complex world. I was trying to offer that sense of affirmation and that sense of heritage, that we are not alone. The passion to be part of change creates its own warmth. Even though you may feel alone, angry, or frustrated, if you can focus on your passion to create a more just world, a safer world, an environmentally better world, a more peaceful world, that passion will sustain and warm you.

Gold: I love the idea that even though you are going someplace where your family members may have never been, you are still carrying them with you.

Mora: Absolutely!

Gold: Older women in your family seem especially important in your work. What did you learn from them?

Mora: I learned a lot about love. I was well loved. And I don't know that there's any substitute for that. In this aggressively commercial world where we are constantly lured to believe that happiness is about things, all of us discover in life that there is no substitute for love. We walk through the world alone, to some extent, but the journey is eased with loving companions — and I had some doozies! I really did. A very quiet maternal grandmother, very quiet, but she would just pat your head and you'd know that she loved you. My aunt was very different, and they always warred. My aunt was the oldest daughter of my grandmother's husband, and so there was a natural antipathy there. My aunt couldn't imagine why her father needed to marry — you know, he had daughters who could take care of him. But this aunt is one of the mythic women in my life. No doubt. She had a capacity for giving that I don't know I will ever be able to document fully. You would give her a present, and before you knew it, she had given it to a cousin, and you would say, "Why did you do this? I gave it to you!" "I know, but I thought she would like it."

Gold: Why is Spanish so important to you and your work, and what does language do for us?

Mora: I heard this line years ago on an NPR program that said every language renames the world. What intrigues me about it is that it is a record of a people's intellectual ingenuity. We struggle, as humans, to name our world. Not literally, but how we feel, what sense we're making of the issues in our lives, how to give counsel to the next generation. We are struggling to name, and languages in the plural afford us different ways to see that and to express it. I feel very fortunate to be bilingual and wish I were trilingual.

Gold: But you do write primarily in English, and with extraordinary command of English, I might say.

Mora: I am English dominant, and I say that outright. My educational experience has been in English, my professional experience has been in English. I don't have the command in Spanish to always be able to express everything that I would want to say in my writing, for example. I could express it, but I don't know that I can always maneuver the complexities and play with the nuances the way I can in English. I'm primarily an English reader, too, and so much of my life, really, is influenced by what I read.

Gold: I noticed you always make a point of letting English readers know what you have said in Spanish in some subtle way so that you never leave anyone out.

Mora: It's a complex issue that I have become more aware of since living in the Midwest. That experience has heightened my sense of people who have never perhaps heard Spanish and who can find *House* a challenge. The editor and I worked hard to have the book be inclusive. She did not speak Spanish, nor did the assistant editor, and so when they felt that it was rough going in a particular spot they would say, "Would you want to suggest, in some way, what is going on?" But they also gave me pretty free rein. I'm hoping that over the book's lifetime — you know, after I'm gone — it will not be too intimidating a struggle. I was interested in communication, not in leaving people out. On the other hand, I built in some extra pleasures for the bilingual speakers — I hope.

Gold: I think you did. You mentioned living in the Midwest; you're living in two places now.

Mora: Right. My husband teaches at the University of Cincinnati; he moved there in 1988. His name is Vern Scarborough, and he teaches archaeology. I left my job as a university administrator in 1989 and moved to Cincinnati. We lived on the Cincinnati side of the Ohio River for seven years. Then a few years ago moved to the Kentucky side for the practical reason that the Cincinnati airport is in Kentucky. Because I fly a lot, that has proved helpful.

Gold: How is it for you being in two places? You do so much border crossing in your work and in your life, how is that for you?

Mora: I am an organized person, and I find it a true challenge to be this disorganized because every move is disconcerting to some extent. On the other hand, I am a true southwesterner. I love Santa Fe and feel very fortunate to live here. It was something I never expected to have happen.

Gold: You've proposed a new national day: El Día de los Niños, El Día de los Libros.

Mora: It is an idea that started in 1996, building on a tradition that exists in many countries of celebrating the day of the child. In Mexico, that day is celebrated on April 30th. I did not grow up knowing that. I learned it on a visit in Tucson, Arizona, when I was being interviewed on the campus radio station. The interviewer was from Mexico, and said, "Would you read something for children in Spanish, and I will play it for Día de los Niños." I said "What is that? What happens?" She said, "There's always a celebration, and it could be a picnic, or it could be candy for everybody, but it's a day that we celebrate *la niñez*, childhood." So I went back to some of my academic buddies and said, "What if we built on that? What if we build on an existing tradition, but link it to literacy?" There are many families in this country — and this is not only Spanish-speaking parents — who do not have a literary heritage to share with their children. It doesn't mean that they don't love those children and want the best for them. Those of us, then, who have that advantage can be part of seeing to it that all children — regardless of background, economics, religion — are linked to books, languages, and cultures. Then we celebrate together on April 30th. So I say to teachers and librarians if you're serving a Vietnamese community, or a Hmong community, then you want to put those words in their languages because it is about this celebration of language, culture, and literacy.

Gold: What a wonderful idea. You freely cross borders in your work: borders of countries, borders between languages and genres, borders between the living and the dead in *House.*

Mora: The presence of the border, the physical presence of the border, is one of the factors that makes me who I am. Having the ease, throughout my growing-up years, to move back and forth, whether it was to eat dinner or to go to the bakery or to go to the market. How many children in this country grow up being able to, willy-nilly, go visit the country that their grandparents were born in? Also, being aware of the tremendous disparities between that world and my world. When I was a little girl in El Paso, there were streets in Juárez that you can see from the freeway today that were dark at night, except for little fires. So we were driving along on what was then not the freeway in our comfortable, though perhaps crowded, car, and looking across and knowing that there was this river that we couldn't see, but it was there. On the other side of that river there were families that did not have potable water, that didn't have that switch to turn up the heat. Often, in cities, I think we have the luxury of not seeing the realities of *all* of the people who live in the city; it's set up to be that way. Those of us in the middle class, we are protected, our eyes are protected. Sometimes when people go to Latin America, for example, they will find it disconcerting that they are being asked to look at people who are poor, as if it's in poor taste, as if the world is a movie set. So I did a piece, which ultimately went into the essay collection *Nepantla,* that was titled "The Border: A Glare of Truth." That's one of the things the physical border gave me. Internalizing that, I think, has created a fascination for all kinds of borders.

Gold: When did you first start writing?

Mora: Probably in elementary school. I liked writing, but I was going to be a nun.

Gold: Me, too.

Mora: Were you?

Gold: Yes.

Mora: I had my name picked out. That went on until I was probably seventeen. So, as I say in *House,* my parents tolerated this child walking around with her black veil all the time and her little clicker, asking her imaginary students to genuflect; I mean there was nothing normal about me! So the idea of being a writer just didn't enter my mind. Schools at that time didn't have visiting writers. For me, authors were in another place. I certainly didn't know one. What I discovered over time was that I knew some wonderful storytellers. My aunt was one of them — probably a key example. My love of poetry comes from my inability to be expansive. I admire these writers who can just write reams. That has never been me.

I have a clear memory in high school of this tall, imposing nun, whose name was Sister Charlotte Marie. We were reading by those old-fashioned school windows that went all the way up to the sky. She looked over in her black habit and veil and said, "What does this poem mean?" as English teachers are wont to do. I raised my hand and whatever it was I said, she said, yes, that was right. I had that sense that this was something that I could do, but I still didn't consider the option of being a writer. When I graduated from eighth grade my parents gave me a typewriter and this beautiful box of stationery. After people went home I sat and wrote all of these rhyming saint poems. So I know that I liked it, yes. When *Aunt Carmen's Book of Practical Saints* came out, I could see that that was a full circle. I don't have any of that earlier work. I wish I did, just out of curiosity.

Gold: What motivates you to write?

Mora: Somebody asked me that recently, and I paused because that's a very difficult question to answer. I said it is the love of language. I love to play with it. It is a source of both delight and consolation. Language nurtures me, and it also frees me.

Gold: What would help you know that you could write?

Mora: What a great question. There were a couple of people early on who, through their faith in me, gave me hope. One was a professor at the University of Texas at El Paso, Robert Burlingame. He was a poet and taught a poetry course. When I was an administrator, I had been playing around with poetry and I showed something to him. He described what I had written with the word "poem." I can remember how that felt, which is why I try so often to say to teachers that they have no idea what powerful people they are. A word of praise as opposed to a look of boredom can make a huge difference.

There was also a young man I met when he and I were teaching part time at the university; his name was Larry Lane. I had started writing poetry. This young man and I — he was from New York — shared an office with a lot of people. One day I must have mentioned the poetry to him and he said, "So let me see it." And I said, "Oh, I couldn't do that." He said, "How are you going to get any better if no one ever reads it?" I remember that moment when I handed him a folder that had some of my poems. We had agreed we would exchange poems.

The sad part of the story is that within a few months he was dead. I'll always be grateful he came into my life, because after that, there started to be some creative writing courses. I audited one, and the writing part of my life began to grow. But the fragility of a writer early in that writer's life, be that writer sixteen or sixty-five, is difficult to fathom, and it is so important for all of us to remember.

Gold: Sor Juana combines two of your desires, to be a poet and a nun. She's a very interesting choice for a children's book.

Mora: She is. I have been fascinated with her since I became aware of her, which was not until after I left college. So much about this woman intrigues me: her wit, her verve, her indomitable belief in a woman's right to an education, her play with language—word games and puns and puzzles that are almost impossible to translate. I admired a lot about her at a distance; then, eventually, I wrote a poem "The Young Sor Juana." The stories we have about her primarily come from her. Most of them from one of her more famous pieces called *La Respuesta*. This was an answer to the church hierarchy that was questioning her behavior. They felt that she should be busier praying than she was writing. Of course the sad part—and that is not in the children's book—is that eventually she does stop writing and she gives away her library. She used the indigenous language Nahuatl in her work; she was omnivorous in her desire to learn from the time she was a child.

Gold: Interesting, too, it connects to *Aunt Carmen's Book of Practical Saints* in the sense that we get that combination of verve, of real practicality, and of fun in these poems that are written by a woman who is a sacristan. She's not a nun, but she's still very involved with the saints. It's very interesting how much you pull into that book.

Mora: Well, thank you for that close reading, because of course that's what I want as an author. I am a great believer in the importance of a good reader. The author floats it out there, but for a casual reader, a quick reader—a lot of what we work very, very hard to do may be missed.

Gold: It's interesting that you've ventured into the world of spirituality a little bit here, something that is certainly an integral part of Mexican American culture, but which many Anglos sort of stay away from. I don't know if you'd want to say any more about that.

Mora: So much is being written about it, and of course in a place like Santa Fe, the word "spirituality" can be tossed around so much that I seldom use it. I do strongly believe, though, that internal spirit or soul or life force or whatever we want to call it needs nurturing and merits attention, and it's difficult to do that in a noisy, consumerist society. It's a gift to have that quiet.

Gold: We haven't talked very much about nature, which is such a powerful presence in your work. I was thinking particularly about the book *The Desert Is My Mother*, which is such an interesting idea because people who don't live in the desert often think of it as a place with no resources. Yet you have this image of it nurturing you.

Mora: The Chihuahua desert is such a strong force in my life. When I'm in the Sonoran Desert—and lots of people don't know there's a difference, but there is a difference—I really love it, too. The space of the desert is liberating. Perhaps for some people it is frightening. I do believe, as I said in *House*, that there's early geographical imprinting on some of us. The desert was such an available place to me because we lived on the edge of town. So it is home. Its sounds are home; the wind is home. In fact, to be in El Paso when the wind is blowing in the evening—not the major dust storms, I have to say—can just be an incredible sensory experience for me. The bareness of the desert—the space, the openness of the desert—I associate with the page. There's this wonderful sense of expansiveness and possibility, which is the way I feel about the page. These are two kinds of spaces that are very important to me. Home, too, I would say; houses are very important to me.

Gold: It's interesting in *House* you get very much a sense of both being closed and being open, and of people being able to walk in and out, but also that sense of being closed in and the sense that the family is closing you in.

Mora: Maybe that's the human experience: that we are closed in, in one sense, in this skin. I recently completed another poetry manuscript and it is a collection of odes. One of the odes—it's in the spirit of Pablo Neruda—is "Ode to My Skin." So I did a lot of thinking about the ways in which our skin is not only made up of cells, it creates a cell. I am enclosed to some extent, at least my physical being is. Then there's the other side, the spirit that can roam and the spirit that can imagine. So maybe that is the human experience.

Gold: You mentioned Neruda. Is there anyone else who has influenced you or inspired you?

Mora: I love the work of Lorca, also. In terms of contemporary American literature, the African American poet Lucille Clifton has been a force in my life as an example of a woman of color who has her own voice. When I get discouraged I think about Lucille. She's done it her way. She says, "My work is not my life." What I would say is that my work is more than my writing. I am always amazed by what the poet Mary Oliver can do on the page. She cherishes the natural world, the wildness of the natural world. That movement that she brings to her work inspires me. So both women have been liberating forces. They bring me great pleasure, aesthetic pleasure.

Gold: Dreams are so important in your work. What are some of your dreams?

Mora: One concrete dream would be that non-Anglo children in this country feel proud of what they are. Books are part of the solution. Media are part of the solution. Rethinking our economic system is part of the solution. I hope that Latino children, in particular, feel that they have more of a place in books because of what some of us are writing. I want them to feel at home there. I want children and adults to feel that language is theirs. American literature will not be what it could be if we are not encouraging all those voices.

I remember my mixed feelings as a young girl whenever my father selected a Mexican station on the radio. I wanted so to *be an American,* which in my mind, and perhaps in the minds of many on the border, meant (and means) shunning anything from Mexico.

But as I grew I learned to like dancing to those rhythms. I learned to value not only the rhythms but all that they symbolized. As an adult, such music became associated with celebrations and friends, with warmth and the sharing of emotions. I revel in a certain Mexican passion not for life or about life, but *in* life—a certain intensity in the daily living of it, a certain abandon in such music, in the hugs, sometimes in the anger. I miss the *chispas,* "sparks," that spring from the willingness, the habit, of allowing the inner self to burst through polite restraints. Sparks can be dangerous but, like risks, are necessary.

I brought cassettes of Mexican and Latin American music with us when we drove to Ohio. I'd roll the car window down and turn the volume up, taking a certain delight in sending such sounds like mischievous imps across fields and into trees. Broadcasting my culture, if you will.

—"The Border: A Glare of Truth,"
Nepantla: Essays from the Land in the Middle
(Albuquerque: University of New Mexico Press, 1993), 11–12.

Frances Nail

My stories remind people of their own stories.

Frances Nail

When I read for people, I'm usually asked to leave time for questions. The listeners don't ask questions; sparks of storytelling burst out of everybody, and they tell their own stories until it's time to go home.

Interview by Leslie Nail

Editor's note: Leslie Nail is the daughter of Frances Nail.

Leslie Nail: You grew up in a reading household, surrounded by books even in hard times, surrounded by storytellers. You studied journalism. It's no surprise that you write. But you didn't become a writer until you were seventy. Most of your life you were an artist. What in your 1920s and 1930s childhood in Memphis, Texas, ever made you say, "I want to be an artist"?

Frances Nail: I think my mother made me do it. She had a friend, Amy, who was psychic, or at least Ma thought she was. Amy told her, before I was born, that I would be an artist. Ma believed it and convinced me. She saw to it that I had watercolors and pencil and paper, even when I was very little. And one summer when I was about ten, an itinerant art teacher came to town and had classes for a week. Ma paid him fifty cents a class for me to attend six times, each time copying a scene off a postcard. It wasn't easy for her to come up with the money. We probably ate beans for a month. However, art has always been part of my life. And still is. I love it and love to paint.

L. Nail: In *God, Cars, and Souvenirs*, you write about seeing a print of Van Gogh's *Portrait of Armand Roulin* when you were a child. Were you always conscious of that moment during the years you were an artist? Or was it as a writer that you recognized its significance?

F. Nail: I never forgot my first sight of Armand Roulin, the postmaster's son, with his blue hat and yellow coat and beautiful eyes. He never left me. But I didn't realize the significance until I started to write. When I started writing, I began to take my memories apart and study them bit by bit, until I could see them for what they are. I began to be a pretty good amateur painter at eleven, the same year I found Armand. My art teacher, who owned Armand, was a good teacher. I wasn't professional, though, until I went to art school at forty. I painted until I began to write at seventy. I seem to be a late starter.

L. Nail: You started writing for the family, the family tales that are our history. When did you notice other people were interested in your work?

F. Nail: I sent the first essay I wrote to *Texas,* the *Houston Chronicle*'s Sunday magazine. The editor published it within two weeks and sent me two hundred dollars. He published eight essays before I had my first book. And I began to get letters from people right away. Fan letters. I couldn't believe it. Still don't. I still get them. I had one today from a woman in Ballinger, Texas, who receives my books as gifts from a young woman in Tucson, Arizona, who knows me from my readings on KUT, Austin's public radio station, which she hears on the World Wide Web.

L. Nail: Your childhood in Depression-era West Texas seems very foreign to me, but then I grew up in the 1950s suburbs of Houston. Who are your biggest fans — those who are like you in age and experience or those who can only imagine what it was like?

F. Nail: I have fans of various ages, though I suppose, more older ones. But I have read in schools, even to third graders, who sent me hand-drawn pictures of mad dogs frothing at the mouth. They had never heard of mad dogs until I read to them. And just last weekend, I read out under some oaks by some hundred-year-old horse stables for an arts festival on the Paleface Ranch at Spicewood. In the front row was a little boy about five. He sat perfectly still, never taking his eyes from me, though my stories were for adults. He either had or had not experienced storytelling. I hope he had.

But my childhood seems foreign because of the changes that have happened so fast. Everything changed fast after I got to be twenty years old. When I was in college at Texas Tech, there were many, many students who never would have been educated except for the war. They would have stayed in little towns and worked for their daddies, and change would have come slowly, as it always had. Education alone changed our lifestyle.

L. Nail: Why are people interested in your writing and your public readings?

F. Nail: It's the simplest thing. My stories remind people of their own stories. And I am a good reader, a ham. I am funny. I inherited a sense of what is or is not funny. I must have passed it down, as you and your sister and her child have it. We are a hoot. In our family, the highest praise we can give a person is to say, "He knows what's funny." My old Texas country voice goes well with my stories. When I read for people, especially book clubs, I'm usually asked to leave time for questions. The listeners don't ask questions; sparks of storytelling burst out of everybody, and they tell their own stories until it's time to go home. Everybody has his own story. They are all good and I'm glad they don't write them down, or I'd be out of business.

L. Nail: What do you like — or dislike — most about the act of writing and being a writer?

F. Nail: I have all these fragments of an essay or story floating about, and I have to catch them, write them down in some order. That is the hard part. I usually have a beginning and end before I begin. The fun part is to work on each sentence until it is as good as I can make it. Which sometimes ain't too good. It's like putting together a jigsaw puzzle. I read an essay called "The Collectors" on John Aielli's radio program. He said it was like listening to a kaleidoscope. There are so many different people doing so many different things, and they seem to be revolving around a center point through that whole essay. I hadn't thought about that until he said it, but I think that's what most of my essays are like — kaleidoscopes. I keep juggling them until they make a picture.

What I like most about being a writer is praise. Nobody ever wrote me a fan letter about a painting. Or told me it changed their way of thinking about life. And it is just delicious to read back to myself something I have written that I know is good.

L. Nail: Besides themes drawn from your childhood or the past, you write about contemporary events. Where do other kinds of inspiration come from? What gets you in a writing mood?

F. Nail: Almost anything that happens gets me in a writing mood. For example, I stubbed my toe and fell down on my driveway on a Friday, the day before the astronauts fell out of the sky over Texas, on Saturday, the first of February. And I saw that same morning a good friend and learned, though I should have known, that he had lost his sixteen-year-old daughter from a fall just after Christmas. So, after I quit crying that bad day, I wrote an essay about falling. And I ended the story with our fall from grace in the war with Iraq. That's another thing that's put me in a writing mood.

L. Nail: You go back to Memphis occasionally. Some of the cousins and old friends you mention in essays are still there. How does it feel to go back?

F. Nail: I love to go to what's left of Memphis. I am the only one left of the Clark cousins, and Ruthie and Mary, the only ones from the Joneses. My cousin Hubert Jones, who kept that town in one piece, has just gone. He was the baby boy cousin. Broom's Creek, that used to flow by the foot of Seventh Street, was diverted to make space for a swimming pool, leaving a little jungle of tall weeds where I used to walk in the creek. And the drugstores with their fountains and the movies, three of each, are gone from the square. The grocery stores and the dry goods stores are gone. The barbershop is gone, and the beauty parlor, where I had my first permanent under a heavy contraption attached to my head. It sometimes burned off big hunks of hair right down to your scalp. You'd have a big sore here, a big curl there.

L. Nail: Those were the days.

F. Nail: Yeah, I miss all that. But really, I still love to go to Memphis, and when I get there, I am home. I stay in the Memphis Hotel, now a bed-and-breakfast, and I go straight to the grand ballroom and listen to the ghosts.

L. Nail: You've probably read hundreds of novels, biographies, and memoirs that describe disappearing times and places like Memphis. Why is it important that you write about your particular life and view of events, past and present?

F. Nail: I think of myself as a folk historian. Since I can write, I feel it is important to tell my story, even though I'm just an ordinary Texas woman who has lived in amazing times. History is told by those who write things down and who paint pictures. Paintings and writings, so far, are all that we know of it. If we don't know anything about everyday life, we don't know much about history. So I feel that memoirs and personal essays and letters are important to the times. It's like we're all keeping a diary. If ordinary people don't tell their stories, history will be told by the lives of celebrities and some politicians.

L. Nail: I heard author Robert Caro describe how he researches important events of the past. He goes to live in the place and with the people who were affected by the events. To write about LBJ's congressional career, he lived in the Hill Country for three years — to get to know people like you.

F. Nail: When you read his first book, you think you've lived in Johnson City. I think that kind of history is important. It's important to tell what you did during the war and what you did when you were a child. And you have to be truthful about it. My publisher asked me if I should be using real names in the essays. But it seems to me that real names give writing a certain truth it doesn't have if you make up a name.

L. Nail: After your third book was published, you said you weren't going to write any more books. Why are you still writing?

F. Nail: I can't stop. Every time I swear off, I read a newspaper story, or something happens to someone, and I'm reminded of some silly or profound event from the past or even the present, and there I go again. It took me seventy years to start writing and now I can't stop. It's ridiculous.

It's not so hard to write a book, but when it's written it must be published, and when it's published, it must be sold. And that is a hard, hard thing to do. I don't like to work. I like to dream around, read, garden, swim, walk around and think about things. I like to putter about all day. My first book changed my life. I became a performer, sort of, when I wrote my first essays. Just in the last four days, I spent the weekend at an arts festival, reading an hour each day and selling my books, and on Tuesday I read for a book club. You can't just write a book and throw it away. If it weren't for that fact, I would just write and putter away the rest of my days.

We were not the poorest in Memphis; we were never hungry, as many were, but we were the poorest among neighbors and friends we knew well. We didn't know that we were poor. My mother considered us exiled royalty on temporary hard times. The hard times were not temporary, but they weren't all bad. For one thing, they smelled like homemade bread. Our house was seldom rid of the heavenly, yeasty smell. Ma made wonderful bread, and sometimes, in a rare good mood, cinnamon rolls, dripping with caramelized brown sugar and butter.

I would take a loaf of bread and go fearfully to Mary King Martin's house down on the corner. She was sister to the undertaker, and I knew that coffins were stored upstairs. The house was in a thicket of unkempt trees and brush; it was old, huge, and gray from lack of paint. It looked like the House of Usher. I knocked timidly on the back door, thankful to see Mary. Her red hair and smiling face didn't go with the house. She gave me a dime for the loaf. I took the dime to Mammy Franks, who gave me a gallon of milk for it. I sloshed home with the milk and Ma took the heavy cream off the top and made whipped butter in a little glass churn. We called it "cow butter." Spread on a piece of the bread, it was worth the fright of the trip to Mary's.

—*Crow in the House, Wolf at the Door*
(Austin: City Desk Press, 1995), 34.

Naomi Shihab Nye

Writing is a way to keep ourselves more in touch
with everything we experience.

Naomi Shihab Nye

Essay by Joe Holley

In "*Ever a Bridegroom,*" *his* 1981 Texas Observer *essay assaying the quality of Texas literature, Larry McMurtry could find only one writer worthy of his "unequivocal admiration." That writer was the Houston poet Vassar Miller. Her best work, McMurtry wrote, was "the product of a high gift wedded to long-sustained and exceedingly rigorous application."*

Miller, who died in 1998, *was indeed a poet of genuine distinction, but in the years since McMurtry passed judgment on Texas writers, the state has seen a proliferation of poets who are producing interesting, innovative work. They include Reginald Gibbons, Leslie Ullman, Lorenzo Thomas, Angela De Hoyos, Harryette Mullen, R. S. Gwynn, Cynthia MacDonald, Wendy Barker, Paul Christensen, Pat Mora, and Rosemary Catacalos.*

One of the most capable is Naomi Shihab Nye, a San Antonian who writes not only poetry but essays, songs, and books for younger readers. The daughter of a Palestinian father and an American mother, Nye was born in St. Louis in 1952 *and moved with her family to San Antonio when she was a teenager. She graduated from Trinity University in* 1974.

Nye's books of poetry include Different Ways to Pray (1980), Hugging the Jukebox (1982), Red Suitcase (1994), Fuel (1998), *and* Words under the Words: Selected Poems. *She also has written a novel for young adults,* Habibi, *and a collection of essays called* Never in a Hurry. *In addition, she has edited prizewinning anthologies of poems from around the world and coedited a collection of paired poems by men and women called* I Feel a Little Jumpy Around You (1996).

Nye's many awards include four Pushcart Prizes, two poetry prizes from the Texas Institute of Letters, and a Guggenheim Fellowship. She has been featured on two PBS poetry specials: "The Language of Life with Bill Moyers" and "The United States of Poetry."

The quiet significance of little things is frequently the focus of Nye's work. Her lighthearted rumination about the differences between men and women, in I Feel a Little Jumpy Around You, *is revealing: "Less is silly to women. Women honor the tiny, the tedious, the particular minutia. (Exactly which B vitamin was it I read*

about?) Women may have greater tolerance for things, which may have some con-
nection to their frequent maintenance of things."

It seems the best gifts and thoughts are given to us when we pause, take a deep
breath, look around, see what's there, and return to where we were, revived.

Interview by Julie Koppenheffer

Julie Koppenheffer: Yesterday when I called, you were out gardening. I'm curious what gardening has to do with your poetry?

Naomi Shihab Nye: Well, everything is connected. You dig, you mulch. I'm really not a good gardener, but I love the feeling of poking around in the earth, picking up leaves, weeding and trimming, and seeing new spaces emerge. Gardening takes a certain discipline and awareness of attention that sometimes I'm not willing to give. Luckily I'm a more devoted writer than gardener because I do work at my desk every day and always have for as long as I can remember. The regularity of working on writing is a very important aspect of it. I like to remain attentive to whatever I'm working on and keep coming back to it. If I have a particular project going on, I'll organize my labors around that project, but I do always feel open to unexpected—blooming—things on the side that do spring up.

I wish more people could feel comfortable just pausing. Many people are so action-oriented. We always have to be doing something productive. But it often seems the best gifts and thoughts are given to us when we pause, take a deep breath, look around, see what's there, and return to where we were, revived. I place a lot of importance on meandering and puttering these days. Maybe it's the pleasure aging brings!

Koppenheffer: You have been not only an inspirational poet for your readers of poetry, but you've taught poetry to students of all ages. How did you get involved in teaching poetry?

Nye: I never planned to be a teacher, and still don't think of myself as one—just as a visiting writer who has spent almost thirty years talking to students about writing. When I was graduating from Trinity University, my professor Robert Flynn asked me if I had ever heard of the "Artists in the Schools" project, which was just kicking off in Texas. I had not. He said, "You know they're looking for people like you, artists in every field who are interested in working with younger artists." I'd been working with high school writers at a summer journal-ism institute at Trinity and loved it. I went for an interview in Austin at the Texas Commission on the Arts without any great expectation, and right on the spot, without seeing any of my poems, or anything—ah, the lovely years before *red tape!*—they said, "Yes, you can do this." My first host school was in Longview, Texas, where I went for two weeks right after I graduated from Trinity.

Koppenheffer: So you were an itinerant teacher?

Nye: An itinerant visiting writer. For years I was on the road in small towns in Texas primarily; then I worked for many years with the San Antonio school dis-trict going from school to school. It's been a huge blessing to get to be with so many young people in the name of something I really believe in. Writing is a tool for how we shape our lives, how we look at the material we have, and how we think. Writ-ing is a way to keep ourselves more in touch with everything we experience.

Koppenheffer: How do the students respond to your request that they write poetry? Do you ask them to write poetry?

Nye: I do when I'm with them longer than one session, and sometimes even during a single session I will. Everything I've said to them means a lot more if they're writing as well. I suggest that all students write at least three lines a day that belong to them, out of the day they just lived. The students have been great, responsive beyond anything I could ever have dreamed. People in our current world are very hungry for expressive experience. I don't think anyone is too hun-gry for tests.

Koppenheffer: Do you give them any triggers, any suggestions?

Nye: Sure, I give them lots of triggers or models and suggestions. There are so many simple ways to invite them into their own experience—writing about family, about the neighborhood, writing out of memory, using difficult material. Many kids I worked with long ago in San Antonio are now adults and can re-member when I made them write about vegetables. And fruits.

Koppenheffer: You don't want to discriminate against fruits.

Nye: Real food! The delectable true names of squash and peppers! We've entered this microwave culture where simply to smell a fruit might seem exotic to some. I lugged vegetable baskets from class to class! Writing invites us to be in close elemental touch with things that make up our lives. Last year I was attend-ing an international teachers conference and someone asked, What have you done when students made fun of one another? I was stumped. I thought about it. *They never have.* In all these years, even in some of the so-called tougher schools, students in my presence have not made fun of one another or one another's voices.

They've *had* fun, they've laughed over things that were written, in a responsive or admiring way, but never scoffed or insulted.

Koppenheffer: In fact, they've derived a lot of benefit. You've compiled a book of poems by some of your students.

Nye: One of my recent books is called *Salting the Ocean*, a presentation of one hundred poems by young poets that were written in schools that I visited during the past years. The title poem is by Bill Collins of San Antonio. He wrote about a wonderful memory with his mother. I'm happy people have said nice things about the book, and I love the artwork, which is by one of my lifelong heroes, Ashley Bryan. I hope the poems in the book encourage other people to share poetry with students and encourage other youngsters to write. That's always the idea, that one poem leads to another. You hear one and it makes you want to write one.

Koppenheffer: Your prescription for writing three lines a day, why couldn't anyone follow that?

Nye: Yes, absolutely, it's not a huge investment in time. What it will give you back is enormous in terms of the way you start noticing things. Writers simply get in the habit of noticing things better. All the little unobtrusive, so-called insignificant things that make up a day are rich material. We *have* to use them when we describe on the page.

Koppenheffer: You said you're disciplined, and you sit and write every day.

Nye: For years I got up at four or four-thirty every day and wrote. I love those early hours because they are so private. Lately (that aging thing again!), I've been leaning toward five or six — ouch!

Koppenheffer: That is your writing time?

Nye: *Early* has always been my favorite time, but I have other writing times. If I'm not busy in the schools or have something else planned, I write later in the day as well. But those early hours feel very pure and precious.

Koppenheffer: How much revision do your poems take? Once a poem is finished, is it finished?

Nye: No, they're always evolving, even after they're published! Sometimes I *read* a poem out loud differently from the way it appears on the page. Our work is always evolving as we return to it. At this stage in my life, revision is the most pleasurable part of writing. But revision is not a young writer's favorite part of writing because young writers are just discovering how much they have to write about, their various voices, stylistic possibilities, and so on. To keep going back over a text is not so attractive to most young writers. As we grow older with our writing, we find how many wonderful things can happen as we go back to it. It's empowering and a great relief not to have to "get it right" in the first draft.

Koppenheffer: Do you have a community of writers that inspire you?

Nye: I'm inspired very much by the writing community in San Antonio, as well as around the country. I'm a big reader, and read everything I get my hands on.

Koppenheffer: Is there any particular poet whom you are enamored of now?

Nye: William Stafford has been my favorite poet since I was fifteen. I have felt heartened and nurtured by his poems for all these years, and they're always changing for me as a reader. I'll read a poem I've read many times, and suddenly it's a little bit different because my life is a bit different. W. S. Merwin is a favorite poet of mine, as is Lucille Clifton. Paulette Jiles, who lives in San Antonio, is one of my favorite fiction and nonfiction writers *and* poets. She's a wizard. She's a terrific writer, and I talk about her wherever I go. You're aware of her?

Koppenheffer: You're speaking to another fan.

Nye: That's great. Paulette Jiles should be read by everybody. I'm very interested in the world community of writers. I've featured writers from other countries in my anthologies, and so am in touch with many of them. It matters to me that young people in the United States read their work.

Koppenheffer: Your poetry has been received and heard around the world also through the Bill Moyers' PBS specials. How did you get involved in that?

Nye: It was the luck of the draw, because he filmed his poetry program "The Language of Life with Bill Moyers" at the Geraldine R. Dodge Poetry Festival in New Jersey, when I was appearing there. He'd filmed an earlier poetry series there as well. I was also lucky because I was the first poet in the series that was presented, along with Sekou Sundiata.

Koppenheffer: Not bad!

Nye: Bill Moyers is a great champion of poetry, as he is of everything in the humanities. I loved the chance to get to know him a bit and hear him speak so eloquently about what poetry gives to our lives, not only to poets but to all of us. He's a firm believer in that.

Koppenheffer: All of your friends speak so highly of you as well. They attest to your generosity of spirit.

Nye: That's kind of you to say. I appreciate that, but I think the world is generous to most of us. So we have an obligation or responsibility to be generous in return, to help find meaning for ourselves, to find a way to convey it to one another.

As a child, I was fascinated by the horizon. Not only because my father was an immigrant and was always staring out to the horizon, missing his home in

Palestine, but also because I had the feeling that there was so much to be found beyond every horizon. If you sent your words out to a magazine it was as if your words were traveling beyond a horizon, and they would find a friend out there.

Koppenheffer: Do you have any words of advice for poets?

Nye: You used the word "generosity." One thing I would suggest to anybody who wants to write is that they be generous with themselves and not confine themselves to a few words or one try at a poem. Often we don't know where our words want to go or what the story is that we want to tell. It's through the writing that we find it. I would urge an expansive spirit of playfulness, discovery, and exploration.

QUIET OF THE MIND

A giant, puffed, and creamy cloud
ignited on the right-hand horizon
from Presidio to Marfa as the western sky
dropped solidly into deepest blue.
We who were driving north on that road
pulled the car over, pulled it over
because the grasses in their lanky goldenness
called for standing alongside them
while the whole sky
held.
Inside that lit stillness,
we drank the swelling breath that would
unfold on its own for months
whenever the cities pressed us,
rubbed us down, or called out
people, people, people.

—"Quiet of the Mind," in *Fuel: Poems by Naomi Shihab Nye*
(Rochester, N.Y.: Boa Editions, 1998), 124.
Reprinted by permission of the publisher.

Karen Olsson — Texas Observer

It's not as if we're a bunch of grumpy,
dour leftists who are always upset that things
aren't going our way.

Karen Olsson—*Texas Observer*

The Texas Observer *is a biweekly progressive publication covering statewide news, politics, and culture. Our community of readers is very intelligent and vibrant. We put out a magazine that speaks to the full* Observer *reader.*

Interview by Teresa Taylor

Teresa Taylor: Can you describe the *Texas Observer*, its mission and its history?

Karen Olsson: The *Texas Observer* is a biweekly progressive publication covering statewide news, politics, and culture. It's been around since 1954; it was started by a group of folks who wanted a forum to articulate political viewpoints that were to the left of the mainstream in Texas at a time when Texas was a one-party Democratic state. So these were Democrats who felt that their views were marginalized within the Democratic Party. Over the years it did groundbreaking work in covering civil rights, LBJ, and a lot of big movements in Texas. Also, when it was founded, the climate of journalism in the state was different. There was not much investigative reporting, in particular covering politics, the Legislature. The *Observer* was one of the first publications in the state that covered political corruption and some of the back-scratching that went on.

Over the years we've continued to be a forum for progressive voices, or voices that are to the left of the mainstream. As time has gone on, we've become less focused on the Democratic Party and more independent, though I wouldn't say that the founders were not independent. More recently we've done a lot of coverage of the problems with the drug war in Texas, of labor, immigration, and environmental issues, and of other issues around the state. We also have a significant amount of the magazine devoted to serious book reviews, art reviews, a poetry page, and I think we're one of the few places in the state where you can find longer reviews and essays.

Taylor: You've been publishing about fifty years now, starting from a pretty brutal period in U.S. history, the McCarthy era. Has the *Observer* shaped the political culture in Texas?

Olsson: Oh, that's a hard one, and one where I feel a little too much of a newcomer to Texas. I wish I had my predecessors here to speak to that. It's interesting. Bob Eckhardt passed away, and I was reading over some of the writings about him that appeared in the *Observer* back in the '50s and '60s. He had a quote that I wish I remembered exactly, but it was something to the effect that liberals never win — they're just right, and the conservatives over time have to move forward. Kind of staking out this position for liberals in Texas as an advance guard. You don't win your battles, but you state for the record what you see as true. The way the state has moved: even though some would say it's more conservative, it's not more conservative. Society in general has come to appreciate more of the values that the editors of the *Observer* were trying to put forth back in the '50s, about civil rights and equality for everyone and desegregation — all these things that have since happened.

Taylor: Now a few years ago I believe there was a change in editorial staff. In what direction has the new staff taken the *Observer*?

Olsson: Well, Nate Blakeslee and I became editors, I think by virtue of our being a little younger and hoping to be read by a somewhat younger audience. One of the first things I wanted to do, even though it seems superficial, was to update the look of the *Observer*. We've done that with the help of our fabulous graphic artist, Julia Austin. We redesigned and are using more color to convey a more modern look. Also, one problem that a lot of progressive publications have is that some of the issues discussed never go away. You keep covering them, trying to convey certain points about the way things are, and over time that starts to seem repetitive. It can become depressing, like a little dark cloud of nothing's-ever-right-with-the-world that arrives in your mailbox. So another thing we've tried to do is to have serious reporting without the gloom-and-doom tone that can sometimes overcome people who are constantly immersed in issues that will not make you happy.

Nate in particular has continued to do really strong reporting on drug issues; we're also continuing to look for different people from around the state, encouraging young writers. The *Observer* has always been a place for young writers to stretch their wings. We are always looking for new writers; we've brought in some younger writers, and some women writers.

Taylor: The comment you made about depressing your readership with the nature of the issues is really important for any kind of activist organization. It's important to identify strength in people even if they're oppressed and to find a way to speak to that strength.

Olsson: That's right. Any magazine stakes out a community of readers. Our community of readers is small, but very intelligent and vibrant. It's not as if we're just a bunch of grumpy, dour leftists who are *always* upset that things aren't going our way. There are a lot of great people who write and read the *Observer*, and they are passionate about political issues, and they also have a sense of humor. I think we can put out a magazine that speaks to the full *Observer* reader.

Taylor: You were mentioning your coverage of drug issues. I read your article on methamphetamine culture in North Texas and was impressed by it on a number of levels. The writing was very seamless, and you worked in a lot of the social fabric. I was also impressed with the interviews you got from people who are users. When you're doing that kind of research, how do you gain people's trust, so that they will talk to you?

Olsson: Thanks a lot for the nice things you just said. I'm always kind of taken aback by how willing people are to open up to reporters. I'm not sure I would do it, but people really do give themselves over to you. Without those people, articles like that could not be written. I don't think that I have any particular strategy for gaining people's trust. You kind of luck into it. If you don't get the interview the first time, maybe if you call back, they'll change their mind.

That was a story I worked on for a long time. At first I didn't find the persons, or they didn't want to talk to me. Sometimes you just show up at their house, and that happened in the case of one of the people I talked to. He was in his house, and he was clearly making meth. He didn't want to talk to me, but he didn't kick me out either, so I was able to do the interview and report on what his place was like. He didn't want to admit to anything, and I never said he admitted to anything. That was his milieu and that's what he was like.

Taylor: It must be tricky then to work that kind of information into a story so that it's available to the reader but not particularly incriminating or suggestive.

Olsson: With those particular subjects, I didn't use their names. You first make sure not to do anything that would incriminate them. If the cops had really been hell-bent on tracking down this small-time dope cook, I'm sure they could have come after me. So part of it is just thinking, "Are they really going to come down to Austin and issue subpoenas to me for this one small-time guy? And if they do, that'll be a pretty good story in itself, even though my personal life will suck for the next year to five years."

Taylor: Does journalism feed your creative energy in ways that fiction does not?

Olsson: I think the two things feed one another. I like to think that some of my better articles have benefited from my being willing to experiment more with the form or a type of sentence that I'm writing. That also goes back to my working at the *Observer*. Stylistically, I get away with some things here that I couldn't at almost any other magazine because their format is tighter and they have a set style, whereas the *Observer* has always been more flexible, going way back. If you look at stuff from the '50s and '60s, they've had a wide range of writers who write different types of things.

Taylor: Have the events of September 11th affected the *Observer*?

Olsson: Definitely. There is a clampdown in the mainstream press having to do with being patriotic and going along with the government's take on things. So the *Observer* and other independent media outlets are really important at a time like this, in order for other viewpoints and critical attitudes to be reflected. Since 9/11 we've run various editorials, open-forum articles, and personal essays on responses to the attack and what the U.S. is doing, and on some of the things that you're not reading so much about in mainstream publications.

Taylor: It's interesting, maybe an interesting comparison between the political climate now and during the McCarthy period when the *Observer* started. It seems in both eras expressing an independent viewpoint means taking a real risk.

Olsson: Yeah, we'll see how much of a risk it is. I heard that Lynne Cheney is putting out a list of professors who do not toe the line, but I'm pretty much an optimist and right now I don't feel any threat that we'll be shut down for saying the wrong thing. I just think it's important that we be able to keep doing that.

Taylor: It's often said in journalism there should be a high standard of objectivity in always presenting both sides of a story. I guess there's an assumption that there are only two sides. What do you see as the role of objectivity and how do you strike a balance between that and your personal feelings about a story?

Olsson: I think that word *objectivity* gets used in a lot of different ways, where what you're really talking about is fairness. If you are going to talk about person A, and person A is saying that person B or district attorney C or corporation D said X and Y and Z, as a journalist you have an obligation to call that person or that entity and ask them for yourself what are they doing. Sometimes *objectivity* is used to imply that the journalist has no point of view, and that's just not the case. Everybody has a point of view. Every article comes from somebody writing it. In your daily newspaper reporters try to mask what they think, but it's there in how they organize the material. I would not enjoy writing for that kind of publication, because I like to make it clear where I'm coming from. To me it feels more honest to acknowledge that I have a particular perspective and to convey that.

He started selling meth to supplement the money he earned working off and on at a mobile home factory and a couple other places. Finally he began stealing anhydrous ammonia from a farmer's co-op in a neighboring county, and he would trade the ammonia—a common fertilizer, and the one thing his meth supplier needed to make a batch that he couldn't buy at a Wal-Mart—for finished product. Eventually, Mike says, "I'd go with him once in awhile when he made it, and after six months of that I tried it myself." The two became partners, bouncing from county to county with their bowls and jars and coffee filters, their ground-up Sudafed pills and lithium strips from Energizer batteries, their salt and sulfuric acid and cans of Prestone antifreeze, looking for some remote, wooded spot out in the country, away from the highway, where no one would see them work.

—"Every Man a Kingpin: Scenes from
Rural America's Drug War,"
Texas Observer, May 5, 2001.

Louis Sachar

My book Holes *is sort of how I look at Texas:*
a hot, hot place.

Louis Sachar

It's like an exaggerated Texas: the tough-on-crime attitudes, the heat, and the wide-openness of the state. I had the setting first, and the story just grew out of that.

Interview by Ramona Cearley

Ramona Cearley: Tell us about *Holes,* your recent screenplay based on the book by the same title. It sounds very exciting.

Louis Sachar: I just came back from a week in the desert on Cuttleback Dry Lake Bed near Ridgecrest, California. We got four hundred holes dug for the filming of *Holes.* It's been really exciting, and I've been there for all but two weeks of it.

Cearley: The book won the prestigious Newbery Medal and the National Book Award for Young People's Literature, among other honors. How did *Holes* begin? What was the process?

Sachar: It's been translated into more than twenty-five different languages and published throughout the world. It began as I was trying to come up with a different setting. I used to set my stories in schools, and I wanted something different. I thought of a detention facility for kids. I had the setting first, and the story just grew out of that.

Cearley: Give us a synopsis of *Holes.*

Sachar: It's ostensibly about a kid sent to a juvenile correction facility for a crime he didn't do. His rehabilitation, the regimen, is digging holes every day under the hot Texas sun. You've got these crazy characters in this juvenile tough-love camp. But there is a lot more to it than that. My book *Holes* is sort of how I look at Texas: a hot, hot place. It's like an exaggerated Texas: the tough-on-crime attitudes, the heat, and the wide-openness of the state. The film site in California was selected over Texas because the potential locations in Texas were so far from towns that travel time would be an issue.

Cearley: What kind of response have you received from your readers of *Holes*?

Sachar: It's a very positive one. The book is sort of a puzzle that pieces together in the end. So some readers may reread it to see those pieces again and see what they missed the first time. I also hear from adults who like it as much as children. In fact, they market it in England with both an adult cover and a children's cover.

Cearley: What led to your writing life? What were your beginnings as a writer?

Sachar: Ever since high school, I liked to write. I was inspired by my favorite authors at the time, J. D. Salinger and Kurt Vonnegut. I enjoyed writing and felt I was good at it. Then my last year of college, I took a class where I was helping out in the classroom at a nearby elementary school and received credit for it. I had a great time with the kids and thought I'd try writing children's books. I've been doing it ever since.

Cearley: We read that you were a practicing attorney during the 1980s. Did you have two full-time careers?

Sachar: I wrote my first book right out of college and sent it out. It took me about a year while I was working at a sweater warehouse in Connecticut and writing at night. Then I decided to go to law school. So I was sending out the manuscript to publishers at the same time I was sending out law school applications. I was accepted to the University of California Hastings College of Law in San Francisco. Then during my first week at school, I heard from a publisher who wanted to publish the book. Do I take the safe route and be an attorney? Or do I try to make a living as a writer? I continued through law school, graduated, and passed the bar exam, but I never actively sought a law job. I did part-time work through friends from law school and mainly concentrated on writing and worried about it a lot.

Cearley: Earlier you mentioned J. D. Salinger as one of the writers who influenced you. What writers or types of writing delight you most today?

Sachar: There are all different kinds of writers who reach me. There's E. L. Doctorow, Rex Stout, and Richard Price. I will read about authors and run out to find something new.

Cearley: From a child's or a young teen's perspective, what do you believe tends to be defining moments at those ages?

Sachar: I guess it's the discovery of becoming independent. I'm not sure it is a precise moment, but rather the period when you are becoming your own person, responsible for yourself.

Cearley: In terms of your writing process, what excites you most?

Sachar: My writing process is very long and drawn out. I write just a little bit each day, and most days I'm not very happy with what I did. It amazes me at the end of the year that I've got something I really like. When I'm in the middle of a book that I feel has potential, that's pretty exciting. Then there are daily discoveries when I think, "Wow, that's a great idea that will work perfectly with every-thing." Those excite me. Then it always feels good when I get the first draft done and go back [to] rewrite it.

Cearley: Share with us a little about your family background. You are originally from New York.

Sachar: Yes, I was born in New York and grew up in East Meadow, a town on Long Island, and lived there until I was nine years old. It was an upper-middle-class background growing up. I had a fairly happy childhood and had a lot of friends. Now I've got a wife and a daughter and live a pretty quiet life except for this year, which has been crazy with the movie. My life normally depends on just having a dull routine.

Cearley: How has this year changed you or your family?

Sachar: The experience has been good for me. Anything that sort of jolts your system is good for you, if it's positive and exciting. I've never been away from home this much before.

Cearley: Are you involved with the directing or the production of the movie?

Sachar: At this point, I'm not that involved. I had written the screenplay, and I did one last polish right before they started shooting. Now for the last month, I've just been there in case some issues arise.

Cearley: Are you very pleased with it?

Sachar: It's just hard to tell. I can't see it the way the director sees it. So, until it's all cut together, I'm not sure what we have. But I've enjoyed the process. I've liked all the actors and the director, Andrew Davis. Everybody seems really into it, so I am real hopeful that it turns out being good.

Cearley: Who play the lead parts?

Sachar: Shia LaBeouf plays Stanley, the main character. Kleho Thomas plays Zero. Sigourney Weaver is the Warden, and Jon Voight is incredible as Mr. Sir. He's constantly coming up with new additions to his character. Tim Blake Nelson plays Mr. Pendanski. Patricia Arquette is Kate Barlow. Dulé Hill is Sam.

Cearley: That is an impressive cast. Best wishes and congratulations to you. [The movie *Holes* was released nationally to wide acclaim in April 2003 — Ed.]

Stanley's hole was as deep as his shovel, but not quite wide enough on the bottom. He grimaced as he sliced off a chunk of dirt, then raised it up and flung it onto a pile.

He laid his shovel back down on the bottom of his hole and, to his surprise, it fit. He rotated it and only had to chip off a few chunks of dirt, here and there, before it could lie flat across his hole in every direction.

He heard the water truck approaching and felt a strange sense of pride at being able to show Mr. Sir, or Mr. Pendanski, that he had dug his first hole.

He put his hands on the rim and tried to pull himself up.

He couldn't do it. His arms were too weak to lift his heavy body.

He used his legs to help, but he just didn't have any strength. He was trapped in his hole. It was almost funny, but he wasn't in the mood to laugh.

"Stanley!" he heard Mr. Pendanski call.

Using his shovel, he dug two footholds in the hole wall. He climbed out to see Mr. Pendanski walking over to him.

"I was afraid you'd fainted," Mr. Pendanski said. "You wouldn't have been the first."

"I'm finished," Stanley said, putting his blood-spotted cap back on his head.

"All right!" said Mr. Pendanski, raising his hand for a high five, but Stanley ignored it. He didn't have the strength.

Mr. Pendanski lowered his hand and looked down at Stanley's hole. "Well done," he said. "You want a ride back?"

Stanley shook his head. "I'll walk."

Mr. Pendanski climbed back into the truck without filling Stanley's canteen. Stanley waited for him to drive away, then took another look at his hole. He knew it was nothing to be proud of, but he felt proud nonetheless.

He sucked up his last bit of saliva and spat.

—*Holes*
(New York: Farrar, Straus, and Giroux, 1998;
reprint, New York: Yearling Books, 2003), 39–40.

Edwin "Bud" Shrake

I had this devil in me that said,
"I want to write a book."

Edwin "Bud" Shrake

So I wrote this novel Blood Reckoning. *It was a Western, came out in 1961. I got a $2,500 advance and bought a white Cadillac. My wife was so mad. She wouldn't even ride in it.*

Interview by Graham Shelby

Graham Shelby: You grew up in Fort Worth and lived in Dallas and New York. When did you come back here to Texas to live?

Edwin "Bud" Shrake: I came back here in 1968 from *Sports Illustrated*, although for the next ten years I maintained an office in New York City. I would live here about half the year and half the year in New York. I was still working for *Sports Illustrated*. So I got the best of both worlds. I went in one day to see my managing editor and said I was going to quit. He said, "Nobody quits here unless I tell them to. What do you want?" "Well, I'm sick of living in New York, so I'm going to leave New York. I'm going to have to quit." He said, "Who told you that you had to live in New York?" I said, "Well, I assumed you had to live in New York." He said, "You have to live someplace where there's an airport." I said, "Wow!" So immediately I thought of three places: San Francisco, Santa Fe, and Austin. Not necessarily in that order.

Austin was a paradise then, it really was. The freedom is nothing like any other city in Texas. Austin has always been seen as the most liberal city in Texas, and it still is, although it's nowhere near like it used to be. So I thought if I come to Austin, I'll be midway between the two coasts, and I have a long history in Austin already. It'll be easier to get to New York in terms of airplane connections and so forth. That's why I came here. There was a *New York Review of Books* symposium where they compared Austin to Athens because of the cedar-covered hills and all the water, and the intellectual climate was very strong then. It still is, maybe even stronger now, but then it seemed more literary to me. Now it's probably more engineering.

Shelby: When did all this start to change?

Shrake: It started to change in the 1980s about the time that MCC came here and started the high-tech consortium to bring high-tech companies in here.

They made a deal with real estate developers to furnish them tax incentives and build roads and wastewater disposals. At its very beginning, Austin was a real estate development. When Mirabeau Lamar founded Austin in 1839, he founded it as a real estate development. He knew this was a much more invigorating climate plus a much more beautiful piece of land. Lamar had the ambition to expand the state of Texas all the way to the Pacific Ocean. What stood between us and the Pacific Ocean were the Comanches, the Comanche Nation. To precipitate a war with the Indians, he came to Austin, the Palm Springs at that time for the Comanche Nation. It was their paradise. They came here to have their R&R, swim, catch fish. It's hard to realize this valley had something like seventeen flowing mineral wells, creeks that never ran dry, and the Colorado River would be a mile wide in the spring. So Austin started as a real estate development.

Shelby: I still think it's the best city in Texas to live in. I regret a lot of things I see going on; things have gotten uglier. This used to be a beautiful city.

Shrake: That's ironic, that the quality of life, the very thing that brings people here, is diminished when so many people move here.

Shelby: What do you still like about the place?

Shrake: I like the people. I like my old friends that are here. I'm lucky that I've been around long enough that I really don't have to have much truck with the new Austin. I don't go west on Highway 71, but I go out to Willie Nelson's. I have such a history with this place. I have so many friends here, lots of wonderful people here. Westlake Hills used to be a hideout for eccentric university types. The head of the architecture department lived right over there. John Wheeler, who won the Nobel Prize working on the atomic bomb, lived right up the street. It was so great. There weren't all these houses; there were more cabins like this one hidden in the woods.

Shelby: How does it feel to have the best-selling sports book of all time, *Harvey Penick's Little Red Book*?

Shrake: It feels unreal. I'm glad of it, of course. It was a phenomenon. It shows what people want. What made it the best-selling sports book is that people fell in love with Harvey Penick, with his philosophy. Harvey, above anybody that I've ever known in my life, tried to live his life by the Golden Rule. That comes across in the book very strongly, as well as his teachings, which are all done in metaphors and parables. People love it that when they read Harvey's book, not only are they learning how to play golf, they're learning something bigger: how to deal with life. I'd bet a large number of people who bought the book don't play golf.

Shelby: You coauthored four books with him, and then you worked on Willie Nelson's autobiography and Barry Switzer's biography. What was your role?

Shrake: The first one I did was Willie's. The reason I did that was because Willie and I were playing golf and running around together almost every day. This publisher offered Willie an enormous amount of money to do his book. This was in 1987, and Willie said no. Then he turned to me and said, "I'll do it if you'll do it with me." I said, "Yeah, why not?" I've known Willie God knows how long. So we went to New York and closed the deal with the publisher. When I sat down to do it, I said, "Wait a minute, I don't know how to write a book like this." Then I thought, "Well, sure you do. You've been training all your life to do this. Consider it being twenty long bonus pieces at the back of *Sports Illustrated*." So that's the way I looked at it.

When Barry Switzer's book came along, it was the same deal. I've known Switzer since he was the assistant coach at Oklahoma, and I've always liked him. I looked at that as a long *Sports Illustrated* story. In *SI*, I did several long first-person, as-told-to stories. The trick is to try to make it sound as much as you can like the person talking. I wrote Willie's book trying to make it sound like it was Willie. Barry's book is very much the same way. I think one of the greatest compliments I ever got, as far as that particular craft goes, was when Barry and I had a squabble toward the end of the book. I said, "Well, I quit. I'm not going to write any more." He wanted to do something I didn't want to do. So Barry asked his brother—his lawyer—who'd wanted to write the book anyway, to take it over and finish it. So I said, "Great." About three days later, the phone rang and it was Barry. Barry said, "Bud, would you come back to work on this and finish it for me?" I said, "What's the matter?" He said, "Here's the real trouble—Donny writes like a fucking lawyer. You write just the way I talk." I thought, that's great. It's great because the book is written in coherent sentences. The book is logical and makes sense. If Barry thinks he talks like this, that's wonderful. Nobody actually talks like that. Switzer's a very controversial person, or so some people would say. I was here not to expose Barry Switzer; I was looking to expose the world to Switzer's side of the story.

Shelby: How does writing a book with someone else compare to writing your own book?

Shrake: It's much easier in a way. They have the material down. They talk, you ask questions. In Barry's case, he had tons of documentation. It uses the same muscles that I've been developing in the process of twenty-five years as a journalist.

Shelby: What separates writers who get to your stage?

Shrake: Luck. You can't leave luck out of it in any equation. Other than luck, and let's assume the amount of talent is equal, then it's persistence. It's perseverance and hard work. The first novel I ever wrote was while I was working as a reporter on the *Dallas Times Herald.* I had to be at work at a quarter to six in the morning, and I'd never get in before midnight. I was married and living in Dallas. I wrote the book sitting at the kitchen table between three-thirty and five-thirty in the morning.

I had this devil in me that said, "I want to write a book." I really wanted to write a book and publish it before I was twenty-eight. Because of Fitzgerald and Hemingway, I thought if you haven't had a book published by the time you're twenty-eight, you're a failure. Also money. I was making almost no money working for the newspaper. My wife was teaching at SMU, and she made more money. We had two little kids, and we needed extra money. So I wrote this novel *Blood Reckoning.* It was a Western, came out in 1961. When I sold it, I got a $2,500 advance and bought a white Cadillac. My wife was so mad. She wouldn't even ride in it. She didn't want me to park it anywhere. We lived in this place that housed SMU students and teachers. All the rest of the cars were Volkswagens. She didn't want me to park it there, and I took a lot of ribbing in doing that. But later on it turned out I was the one with foresight, because I wound up living in it. Lots of times I slept in it in the parking lot. Not every night, but there were times when I was dead broke.

President Lamar admired a half inch of glowing ash on his cigar.

"Captain, you say we are going to have to fight the Comanches if we intend to plant our capital in Austin. To that end, you have seen the pitiful stockade fence they tried and failed to build in Austin. Austin has no defense against the Comanches. We have General Savariego and his Mexican army marching somewhere in Texas, and more Mexican armies with more generals behind them, and trouble with savages everywhere, even with the Cherokees, who were supposed to be our allies.

". . . But I have an idea of a way we can avoid a war with the Comanches and expand and solidify our Republic at the same time."

Matthew waited, a foot on the railing, smoking the Cuban cigar and looking at the desolate prairies dotted with pools of water outside the city. For an instant Matthew feared Lamar might be suggesting a union with the United Sates.

"The Republic is going to buy all the land up to a line fifty miles west of San Antonio," Lamar said.

—*The Borderland: A Novel of Texas*
(New York: Hyperion, 2000), 232.

Evan Smith — Texas Monthly

_____

In Texas, there is this genuine pride.
It's unlike any place else.

Evan Smith—*Texas Monthly*

The magazine is trying to speak to the people who've been here for three generations and also for three minutes. The people that have been here for a long time see Texas as a state of mind. The people that just got here see Texas as a state.

Interview by Graham Shelby

Graham Shelby: As a transplant from New York, what were you surprised by when you came to Texas?

Evan Smith: It is a cliché, but the sky. The sky in Texas just seems bigger to me. When I go to other places I feel hemmed in. When I come back to Texas after being in New York or California or some place, the first thing I notice is the openness of the land. The sky is so much. I have a real affinity for the physicality of Texas, for the physical nature of the land and the sky. It does something to me. It makes me feel good. And now it makes me feel at home, which I'm glad to say is the right way to feel.

Shelby: In one of your columns as editor of *Texas Monthly*, you wrote about the sign in the lobby. Does that sign serve to define the magazine?

Smith: There's a sign in the lobby of *Texas Monthly* when you get off the elevators that says "*Texas Monthly*, A Great Magazine," and I wrote somewhat jokingly that my responsibility is to make certain every issue lives up to the sign, that it be a great magazine. Clearly slogans are just that and not meant to be taken literally. Every issue can't be "great," but we'd certainly like to set a high mark for ourselves and meet it every month in terms of the quality and ambition of the magazine.

Shelby: And if it's perceived that it's not, you take the blame?

Smith: *If* it's not the case, I take the blame. *When* it's not the case, I take the blame. We have had issues since I've been editor where there have been stories with which people haven't been happy. So in their minds, the magazine was less than great that month, and boy, did I hear about it.

Shelby: Do you think that people from outside the state have more of an image of what Texas is than they do of states that may not have as distinctive a myth?

Smith: Sure, that is one of the great things about Texas. When *Texas Monthly* began in 1973, our founder, Mike Levy, in essence sold the magazine on this basis. There are these people called Texans in this place called Texas. They self-identify as Texans first, and as Austinites, Dallasites, or Houstonians second. It's just what makes us different. In Texas there is this genuine pride. It's unlike anyplace else. I will say that the myth is itself a myth. The mythic Texas that so many people talk about — life on the ranch — is legitimate in some sections of Texas today. There are many people in Texas who are several generations Texan, whose kin were of that world. But at the same time Texas is a modern state. I'm not so sure if the myth really has any resonance for a lot of the people who are here today — natives or not. The problem we have as a magazine is trying to speak to the people who've been here for three generations and also for three minutes, because those folks want different things and think of Texas differently. The people that have been here for a long time see Texas as a state of mind. The people that just got here see Texas as a state.

Shelby: Do you think there's a particular feel or flavor that comes out of Texas?

Smith: I do. For one thing, we are very lucky and blessed as a magazine to have such a deep pool of talent. There are a lot of folks in Texas, many more than we can ever publish in a given issue of *Texas Monthly*, who have the ability to write wonderful magazine stories. I mean magazine stories as opposed to simply any story. The difference between magazine and newspaper writing is very great. Magazine folks are people with an innate magazine talent, with the ability to tell stories in a feature-oriented way. Much of the writing that I've seen while I've been here is like the state itself, kind of outsized in its countenance, almost arrogantly so, though I mean that in the best possible way, people who are themselves big. They feel very comfortable being present in their stories and being on display, having that confidence drive their writing. That is something that you just don't find in many places. There are other places, for example in New York, that experience a similar phenomenon. Perhaps in California and Montana, there's a particular type of writing that is inherently self-confident, but it is relatively rare. In Texas it exists in great amounts.

Shelby: How do you determine which topics to cover? For example, what was discussed at the magazine to cover the presidential campaign of 2000?

Smith: For us the campaign was something we knew we had to cover, but it was not going to be possible to cover as news. So it became for us not so much delivering news as putting things in perspective. At the same time, we live in a world overtaken by punditry. Everyone now is a pundit. Everyone is trying to put things in perspective. The difficulty for us is in figuring out a way to have our particular perspective be fresh and interesting. That was really the discussion that went on around here. We as a magazine don't endorse candidates. As a magazine we have to go a long way toward staying neutral in such elections. [Yet] at the same time [we] exert our right to take on things that we think are not fair.

A number of issues were raised during the campaign that I think are going to get addressed in the legislative session, that are probably good for Texas. Two come to mind immediately. One is the competency of counsel in death penalty cases. The question concerns whether defense lawyers for death row inmates are not reviewing files and whether [they] are falling asleep during the trials. There are accusations that death row inmates were not well served by these appointed defense lawyers. That issue may get rectified in the session. The other one involves DNA testing of inmates on death row, to make absolutely certain before we put them to death that they are the ones who committed the crimes. DNA testing, of course, is not something that happened in many cases; either the technology didn't exist or there was not a law in place that allowed them to get tested. Both of those issues raised legitimate questions about the way the law is conducted in Texas.

Shelby: What does a good magazine writer need to be able to do?

Smith: A good magazine writer needs to take a subject and make it into a story. Too many people misunderstand the mission of a query letter or a pitch letter to a magazine editor. They simply propose writing about a subject, "I want to write about George W. Bush." The difference is being able to understand that in order to write a story for a magazine you have to have a spin, a take, or a particular angle to the story that makes it different from every other story you've read. The story has to be about something specific, not general. The first thing that a magazine writer does, at least for us, is to understand what the story is.

The second thing is to understand who the audience is. With us, the thing that makes people want to read a story in *Texas Monthly* is that it is authentically Texan and understands the nature of the state. In the story you understand essentially what it means to be in Texas and what it means to be Texan. This is a magazine about Texas. We give people the tools and information that they need to live in Texas and to feel more like Texans. So understanding the audience is a critical element to writing for this magazine. The third thing is can you tell a good story? Can you create a scene? Can you get people to give you good quotes that you can then use? Can you find really wonderful characters? Can you be vivid in the way you use language, in the way you describe folks? Those are things that can be taught but most of it is innate. We just hired a young woman to join the staff. She's twenty-four years old and has not been writing very long. The minute she picked up the pen and paper to write a story for us we knew that she would be able to tell a story. That is a wonderful thing to discover, and that is an incredibly important aspect of writing for a magazine: Can you tell a story?

Shelby: What are some other common mistakes you see writers make?

Smith: Incomplete reporting. We pride ourselves on thoroughness and accuracy and telling the whole story. I am always sorry when good writers with good intentions are lazier than they ought to be in terms of their writing. Any editor worth his or her salt can read a story and know that there are gaping holes. Be sure that you've done all your homework. Be sure that you don't present half a story or three-quarters of a story. The flip side of that is you may do a great job of reporting, but you do a notebook job of it. You don't edit yourself. Every single quote, every single conversation gets in the story, and the story becomes this great big mess of reporting.

Shelby: One aspect of being a freelance writer that causes people a lot of anxiety is the query letter. What is your advice?

Smith: First of all, don't tell me the whole story. That's not called a query letter; that is called a submission. If you are attempting to get me to publish your story, don't give me the story itself, although that is one strategy that people undertake. Save yourself the time and trouble. Pitch me the story in a way that makes it irresistible. Always know what the magazine has done so you know you are not replicating it. Know who the audience is, that's critical. Be an authority on the subject that you are querying us about. Do enough reporting to make the query letter attractive and substantive so that I am just blown away by it. Really write it. Show me in the query letter that you can write. People send clips all the time as a way to say, "Hire me." The problem is that when you see a published story you don't know if that published story reflects the writer's work or the work of a really good editor. I discount clips, personally. A query letter is you, unedited, unvarnished, writing to me that you want to write a story. One of the best query letters I've ever gotten came from one of our writers, Pam Colloff. She pitched me a story that the magazine had done many years ago, but the query letter itself said to me this woman should be writing for *Texas Monthly* whether it's on this subject or any other. So I called her up, and I said no to the idea, yes to you. You don't want me to walk away from the query letter thinking you're not somebody that should be writing for the magazine regardless of whether I like the idea.

Shelby: What are some of the perceptions you think writers have about the process?

Smith: That they are not going to be edited. That they are not going to be cut. That they are going to be able to do whatever they want, and that they will turn in the story and it will go in the magazine untouched. It is amazing how the least-experienced writers are the ones who balk the most at the editors, writers who don't understand that fact checking actually helps a story. The people with the most experience understand that editors, fact checkers, and copyeditors are there to help you make your story better. So that is the biggest misperception: that you are going to turn in your story and it's going to go in the magazine untouched.

Shelby: Any suggestions for people who want to be freelance writers, magazine writers?

Smith: Be persistent. Have patience. Read lots of magazines to get a sense of what sorts of stories are getting published. Don't give up the hope of writing for a magazine. Even if you can't do it today, in five years you may wind up there. No job is too small. You can only get better by writing. All those things, or some combination, are the basics of what we all do. Writing for a magazine is a great thing. Not everybody gets a chance to do it, but it is certainly worth trying. All good editors like to consider submissions from people with no experience. That's why it's important to keep trying.

I've known Kinky Friedman for years, mostly in the context of his career as a mystery novelist. Before he put pen to paper, he was, of course, a cult country singer with a nasty habit of offending an array of demographic groups. (To hear him sing "They Ain't Makin' Jews Like Jesus Anymore" or "Homo Erectus" is a rare pleasure indeed.) In five pieces for us to date, he's shown himself to be witty, literate, and more professional than most so-called writers. I've asked him to help us leaven what is often a hyperserious magazine by tackling topics of his choice in short-essay form. Trust me: He may tick you off now and again, but you won't be able to stop reading—or laughing.

The Kinkster a columnist for *Texas Monthly?* You must be thinking, "This *is* going to be a different magazine." You're right. And we hope you like it.

—Behind the Lines: "Grand Designs,"
Texas Monthly, April 2001, 7–10.

Bruce Sterling

I've got a Texana shelf that I keep in the guest room for people that have shown up and can't believe that Texans really do write.

Bruce Sterling

Essay by Joe Holley

If there is a twenty-first-century successor to the prolific Robert Howard, it is the prolific Bruce Sterling, an Austin science fiction writer who is one of the founding fathers of cyberpunk. In addition to numerous near-future science fiction novels and short stories, Sterling is the author of The Hacker Crackdown: Law and Disorder on the Electronic Frontier (1992) and numerous articles and columns for Wired and other publications.

"Cyberpunk," Sterling has written, "was a voice of Bohemia—Bohemia in the 1980s. The technosocial changes loose in contemporary society were bound to affect its counterculture. Cyberpunk was the literary incarnation of this phenomenon. And the phenomenon is still growing. Communication technologies in particular are becoming much less respectable, much more volatile, and increasingly in the hands of people you might not introduce to your grandma."

Science fiction allows Sterling to explore the strangeness and unpredictability of the bewildering, relentlessly changing world that is inexorably changing us in ways we don't always comprehend.

"We're not into science fiction because it's 'good literature,' we're into it because it's 'weird,'" Sterling once told an audience of computer-game developers. "Follow your weird, ladies and gentlemen. Forget trying to pass for normal. Follow your geekdom. Embrace your nerditude. In the immortal words of Lafcadio Hearn, a geek of incredible obscurity whose work is still in print after a hundred years, "Woo the muse of the odd."

Sterling, who was born in Brownsville in 1954, woos the muse of the odd in Austin, where he lives with his wife and daughter.

I quite commonly run into people who are aware of my work and alarmed and surprised to find out I am not merely a Texan but a native Texan from Brownsville, a border child.

Rick Klaw: Besides the fact that you live in Texas, would you consider your work Texas fiction?

Bruce Sterling: No. I always figured being a genre writer is delineation enough. I figured it would be professional suicide to be seen as a Texas regionalist. Although in point of fact, I am interested in Texas regional writing. I've got a Texana shelf that I keep in the guest room for people that have shown up and can't believe that Texans really do write. I quite commonly run into people who are aware of my work and alarmed and surprised to find out I am not merely a Texan but a native Texan from Brownsville, a border child.

Klaw: Have you lived in Texas all your life?

Sterling: No, I lived in India over a year as a teenager.

Klaw: How did you end up in India?

Sterling: Oh, by diaspora, a very Texan thing. I've still got an aunt right now who's out in the Persian Gulf. Another uncle of mine worked on offshore oil rigs in the North Sea. There are Texans all over. Mechanical industry. Petrochemicals.

Klaw: When and where did your first story appear?

Sterling: I had a story that was published by a regionalist Texas thing [*Lone Star Universe*, 1976] but mangled in the press. I had to disown it because several of the pages were mixed up before the thing went to print. Chunks of pages were mixed up. If you read the story now, it doesn't make any sense. It was reduced to gibberish. That was the first piece of print that ever appeared in my name between hard covers. But of course I used to do a lot of fanzine writing.

Klaw: What was your first novel? How old were you then?

Sterling: Twenty-three, actually. It was *Involution Ocean*, which came out in late 1977. That was really my first published work. I wrote a lot of it when I was twenty, when I was a junior at UT.

Klaw: Your next book was *Artificial Kid*. How much of a gap is there between those two?

Sterling: A couple of years. *Schismatrix* was next. I wrote it when I was twenty-nine. So that took a pretty good long time there.

Klaw: What about your recent books?

Sterling: One of my recent books, *Zeitgeist*, that I'm particularly happy with now was written in 1999. It's about the culture war between the pop culture of the G8 and Islamic fundamentalism. People at the time were asking, "What's this thing with you going on and on about Islamic fundamentalism and these women and everything?" Osama bin Laden is actually a minor character in that book. He's referred to at one point. The thing cannot look more prescient now. It's so prescient it almost scares me.

Klaw: What is your favorite Bruce Sterling book?

Sterling: I like *Crystal Express* actually. It's my first short story collection. It packs more weird fireworks per printed page than most of my stuff. I like shorter forms. I used to, anyway. It's a nice way to toss off intellectual squibs. The variegated stuff appeals to me. There's historical fantasy in it and weird sapier-mechanist stuff, peculiar space opera.

Klaw: Do you think your journalist background is the reason for your preference of the shorter form? Get your idea out and then move on?

Sterling: It's more a matter that short material is good for really hot and incandescent ideas and conceits. You know, really weird, peculiar notions that couldn't stand a whole novel's worth of exploitation but that hit hard—what Stanislaw Lem calls the spearhead of cognition. You think differently. It's not the sort of rising tension curve, arch with denouement, and secondary love interest and all the palace intrigue. It just comes in, bombs you into submission and leaves.

Klaw: Genre fiction seems to lend itself to that really well.

Sterling: Yeah. William Gibson always said his idea of writing science fiction is that it should be like somebody stumbling out of the alley, grabbing you by the lapels, and slamming you up against the wall. And you know, if that happens, and the guy then departs in short order, it's a very interesting encounter. If he actually stands there and slams you against the wall for two or three hours, you begin to wonder, "All right, come on! What exactly is your point here?"

Klaw: What Bruce Sterling book would you recommend to someone unfamiliar with your work?

Sterling: Geez, that's a good one. I'd have to ask them what they did, because my work is all over the map and a lot of my books have different fandoms. But if they're into science fiction, they've surely heard of me by now. If they're into traditional space opera, futurist kind of stuff, they should probably read *Schismatrix*, which is probably my most famous book. Or the easiest to get, because it's out in a version that has all the related short stories with it.

Klaw: The *Schismatrix Plus*?

Sterling: Yeah, it's what's known as the sapier-mechanist series. It's five stories that I wrote in the early eighties. If you're into political satire, you ought to read *Distraction* and if you're a woman, I would definitely recommend *Holy Fire*. That's the book that has the strongest following from women. I get a lot of fan mail from women about that book.

Klaw: Did you expect that when you wrote it?

Sterling: It's written from a female point of view, very deliberately so. It also deals with a lot of traditional women's issues — woman's struggle to affirm herself and become an artist in the face of social disapproval and so on. It's a very powerful work along genre lines, and it's rare to see that done from an intimate, feminine point of view.

Klaw: Certainly from a male writer.

Sterling: I'd have to say I do get a lot of kind remarks from women. That's definitely the book of mine that Oprah would want out on the list. Which is saying something, considering my other books are like *Heavy Weather*, my Texas regionalist book. It's mostly set in West Texas, and it definitely has powerful, J. Frank Dobie elements in it. It's a Texan folklore study, a very powerful regionalist sense of place.

Klaw: Are there Texas writers that you enjoy?

Sterling: I like Dobie, Bedichek, and Webb. These guys were the first professional littérateurs, genuine, no-kidding, straight-up-and-down Texas intelligentsia. I'm not nuts about the lost silver mines of San Saba stuff. But there's a Dobie book, *A Texan in England*, where he writes about his experiences teaching — it was Oxford or Cambridge — which I thought was genuine, interesting, social reportage. He's not sitting there making up nonsense about border knife-fighters and all this corny stuff. This shows this guy had global-style capacity. He was able to go to Europe and hang out in Britain with the top intellectual people of the period. He had something to tell them that they were interested in hearing, and he made some very astute remarks about British society. That's something I admire. I like that book a lot, if anything, more than the books about mustangs and rattlesnakes and coyotes.

Klaw: Many of your readers would be surprised to discover that you are a fan of those writers.

Sterling: One of the great secrets of originality is being able to hide your sources. If they don't know where you got it, it looks really sexy. Most science fiction people certainly never read any J. Frank Dobie. They wouldn't recognize the riffing that they see in *Heavy Weather* as being Dobie-like stuff. When it's interpreted through a science fictional context, I think it holds up quite well. It doesn't come across as the kind of weird western stuff where people are deliberately riffing on Western fiction.

There really is science fiction that happens to be set in the Panhandle, West Texas, and Oklahoma, which have been changed, a socially changed area. At one point the Texas Rangers show up and they're not kidding! It's just like being pulled over by the Rangers now. It's a scary experience except these guys have got shoulder-launched rockets and multiband cell phones. They're pursuing genetic smugglers from Mexico, and it works great. I was really pleased at the effect it had. That material stood up well.

Klaw: You're right. A talented, creative writer is going to take stuff from other sources and meld it in.

Sterling: Well, if you don't have much talent, you "borrow." If you do have some talent, you "steal." Just steal. Everybody does it. It's not like you ever made up the English language.

Klaw: Legend has it that cyberpunk emerged from Texas in the '70s. Is that true?

Sterling: I have no idea. Nobody used the term until the mid-eighties in any kind of way. But definitely the Turkey City group that started up in 1973 or 1974 was the launch pad of Texan science fiction as a going thing. Lewis Shiner and I, the only two cyberpunks that ever lived in the same city, were very ardent people in that group. Still running today, it's one of the longest lasting regional science fiction workshops in the United States.

Klaw: What is Turkey City?

Sterling: It was a spontaneous thing by a bunch of fans at some convention in Dallas. Somebody cleared off a corner of a table and asked people to put manuscripts there. It wasn't at that time an organized group where people sat down and used the Milford workshop method as we now do.

Klaw: Why is it called Turkey City?

Sterling: Because some unknown genius put up a sign indicating where the manuscripts should be laid saying "Welcome to Turkey City" and because the manuscripts were all turkeys, none of them was any damn good. No particular manuscript as far as I know that was shown at that particular event was ever published.

Klaw: When people talk about Bruce Sterling, what would you like them to be saying about your career and possible legacy?

Sterling: I would like them to think that I was doing my best. I would like them to think that I did not slack off and that even though my attitude is sometimes impolite and regrettable, I took my literary calling seriously. I work in a minor genre in a peculiarly minor key, and it's something that suits my temperament. Generally, I tend to write books which are funny but with black humor. People are sitting there trading witticisms with terrorists and zeitgeists for instance. I'm really pleased to be working in the area that I do, and I'm giving it the best I've got.

Klaw: What does the future hold for Bruce Sterling?

Sterling: Age, decline, and death. It's funny, I'm pushing fifty here. I don't know how much more work I'll get done. I've done fourteen books already. If I do another fourteen, it'll be pretty remarkable. I never imagined myself as being particularly effusive, productive, or verbose, but I have turned out to be a quite prolific writer. In point of fact, I'm a guy in mid-life, and I'm at peace with that.

Klaw: For a guy who is "stuffy and satisfied," you are very active politically.

Sterling: Sure, I'm an activist. I run Internet lists and work for magazines. I travel quite a bit. People think of me as a chrome-and-matte-black cyberpunk and a menace to something-or-other, or else a bohemian literary type. From a personal point of view, my life has been very consistent. I've lived in the same city more than half my life. I have only one wife — not the usual authorly three or four. I've never been drafted. I've never been in a race riot. I've never been arrested. I never was in the Betty Ford detox clinic. I consistently produce a book every two years or so. I'm well known, but I've built up to it slowly and consistently. I never had a book come out that was so horrible that everybody fled. Never had a movie come out that suddenly revolutionized what people thought of me. So yeah, I'd say "quiet" and "stable" are pretty good terms in a lot of ways.

Klaw: What do you see in the future for science fiction?

Sterling: I'm really worried about the magazines. The magazines have always been the recruiting ground for the field, and they are shrinking badly. If the Web ended up picking that up and breaking people into print, that would be good, but I don't see evidence of that. The publishing and distribution infrastructure is under severe stress right now. It's tough on authors, and it's especially tough on authors who want to break in. On the other hand, I'm pleased and encouraged by what's been going on in Austin over the past year. I made an effort to kick this little writers' group, Turkey City, into higher gear here. Now we've got a new writers' group starting up which has been founded by some guys in town who were quite serious about breaking into the genre. My feeling is that as long as there are young people around who are interested in science fiction — new voices that want to make something happen — they will create an audience.

Viktor laughed harshly. "Hah! Can you imagine a Turkish heroin-smuggling scandal when the Balkans are on fire? No American cop is that stupid! They're crushing a heroic Slavic people in their innocent heroic homeland. Heroin means nothing to the Yankees now! Their new Yankee darlings are the KLA, an Albanian terrorist mob. They steal cars and sell heroin! It's how the KLA bought the guns to massacre pregnant Serbian women and gouge the eyes out of children."

"Yea, that's some story, all right."

"The KLA were all trained by Osama bin Laden. You know that, don't you?"

"Oh, yeah, millionaire philanthropist and all that, he's a heavy guy, Osama bin Laden. Look, Viktor, I can see you're taking this temporary air strike pretty hard, and I'd love to discuss regional politics with you some other time. But frankly, I just called to see how the band is doing."

—*Zeitgeist: A Novel of Metamorphosis*
(New York: Bantam, 2000), 188.

Katherine Tanney

---

*For me, writing is a soul-searching activity
that takes a long time.*

Katherine Tanney

I like dark subject matter. It's funny too because at the same time I'm more inter-ested in generosity and kindness in characters. That doesn't negate the darkness that's in the world and in my stories. Maybe it enhances it.

Interview by Kyra Edeker

Kyra Edeker: Stephen Longstreet, who died in 2002, was your grandfa-ther. He seemed like a major figure, being a novelist, screenwriter, painter, and collage artist. What role did he play for you?

Katherine Tanney: He was nothing but supportive. My grandfather was very fond of me and always had something nurturing and nice to say to me in difficult moments of my life. Financially, my grandparents were a big source of support in my life. They provided the extras, like piano lessons and camp and art school. My granddad was a screenwriter and had stories about going to parties and knowing all these big-name people. But the Stephen Longstreet that *I* saw was the guy who lived in his room and wrote all day. He made collages and painted and didn't go out very much. To me he was like a hermit misanthrope.

He had a different philosophy than I do about writing. He was prolific; he wrote more than a hundred books in his life. It took me five years to write my novel and he just couldn't understand why it was taking so long. He used to say to me, "I don't understand. Twelve words makes a sentence, four sentences is a para-graph, six paragraphs you got a page, twenty pages you got a chapter, fourteen chapters you've got a book!" Doesn't that make it sound so simple? He didn't un-derstand. But at the very end of his life, around the time my book came out, he told me he thought he might have written better books if he had slowed down. He wrote more plot-driven books, and for me, writing is more of a soul-searching ac-tivity that takes a long time.

Edeker: So what was your reply when he told you that it should be easy?

Tanney: Oh, nothing. We were from completely different generations and had completely different interests in what we wanted our work to be about. I've read some of his work and he's a great stylist, but his books are superficial to me. I'm more interested in the psychological depths of people, so we were up to different things.

Edeker: You not only share writing with your grandfather but also you create collage as he did.

Tanney: He used to describe himself as an artist who writes as opposed to a writer who paints. I think of myself as a writer. Even though I went to art school and love visual art, I don't think that's where my strongest talents lie. It was probably a stronger talent for him. I grew up in this aesthetically sophisticated family with a huge art collection. They cared about art and beauty.

Edeker: You've written you were the "product of Jewish Atheist Culture Hounds who didn't blink at treating their kids to cutting edge theater, film, visual art, and music." What were you exposed to that was so unusual?

Tanney: *Oh, my!* My parents didn't seem to think very much about exposing us to really inappropriate movies when we were kids. I remember them taking us to what must have been R-rated films that had dark, psychosexual subject matter. It's strange, but at the same time I'm thrilled that they exposed us to that. I was also taken to theater that was very avant-garde at the time. My mom took us to a matinee of the original Broadway production of *Hair* when I was a kid—with all the naked people. My parents were kind of wanna-be hippies. I remember going to giant events in public parks with hippies going all around, dancing, smoking pot, and passing around their peanut brittle and daisies. Looking back, my parents weren't part of it. At the time I didn't think about it because everyone was welcome. But they weren't painting their faces and they weren't wearing hippie clothes. My dad was an aerospace engineer for McDonnell-Douglas. He had a straight job and worked on the space shuttle. It was more like entertainment; they just liked the whole groovy scene of it. Their record collection had Janis Joplin and The Doors. That was the music I grew up with.

Edeker: Did they also expose you to avant-garde books at a young age? Did they have a large library?

Tanney: They did, but I didn't go near their books. I wasn't a reader. I was one of those kids that grew up on TV and comic books. I didn't start reading until I was in my teens.

Edeker: When you started reading, was there one book that made you think "I can do that" and made you want to write?

Tanney: It's so low-brow. It was in junior high, and I was so miserable. I hated it—we all hated it. I was tall and skinny and people were so mean to me. On the first day, my first-period math teacher said, "Cut the apron strings! You're not a kid anymore!" and I felt really homesick. Then I got to my second-period class—

an English class with this really weird teacher, Mr. Chernow. He read aloud to us from *Alfred Hitchcock Presents*. His readings were like performances. He walked around the room with his yardstick in his hand and slammed it on your desk if you weren't paying attention. Then he'd go over to the window and pretend that he was eating a fly out of the Venetian blinds.

The stories were so creepy and he was such a goofball that it was the beginning for me. I was mesmerized and escaped into those weird worlds away from that horrible school. I did and still do have a love of those kind of stories, stories that are scary and thrilling and creepy. I think my new novel is starting to lean in that direction.

Edeker: How's it going?

Tanney: Very, very slowly. I have a feeling though that when I finally write it, it's going to come out fast. I keep starting it and writing a lot of it and then deciding, no. By the time I get on the right track I will have spent so much time working it up that hopefully I'll have the time and the focus to just write it.

Edeker: You spent a month in residence at the Millay Artists' Colony working intensely on *Carousel of Progress*.

Tanney: When I got there I was so ready. The timing was the best thing. I had one month to get the lead out, and I'd been craving that kind of concentrated time. I was so determined not to waste even a minute. I was meditating every day and reading a lot about Buddhism. It got my mind in writing mode — it calmed me so I could focus and gave me a lot of clarity. Meditation is a great alternative to therapy. In a way, I approached my time at the colony as a monastic opportunity. It's deprivation; you have to be ready for it.

Edeker: After your book was published you won the Texas Institute of Letters prize for a first book of fiction. Did that surprise you, being born and raised in L.A.?

Tanney: That was a huge welcome for me. It was like they were saying "It's okay that you're from L.A., we like you, we like your writing." I felt included. I was eligible because I'd been living here more than two years, but it was incredibly surprising. It was from the *Texas* Institute of Letters and I always felt there was no chance of winning because my book was so strongly about another place.

Edeker: Do you feel like a "fish out of water" being a writer from Los Angeles in Texas, especially since Texas has such a strong story and myth about itself?

Tanney: I do. It's prevalent all the time. I'm different from a lot of the people that I interact with. I have an edge that doesn't exactly cut it here, to use a nice metaphor. I can be more abrasive than people like. I like being here, so I think I must like the fish-out-of-water thing a little. It might be good for me, and it's probably good for my work. It helps me define myself. It comes from my side too, being out of place. I could probably change, but I have found the places I fit in. I feel good here, but at the same time I don't really feel like I have to give up anything. The things that I have given up, I've wanted to let go of them. They've dropped away through some natural process. If my writing's changing, it's changing by virtue of the people I've come into contact with and the relationships I've made. Maybe it's getting a little kinder.

Edeker: Less dark?

Tanney: I don't want it to become less dark. I would like my writing to become *more* dark.

Edeker: In your novel, I enjoyed your slow examination of uncomfortable situations.

Tanney: I'm going more in that direction. I *like* dark subject matter. It's funny too because at the same time I'm more interested in generosity and kindness in characters. That doesn't negate the darkness that's in the world and in my stories. Maybe it enhances it.

Peter and I looked at each other hard. It seemed they were playing at being apart, using their separation to spice up their relationship. A half hour passed, then my father and I got cozy on the couch, sitting closer together than normal so we could both see the textbook propped in his lap. My mother stayed close by, reading a magazine.

"You know, the two of you look like newlyweds." She interrupted our discussion of algebra. "No, really. You look like sweethearts poring over honeymoon brochures." It was her specialty. I don't think she had any idea how uncomfortable comments like that made me. She saw everything between the sexes—even between father and daughter—as sexual, so it was no wonder that instead of seriously considering the number of apples among Tom and Patty in the equation my father was explaining, I gave them faces and a neighborhood with trees and wondered why they were selling apples at all when they could have been doing something better, like kissing.

—*Carousel of Progress* (New York: Villard, 2001), 85.

Lorenzo Thomas

---

*We all have something to say, and we have
our own way of saying it.*

Lorenzo Thomas

The poet's job is to listen and record that which is, in its own way, a celebration of our consciousness. [Poetry is] about expressing feelings that are open to everybody—making statements that will somehow make a change in the world. Poets make a change in the world by making people aware of something they weren't aware of before.

Interview by Ayo Bain

Ayo Bain: When did poetry first embrace you?

Lorenzo Thomas: I grew up in New York City (originally I'm from Panama) in a family that was always interested in reading. I became interested in poetry and found lots of activity around New York. I would read everything I could find at the library. When I was old enough, I started to go to poetry readings held in coffee shops, and that's what got me involved in that scene. I'm still involved in that today.

Bain: Places such as the Nuyorican Poets Cafe must have offered a literary carnival around the clock.

Thomas: That's very much how things were back in the 1960s. There were many such places, not as entirely devoted to poetry as the Nuyorican Poets Cafe is, but every one of them has a night of the week when they feature poetry, probably because it was cheaper than featuring music. The poets came for nothing. I had an opportunity to read at the Nuyorican Poets Cafe a couple of years ago with David Henderson, who is a friend from the era when we both started out together reading poems at various places, and also at St. Mark's Church, which was the central place where younger writers could meet, and older ones, too. They had something called the Poetry Project, which still exists and is now some thirty years old. That was the kind of place where organized readings and publications assisted people. Poets who had problems or were down on their luck could be assisted in material ways as well, when necessary, so it was very much like a community as far as writers were concerned.

After I left New York and moved to Texas, I worked all over the state and all over the country. For the state, I worked for the Texas Commission on the Arts doing Poetry-in-the-Schools programs in East Texas and small towns. I did the same thing in Arkansas and Oklahoma. Here in Houston I also discovered a community of writers and artists. That, also, is still very strong here in Houston. It changes from time to time because people come and go, but there is always a sense here of an artistic community and a community of poets and writers, which makes it a good place to be.

Bain: Does the poetry scene in New York keep you traveling there?

Thomas: I find myself in New York quite frequently. I still have a brother who lives there, and the poetry business, if you can call it that, takes me to New York quite often. I was there last fall to give a reading at Columbia University. I presented a workshop and a reading at the St. Lawrence Poetry Project. So there are often occasions for me to be in New York, and it's always exciting there.

But again, the literary scene in Houston is also very exciting. There was a time after I first moved here that people felt that not much was happening. There was radio, but it was not as well publicized as in other places. At the present time though, if you are really interested and want to check it out, you can find poetry readings every day of the week in Houston too. You need to know where they are — and you can do that on the Internet by the way. There is a Spoken Word newsletter that is run by a group that runs *Tongues* magazine. You can check into that on the Internet, and it will tell you where poetry readings are every night.

Bain: Why Houston?

Thomas: I came to Houston because I was asked to be the writer-in-residence at Texas Southern University. I actually intended to fulfill that job and return to New York, but I'm still here in Houston because I kept finding things to do. I've been at the University of Houston since the late '80s.

Bain: Who were your early influences?

Thomas: The first people to influence me were poets who were on television, and they were Langston Hughes and Carl Sandburg. I was fascinated to learn later on from reading that Langston Hughes, as a high school boy, was influenced by Carl Sandburg. Sandburg was a really tremendous personality on television. He was a strange old man who had a very dramatic style of elocution in the recitation of his poems. Langston Hughes was also a dynamic personality when he appeared on television, and both of them fascinated me. Then I went to the library and read what they wrote. Later on, after I became involved in hanging around the poetry readings, Frank O'Hara and Amiri Baraka were people I was excited by, in terms of what they wrote and how they declaimed their work. I had the fortune to become friends with them, and they were both very generous men in terms of turning on a young guy to poetry. They really showed me around. Allen Ginsberg, also.

I remember publishing a poem in a little magazine that came out from San Francisco, and I got a postcard from San Francisco that said, "I liked your poem, it was very good." It was from Allen Ginsberg, who did things like that. He said that he had just come back from India and "if I am ever in New York, I hope to meet you." All of his life, he did things like that. If he was reading a magazine, and he saw something he liked, he would send the person a postcard and say, "I like that. It's good." He would encourage people. I remember once at the University of Oklahoma in Norman, Allen was doing a reading. He was traveling around the state with Ted Berrigan, who was a poet from New York and also a good friend. I was doing Poetry-in-the-Schools programs in a nearby town, so I drove up to hear the reading. We all went to dinner, and Allen says, "Oh, by the way, you guys come up on stage." We said, "No way, this is your gig." And he said, "Oh, that's okay." So he insisted, and Ted went up on stage and read a couple of poems. I read a couple of poems, and Allen did his gig. He was very generous and gave us some of his time, and that is what I have in mind when I say there is a community of poets. You can find it in certain locations, but obviously it is something that travels with the poets if they are so inclined, and people like that were. People like that encouraged me to continue doing what I was doing.

Bain: Who are your favorite poets from the Caribbean?

Thomas: The Panamanian poet I've found most interesting is a poet named Roberto Miero. I've made English versions of some of his poems. Certainly, I thought Claude McKay was an extraordinary poet when I encountered his work and Derek Walcott, an absolutely tremendous poet. I taught his poetry for a long time. I remember seeing *Ti-Jean and His Brothers* performed in Central Park in New York during a summer-theater festival. Derek Walcott is fantastic. It's no wonder he won a Nobel Prize; his work is just so skillful and so attentive to all of the sounds of the English language from dialect to class. He manages to record those ways of speaking and presents them on equal footing because we all have something to say, and we have our own way of saying it. The poet's job is to listen and record that which is, in its own way, a celebration of our consciousness. Each one of us is a contributor to the consciousness of our time, and we don't discount somebody because we don't like the way someone talks.

Bain: In what manner do you encourage students to write creatively?

Thomas: When I do a poetry workshop, I think of the art form in the same way as people who are involved in the art of music and the visual arts think of their disciplines. That is, one learns by imitation. You practice by copying the great masters until you have the vocabulary and skills to create what you want to create. I have an article I wrote about how to teach a Derek Walcott poem as a model for writing. No one can recapture what Derek Walcott does in a poem, but by copying it and intensely analyzing it, you learn what he did and you can apply those skills to what you want to do. I don't believe in the idea that people sit down and wonderful ideas pop into their heads, and they write it down and they are geniuses. That's not the way it works. You learn by looking at the best examples of the art form and learning how those were achieved.

Bain: Describe your daily life as a poet.

Thomas: I'm always scribbling down lines that come to me that I find interesting, and someday I'll collect those into something that looks like a poem. I work on poetry the same way I work on other things. I need deadlines. So if I know there is a reading I have to do, then that becomes the deadline to work to. If I have to submit something to a publication, that becomes a deadline to work toward. Any open time, I polish up the things I have in notes or in progress or unfinished things. I'm always scribbling down things on index cards or notepaper, working toward a point.

Bain: Would you take a moment to share some of your poetry?

Thomas: This is a sequence of double haikus as one haiku runs into another haiku so that they end up being cyclic poems:

> *We puzzle each other*
> *wanting to know all we share*
> *Pretty with sun stripes*
> *Cat on armchair*
> *When mystery visits your face*
> *That measuring stare*
>
> *Smiles flutter from me*
> *You knew that you were needed*
> *A hectic schedule blur of business*
> *A sorceress to claim them*
> *from my doubting eyes*

I was interested in doing those not because it was a form I wanted to play with, but to find out what would happen if you allow one haiku to run into another. If you count them out, you would find that they are haikus, but they are all supposed to carry the same thoughts around—just something a little different to do.

> *What women could be*
> *If any less demanding*
> *Be just wonderful*
> *First there are questions*
> *Soon just as I found your lips*
> *You will find your mouth*

Bain: How have your views on poetry changed over time?

Thomas: I used to think poetry was something that was for self-expression. That was when I was in high school, and I thought what I was writing was expressing myself, my moods. Soon thereafter I began to learn from other people like Calvin Hernton, a wonderful poet, that poetry is more than that. It's not just expressing your own personal feelings. It's about expressing feelings that are open to everybody—making statements that will somehow make a change in the world. Poets make a change in the world by making people aware of something they weren't aware of before.

Bain: How would you encourage a young person to get started in poetry?

Thomas: You have to read everything that is out there. You have to read it with an open mind and learn from it whatever it has to teach. I know some poets who are talented, and they write some very good stuff, but they don't read anything. I've known these people for twenty-five years, and what they are doing now is no different or no better than what they were doing twenty-five years ago. They don't read anything, and they are still working off the same two ideas. You have to read everything and know what's happening. You take what is good for you and what you think is beneficial to others. You discard what is detrimental.

In my workshops, people have to read poetry other than their own. We read, commiserate, and congratulate each other. People have to make reports on other writers. They have to bring in work by other people and talk about why it is important or not. Then we do our own work in a similar manner. It involves being a member of a community that reads and hears about literature. That's very important.

"Been up North!" opens Calvin Hernton's poem "Remigrant" (1954), echoing the ebullient vernacular of Langston Hughes:

Been up North!
Chicago, New York, Detroit—

The poet's mood changes dramatically in the next stanza,
however:

But I'm back down home now
Back down South—to stay.
Down South:
I'll make my stand
As a human being, as an
Equal man.

Hernton's echo of the song "Dixie"—and the title of the reac-
tionary 1930 manifesto by the Nashville Agrarians—adds resonance to
the poem's defiant reclamation of the South as *home* to African Americans, terrain worth fighting for with the nonviolent tactics of the civil
rights movement.

A year later, while a graduate student in sociology at Nashville's
Fisk University, Hernton began to define a personal aesthetic—a vision
of poetry as both political necessity (the authorized voice of collective
struggle against economic oppression and racial discrimination) and in-
dividualized Romantic torment. His poems attacked the same targets
that New York's Beat poets were assailing. Hernton knew that all was *not*
well in Eisenhower's apparently placid America.

—*Extraordinary Measures: Afrocentric Modernism
and Twentieth-Century American Poetry*
(Tuscaloosa: University of Alabama Press, 2000), 133–134.

Lori Aurelia Williams

The circumstance of my growing up influenced me the most to become a writer.

Lori Aurelia Williams

I had these stories about young people that I wanted to tell. Some really uncomfortable things happen to young people, and a lot of times I don't think that they have anybody with whom to talk. That was my biggest motivation for becoming a writer.

Interview by Gary Kent

Gary Kent: You just flew in from New York where you received the 2002 PEN Phyllis Naylor Working Writer Fellowship. How did that go?

Lori Aurelia Williams: Oh, that was actually very nice. It was at the Lincoln Center in New York, at the Walter Reed Center, near the Juilliard school. It was packed. Lots of people came, and most of the writers that were awarded fellowships were playwrights and very established writers, so you know I felt like I was among greatness.

Kent: It is a great honor, and congratulations to you.

Williams: I did feel very honored, and very blessed also, because I won — and I won by unanimous vote, which really surprised me. So I was just very happy, and people were nice. They just kept coming up to me and congratulating me and asking me about my career.

Kent: In terms of your career now, what does this award mean? Will this give you some financial help to write your next work?

Williams: Yes, the award is five thousand dollars, and it's meant to help you finish the book that you are working on — a work in progress. It's given by Phyllis Naylor, who is a very well-known writer for children and young adults. She wanted to make it a little bit easier for writers starting out in young adult fiction, who haven't had a lot of financial success right away, because it takes a bit of time. What it means to me is that I will be able to take time off just to write, something I haven't been able to do. When I'm working — which is actually quite a bit — I work eight hours a day. And when you work eight hours a day and try to come home and write, it's almost impossible. So hopefully I can take a little time off to write, and that means a great deal to me.

Kent: In that vein, let's go back to your childhood. First of all, where were you born; where are you from?

Williams: I was born in Houston, Texas, a place called the Fifth Ward. The area that I lived in was called the Bottom, and primarily ghetto, I'll put it that way.

Kent: Were there any brothers, sisters?

Williams: I'm the youngest of four. I have one brother and two sisters.

Kent: Are there any other writers or artists?

Williams: No, no writers. My brother is a psychiatrist, and one of my sisters teaches school, and the other one works for the state.

Kent: Your work seems to be centered on the trials and tribulations of young people. You expressed in one interview that you wish you had had the naiveté that Shayla has in your stories, and her knowledge that she was going to be a great writer, to get her through the hard times. Well then, what *did* get you through the hard times? If at that early age you weren't looking forward to being a writer, what got Lori by?

Williams: I would say it just has to be faith. I had a very religious mother, and she taught us that you just have to trust in God, that no matter what the situation, you could get through it. That's how we all got through.

Kent: When did you first become aware that you should write some of this down or be a writer? Was that early on?

Williams: I started writing when I was in college. I loved English. I loved books and reading.

Kent: What was the plan? Were you going to be a teacher?

Williams: My plan originally was to be a teacher, but I found out I just wasn't cut out to be a teacher. I love kids, but they kind of take advantage of me. I'm not that great at discipline when it comes to kids. I was taking regular English classes, and I'd taken so many that I wanted to try something different. So I started taking creative writing courses, and I just started writing stories.

My first story was about a little girl that lived in the ghetto, and it's called "No More Hunger." It's actually my favorite story. She's very hungry, and she wants to eat because she lives in a very impoverished environment. She eats cold, rat-infested cereal everyday. This guy comes around, a gangster kind of guy. He's actually a drug dealer. He tells her he's going to take her out on the town, and he's going to give her food. So she goes with him, and she ends up getting shot in an alley. Not really knowing what was going on, she just wanted to try to get a better life for herself. I had to get up and read that story in front of a class, and I hated doing that. I always sat in the back of the class, but my teacher made me get up and read it. So I read the story, and when I got through reading, the room was silent. Nobody said anything, and I thought, "Was it that bad?" Then I realized that it wasn't. It was good, and they were affected by the story I told. I thought, "Well, I can do this. I can write these kinds of stories." And I just continued to do it.

Kent: Well, obviously you're very good at it, because your work has been almost an immediate success. How has that changed your life? Does the other end of writing—marketing, publicity, promotion—interfere with a writer's life or are you able to take that in stride?

Williams: I take it in stride. When I first started, because I was writing young adult fiction, I was told by a lot of people, "Don't expect a lot because those kinds of books don't get a lot of attention." And then I got mega attention. At first it was really overwhelming. People were calling, asking me to come for interviews. But after awhile, I just stopped reading the reviews. I didn't want them to affect me.

Kent: You're credited with giving a voice to young people—a true voice. I loved your comment about why Tia ends up with Doo-witty. What you had to say about that is that she could look past all the failings in his appearance and find a true heart and a true soul. Do you get any interference from the publisher or from an editor with what you want to say? Do they try to guide that, or is their guidance mainly marketing, while the writing is strictly left up to you?

Williams: I've been lucky because they haven't really interfered much in my writing process at all. I've had a little editing where maybe I needed to say this or clarify that, but I've been lucky saying what I wanted to say.

Kent: Do you know when you start to write where you're going? Do you have an outline first? What creates the spark in you?

Williams: I usually know where I'm going, what it is I want to do with the text. I think most writers know what they want to do. I have an idea of where I want to end up before I start anything.

Kent: Who are some of the people, what are some of the circumstances, that influenced you most to become a writer?

Williams: I suppose the circumstance of my growing up probably influenced me the most to become a writer. I've always said that I had these stories about young people that I wanted to tell, and I was one of those young people. I was one of those kids that grew up in a bad situation, who really had nobody to talk to about it, and I think that's the biggest influence on my writing. Sometimes you have to write things that make people uncomfortable to get them out in the open. Some really uncomfortable things happen to young people, and a lot of times I don't think that they have anybody with whom to talk. That was my biggest motivation for becoming a writer.

Kent: Since you write primarily about young people, do you keep up alliances or affiliations with young people? Your use of language and your use of dialogue are right on target. And you are a young person yourself, but it seems like the patois of young people changes every three or four years. Is that a problem?

Williams: Well, one thing that happens as a young adult writer is that you end up all the time around young people. It's almost impossible not to, so I just listen and talk. The more you listen and talk, the more you pick up. I'll always just be a young person at heart.

Kent: What do you see in the future for your writing projects? Have you been approached by filmmakers, or have you been interested in having something done in film with your work?

Williams: I'd love it, that would be great, but maybe that would be in the future. Right now I just take one day at a time, writing. I started off writing adult literature. I've written memoir, and at some point maybe I'll do some more of that.

Kent: What's been the most fun about a writing career for you?

Williams: I would say the travel. I didn't travel a lot before I wrote, and I've gotten to go to some pretty nice places. The travel and meeting people who've read the book. Especially when I go to conferences where there are teachers and librarians and students, you get really good feedback about the book. That feels good because then I feel like I'm actually doing something, accomplishing something. I want to make a difference.

Kent: Obviously you're doing that. Who is the living person you admire the most?

Williams: It would have to be my sister. When my mother died she kind of got stuck with being a sister/mother, and she never really complained about it. Whenever I need anything, she's willing to get it for me, whatever I need. You know writing is difficult, especially when you're starting out and you don't have the finances. When I can't pay for something, she does. She just does a really great job with her students and everything else. So I admire her more than anybody.

Kent: Is there a writer that you admire, living or dead, more than other writers, or are there several that come to mind?

Williams: I admire Zora Neale Hurston. She was actually one of the first writers that inspired me. She does just amazing things with writing, that I think nobody's ever done. Her fiction just has life to it. She proves you can do anything with words. When I started out writing *When Kambia Elaine Flew In from Neptune*, I remembered that you could do anything you wanted to do with words and character. Anger could become Mr. Anger and things like that. I got that a lot from her. Then I also admire and read books by Sandra Cisneros. I like her writing a lot. She's a very open and down-to-earth person when she writes. Her characters are great. I love the dialogue and the way they talk. Another one is Rudolfo Anaya.

He's another writer that does great things with literature. His book *Bless Me, Ultima*—which is one of my favorite books—was adopted by the mayor's office and the Austin Public Library as the first annual selection of The Mayor's Book Club.

Kent: Is there a hidden talent you have that we don't know about, that you wish you could express? What is it, Lori, about you that we need to know?

Williams: Hidden talent? When I was younger, I really wanted to be a singer. You know, I've got a pretty good voice. I used to have a really good voice, but I stopped using it. Maybe that's my hidden talent.

Kent: That kind of figures though because of your love of words.

Williams: I was thinking about what you were asking me about writing for young people, and I think young people don't really change that much. I mean it looks like they do, maybe some of the phrases change, but they don't really change that much. The way you feel at that age never changes, kind of that awkward, unsure-of-yourself age.

Kent: That's a good point. What advice do you have for writers that are just starting out now?

Williams: I hear a lot of writers tell me that they get discouraged because they get rejection letters. I would say just don't give up. A lot of times rejection letters have absolutely nothing to do with your writing. It has to do with the persons that read it. Maybe they didn't think it was right for the magazine or right to be published by them. You should never give up; keep going.

I remember taking a class from Rolando Hinojosa, and one of the things that he said was write about what you know. For writers that are just beginning that's probably one of the best pieces of advice that you can get. Write about what you know because that's going to be the thing that's closest to you, the thing that you understand best and have the most heart about. Not that people can't write different kinds of fiction, but if you're really unsure what to write about, just take it back to your roots. Take it back to what you understand.

Kent: I cannot let you escape the interview without asking you where you come up with these great titles. *When Kambia Elaine Flew In from Neptune* and *Shayla's Double Brown Baby Blues*—those are great titles. Where do you find them?

Williams: I like things to be unique for one thing, and I like them to reflect the book. *When Kambia Elaine Flew In from Neptune* was a perfect name for that book because of Kambia, who's a little girl who lives in a fantasy world because of the abuse that she suffered. She's the spacey kid. *When Kambia Elaine Flew In from Neptune* was perfect for that. It's a line that the main character actually utters in the book when she refers to Kambia, so it was perfect to give the book this kind of other-worldly feeling. For the second book, it's a bit more complicated book. It has a whole cast of characters that have a lot of different personalities. So *Shayla's Double Brown Baby Blues* actually worked well for that book because it's a book in which everything doubles, and also there are at least three babies. There's a set of twins, and the book begins with Shayla, who is upset over the birth of her new little sister who gets born on her birthday. So she refers to it as being two Shaylas—herself and the other baby that gets born.

I pulled Kambia to me and gave her a big hug, the way Tia used to do me when I was really upset about something. She felt cold. I closed my eyes and tried to make sense, once again, out of her Wallpaper Wolves story and her mom. What really went on in her house? I thought about going into the kitchen and telling Mama the wolves story, but I had promised Kambia that I wouldn't. "Your word is your bond," Grandma Augustine always says to me. "If people can't trust the words that come outta your mouth, they can't trust you." I pulled Kambia closer to me. I could feel her bony ribs through the thin material of her dress. It felt like she hadn't eaten in a while, but then if I had Wallpaper Wolves hanging on my walls, I guess I probably couldn't either. I took a deep breath and let it out, and pulled her dress straps up over her shoulders for the second time. As I did the sound of pounding came from the window.

"Kambia Elaine!" Kambia's mom's shrill voice yelled out, between her blows to the side of her house. Kambia flinched, but she didn't move. "Kambia Elaine," her mom repeated. "If you're under that house, you better bring your behind out! If you don't come out, I'm gonna make you real sorry!" Kambia already seemed pretty sorry to me. I wondered what her mother could do to make her feel worse.

—*When Kambia Elaine Flew In from Neptune*
(New York: Simon and Schuster, 2000), 115.

Mary Willis Walker

What helped me become a writer were
the secret things I did.

Mary Willis Walker

It was keeping a secret journal that I would have died if anyone had seen. Or steal-ing my father's adult mysteries and reading them at an early age under the covers with a flashlight. Having a rich imaginary life when I was a child. Being able to imag-ine myself in other worlds and being other people.

Interview by Gary Kent

Gary Kent: Your critical reviews—"superb suspense, masterful writ-ing"—are grand. *Publishers Weekly* informs us that your readers are left cheering, weeping, gasping for breath.

Mary Willis Walker: Oh, I'd like to think that's true!

Kent: Those are great comments. Where did this all start?

Willis Walker: It all started when I used to steal my father's hard-boiled mysteries from his bedside table and read them at an inappropriate age. This was in Milwaukee, Wisconsin, where I was born. I grew up and lived there until I went to college.

Kent: Do you remember some of those authors your father had?

Willis Walker: Oh, yes! He used to have on his bedside stand John D. McDonald and Mickey Spillane. I was reading Mickey Spillane when I was ten, and of course I read the Nancy Drew series with great interest. So I grew up very early reading all kinds of fiction, but especially, I've always loved mysteries.

Kent: Was there a period or a time you decided to become a writer?

Willis Walker: I thought about it for decades. I would finish reading a book, often a mystery, and think, "I could do that." I might even be able to do that better than the particular book that I just finished. But I didn't know how to get started. I was really a late starter. I didn't write a word of fiction until I was in my early forties. My first book was published when I was forty-nine, so as these things go, that's a very late start.

Kent: Had you been writing in some other field before then, or did you just come very late to writing?

Willis Walker: I had done some newspaper writing for some years, working for small newspapers, but never fiction until I sat down and started to write a mystery in midlife.

Kent: How did you feel when you finished that first book?

Willis Walker: It was a combination of being set free from prison and losing your best friend all at the same time. You've lived within that story for a long period of time. You've been a slave to it, then suddenly your time frees up.

Kent: Did you send it off to publishers or to agents?

Willis Walker: When I thought *Zero at the Bone* was ready for me to send out, I didn't know anyone. I read this article in *Publishers Weekly* on how to get an agent because people told me you needed an agent to sell fiction. I followed what that article said. I wrote query letters to thirteen New York agents and sent the first ten pages of the manuscript, even when they didn't ask for it. The man who became my agent called me from a street corner in New York. He said he'd just read it, and would I send him the manuscript? So I did. He liked it, thought he could sell it, and did I want him to? I did want him to, and he did sell it. So this is not your typical story. It was a fantasy story—I was afraid I didn't pay my dues on the selling of a first manuscript.

Kent: What other influences did you have in becoming a writer?

Willis Walker: It's funny that you asked that. I was recently at an elementary school talking to fourth graders. I was the visiting writer. After I told them about how books are published and showed them drafts, a little girl with glasses in the back raised her hand and said, "Did the things you did in language arts in fourth grade help you to become a writer?" The teacher was standing in the back of the room with her arms folded, but I had to tell the truth. And the truth was no. What helped me become a writer were the secret things I did. It was keeping a secret journal that I would have died if anyone had seen. Or stealing my father's adult mysteries and reading them at an early age under the covers with a flashlight. Having a rich imaginary life when I was a child. Being able to imagine myself in other worlds and being other people. So school activities, English classes, did more to deter me than to encourage me.

Kent: Did you have formal writing courses geared to becoming a writer?

Willis Walker: I was an English major, but I never had a writing course. Then when I started to write *Zero at the Bone,* I discovered I didn't know how to do it. I thought that because I had been a voracious reader, appreciator, and critic, I would know how to write, but I didn't. So I started going to writers' workshops and found a group of first-time writers. We made a critique group, and gradually I taught myself with some help.

Kent: *Zero at the Bone* was your first book?

Willis Walker: It was my first book, and the seed of that, the kernel, was that I wanted to have a woman character who was independent and brave, but who had one thing that really scared her. Then I read in *Texas Monthly* an article that Stephen Harrigan had written about a tiger attack at the Houston zoo. A keeper was pulled into the cage by a tiger and killed. I got to thinking, what if that were murder and not the accident that it looked like? So those were the things that worked together for me to build the story.

Kent: Your books are bestsellers: *Zero at the Bone, All the Dead Lie Down, Under the Beetle's Cellar, The Red Scream.* Where do your ideas come from?

Willis Walker: Sometimes it is from articles in the newspaper, and sometimes from little things that happen. *All the Dead Lie Down,* for example, started when I was out having dinner on a porch. There were some homeless people who were camped out under the deck of the fancy restaurant. One of the waiters told me that they'd had a lot of trouble because the homeless started fires down there to cook on and keep warm and had set the deck on fire. So they'd made an arrangement with them that they wouldn't build fires under the deck. I just saw this level with the homeless camped out, and all the wealthy people up above drinking wine. It was an image that I wanted to explore, and it developed into that book.

Kent: What sustains you as a writer? When it gets tough and you're sitting there, and nothing comes? Have you ever experienced that?

Willis Walker: Oh, yes, I have experienced it, and the tough times are really tough. What has sustained me in the past is that to some degree you fall in love with what you are writing. If I go back to a passage or scene that I really like, and read or rework it a bit, it helps me get over the humps where it's hard going. Sometimes if I'm having a hard patch in the writing, I skip that for a while and move forward in the work. It's such a delightful freedom to know that you don't have to do it sequentially, you can move around. I thought when I started writing that it was a very linear, sequential activity, but it doesn't have to be.

Kent: Which living person do you most admire?

Willis Walker: My father. I have watched him become more flexible and understanding and compassionate with age rather than having the reverse happen. He's in his nineties now, and better than he has ever been. I admire his ability to grow and change and weather difficulties with good humor. He has actually gone with me on some of my book tours. On one occasion, we arrived in Denver in September, and there was a snowstorm. It was an unexpected early snow and ice storm. My father lives in Florida and thought he'd never again in his lifetime have to endure snow, but there it was. So we went to a signing at a bookstore in Denver, and the electricity was off. I looked over at my father, and he, all bundled up, was talking to people and showing them pictures of my daughters and me at the Edgar Awards ceremony, saying, "Mary won the Edgar you know."

Kent: What advice do you have for writers just starting out in their career?

Willis Walker: My advice to writers is the same I give myself. Identify your obsessions, your passions, and write about those things that you know to be true. Enjoy the process because that's often the best part of writing, and sometimes it is the only part.

Sarah Jane looks up at the wooden deck, at the thin stripes of harsh floodlight between the slats. Carefully she turns over on her back, keeping her big canvas bag under her head. She tries not to make any noise, not to rustle the flattened cardboard refrigerator carton she is lying on. She stares up at the deck, three feet above. Black forms break up the yellow stripes. The lines of light flicker. A clopping right over head makes her blink. Then a scraping noise.

Someone's sitting down. Damn. This has never happened, in the . . . how long has it been? More than a year. No one has ever sat down on the deck after dark. Occasionally someone would wander out, but they would see it was closed and leave.

Now there are voices overhead, male voices. A smooth, phony-type voice is droning. She catches some words. "Full moon tonight, sir. Real pretty. Sure it's not too cool for you out here? Technically, the deck is closed, but since your friend needs to smoke—"

A loud laugh barks out. "Fine. Real fine. You just be sure and tell Mr. Vogel I'm out here when he comes. And, pardner—let's keep it private out here, know what I'm saying?" This voice is one of those bossy, king-of-world voices Sarah Jane hates the most. It's the kind of voice that tells you to get off the bench, get out of the park, leave the library, move along, 'cause he owns the world and you don't.

—*All the Dead Lie Down*
(New York: Doubleday, 1998), 2–3.

Bill Wittliff

All along I wanted to tell stories, and as it happened my best way turned out to be film.

Bill Wittliff

I was raised in a time before television was around. People sat on the porch in the evenings and told stories. I would sit there, just rapt, listening to these wonderful stories about people and about places that I knew.

Interview by Gary Kent

Gary Kent: You've done so much work in film and in writing. Much of your work has been connected with people such as cattlemen, drovers, ranchers, and fishermen. What is it in your background that gives you such an identification with all of these people? Where were you born?

Bill Wittliff: I was born in Taft, Texas, which is down on the Gulf Coast. My mom and dad were divorced when I was eighteen months old. Mother ran a little telephone office in Gregory during World War II, so my entire background, including my family and how I was raised, is ordinary folk.

Kent: Is Taft a relatively small town?

Wittliff: Yeah, it is. We didn't live there long, so I don't really have any recollection of Taft at all. I was born there, but that's it.

Kent: When you were a youngster in school, did you have any idea that you wanted to be a writer, or in the film industry?

Wittliff: No, but all along I wanted to tell stories and, as it happened, my best way turned out to be film. I tried to write in any number of other mediums, but screenplays worked for me in ways that other forms didn't.

Kent: Were you a moviegoer when you were a kid? Did you hang out at the theater?

Wittliff: Oh, yeah, the Saturday matinees. I loved the *Durango Kid* and all the B Westerns. Incidentally, I was a Roy Rogers man rather than a Gene Autry man.

Kent: Did you study screenwriting?

Wittliff: No.

Kent: How did you pick it up?

Wittliff: I just simply wrote one the way I thought I might see it. Bud Shrake was the first person to read any of my stuff other than my wife, Sally, and he gave me a few pointers here and there about crafting a screenplay.

Kent: What is it that connects you so strongly to people?

Wittliff: As I mentioned a while ago, my mom ran the little telephone office in Gregory, and then later the one in Edna. At that time very few people had telephones; it was during the war. When someone got a call from Washington that their son had been lost in battle, or got a call that that son had been found and was alive, almost without exception, those people would come to our house to get the news. So the whole world came through our house, which was also the telephone office. This whole world was made up of the greatest variety of humankind you can imagine; I mean, solid, hardworking poor folks, and also people who were well-to-do. That was true in Gregory; it was also true in Edna.

Kent: Were there other writers or artists in your family?

Wittliff: Not writers. My mother was a wonderful artist. She painted and was great at crafts, too. My grandfather was the one who loved to tell stories, and I'm sure I get my love of storytelling from him. I was raised at a time before television. Radio was there, certainly, but television was not. In my childhood, people still sat out on the porch in the evenings and told stories. I would sit there, just rapt, listening to these wonderful stories about people and about places that I knew. A good storyteller was always a special person to me, and still is.

Kent: When you were a lad, you say the war was going on. Do you remember much about it? Was it a frightening thing lurking off in the dark somewhere?

Wittliff: Gregory is near Corpus Christi, and from time to time there would be blackouts where we would have to pull black shades down over the windows so that no light could get out. Everyone feared there was a Japanese submarine out there in the Gulf near Corpus Christi, and that was frightening. And, of course, the calls that came through. Very early you had a sense of life and death, because life and death were coming through that little office, through the telephone lines — a son missing in Guadalcanal, or lost in Guadalcanal, or found somewhere else still alive.

Kent: I think we saw or felt some of these things you're discussing in *Raggedy Man*.

Wittliff: That was based in part on my childhood, and it was really meant to be a thank you to my mom because she lived that life. That was Mom at the switchboard. She literally worked it twenty-four hours a day, with no help. She even slept at the switchboard.

Kent: Did your mother see *Raggedy Man*?

Wittliff: Oh, yeah.

Kent: What was her response?

Wittliff: She was moved by it, and she just adored Sissy [Spacek]. Sissy and my mom became friends during preproduction. Mom talked to Sissy a lot about what it was like to run a switchboard during the war and to have to raise two little boys at the same time. I don't think Mother really realized what she had been through until she saw the film.

Kent: What was the first thing you wrote, period?

Wittliff: As far as film, you mean? *Barbarosa*.

Kent: Did you just send that off, or did Bud Shrake help you get that going?

Wittliff: Bud popped over here — actually the day after I finished it — and saw it on the desk. He said, "Damn, you're writing screenplays!" I said, "Well, I'm piddling around." So Bud took it home and read it. The next morning he called me and said, "This thing'll sell." Bud sent it to his agent in New York, who didn't like it, but she sent it to a couple of producers who did. Nothing came of it, but it gave me a certain confidence to try another one. Bud was the first one to be my mentor, my supporter, and my helper, other than my family.

Kent: Someone said the other day in an interview that the written word was the best way to express feelings and emotions to the public at large, and I've wondered about your thoughts on that. Is the visual impact equally important?

Wittliff: It's all a matter of combinations: the right words with the right visual images. I've pretty much decided that — in film writing — it's not so much what you say as it is what you don't say. You don't want to tell the audience everything; you just make them observers if you do. But if you leave things for them to figure out, then they become participants in the story. They get involved, and of course that's what an audience wants. They want to disappear from their daily lives for an hour or two. Art in any form seeks to do that — transport the audience, absorb them.

I'm repeating myself now, but it's never what you tell an audience, but what you allow them to tell themselves. You try to remind them of things they knew but didn't remember they knew. It's why the first response to great art in any form — writing, film, poetry, music, painting, whatever — is always an instant "yes." It's an "ah, yes." It's a recognition of something that was already in us as fellow beings on this spinning globe. It's the artist's job to pull that out of us so we can look at it, maybe see ourselves deeper, fuller.

Kent: How did you get started in photography?

Wittliff: I've always been interested in the visual. When our son Reid was born I bought a used Nikon, which was the first good camera I ever had. Shortly after, Joe Frantz invited me to go with him to a ranch down in Mexico where they were still ranching and cowboying in the old ways, ways that had disappeared in Texas a hundred years ago. I was absolutely transfixed by what I saw. For three years I went back and forth to Mexico to photograph the vaqueros, the Mexican cowboys. It was a great adventure.

Kent: Your film work is excellent, and it seems to come to you naturally. What should a novelist who decides to be a screenwriter know about writing for the screen?

Wittliff: To my mind, the best screenplays are closer to poetry than they are to novels or any other form. They're closer to poetry because you have to pack a lot of meaning in the silences between the lines. It's the art of omission. It's all the things you could say but don't. What you're really doing is setting up poles. If you set the poles just the right distance apart and the meaning lies in the jump between them, then the audience can make that jump.

Kent: I see. Very well put.

Wittliff: But awkwardly expressed.

Kent: Who were your favorite writers when you were a youngster? Were there people you absolutely loved and couldn't wait to get their books from the library?

Wittliff: Mark Twain comes instantly to mind. Then of course I read the Texas writers: J. Frank Dobie, Fred Gibson, and Tom Lea. Dobie had a huge influence on me because he was the first Texas writer — that I came across, anyway — who wrote about things and places I was familiar with. It was the first time that I realized writing could come out of my own piece of ground, my own experiences. I was maybe eleven or twelve. It absolutely set me on fire, to realize that. Prior to that I thought all writing came from across great oceans, and that all writers had the finger of God on them, and it just poured. It was only later that I realized that writing is writing. You write and you write and you write. When it's good, you're glad, and you keep writing. When it's bad, you throw it away and keep writing.

Kent: Other than writers, who are some of the people that affected you most in your life?

Wittliff: First of all, my mom. I'd say "I want to do this, I want to do that," and she'd say, "Well, you have to know." She never said, "Oh, you can't do that" or "That's a silly dream" or "a silly idea." She'd say, "Well, you have to know," or "Go on with it." I met Dobie when I was in college. Dobie ignited my interest in all things southwestern. John Graves is a dear friend whose writing I admire hugely. John is a father figure to me. Bud Shrake's been helpful in so many ways. There have been so many people, so good to me, all my life.

Kent: What is it about the Texas mystique that you find so intriguing?

Wittliff: That my people are from here and go all the way back to Austin's Old Three Hundred. This is my home; I'm at home here.

Kent: For a rough-and-tumble state, Texas has a lot of people with their eye on larger horizons, and you're certainly one of the people they admire the most. Is there something about Texas that breeds this kind of frontierism, artistically?

Wittliff: The atmosphere of unlimited possibilities is still in Texas, and for an artist or writer or anybody who wants to lead a creative life, that's real food, real nourishment.

Kent: What's in the future, now, for Bill Wittliff?

Wittliff: More writing. More photography. More trying to make deals with the muses for inspiration. Those guys can be tough little bastards. Also staying involved with the Southwestern Writers Collection and the Wittliff Gallery of Southwestern and Mexican Photography, which Sally and I founded over at Texas State University in San Marcos. It's our hope that both collections will serve to inspire young people who have the urge to create, but maybe not yet the courage to try. I was like that. I know I would have found my courage much sooner if I'd known how every writer sweats to find just the right words, the right sentences to express his or her intentions.

Kent: Where and when are you the happiest?

Wittliff: With my family. And it's wonderful when the writing's going well. For me there's nothing quite like disappearing into a story, letting it take me rather than me taking it. That's great happiness.

Nita (v.o.):	I been working this switchboard night and day for two solid years. What more experience you want?
Mr. Rigby:	A war's going on, Nita. Don't you know that? Nobody's on easy street.
Nita (v.o.):	(angrily) I'm not asking for easy street. I'm asking for a chance to kiss my boys goodnight without being interrupted by a telephone switchboard.
Mr. Rigby:	I can't help you. I told you that. You're frozen in this job till the war's over or till the Employment Agency says you're unfrozen.

Nita (v.o.):	They'd change my status if you'd recommend it.
Mr. Rigby:	I can't do that.
Nita (v.o.):	I'll just quit, then . . . I'll walk out.
Mr. Rigby:	Go ahead . . . but you won't get no job nowhere else, not if you violate the law.

—*The Raggedy Man* [screenplay]
(Doty-Dayton Productions, [n.d.]), 15–16.

Bill Wright

---

*We fancied ourselves explorers and delighted
in trying to find a place where no one else
had ever been.*

Bill Wright

My high school friends and I delighted in hiking on area ranches and imagining that we were the first persons to place our foot along that creek or climb that hill. My natural curiosity drove my interest in exploration.

Interview by Ramona Cearley

Ramona Cearley: In your writing, you credit members of your family for their influence on you. Would you tell us about those family influences?

Bill Wright: I would say that there were many. My mother encouraged my love of natural history by tolerating a wide variety of pets: Flower the skunk, miscellaneous rats and mice, guinea pigs, hamsters, fish, orphaned sparrows, snakes, and insects. I developed a large mineral and fossil collection, and she enabled me to contact adults who guided my interest with recommendations, books, and time. My mom introduced me to a man who developed pictures and launched my love of photography. She tolerated chemistry in the bathroom and the smells of hypo and toners and other exotics alien to the normal household.

Perhaps the most important thing my parents gave me was example. They were both honest, hard working, and dedicated to their church and community. My dad was a tireless civic worker. He chaired many important local committees of the Chamber of Commerce and Hardin-Simmons University and was responsible for much of the economic development of Abilene during the time I was growing up. They had a strong marriage, as did my grandparents, and saw to it that my sisters and I received an excellent educational opportunity.

Cearley: Did your passion for writing, photography, and exploration develop similarly, from family interests?

Wright: I developed a love for reading early in my life that I am sure led to an interest in doing some writing myself. I heard stories from my grandmother and grandfather Bruyere about our famous relative, supposedly, the French writer La Bruyere. My interest in photography grew also from my grandfather Bruyere, who himself was a photographer and printed many pictures in his home darkroom. I was heir to a fancy certificate that he won in a county fair competition, and it hung in my own darkroom for many years. I have since passed it on to my own son, Mitchell, who follows in the photographic footsteps, or should I say tripod holes, of his father and great grandfather.

I suppose that my natural curiosity drove my interest in exploration. My high school friends and I delighted in hiking on area ranches and imagining that we were the first persons to place our foot along that creek or climb that hill. It was a natural complement to my interest in natural history.

Cearley: In *Portraits from the Desert* and in *People's Lives*, you discuss the relationship of people with the land or their environment. Would you give us an example, particularly in terms of change over a period of time?

Wright: My interest in natural history — geology, biology, for example — made the Big Bend area of Texas a magnet attracting me there as often as I found the time after my graduation from college. I have seen the land change in those fifty years. Tamarisk and other alien plants have invaded, the Rio Grande has dried up, and the droughts have come and gone, leaving the land progressively more desert-like.

The people have changed also. Once there were a few hardy souls who moved to the area to seek their own muse and escape the frenetic pace of city life. They joined the widely dispersed ranching families that began coming after the Civil War when the beef industry grew in momentum. They have now been diluted by swarms of retirees and affluent city dwellers wanting summer homes in an exotic spot. Marfa has lured artists and writers, and Fort Davis, summer tourists. Alpine has grown with the university and retirees, and Marathon has become the jumping off place for the Big Bend National Park, which continues to attract visitors from across the nation. As the years have passed, I have seen the air quality decline, traffic increase, local ranchers become more protective of their privacy and the land. I understand their concerns.

Cearley: What is your involvement with conservation efforts and wildlife sanctuaries?

Wright: Two organizations, to which I belong, the National Parks Conservation Association and the Sierra Club, both devote substantial resources to overcoming these consequences of industrialization. In my lifetime, I have seen air quality in the park degrade because of power plant emissions, from routine visibilities of over two hundred miles to present days when a visitor might be lucky to see past ten miles.

Cearley: You're working on a book now in terms of the Big Bend. What does that involve?

Wright: Presently I am making the final revisions to a manuscript to accompany June Van Cleef's photographs of the ranchers and cowboys of the Texas

Big Bend. The title is *The Texas Outback: Ranching on the Last Frontier.* Expected release date is the spring of 2005 by Texas A&M Press.

Cearley: Sam Abell, noted photographer for *National Geographic,* praises highly your storytelling and photography. Would you share with us some of your most memorable encounters in your travels?

Wright: There have been many great stories over the years. The encounter that shaped me the most I relate in my book *People's Lives,* for which Sam Abell wrote the introduction. It was 1978. I had traveled to Nepal to trek around the Annapurna Range through territory that had only recently been opened to westerners. Six months before, I had undergone major surgery for stomach ulcers, but I was determined not to let that interfere with the trip. I was tired and discouraged. My three companions were ahead of me on the trail. As I started up a particularly steep section I saw a man coming down carrying a large wicker basket of oranges on his back. I stepped aside to allow him to pass, and without my asking, he reached into the basket behind his head, withdrew a couple of oranges and handed them to me. I tried to pay him, but he refused, saying "Nameste," which means "I salute the god within you." Stunned by his generosity, I watched him disappear down the trail. I never saw him again.

As I continued up the trail, and over the days ahead, I reflected on the significance of this act of generosity. I had come to Nepal believing myself to be superior to these uneducated and simple people, but the encounter proved otherwise. That day this Nepalese bearing a heavy load on a lonely trail high in the Himalayas was the better man. I have never forgotten that lesson.

Cearley: How did this encounter influence your work? What is your approach to photographing people from such diverse communities?

Wright: It was this lesson, taught me by the kindness of a stranger, that has led me to photograph the many people I have met who reflect positive attributes of life. The survivors. These men and women, often in the worst of circumstances, still were able to experience kindness, joy, love, and hope. Certainly there are personal tragedies—victims of disease and misfortune. But the world has many writers and photographers who direct our attention to our problems. I want to show that despite the wars and conflicts that beset us, there is a positive dimension that is often overlooked. Finding this and sharing it drives my creative life.

During my high school days, friends and I sometimes camped out along Elm Creek on one friend's family ranch. We fancied ourselves explorers and delighted in trying to find a place where no one else had ever been, a place where our footsteps were the first. We added to our bird lists and fossil collections and photographed the lizards and snakes we found. We developed a taste for adventure, and within the limitations of our youth, we traveled and explored much of western Texas.

—*People's Lives: A Photographic Celebration of the Human Spirit*
(Austin: University of Texas Press, 2001), 8.

Lawrence Wright

---

*I was made to practice the craft of writing
before I had the chance to learn about it.*

Lawrence Wright

I began writing at the Race Relations Reporter *in Nashville covering the end of the civil rights movement. It was a terrific education. I got my education on the run.*

Interview by Ramona Cearley

Ramona Cearley: How do you define yourself in terms of your writing?

Lawrence Wright: I'm a writer that covers many different subjects in many different forms. Mainly I'm just interested in exploring the world, what I find curious. So anything that really captures my attention, I have the opportunity through this wonderful profession to look into it.

Cearley: How does the work come to you?

Wright: It depends. Sometimes editors call me up and ask me to write a particular subject, or someone commissions a movie screenplay. But just as often there are things that originate with me out of my own life or my reading or just my curiosity about what's going on in the world.

Cearley: What were the beginnings of your writing life?

Wright: I began my writing life at the *Race Relations Reporter* in Nashville covering the end of the civil rights movement in the early 1970s. It was a really great education. I had little experience — no experience — as a reporter. But suddenly I was thrown in and sent all over the country writing stories about Indian rights, desegregation, legal stories. It was a terrific education. I was made to practice the craft of writing before I had the chance to learn about it. I got my education on the run.

Cearley: What are some experiences that you can share with us based on your tenure there?

Wright: I had this crotchety old editor named Jim Leeson and really for a while I was the only writer he had. Because [the publication] was called the *Race Relations Reporter,* he liked to call me his only white writer. But I would go out and come back with, I thought, good articles. He would force me to take out the word "I" — the first-person singular. He forbade that word from ever being used. It was taboo to use the first-person pronoun. Till this day it's hard for me to use the word in writing, even though I wrote a memoir about growing up in Dallas during the Kennedy assassination. So I learned that from him. I learned that I need to talk to everybody, even people that I think I won't agree with. It's terribly important to get everybody's perspective in a story. That way I was able to become a reporter and see other people's points of view.

Cearley: Along those same lines, who are your early influences?

Wright: When I was in college doing a paper for a philosophy class, my philosophy professor said, "There's a writer that you might be interested in here in New Orleans named Walker Percy." He'd won the National Book Award in 1962, but he was at that point still a pretty obscure writer. I was interested in Kierkegaard in this philosophy course. Apparently there was a quote from Kierkegaard in one of these Percy books, and so the philosophy professor said, "You might be able to find something to write about by interviewing Walker Percy."

So I went across the Pontchartrain to Mandeville, Louisiana, where Percy lived — in this wonderful Old South manse that his uncle had left him. I met, for the first time, a real writer. Somebody I genuinely admired. I just loved Walker Percy's work. He was very gracious, and we kept up a correspondence for some years. So I would say that was my first big influence.

Then there were people I read that I just adored. A. J. Liebling, one of those great *New Yorker* correspondents, had written a book that was a model for me as a young writer, *The Earl of Louisiana*, about Earl Long, former governor of Louisiana. I just was crazy about that book. And Robert Penn Warren was possibly as great an influence, if not greater than the [other] two, because I was so deeply in love with the book *All the King's Men*. It just spoke to me in a way that nothing else ever had.

Cearley: One of your books, *In the New World: Growing Up with America from the 60s to the 80s*, reflects on coming of age in the sixties. Would you speak about the influences on this work and place in context some of the defining moments of these monumental times?

Wright: I grew up in Dallas during the Kennedy assassination, and twenty years after the death of the President, I did an article for *Texas Monthly* about what it was like to be in Dallas during that time. Nobody had ever really addressed that. Dallasites were hated for years, for decades, after the Kennedy assassination and held responsible for his death, and it was true that we had kind of a fascistic climate at that point. I remember those days starkly.

I set out to write a little account about it and, as I said, had a hard time writing about myself. But it was a very meaningful story for me, to go back and revisit those times. For instance, there was a rumor, and it may have happened. It appeared widely in a number of magazines and newspapers in America that when the news came over the radio in Dallas schools, the schoolchildren laughed at the news. That's one of the reasons that people were so angry at Dallas. They thought that we were rejoicing in Kennedy's death. Twenty years later I had myself hypnotized to see if I'd laughed, I was so traumatized by that. As it turned out, I don't think I did. But I was insecure enough because of that reaction, the way people felt about Dallasites in the wake of that tragedy. So when I finished [my] article, an editor at Knopf, Ann Close, asked if I would do something with it. I didn't think I had anything more to say about the assassination so I decided to continue writing a memoir. It was a mutual memoir of my life and that of my country. It starts with the early days of Dallas, the Kennedy assassination, goes through Vietnam, ends with the Reagan election and the convention in Dallas, and returns to Dallas at the end.

Cearley: In addition to journalism and memoir writing, your screenwriting is well noted. September 11, 2001, the nation endured terrorist attacks in New York City and Washington, D.C. Your 1998 screenplay *The Siege* reflects strong parallels to these events. Give us the basis of the film and possible implications of exploring terrorism through film and other media.

Wright: In 1993 or 1994 Lynda Obst, who was the producer of *The Siege*, came to Austin, and we met. She was interested in a movie about a woman in the CIA. That's all she had. She did have a Jane Doe sexual harassment suit against the CIA that she thought might be useful, but it turned out not to be. There was a real problem for a screenwriter to write about a CIA woman in the late '90s because the Cold War was over. Who was the antagonist?

I wanted to make a story out of it. It took me a year to come up with the idea that the CIA does have a real-life antagonist and it's the FBI. What they are really doing is struggling for turf. It's a bureaucratic battle. In real life what they were fighting over was who was going to be in charge of fighting terrorism, especially in this country. So that's how the movie idea got started. I then went out to interview people in the FBI, the CIA, and the counterterrorism strike force. I found out in 1995 or 1996 that the pieces of the puzzle were already on the table. They had already seen the World Trade Center being bombed in 1993. There was only a series of fortunate accidents that had kept [more] things from happening.

For instance, there was a fire in a Manila hotel room that led to the arrest of the mastermind of the Trade Center bombings. He had a plan of highjacking eleven jets; they planned to ram one into the Pentagon. Some of this is only now coming out. But had it not been for that fire, a random accident, we might have been facing this a lot sooner. The scenarios that these experts were describing were really far worse than what took place. Things that we're now scaring ourselves to death about—nuclear bombs, bioterrorism—those things were very much on their mind.

It was the director's decision that we had tone down the movie a bit because it didn't seem realistic, it didn't seem plausible. In fact, if we had done what the terrorists actually would do, it wouldn't have seemed realistic at all. What they did was too "Hollywood," in our opinion at the time. So it was not guesswork. It was already evident that terrorists could strike in the United States. We were vulnerable, and it wasn't clear how we'd react.

It was strange for me when September 11 happened. As the day unfolded, these familiar scenes began to make themselves evident. I realized there was a startling parallel with scenes in the movie. It got even more creepy in the days that followed, with Humvees in the street, Arabs being harassed and pulled in and detained. All those things that I'd envisioned as likely consequences started to happen. That was very unsettling for me. When *The Seige* came out in 1998 Arab Americans and Muslims were tired of being stereotyped in Hollywood films as terrorists. And they were just waiting for the next such movie to come out. Unfortunately, mine was the next one. But it was not at all stereotypical. It was a very sophisticated look at what was possible. It was very compassionate to Arabs, but it did imagine a great nightmare for them, one that did unfortunately come to pass. There are things that happened in the movie that have not yet come to pass; at least I hope that we haven't started torturing suspects. But the reason that was in the movie is that in Israel that's a reality. In other countries that have suffered terrorism—at a level beyond what we have experienced—indefinite detention, suspension of civil rights, and even torture, are real life features of those societies. I was imagining what would happen in our society if we had that same level of violence and had to react to it. So that the serious question that the movie asks is, What would happen to us if this happened here? [This interview was conducted in November 2001—Ed.]

Cearley: How do you decide which issues to explore? Give us a frame of reference for some of them—for example, hysteria in *Remembering Satan*?

Wright: Every writer who wants to be a part of the national conversation, whatever it is at that moment, has to find a way to address it in his own manner. For me, the early experience of being involved in *Race Relations* and the controversies over civil rights taught me the importance of objective reporting in controversial situations and the usefulness of a clear-headed reporter in such an environment.

It's just rare to get good reporting out of over-excited situations. I found that I had a certain kind of strength as a journalist, because I was unafraid of controversy. It's not that I look forward to people getting angry at me, but that is part of the price you pay for entering into the conversation. A good example of it, as you point out, is recovered memory phenomenon. That was something that happened in the late '80s and early '90s. There was a phenomenon of people remembering events that didn't actually occur. Oftentimes these memories were produced in therapy, frequently under hypnosis. They would seem to be exaggerated, a little divorced from reality.

I remember when I first got interested in it here in Austin. Some friends of mine who were therapists, whose opinion I value very highly, said that they were getting the most amazing stories from patients who had been diagnosed with multiple personalities. The patients were remembering satanic events, murdering children, slaughtering other people. They said that these satanic crimes were accounting for more than fifty murders a year in Austin alone. It's very rare that we have that many murders in total in this city.

Then I went to a workshop where a policeman was talking to other cops and social workers, and he was saying that satanists in this country were responsible for fifty thousand murders a year. That exceeds our total murder rate. I thought, "How can these people, even responsible people like policemen, be making statements like that? Maybe there's something to it." I didn't know. And obviously there was a great deal of anxiety in the country. It was fed a lot by patients in therapy who were reporting really horrible events in their childhood. So I was talking to the editor of the New Yorker, Tina Brown at that time, and I was interested in writing about multiple personalities. I told her that they often had these satanic memories, and she was mainly interested in that. So she said in her British accent, "Oh that's hot, hot, hot. Find me something like that."

I started looking through Nexus clips of stories in the country, and there were hundreds of cases around the country where people were being prosecuted for crimes that had been remembered, recovered in therapy. Soon there would be thousands. I began calling people — lawyers, cops, victims who were involved in those stories — to see which would be the most interesting and revealing story to tell. I finally found this case in Olympia, Washington, where a deputy sheriff who'd been the Republican county chairman had been convicted of crimes with satanic involvement that he'd confessed to; they were crimes of abuse against his daughters. But they escalated into these amazing charges that involved the entire county, even officials in the state.

I talked to the deputy sheriff there about what had happened. He said satanic ritual abuse exists, and this case proves it. They did have a confession. And they had a man in prison for the crimes. It seemed to me if there was a signal case in the country that would either prove or disprove the existence of these kinds of crimes based on recovered memory, that would be the best example. So that's where I went. That's where the book *Remembering Satan* takes place.

At that time it wasn't clear exactly what was going on in this country but as I began to look into it, it was obvious to me these events did not actually occur. We were in the grip of this national hysteria propagated through therapy and talk shows, popular entertainment, that suggested that people could have these appalling early childhood experiences and completely forget them, repress them, only to be remembered later in life in therapy. I'm proud of the effect that that work had in puncturing the fantasy this country was gripped by.

Cearley: What kind of feedback have you received from the book itself?

Wright: The book got a lot of acclaim, and also there were a lot of people who were very angry at it. I remember once, at a meeting of psychiatrists here in Austin, I secured an invitation from a friend. This psychiatrist from Dallas was here to address the local psychiatric association. I was interested in him because he had a book proposal in which he'd conceded that the satanic abuse didn't actually happen. He proposed that memories were fed into people that the CIA had groomed in order to make them have multiple personalities, so that one personality could carry secrets and another personality wouldn't be aware of them. I thought that's the most frightening scenario imaginable. But he was down here talking to our local psychiatrists.

What he was speaking on was really the reversal of the therapeutic triangle, the relationship of the victim, the victimizer, and the therapist. The therapist was supposed to help the victim understand the actions of the victimizer, but, according to his speech, it had been all turned around so that the therapist was now becoming, in the minds of the victim, the victimizer. Lawsuits were being launched against therapists and psychiatrists by people whose children were now accusing them of committing crimes only just now remembered, crimes of abuse typically. At the end of this speech I stood up to ask a question, and he said, "Before I call on you I want everyone in this room to know that this is Lawrence Wright, whose book *Remembering Satan* is being used in lawsuits against psychiatrists all over this country." The most wonderful introduction I've ever had. Every eye in the room turned to me and some woman said, "People are denying the Holocaust too." Well, there are bodies in the Holocaust; there are no bodies in the satanic scare. But there was that kind of criticism as well. The net effect was that it caused people to reassess what was essentially a hysterical outbreak in this country. It helped bring the chapter to a close.

By the time the interview ended, many hours later, Paul Ingram had confessed to having sex with both his daughters on numerous occasions, beginning when Ericka was five years old. He had also talked about having impregnated his younger daughter, Julie, and taken her to have an abortion in the nearby town of Shelton when she was fifteen. All of these statements accorded in a general way with the charges his daughters had made, although Ingram's confessions were still maddeningly mired in conditional phrases. Brian Schoening, who is a talkative and emotional man despite his hard-bitten exterior, said later that he was deeply affected by Ingram's detachment in describing the sexual abuse of his daughters. Schoening had never seen such apparent remorselessness on the part of an offender, and it was even more galling to him because Ingram wore the same uniform that he did. Still, there was nothing very unusual about a community leader's being caught in a disgraceful act. If the case had ended that Monday, with Ingram's tentative confession, it doubtless would have caused only a brief sensation at most. In the ordinary course of things, he probably would have been spared a prison sentence and assigned instead to psychological counseling. His case would long since have been forgotten. But no one realized then where the hole in Ingram's memory would lead.

—*Remembering Satan: A Case of Recovered Memory
and the Shattering of an American Family*
(New York: Knopf, 1994), 10–11.

Sharon Wyse

"I can put my eyes just at the top of the wheat
and see the world stretch out flat to the sky."

Sharon Wyse

I saw that Lou Ann was writing on a scrap of paper there in the wheat field. And the book took off from there, once I found her voice. Every day I was always able to find her again after a few minutes at the table, strong and true.

Interview by Linda Evans

Linda Evans: How does it feel to have published your first book, *The Box Children?*

Sharon Wyse: It's wonderful to have written a book that said what I meant to say, and to know that what I wrote is reaching people who are moved by it. Recently I received an e-mail from a college freshman in New Hampshire who wrote a paper about facing adversity, using *The Box Children* as her literary example. I met a middle school librarian who said that the book is finding a strong readership among young teens at her school. A man at a book club meeting told me he'd turned off a football game he was watching so he could finish the book! Publication made all of this possible, and that is what's best about it for me.

Evans: As a newly published author, how has your life changed?

Wyse: It feels pretty much the same. I'm busier, because I'm still working full-time in my own business, doing new writing, and doing quite a bit of book promotion. But I am still me, with my daily stuff to get through, highs and lows. I have never had a serene, writerly lifestyle, and I definitely don't now. A nice change is that now I'm being offered opportunities to speak about the book and to lead writing workshops. It turns out that I do love these gigs.

Evans: Who were the most influential people and/or events in your life?

Wyse: My parents are no doubt the most influential. Their imprint is on me with every breath I draw. I don't know how that could not be true, for anyone, and to an extent beyond which they can even imagine. Trees have been vital to me. And my son, and my husband, David.

Evans: How do you think growing up in Texas has affected you personally and professionally?

Wyse: Growing up in Texas, I had a sense that I was at the center of the universe. Maybe every child feels that? But there were songs like "Texas, our

Texas, all hail the mighty state! So wonderful, so great!" that I grew up with, and I just thought everybody in the world knew that Texas was the biggest and best thing there was. I think believing that gave me a bit of a swagger that I still have. The self-confidence part of it is great, but the I'm-better-than-you part had to go. Coming to terms with that has demanded that I listen more to others, have an enthusiastically open mind to the value and values of others. When I moved to New York City and started going on job interviews, potential bosses told me they liked to hire former Texans, that we fit right in: a little pushy, intent on getting our way, proud of ourselves. I thought it was funny, given how much anti–New York sentiment I'd absorbed from living in Texas, to be seen as similar in nature to New Yorkers! Most of my writing is set in Texas. It is more than a place — it is almost another character. It influences everything. I have a deep and abiding sense of belonging to the land and to what grows there.

Evans: You are a classically trained singer and have degrees in music, journalism, and English. Tell us more about these aspects of yourself and your life?

Wyse: I sing for the same reasons I write, because it is in me to do it, and I don't feel like myself if I'm not singing. I'm a soprano; I sing opera and oratorio repertoire. In the past ten years, parallel to my learning to write well and deeply, I have learned to use all of my voice — high, low, middle, really loud and really quiet, scary and soothing. It's amazing to make these sounds in your own body and to feel what comes up emotionally. So "finding my voice" has happened with singing and writing at the same time, part of the same big process.

My husband and I share a joke in which I come in after every voice lesson and say, "I'm finally learning how to sing!" Over and over again I feel like a raw beginner, and over and over again I feel that I have found the ultimate answer, Aha! All of it passes, and I'm left with more inside myself than I had before, feeling more, being able to do more, not from any one revelation or accomplishment, but from showing up over time to do the work. It is the same with writing.

Evans: How would you compare writing to your other personal or professional pursuits?

Wyse: Every time I start a sentence saying writing is harder or writing is more personal or writing takes the most honesty, I think of how other things really are and I think it is all the same challenge. It is hard to be disciplined, to do the things that the world isn't asking for, that are only to be done because you have it in you to do them, and you know you can't be all of who you are if you are not doing them. With writing, it is hard that you have to write things that you know are not "it" to get to what is "it." You have to keep going through the muck. I used to think I could never be a writer because I didn't feel like I knew what I was doing in advance. I thought if I were supposed to write a novel, I'd know how already. The challenge was learning to trust in my ability to find my way as I went along. So far, it isn't any easier with the second novel; the process is exactly the same. But I do have the example of myself to follow, that if I just keep showing up to the page, I'll get somewhere eventually. I think that's true for any creative endeavor.

Evans: I was intrigued by the subject of your book in *The Box Children*. What inspired you to write this book, in particular?

Wyse: I don't know the "what" of inspiration. The book grew out of my working over a number of years to find my material, the subjects and emotions that run the deepest in me, which feel like imperatives. And then, over time, to find a way to tell a tale that would have those things in it. The "finding a way" is, for me, not at all linear or explainable. If I were to show you boxes of my writing over the past fifteen years, you'd find traces of Lou Ann and the farm and other characters throughout. This particular book came out of who I am, what I think and write about, and what I wanted to say.

Evans: How much of your own experience, if any, is reflected in *The Box Children*?

Wyse: A lot of my experience is reflected in the novel. I lived on a wheat farm every summer until I was fifteen, and the farm I lived on is the one I re-created in *The Box Children*: the house, the bunkhouse, the windmill, the barn, the garden, the driveway, even the survivor rose bush; the particulars of the wheat harvest, weather, rural life in 1960. The plot of the novel is fictional, however. I didn't have a diary, there were no "box children," my mother didn't have six miscarriages, etc. The emotional truths of the novel come from my own experiences, transformed. As fellow-Texan Edward Swift, author of *Splendora*, has said, "Truths are far more interesting when you leave out the truth."

Evans: What enabled you to develop your characters and to give your main character, especially, her distinctive voice?

Wyse: I had been working with the material for a year, and it had no consistent voice or point of view. I shared it with my writing mentor, Lisa Shea, and she said, "Who is telling this story? You need to put your narrator somewhere and let her talk, see who shows up." In my mind's eye, I saw Lou Ann in the wheat field, and wrote, "I can put my eyes just at the top of the wheat and see the world stretch out flat to the sky" — the first line of the novel. I saw that Lou Ann was writing on a scrap of paper there in the wheat field. And the book took off from there, once I found her voice. Every day I was always able to find her again after a few minutes at the table, strong and true. The other characters developed as she saw them, undergirded by my years of writing in that territory.

Evans: Why did you write the story in diary form?

Wyse: Once I saw Lou Ann writing in the wheat field, it was clear to me that this was the only way she could tell her story. She had no privacy. She was barely allowed her own thoughts, and she had to find a way to record them and have them matter. She wasn't going to tell her tale as a grown-up looking back on this time — she had to be in it, each day. And there was no other way that she could be talking to the reader directly. She had to leave a record for others to read later, "people I don't know yet," as she said. Several publishers recommended that I should take *The Box Children* out of the diary form. I couldn't. The book is the diary; I knew I couldn't write it in any other way. So I had to find a publisher who valued that.

Evans: Is there anything else you would like to share about your thoughts on writing?

Wyse: For years, I wrote and hated what I wrote and wasn't able to read it, and didn't understand how it would ever become anything good. I'd write, "How will this ever turn into a book?" Even when I was working steadily on the actual novel, it felt like that a lot of the time. Yet the fact is that when I finished it, I knew it was good and whole, and it was published as I wrote it, with very few changes. All of this is to say to anyone who is trying to write but feels lost: keep going. You don't have to know what you're doing to be doing it.

Another thing is that while my son was growing up, it was very hard to find writing time. It's extremely hard to tell your child, "Don't open the door, don't come in here, I have to write now, I have to be alone to do this." It is so hard to do and yet women writers, in particular, have to do it. For this reason, it can take a far greater number of years for a woman to create a body of work. The situation also contributes to her not feeling like a "real writer" in the meantime. I don't have a solution; I just wanted to acknowledge the difficulty and to express my respect for anyone who keeps at it.

For helping me, and so many others, I want to thank writers' colonies, in particular the Ragsdale Foundation in Lake Forest, Illinois, and Byrdcliffe in Woodstock, New York. Anyone who wants to found a writers' colony with extra income or estate should do so. Writers need this kind of space and time and support so very much.

What you are reading is my diary.

I have started it just to see what will happen. I will have to be careful. Mother hunts through my room all the time to make sure I'm not hiding things from her. Her rule is Never write anything down because you never know who will see it. That rule won't work for me. I want to write everything down and I want people to see it. Not her, but other people. People I don't know yet.

—*The Box Children*
(New York: Riverhead Books, 2002), 2–3.

Suzan Zeder

I knew from childhood on that the theater held a magic and allure the likes of which I had never seen.

Suzan Zeder

When I was five, my mom gave me the option of going to New York to see a Broadway show or having a birthday party. I took the show—and my life was changed forever.

Interview by Gary Kent

Gary Kent: Suzan Zeder is an award-winning playwright whose works have been produced successfully worldwide. A professor of playwriting at the University of Texas at Austin, you hold an endowed chair in the art of playwriting. Suzan, where are you from? Early on, was there an interest in theater?

Suzan Zeder: I was born in Los Angeles but left there when I was about two years old. I grew up in Connecticut, just over the New York line, which is important only because it had a major impact on me growing up. When I was five, my mom gave me the option of going to New York to see a Broadway show or having a birthday party. For some unknown reason, I took the show — and my life was changed forever. I knew from childhood on that the theater held a kind of magic and allure the likes of which I had never seen. So all during my growing up years I would save my allowance to go into New York and see the theater.

Kent: Do you remember that first show?

Zeder: I do! Absolutely! As a matter of fact it was called *Happy Hunting*, and it starred Ethel Merman and Fernando Lamas; it was wildly inappropriate for a child. I not only remember that show, I could probably sing you every song, but I will spare you because it's nothing you'd like. It was just electric! I mean to be in that theater, to sit there and hear the downbeat of the orchestra, to see the actors coming out, to watch the dance numbers. I have never, never forgotten it. I think a lot of my own work, which has a good deal to do with the intersection of theater and young people, was probably influenced by those very early years.

Kent: Why the theater over movies? Most kids then were absolutely nuts over movies, but the theater?

Zeder: It was something about theater being live. There was something about the audience having to be there for the event to happen at all. If everybody in a movie house gets up and walks out, the movie is going to go on. But in theater, the audience is absolutely essential.

Kent: When you were this young girl going to see these Broadway shows were you thinking of yourself already as a writer?

Zeder: No, not at all. I was convinced that I would be a Broadway star and that everyone that I had ever known in my whole life would come to my dressing room and ask for my autograph. In my undergraduate years of college, I concentrated on acting. It was only when I got to graduate school at Southern Methodist University that I really discovered my own voice. By that time I had pretty much decided I wanted to write. I think as an actress I was always typecast: I would play the bossy best friend or the loud-mouth aunt. I just felt I had more voices inside me than I would ever be allowed to play.

Kent: So writing opened up a whole new, deeper place for you. Did you change your major then?

Zeder: No. It was just a sideways shift. I was very much focused on writing for adults during my first year of graduate school. But also at SMU I worked with a wonderful children's theater program. They asked me if I'd write a kids' show, and I thought, "How hard could that be?" So I wrote a play called *Wiley and the Hairy Man,* based on an old Louisiana folktale. In that experience of trying to write a child character with some fullness, some depth, some vitality, it was as if I suddenly discovered my own voice. I think that my work up to that point had been seeking a voice. I was really influenced by other writers. If I were reading Tennessee Williams, then I would sound like Tennessee Williams. It was only when I came to write *Wiley* that I found a voice that was far more authentic, that truly satisfied me as a writer.

I have always been attracted to writing about young people because of their vitality and imagination. I think that going back to that fourteen year old who was just so in love with the theater that she couldn't sleep at night, tapping into the confluence of theater and that kind of passion, set me on the career course that I have been on for the last thirty years.

Kent: That's wonderful. What was unique in your background that took you into those magic areas that children inhabit?

Zeder: Well, the dividing line between fantasy and reality — it's not even a long-distance call when you're a kid, you know? It's a very open border. The other thing is, I have always been fascinated by family relationships and how extraordinarily complicated they really are. Of course, that's been the source for dramatists since Medea threw the kids out the window and Oedipus poked his eyes out. People have been writing about parents and children forever. What was different about me was that I seemingly was able to write from the viewpoint of the child. I could take a situation and actually look at it through those lenses and have it be very fresh.

A really important play that I wrote a year after I left graduate school is called *Step on a Crack*. It's about a little girl whose father has remarried — her mother died when she was very small. She's a having a perfectly beastly time adjusting to her stepmother. The play goes in and out of fantasy and reality. The stepmother's a really lovely person, but Ellie can't see that at all. She sees the wicked stepmother. Ellie has two imaginary friends called Lana and Frisbee. They play out with her in her fantasy world and allow us to see her feeling world in a much broader and much more tangible way. That play, which was written in 1975, revolutionized my way of looking at theater. It also had a very big impact on the field, because up until that time most plays for young people were adaptations of fairy tales. But here was a three-dimensional kid, and here was a play that looked at the psychological realm of childhood in a way that touched both fantasy and reality.

Kent: What was the reception to that play?

Zeder: It took a while before producers could understand what it was about, but it just caught on like a house afire with children themselves and adults. This is what I passionately feel, that theater should be a banquet that people of all ages can come to and take what they hunger for. A really well-written play about a young person should also have points of access and recognition for adults as well. My hope is that both children and adults enter my plays with different perspectives but leave fulfilled and moved emotionally and intellectually. What was fascinating for me was to find and fully franchise both voices, the adult voice and the child voice, within a particular situation.

You asked how *Step on a Crack* was received? That was pretty positive because it was a stepmother relationship. A play I wrote several years later called *Doors* deals with a divorce from a child's point of view. That play became very popular in Canada, but I couldn't get a production for many years in this country because people felt it was just too emotionally charged for kids. Adults would say, "Oh, it has such a sad ending because it takes place on the day the dad actually leaves." Well, it was exploring some pretty painful territory for children, but the response that we got from kids was just incredible, because children would come up to me and say, "Thank goodness you're telling the truth! I know exactly how that feels because I've felt that way."

Kent: You say that you had difficulty getting it mounted at first. What does that mean?

Zeder: We originally produced it in Seattle, where it was well received. I sent the script to several other theaters, and people were a little bit frightened of it. What happened is that the Carousel Theatre Company from Vancouver came down and saw the show in Seattle and picked it up for production the next year. Then it just traveled like wildfire: it was done in Saskatchewan, it was done in Toronto, and a sort of buzz got started. Then it began to filter back down to the United States. A couple of university theaters did it next, and it was given an even fuller production by Seattle Children's Theatre. Then it won an award, and it was produced quite a bit.

Kent: By this time were you no longer thinking about writing adult plays?

Zeder: I think as I have evolved that I don't make a distinction between writing "adult" plays and "children's" plays. I am fascinated writing about children, but I don't necessarily write for them, although I do. The paradox is that if you start off writing *for* a target audience, no matter what that audience is, you automatically condescend to them. I feel that as a writer it takes all of my intellectual powers, all of my creative powers, all of my imaginative powers to fully evoke a three-dimensional child character. And if I have done that effectively, then I will be writing for children, because a child will recognize the child. I will also be writing for an adult, and I will be writing for an older person.

Many of my plays feature cross-generational roles and look at cross-generational subjects. Twenty years ago I wrote an adaptation of one of the *Oz* books, *Ozma of Oz*. I focused in that one on the relationship between Dorothy and her aging Uncle Henry. I just re-did that last year as a very large-scale musical called *Time Again in Oz*. This version is intergenerational too.

Kent: What inspires you? What makes Suzan say, "Okay, now I know what my next project is"?

Zeder: Oh, there are different points of entry for different plays. Actually the play *Doors* that I told you about, the play about divorce, occurred to me out of a conversation I had with a close friend who at that time was going through a divorce. She turned to her seven-year-old son and said, "Chris, what do you do when you're really feeling blue?" And he said, "I don't know. I just take a walk, and I look for something I like, and it just makes me feel better." Then he asked her if she'd like to take a walk, and they took a walk. I knew that this was the end of the play.

I have another play called *Mother Hicks*, whose primary narrator is deaf and speaks in sign language. That play arose from a visual image: I saw a character walking into a stage space pulling a wagon. He stops; then he comes forward to the audience and begins to sign. I really didn't know anything else about the play except that was how it started. Sometimes the inspiration comes from a commission. I was approached by the AARP to do a play about an intergenerational re-

lationship. *Do Not Go Gentle* is about a military family and the relationship between a grandmother and granddaughter and the grandmother's relationship with
another child who lives in her neighborhood. So plays have all different points of
entry: an image, a word, an idea, a theme that won't let me go, and I have to write
the play to find out what it's about.

Kent: Do you know the beginning, middle, and end before you start, or
do you just let it take you along?

Zeder: It's a combination. I do an enormous amount of research for whatever play I'm working on. My husband likes to say I'm keeping my conscious mind
out of traffic while my subconscious mind writes the play. I will read anything I
can get my hands on that is in any way related to the subject. I keep notes in those
blue bound notebooks that you use for chemistry assignments. I always try to keep
two colors of ink with me. One is to take notes on whatever I'm reading, and when
an idea occurs to me I write it in a different color. That is so that I can go back and
pick up those ideas. So I spend a lot of incubating time. People ask me, "How long
does it take to write a play?" I say, "As long as I've got." Then I write and rewrite,
and rewrite, and rewrite. I'm still rewriting pieces that I've written ten or fifteen
years ago. That's a little tricky because they're published; my publisher eventually
pulls it away from me and says, "You have to stop this now!"

Kent: How about dialogue? Writing what children say, and what adults
say? I know that's been complimented in your work. Do you have an ear or did that
come from your acting background?

Zeder: I don't think it has much to do with me. I know it sounds silly but
it's true: when I fully know my characters, they really speak through me. It's this
funny feeling that you can almost hear them; it's like taking dictation. The character's voice is the easiest thing. It is also connected to the fact that I philosophi-
cally believe that somewhere in a parallel universe the play exists. It's not my job
to create it; it's my job to find it. When you learn more about a character, or when
an actor gives you an idea, or you hear something in rehearsal that's much better,
then you can be flexible enough to get rid of that old idea and get on to what is
really true.

Kent: Do you have special places where you go to write?

Zeder: Particularly now I do, because of the demands on my life here at
the university. I really can't write while I'm in school. When I write, I put all of my
head and all of my heart in that place and time, and I can't be that divided. So my
husband and I have a place in Colorado — way, way out in the country. I go there
every summer, from the end of May until the end of the first or second week of
August. That's my writing time. That's what I consider to be the other half of my

job here. Every day begins with a long, vigorous walk, and then I usually go to the back porch if I'm doing the early process work. If I'm actually working scenes, then I'm in my study. I'll do eight-to-twelve hour days.

Kent: Have you got a word for people that are considering writing for the theater?

Zeder: Yes. Keep writing. Just keep writing. Writing defines itself in the writing. The writing will tell you what it needs, if you really trust it. The most important thing you could do as a writer is to keep that voice open and communicating, just keep writing.

Girl:	What's he saying now?
	(Tuc speaks in sign language as *Mother Hicks* interprets.)
Mother Hicks:	(Voicing for Tuc) You look at me and only see things I cannot do, things I cannot be; but I can taste the cool spring water and know what month it is. I can smell the difference between the smoke of hickory and apple wood. I can see the sharp sting of honey, and I can taste the sunrise.
Girl:	Don't he mean he can taste the honey and see the sunrise?
Mother Hicks:	He means what he says. That's the trouble with you town folks; you see and you hear, but you don't know nothing!

—*Mother Hicks*
(Louisville: Anchorage Press, 1987), act 2, scene 3.

Project Notes

IN MAY 2000 Frances Leonard, director of the Texas Council for the Humanities Resource Center (now Humanities Texas Resource Center), invited me to contribute to the "Texas Writers" exhibit by contacting writers for their promotional photographs to use in the exhibit and, later on, by taking informal portraits of the writers for inclusion in this book. The project was one I could not turn down, and it would only grow as the book slowly came into being. The journey is best described as one of community, particularly defined by the generosity of the writers and contributors.

At the 2000 Texas Book Festival I encountered Dave Hamrick, Texas literature enthusiast and editor of *John Graves and the Making of Goodbye to a River: Selected Letters, 1957–1960* (Taylor Publishing, 2000). On meeting, in his characteristic optimistic manner, Dave asked, "What's new?" I told him of the exhibit on Texas writers under way by Humanities Texas. Learning of the project, he encouraged us to expand the work into book form. From that point forward, we approached the writers with both the exhibit and the book in mind. Through Dave's guidance, we eventually met editors at the University of Texas Press and submitted our proposal manuscript in 2003. Bill Bishel, sponsoring editor, and Jan McInroy, manuscript editor, at UT Press, along with Lois Rankin, copyeditor, provided us invaluable direction and support throughout the publication process.

Early on, to develop the book, we invited a team of interviewers — many of whom are members of the Writers' League of Texas Radio Collective — to conduct informal interviews of the authors originally featured in the exhibit. In a few cases interviews were conducted via e-mail; the majority were conversations taped during in-person visits. At every turn, the writers shared their passion for reading and writing. In some instances, interviewers entered into mentoring relationships with writers whom they met through their work on the project.

The book came to fruition through the collaborative efforts of many people, in particular the interviewers who volunteered much of their time. Teresa Taylor, Gary Kent, and Graham Stewart contributed the majority of interviews.

They were available from beginning to end, and we followed their exceptional lead. Ayo Bain, K Bradford, Susan Daniels, Kyra Edeker, Linda Evans, Mark Finn, Liz Gold, Joe Holley, Rick Klaw, Julie Koppenheffer, Bryce Milligan, Henry Mills, Leslie Nail, Graham Shelby, Bruce Snider, Don Webb, and Ric Williams all contributed one or more interviews. Peggy Hailey did the outstanding research for the bibliography section. Mashon Carter, Audrey Smith, Kayla Rivera, Bobby French, and Eduardo Vera contributed transcripts of the taped interviews. The Writers' League of Texas, most especially Sally Baker and Beverly Horne, gave immeasurable support throughout the project. Jill Bartel, Barbara and Jack Baum, Lisa Germany, Zara Houshmand, Krista Keosheyan, Rich Levy, Glenn Lord, and Amy Tharp Nylund provided assistance. Staff at the Southwestern Writers Collection at Texas State University—San Marcos provided information for exhibit panels. Humanities Texas funded in part production of the exhibit and the book. Humanities Texas Resource Center director Frances Leonard and staff members Jic Clubb and Henry Mills are credited for the development of the exhibit and its touring schedule, along with contributions to the book.

On a personal note, a special thanks is due my family, whose love and unconditional support are gratefully acknowledged.

In the making of this book to showcase Texas literature in its diversity and at its finest, our journey began quietly. We showed up at each writer's door and were welcomed inside. This book is a reflection of their gifts to us.

In *Goodbye to a River*, John Graves indicates that the point of his trip down the Brazos River was simply to be there. "It is as purely Texas country as you can find," he writes. Our sentiments precisely.

—Ramona Cearley

WENDY BARKER

Wendy Barker was born September 22, 1942. She received her B.A. and M.A. from Arizona State University and her Ph.D. from the University of California at Davis. Her collection of poems, *Way of Whiteness*, received a Violet Crown Award for poetry from the Writers' League of Texas in 2000. As a critic, Barker is the author of *Lunacy of Light: Emily Dickinson and the Experience of Metaphor* and a coeditor of *The House Is Made of Poetry: The Art of Ruth Stone*. She has received grants from the National Endowment for the Arts and the Rockefeller Foundation and has published widely. Barker lives in San Antonio, Texas, and is a professor of English at the University of Texas at San Antonio.

SARAH BIRD

Sarah Bird was born in Ann Arbor, Michigan, December 26, 1949, and raised within a military family. In 1973 she received a B.A. in anthropology from the University of New Mexico and in 1976 her master's degree in journalism from the University of Texas at Austin. Bird is the author of novels and screenplays, as well as magazine features in such publications as *Cosmopolitan*, *Mademoiselle*, and *Ms.* Her career as a fiction writer began with five romance novels under the pseudonym Tory Cates and a mystery thriller under her own name, Sarah McCabe Bird. With the publication in 1986 of *Alamo House: Women Without Men, Men Without Brains*, Bird turned toward literary fiction, where her wit and comic satire found greater range. Her next three novels, *The Boyfriend School* (1989), *The Mommy Club* (1991), and *The Virgin of the Rodeo* (1993), established her reputation as one of Texas' most lively and entertaining contemporary writers. In 2001, Bird published *The Yokota Officers Club*, a critically and popularly acclaimed novel drawing on the author's experiences as a young adult in Okinawa. The novel received the Jesse H. Jones Award for Best Book of Fiction from the Texas Institute of Letters in 2001. Bird lives in Austin with her husband, George, son, Gabriel, and loyal dog-friend, Porgy.

JAY BRANDON

Jay Brandon was born September 30, 1953, in Dallas, Texas. One of the country's best-regarded writers of legal thrillers, Brandon was nominated for an Edgar Award for his 1990 novel, *Fade the Heat*. His first nonfiction book, *Law and Liberty: A History of Practicing Law in San Antonio*, was published in 1997. In addition to his law degree, Brandon holds a master's degree in writing from Johns Hopkins University. His books have been published in more than a dozen foreign countries and have been optioned for movies by Steven Spielberg, Bill Cosby, and Burt Reynolds, among others. Brandon has practiced law at the Court of Criminal Appeals, the highest criminal court in Texas, as well as at the Bexar County District Attorney's Office and the San Antonio Court of Appeals. He is now in private practice in family and criminal law.

BOBBY BYRD

Bobby Byrd was born April 15, 1942, in Memphis, Tennessee. The author of nine books of poetry, he has received a fellowship in poetry from the National Endowment for the Arts, a D. H. Lawrence Fellowship, and an International Residency Fellowship to live in Mexico, the latter funded jointly by the NEA and the Instituto Nacional de Bellas Artes de Mexico. Raised by his widowed mother and a black female servant (Darthula "Tula" Baldwin), he grew up in Memphis during the golden age of that city's music. In 1963 he went to Tucson, where he attended the University of Arizona. Since then he has lived in the American Southwest. El Paso and the border region have become home to Bobby and Lee, his wife. With his daughter Susannah Mississippi Byrd, Bobby coedited *The Late Great Mexican Border: Reports from a Disappearing Line*.

LEE BYRD

Lee Merrill Byrd was born and raised in New Jersey but has spent most of her life in the Southwest and Texas. Lee and her husband, poet Bobby Byrd, are publishers of Cinco Puntos Press. The Byrds publish fiction, nonfiction, poetry, and children's bilingual literature from the American Southwest, the U.S./Mexico border region, and Mexico. They have three children and four grandchildren and live in El Paso. Lee's collection of short stories, *My Sister Disappears*, was published by Southern Methodist University Press in 1993. It received a Southwest Book Award and the Stephen F. Turner Award from the Texas Institute of Letters for the best first work of fiction in 1993. In 1997 she was the recipient of the Dobie Paisano Fellowship.

VIOLA CANALES

Viola Canales is a native of McAllen, Texas, who left home at age fifteen to accept a scholarship to St. Stephen's Episcopal School in Austin. She graduated from Harvard and Harvard Law School and has worked as a litigation and trial attorney, as well as a community organizer for the United Farm Workers. *Orange Candy Slices and Other Secret Tales* is her first book. A novel, *Angels with Mexican Faces*, and a children's book, *A Child's Christmas in Magical Mexico*, are forthcoming. She currently lives in Stanford, California.

GARY CARTWRIGHT

Gary Cartwright was born August 10, 1934, in Dallas, Texas, and reared in nearby Arlington. A senior editor at *Texas Monthly* since 1982, Cartwright is the author of several books. His work has appeared in *Harper's, Life,* and *Esquire.* A former newspaper reporter and sportswriter, Cartwright is the recipient of numerous writing awards, including the Dobie Paisano Fellowship, the Texas Institute of Letters Stanley Walker Award for Journalism, and the Carr P. Collins Award for nonfiction. He lives in Austin, Texas, with his wife, Phyllis.

PAUL CHRISTENSEN

Paul Christensen was born March 18, 1943, in West Reading, Pennsylvania. He received his B.A. at the College of William and Mary in 1967, his M.A. at the University of Cincinnati in 1970, and his Ph.D. at the University of Pennsylvania in 1975. A poet, essayist, and professor of English at Texas A&M University, Christensen has lived in Texas since 1974. A member of the Texas Institute of Letters, he has received three Pushcart nominations and served as a Fulbright senior lecturer in Austria and Norway. His poems and essays are published in numerous journals and reviews throughout the United States and abroad. He lives part of the year in France, where he is a contributing editor to *France Today.*

J. CALIFORNIA COOPER

J. California Cooper, recognized as one of America's premier storytellers, was born in Berkeley, California. From 1987 to 1994 Cooper lived in Marshall, Texas, her father's hometown, where she continued writing her novels and short stories. She is the author of the novels *Family* and *In Search of Satisfaction* and four collections of short stories, including *Homemade Love* and *Some Love, Some Pain, Sometime*. Cooper has written seventeen plays and was honored as Black Playwright of the Year in 1978. In 1988 she received the James Baldwin Award and the Literary Lion Award from the American Library Association, and in 1989 received the American Book Award. Cooper was honored at the Texas Book Festival in 2000 and was a featured speaker at the National Book Festival in Washington, D.C., in 2001. Cooper lives in northern California.

ELIZABETH CROOK

Elizabeth Crook was born April 9, 1959, in Houston, Texas. She attended Baylor University in Waco, then Rice University in Houston, where she studied creative writing under Max Apple and graduated in 1982 with a B.A. in English. Her best-selling first novel, *The Raven's Bride*, was published in 1991 by Doubleday and edited by Jacqueline Kennedy Onassis. In 1993 Crook was inducted into the Texas Institute of Letters. Her second novel, *Promised Lands: A Novel of the Texas Rebellion*, also edited by Ms. Onassis at Doubleday, was published in 1993. Both books have been reissued by SMU Press as part of the Southwest Life and Letters Series. Crook has published in periodicals such as *Texas Monthly*, *Publishers Weekly*, and the *Southwestern Historical Quarterly*, a publication of the Texas State Historical Association. Crook lives in Austin with her husband and two children.

ANGELA DE HOYOS

Angela De Hoyos, poet, publisher, and editor, was born in Coahuila, Mexico, and came to the United States as a child. Influenced by the Texas farmworkers' struggle and the Chicano literary movement, De Hoyos' early poetry highlights political issues. As publisher and editor of M&A Editions, De Hoyos served a critical role in publication of Chicano writings; her contributions to Chicano letters were recognized in 1993 by the National Association of Chicano Studies. During the San Antonio Poetry Festival in 1994, De Hoyos received a Lifetime Achievement Award and recognition by the Texas Commission on the Arts. In Europe, she is among the best-known United States Latina writers, and her work has been translated into fifteen languages. Two book-length studies of her writing have been published, *Angela De Hoyos: A Critical Look* (1979) and *The Multi-faceted Poetic World of Angela De Hoyos* (1985). De Hoyos is one of the coeditors of *Daughters of the Fifth Sun: A Collection of Latina Fiction and Poetry* (1995) and *¡Floricanto Sí! A Collection of Latina Poetry* (1998). She lives in San Antonio, Texas.

MYLÈNE DRESSLER

Mylène Dressler was born in The Hague, The Netherlands, and as a child emigrated with her family to the United States, spending many years moving back and forth between California and Texas. After an early career as a professional ballet dancer, Dressler turned to her other serious love, the English language, receiving her B.A. in English from the University of San Francisco and her Ph.D. from Rice University. Her first novel is *The Medusa Tree*, completed while she was a Fulbright Fellow in Mexico. After teaching for several years as a professor at Rice University and the University of St. Thomas in Houston, Dressler devoted herself to writing full-time. Her second novel, *The Deadwood Beetle*, was well received and named a Book Sense Pick as well as one of the best books of 2001 by the *Christian Science Monitor*. In 2002 Dressler was a recipient of the Dobie Paisano Fellowship and was inducted into the Texas Institute of Letters.

HORTON FOOTE

Horton Foote, awarded a National Medal of Arts by President Bill Clinton in 2000, was born March 14, 1916, in Wharton, Texas. Foote's writing career spans more than sixty years as an acclaimed and prolific writer whose work is primarily for stage, screen, and television. He received best screenplay Academy Awards for *To Kill a Mockingbird* (1962) and *Tender Mercies* (1983); a Pulitzer Prize for drama for *The Young Man from Atlanta* (1995); an Emmy Award for the teleplay *Old Man* (1997, based on the novel by William Faulkner); and an American Academy of Arts and Letters Gold Medal for Drama for lifetime achievement (1998). Most of Foote's plays center on human relationships and small-town life in the imaginary town of Harrison, Texas. He began his career as an actor in Broadway plays from 1932 to 1942, and his later work includes his memoirs, *Farewell: A Memoir of a Texas Childhood* (1999) and *Beginnings: A Memoir* (2001). Foote resides in his boyhood home in Wharton, Texas, as well as in New York City.

KINKY FRIEDMAN

Kinky Friedman, musician, author, and philanthropist, was born in 1944 on a ranch near Kerrville, Texas. Known for his iconoclastic views and ribald humor, he began as a country-and-western singer with the group Kinky Friedman and the Texas Jewboys. With songs such as "They Don't Make Jews like Jesus Anymore" and "Get Your Biscuits in the Oven and Your Buns in the Bed," he established himself as a social commentator and satirist. Friedman began his career as a mystery writer in 1977 and has since published fourteen mystery novels, including *Roadkill*, which made the *New York Times* best-seller list. Friedman raises money to support the Utopia Animal Rescue Group, which rescues abandoned, old, or injured animals and places them in loving homes. He lives and works at Echo Valley Ranch near Medina, Texas.

LAURA FURMAN

Laura Furman, award-winning novelist, short-story writer, and essayist, was born November 19, 1945, in Brooklyn, New York. Beginning her literary career in the 1970s with stories first published in the *New Yorker*, Furman continues to receive critical praise. Her fiction and essays have appeared in *Ploughshares, Southwest Review, Threepenny Review, Yale Review, Mirabella, House and Garden, GQ*, and other publications. She was a founding editor of *American Short Fiction*, a recipient of Guggenheim and Dobie Paisano fellowships, and president of the Texas Institute of Letters. Furman moved to Houston in 1978 to work on a new magazine and has been in Texas ever since. She lives in Austin with her husband and son and is associate professor of English at the University of Texas at Austin.

DAGOBERTO GILB

Dagoberto Gilb was born in Los Angeles, California, and began his writing career while living in El Paso, Texas, and working as a construction laborer. Gilb won wide acclaim for his first short story collection, *The Magic of Blood* (1993), for which he received the PEN/Hemingway Award. His novel *The Last Known Residence of Mickey Acuña* (1995) was a *New York Times* Notable Book of the Year. Critics applaud his recent work, *Woodcuts of Women* (2001), and *Gritos: Essays* (2003). Gilb was the recipient of a Guggenheim Fellowship and a Whiting Writers' Award. He teaches at Texas State University–San Marcos and lives in Austin, Texas.

WILLIAM H. GOETZMANN

William H. Goetzmann was born July 20, 1930, in Washington, D.C. He is a Pulitzer Prize–winning historian (1967), acclaimed scholar, and author of numerous books and articles, including *The West of the Imagination; New Lands, New Men: America and the Second Great Age of Discovery;* and *Exploration and Empire: The Explorer and the Scientist in the Winning of the American West.* Professor Goetzmann is the Jack S. Blanton, Sr., Professor of History at the University of Texas at Austin and a Fellow of the Texas State Historical Association.

JOHN GRAVES

John Graves was born August 6, 1920, in Fort Worth, Texas, and grew up there. He graduated from the Rice Institute [Rice University] in 1942 and received his master's degree in English from Columbia University. Graves has contributed to magazines and literary collections for more than four decades. Considered one of the most important Southwestern writers, Graves received a lifetime achievement award from the Texas Book Festival in 2000. The Texas Institute of Letters honored Graves in 1961 with the Carr P. Collins Award for his first book, *Goodbye to a River,* often called the best book ever written about Texas. His second book, *Hard Scrabble,* was awarded the Parkman Prize. In 1984 Graves served as president of the Texas Institute of Letters, which honored him with the McCombs-Tinkle Memorial Award also. Graves' third major book, *From a Limestone Ledge: Some Essays and Other Ruminations about Country Life in Texas* (1980), was nominated for an American Book Award. Graves is married to the former Jane Cole of New York. They have two daughters, Helen and Sally.

JAMES L. HALEY

James Haley was born in Tulsa, Oklahoma, and grew up near Fort Worth, Texas. Now a resident of Austin, Texas, Haley graduated summa cum laude from the University of Texas at Arlington with a degree in political science. He began graduate study at the University of Texas at Austin Law School but withdrew to concentrate on a literary career. Haley's work includes biographies, historical novels, and books of history, which are often used as reading texts in teaching the history of the Southwest. Haley's *Sam Houston,* the largest and most complete biography ever written about that legendary icon, was published in 2002 by the University of Oklahoma Press to wide acclaim.

STEPHEN HARRIGAN

Stephen Harrigan was born October 5, 1948, in Oklahoma City. At the age of five, he moved to Texas and grew up in Abilene and Corpus Christi. A 1971 University of Texas graduate, Harrigan is a former *Texas Monthly* staff writer and senior editor. His essays and articles appear in many publications, including the *Atlantic, Life, New York Times Magazine, Condé Nast Traveler, Rolling Stone*, and the *Texas Observer*. The recipient of a Dobie Paisano Fellowship in 1977, Harrigan is the author of six books, which gained critical praise. For his best-selling novel *The Gates of the Alamo*, Harrigan received the TCU Texas Book Award, the Western Heritage Award from the National Cowboy and Western Heritage Museum, and the Spur Award for the Best Novel of the West. He has written numerous screenplays and movies for television. Harrigan and his wife, Sue Ellen, live in Austin, Texas. They have three daughters.

JIM HIGHTOWER

Jim Hightower, political columnist, author, and radio commentator, was born January 11, 1943, in Denison, Texas. His populist viewpoint is published in a monthly political newsletter, "The Hightower Lowdown," which has received the Alternative Press Award and the Independent Press Association Award for best national newsletter. In addition to commentaries he has broadcast on more than ninety commercial and public radio stations, Hightower writes a monthly column for the *Nation*, a leading progressive journal. From 1976 to 1979, Hightower served as editor of the *Texas Observer*. He was elected to two terms as Texas agriculture commissioner and served from 1983 to 1991. The *Houston Chronicle* notes that Hightower views "the true political spectrum [as] not right to left but top to bottom." Hightower is a best-selling author, whose books include *If the Gods Had Meant Us to Vote, They Would Have Given Us Candidates* and *Thieves in High Places: They've Stolen Our Country and It's Time to Take It Back*. He lives in Austin, Texas.

ROLANDO HINOJOSA-SMITH

Rolando Hinojosa-Smith was born January 21, 1929, in Mercedes, Texas, a small town stitched onto the edge of the sprawling Rio Grande Valley along the U.S.-Mexico border. "I was born into an environment filled with reading and readers," says this son of a Latino father and an Anglo mother. A world-class writer and educator, Hinojosa-Smith is currently the Ellen Clayton Garwood Professor of Creative Writing at the University of Texas at Austin. Best known for *The Klail City*

Death Trip, his fascinating series of loosely linked short novels, Hinojosa-Smith has been praised by critics as "simply the best we have."

EDWARD HIRSCH

Edward Hirsch was born January 20, 1950, in Chicago, Illinois. A highly acclaimed poet, scholar, and author, Hirsch was named a MacArthur Fellow in 1998 and has received numerous literary awards, including the American Academy of Arts and Letters literature award in 1998. Hirsch received his Ph.D. in 1979 from the University of Pennsylvania and taught at the University of Houston from 1985 to 2000. In 2003 Hirsch began serving as the director of the Guggenheim Foundation. Among his collections of poetry, Hirsch received the National Book Critics Circle Award in 1987 for *Wild Gratitude*. Critics recognize Hirsch's poetry for its "intelligence," "tenderness," and "immense wonder and rigor." His prose also meets with broad critical acclaim. In *How to Read a Poem: And Fall in Love with Poetry*, Hirsch discusses how to understand and appreciate poetry from diverse times and places. Having lived in Houston, Texas, since 1985, Hirsch and his family now reside in New York.

ROBERT E. HOWARD

Robert E. Howard was born January 22, 1906, in Peaster, Texas. His father, a country doctor, moved the family to Cross Plains, Texas, when Howard was a boy. From the small oil-and-cattle boomtown, Howard single-handedly invented the genre of heroic fantasy. His stories appeared in the pulp magazines of the day: *Argosy, Weird Tales*, and others. His most famous creation, *Conan the Barbarian*, became an international success. A prolific and energetic writer, Howard is considered one of the greatest adventure writers of the twentieth century. He died in 1936 at the age of thirty.

MOLLY IVINS

Molly Ivins was born August 30, 1944, in Monterey, California. Known for her sharp wit, humor, and irreverent style, Ivins is a columnist, political commentator, and regular contributor to publications such as the *Progressive, Nation, Esquire, Atlantic*, and *Mother Jones*. She served as coeditor of the *Texas Observer* and as a political reporter for the *New York Times*. Ivins has written several books of collected columns and essays, including *Molly Ivins Can't Say That, Can She?* and *You Got to Dance with Them What Brung You*. With Lou Dubose, she has coauthored two books on George Bush: *Shrub* and *Bushwhacked*. Ivins received a master's degree in journalism from Columbia University and in 1976 was named Outstanding Alumna by the university's School of Journalism. She has been a finalist for the Pulitzer Prize three times and was recipient of the 1992 Headliners Award for best column in Texas. Ivins lives in Austin, Texas.

MARY KARR

Mary Karr grew up near Port Arthur, Texas. Her poetry, essays, and memoir writing have been recognized with numerous awards. She has won Pushcart Prizes for her poetry and essays, and her work is featured in publications such as the *New Yorker, Parnassus, Esquire, Poetry, American Poetry Review, New York Times Magazine,* and *Harper's Bazaar,* among others. In 1995 *The Liar's Club,* her memoir of growing up in East Texas, won the PEN/Martha Albrand Award and the Texas Institute of Letters Prize for Best Nonfiction. It was selected as an American Library Association Notable Book and was named a finalist for the National Book Critics Circle Award. *Cherry: A Memoir,* her prizewinning sequel, was released in 2000 to broad acclaim. Karr has been the recipient of grants from the National Endowment for the Arts, the Whiting Foundation, and the Bunting Institute at Radcliffe College, among others. Karr teaches literature and creative writing at Syracuse University, where she is a full professor. She lives in upstate New York with her son.

ELMER KELTON

Elmer Kelton was born April 29, 1926, in Andrews, Texas. Kelton is a world-renowned writer whose novels, stories, and touching musings cover half a century of Texas journalism. Considered the state's foremost pastoral novelist, he acquired a degree in journalism from the University of Texas at Austin, followed by forty years as an agricultural reporter for the *San Angelo Standard Times* and *Livestock Weekly*. His novels, including *The Time It Never Rained, The Day the Cowboys Quit,* and *Buffalo Wagons,* have won six Golden Spur awards from the Western Writers of America. In 1990 Kelton received the Distinguished Achievement Award from the Western Literature Association. In 1995 his novel *The Good Old Boys* was made into an award-winning movie for TNT, starring Tommy Lee Jones and Sissy Spacek. Kelton is a member of the Texas Institute of Letters and is a popular speaker on the art of writing throughout the country. In November 2001 the Texas Book Festival honored Kelton with the TBF Bookend Award for lifetime achievement in literature.

JOE R. LANSDALE

Joe R. Lansdale was born October 28, 1951, in Gladewater, Texas. Lansdale's writings include science fiction, horror, Westerns, and mysteries, all of which are informed by his upbringing in deep East Texas. In addition to novels and short stories, Lansdale has written screenplays, stage plays, and comic scripts. In 1989 Lansdale received the Bram Stoker Award for short fiction with "The Night They Missed the Horror Show" and in 1990 for long fiction with "On the Far Side of the Cadillac Desert with Dead Folks." He has since been nominated for and received other Bram Stoker Awards.

DAVID LINDSEY

David Lindsey was born November 6, 1944, in Kingsville, Texas. He spent his early years a few miles from the Mexican border, in Starr County, and grew up in West Texas near the Colorado River Valley north of San Angelo. Lindsey has published more than a dozen mystery and suspense novels since 1983. From the outset, Lindsey's writing has garnered acclaim. *A Cold Mind*, the first in a series featuring Houston homicide detective Stuart Haydon, has been called "one of the best suspense novels of all time" and "a classic of the genre." Lindsey's popularity has grown along with his international reputation, and his books are now translated into twenty different languages. *Mercy*, a critically acclaimed novel published in 1990, was released as a feature film in 1999 and served as a watershed book for his career. A graduate of North Texas State University (now the University of North Texas), Lindsey spent a year in graduate school there before moving to Austin, where he and his wife presently reside.

ARTURO LONGORIA

Arturo Longoria was born December 5, 1948, and grew up in Mission, Texas. A writer and journalist for more than twenty years, Longoria has published articles in more than five hundred newspapers across the country, as well as in national and state magazines and journals, including *Time, Texas Highways, Texas Parks and Wildlife*, and *Borderlands: Texas Poetry Review*. He has authored two books, both from Texas A&M University Press. His first book, *Adios to the Brushlands* (1997), won the Carroll Abbott Memorial Award presented by the Texas Native Plant Society. It also won the Webb County Heritage Award. His second book, *Keepers of the Wilderness* (2000), was a finalist in the literary nonfiction category of the Violet Crown awards given by the Writers' League of Texas. Selected as a Notable Valley Hispanic by the University of Texas–Pan American, Longoria was recognized by the National Audubon Society for his investigative articles on the environment. At work on his third book, a novel set in South Texas, Longoria divides his time between homes in McAllen and the Texas Hill Country near Leakey.

PHILLIP LOPATE

Phillip Lopate was born November 16, 1943, in Jamaica, New York. Perhaps best known for his personal essays, Lopate receives high praise as a writer of novels, poems, essays, nonfiction, and film criticism, as well as an editor. He is a recipient of Guggenheim and National Endowment for the Arts fellowships. Lopate is the author of numerous essay collections, including *Bachelorhood: Tales of the Metropolis*, *Against Joie de Vivre*, *Portrait of My Body*, and *Being with Children*, the latter an educational classic about his teaching experience with the Teachers and Writers Collaborative Program in New York City schools. His works have appeared in numerous publications, such as *Best American Essays*, the *Paris Review*, and Pushcart Prize anthologies. Currently Adams Professor of the Humanities at Hofstra University, Lopate taught creative writing at the University of Houston, Columbia University, and Bennington College. He lives in Brooklyn, New York, with his family.

JAMES MAGNUSON

James Magnuson was born August 24, 1941, in Madison, Wisconsin. He is the author of numerous novels, including *Without Barbarians*, *Ghost Dancing*, *Open Season*, and *Windfall*. The author of a dozen plays, Magnuson has also written extensively for television. He was the recipient of a National Endowment for the Arts fellowship for his fiction, in addition to the Alfred Hotter Fellowship from Princeton University and the 1990 Jesse H. Jones Award from the Texas Institute of Letters for the outstanding novel published that year. Along with his work as a writer, he is the director of the Michener Center for Writers at the University of Texas at Austin, where he teaches fiction workshops.

LARRY MCMURTRY

Larry McMurtry was born June 3, 1936, in Wichita Falls, Texas, and grew up on a ranch outside of Archer City. He received his B.A. degree from North Texas State University (now the University of North Texas) in 1958, and his master's degree from Rice University in 1960. A 1960–1961 Stegner Fellow at Stanford University,

McMurtry was awarded the Texas Institute of Letters Jesse H. Jones Award in 1962. McMurtry's novels, essays, and screenplays are critical and popular successes. In 1972 he wrote the Academy Award–winning screenplay adaptation of his novel *The Last Picture Show* and in 1985 won the Pulitzer Prize for his novel *Lonesome Dove*. That novel was brought to television as a very popular miniseries of the same name. In 1970 McMurtry bought a rare-book store in Washington, D.C., and named it Booked Up; then in 1988 in Archer City, where he now resides, he opened a second Booked Up for his large collection of used books.

PAT MORA

Pat Mora, born in El Paso, Texas, is an award-winning author of poetry, nonfiction, and children's books who believes in connecting communities through literature and literacy. She speaks often at conferences, universities, and schools about creative writing, multicultural education, and leadership. Mora has published more than twenty books for young readers and actively promotes April 30 as Día de los niños/Día de los libros (Children's Day/Book Day), a celebration of children, books, languages, and cultures. In 2003 Mora received a Civitella Ranieri Fellowship to write in Umbria, Italy. She has been a judge of the poetry fellowships granted by the National Endowment for the Arts, has served as an advisor on Kellogg National Leadership fellowships, and has herself received both of these fellowships. The mother of three grown children, Mora lives in Santa Fe, New Mexico, and also spends time in the northern Kentucky–Cincinnati area.

FRANCES NAIL

Frances Nail was born in Memphis, Texas, in 1924 and now lives at Lake Travis in the Central Texas Hill Country. After many years spent as a painter, she began to write essays at age seventy. Her autobiographical and personal essays have appeared in the *Houston Chronicle* and various Texas periodicals. They also have been published in book form, both hardcover and audio. Her books are edited by her daughter, Leslie Nail, who contributes a poem for the forewords. The hardcover books are illustrated by her painter daughter, Katy Nail, and her granddaughter Carrie Rodriguez creates the music for the audio books with her violin. Nail is frequently in demand as a reader throughout the Texas literary community.

NAOMI SHIHAB NYE

Naomi Shihab Nye was born March 12, 1952, in St. Louis, Missouri. Her recent books include *Come with Me: Poems for a Journey, Fuel: Poems,* and *Habibi,* a novel for teens that won six Best Books awards. She has edited prizewinning anthologies of poetry for young readers, including *This Same Sky, The Tree Is Older Than You Are, The Space between Our Footsteps, Poems and Paintings from the Middle East, What Have You Lost?* and *Salting the Ocean.* A Guggenheim Fellow, she was a Library of Congress Witter Bynner Fellow for the year 2000 and recently received a presidential appointment to the National Council on the Humanities. Nye says, "Poetry is my breath, map, and friend. Encouraging and collecting poetry of others is my passion." She lives in San Antonio, Texas, with her husband, photographer Michael Nye, and their son.

KAREN OLSSON

A native of Washington, D.C., Karen Olsson moved to Austin in 1996 and has lived there most years since. She is a former coeditor of the *Texas Observer* and a writer-at-large for *Texas Monthly.* Her first novel, *Waterloo,* set in a city not unlike Austin, will be published by Farrar, Straus, and Giroux in 2005.

LOUIS SACHAR

Louis Sachar was born March 20, 1954, in East Meadow, New York. As a writer for youth, Sachar has received numerous awards for his books, including the prestigious Newbery Medal in 1999 and the National Book Award for Young People's Literature for *Holes* in 1998. The screenplay based on *Holes* was written by Sachar, and the movie, released in April 2003, received wide acclaim. In addition, *Holes* was chosen by the Austin Public Library, along with the mayor and residents of Austin, Texas, as the second annual book selection of the Mayor's Book Club. Sachar's work includes the "Marvin Redpost" series, as well as *Sideways Stories from Wayside School* (1978) and *There's a Boy in the Girls' Bathroom* (1987), among many others. Sachar and his family live in Austin, Texas.

EDWIN "BUD" SHRAKE

Edwin "Bud" Shrake was born September 6, 1931, in Fort Worth, Texas. A journalist, novelist, sportswriter, biographer, and screenwriter, Shrake earned degrees in English and philosophy at Texas Christian University while working full-time for legendary sportswriter Blackie Sherrod at the *Fort Worth Press* sports department. Following stints at the *Dallas Times Herald* and the *Dallas Morning News*, Shrake moved to New York in 1964 to work for *Sports Illustrated*. Shrake continued his association with the magazine after returning to Texas in 1968. During the late 1980s Shrake coauthored several best-selling celebrity autobiographies, including *Harvey Penick's Little Red Book*, the best-selling sports book in American publishing history. His fiction includes *The Borderland: A Novel of Texas* (2000) and *Billy Boy* (2001). Shrake lives in Austin, Texas.

EVAN SMITH

Evan Smith joined the staff of *Texas Monthly* as a senior editor in January 1992. In February 1993 he was promoted to deputy editor, and in July 2000 he was promoted to editor. In May 2002 he added the title of executive vice president.

Since Smith took over as editor, *Texas Monthly* has been nominated seven times for a National Magazine Award, the magazine industry's equivalent of the Pulitzer Prize. In April 2003 *Texas Monthly* was awarded the National Magazine Award for General Excellence for the third time in its history.

A New York native, Smith has a bachelor's degree in public policy from Hamilton College (Clinton, New York) and a master's degree in journalism from the Medill School at Northwestern University (Evanston, Illinois). He previously held editorial positions at a number of national magazines, most recently at the *New Republic*, where he was deputy editor. He has written for *GQ*, *Mother Jones*, and other national magazines. He hosts a weekly interview program, *Texas Monthly Talks*, that airs on PBS stations all across Texas, and he is a recurring guest on numerous other TV and radio shows, from CNBC's *Hardball* to CNN's *NewsNight with Aaron Brown*.

Smith is on the boards of the American Society of Magazine Editors, the Jack S. Blanton Museum of Art at the University of Texas at Austin, Ballet Austin, the Headliners Club, and Austin public television station KLRU, whose board he chairs. He is also the founding co-chair of the Texas Film Hall of Fame.

BRUCE STERLING

Bruce Sterling was born April 14, 1954, in Brownsville, Texas. He attended the University of Texas at Austin from 1972 to 1976. Sterling's work includes science fiction and nonfiction books. He received the Hugo Award for Best Novelette for "Bicycle Repairman" in 1997 and again for "Taklamakan" in 1999. Sterling is considered the "standard bearer of the cyperpunks, a cadre of science fiction hot-shots who have taken the genre by storm," and he sums up the cyberpunk aesthetic in

Mirrorshades: The Cyberpunk Anthology. Sterling's science fiction includes *Schismatrix* (1985), *Distraction: A Novel* (1998), and *Zeitgeist: A Novel of Metamorphosis* (2000). He is also a frequent contributor of stories to periodicals, including *Omni, Magazine of Fantasy and Science Fiction,* and *Interzone.* Sterling lives in Austin with his family.

KATHERINE TANNEY

Katherine Tanney was born in Los Angeles. She began keeping a journal at the age of nine and could usually be found writing stories, drawing pictures, or making up strange games to play with her friends. Her grandfather was the artist and writer Stephen Longstreet. Tanney's first novel, *Carousel of Progress* (2001), was awarded the top prize for a first book of fiction from the Texas Institute of Letters. She has lived in Austin, Texas, since 1996, where she is also a producer and interviewer for the radio program *Writing on the Air.*

LORENZO THOMAS

Lorenzo Thomas was born August 31, 1944, in the Republic of Panama. He is a poet, author, and professor of English at the University of Houston–Downtown. In addition to teaching creative writing and literature classes, Thomas is director of the Cultural Enrichment Center on campus. He leads poetry workshops throughout the country and is in demand as a lecturer and a poet. His work has appeared in *African American Review, Arrowsmith, Blues Unlimited, Living Blues, Ploughshares,* and *Popular Music and Society. Extraordinary Measures: Afrocentric Modernism and 20th-Century American Poetry* is among his most recent publications. A regular book reviewer for the *Houston Chronicle,* Thomas has also contributed scholarly articles to the *African American Encyclopedia, American Literary Scholarship, Gilliver* (Germany), and the *Dictionary of Literary Biography.*

LORI AURELIA WILLIAMS

Lori Aurelia Williams was born in Houston, Texas. She holds a master's degree in English from the University of Texas at Austin, where she was awarded both a James A. Michener Fellowship and a scholarship in creative writing. In 2002 Williams received the PEN Phyllis Naylor Working Writer Fellowship. Her fiction is set primarily in urban areas and combines African American storytelling with street slang. Williams lives in Austin, Texas.

MARY WILLIS WALKER

Mary Willis Walker was born May 24, 1942, in Fox Point, Wisconsin. The award-winning mystery novelist began her writing career in the late 1980s after her children were grown. In 1991 Willis Walker's first novel, *Zero at the Bone*, received the Agatha Award. In 1995 *Under the Beetle's Cellar* won both the Anthony Award at the Bouchercon World Mystery Convention and the Hammett Award of the International Association of Crime Writers, and that same year the Edgar Award of Mystery Writers of America also went to Willis Walker, for *The Red Scream*. Her novels have been translated into several languages. She resides in Austin, Texas.

BILL WITTLIFF

Bill Wittliff, screenwriter, photographer, and publisher, was born in Taft, Texas. Wittliff's film credits include *Raggedy Man, Redheaded Stranger,* and *The Perfect Storm.* His television adaptation of Larry McMurtry's *Lonesome Dove* received seven Emmys, a Golden Globe, and the George Foster Peabody Award. Wittliff and his wife, Sally, founded the award-winning Encino Press in 1964 to publish regional books about Texas and the Southwest. In 1985 they donated their collection of original manuscripts, paintings, and books to Texas State University–San Marcos, founding the Southwestern Writers Collection and the Wittliff Gallery of Southwestern and Mexican Photography. Wittliff is a former president of the Texas Institute of Letters.

BILL WRIGHT

Bill Wright was born April 2, 1933, in Harlingen, Texas. He received his Bachelor of Business Administration degree from the University of Texas at Austin in 1956. He attended photographic workshops led by Ansel Adams, Cole Weston, Sam Abell, and Mary Ellen Mark, among others. For thirty-five years, Wright led a successful business career in West Texas, and since 1990 he has worked full-time as a photographer and writer. His work includes numerous exhibitions, publications, workshops, lectures, and awards. His photographs are in museum and university collections throughout the world. Wright serves on the board of the Texas Commission on the Arts and the Texas State Historical Association, as well as on advisory councils of many state and national organizations. Wright lives in Abilene with his wife, Alice.

LAWRENCE WRIGHT

Lawrence Wright was born August 2, 1947, in Oklahoma City. A graduate of Tulane University, Wright received his master's degree in 1971 from the American University of Cairo. A *New Yorker* staff writer, Wright is the author of fiction and nonfiction, as well as screenplays. His work includes *In the New World: Growing Up with America, 1960–1984* (1987), *Remembering Satan: A Case of Recovered Memory and the Shattering of a Family* (1994), and *Twins: And What They Tell Us about Who We Are* (1997). In 1993 most of *Remembering Satan* appeared in the *New Yorker* and won the National Magazine Award for Reporting and the John Bartlow Martin Award for Public Interest Magazine Journalism. His first novel, *God's Favorite* (2000), is based on political and religious intrigue during the United States' invasion of Panama in 1989. Wright is a regular contributor to *Texas Monthly*, among other periodicals. He lives in Austin, Texas, with his wife and children.

SHARON WYSE

Sharon Wyse is a native Texan who spent her summers on a wheat farm until she was fifteen. A classically trained singer and former disc jockey, she holds degrees in English, journalism, and music and has received two fellowships to the Ragsdale Foundation writers' colony. *The Box Children* is her first novel. Wyse lives in Brooklyn with her husband, David Satz.

SUZAN ZEDER

Recognized internationally as a leading playwright for family audiences, Suzan Zeder is a professor at the University of Texas at Austin and is the first holder of an endowed chair in Theatre for Youth and Playwrighting at UT-Austin. The three-time winner of the Distinguished Play Award given by the American Alliance of Theatre and Education, she was inducted into the College of Fellows of the American Theatre in Washington, D.C., in 1996.

Contributor Biographies

AYO BAIN

Ayo Bain is a graduate of Huston-Tillotson College, Austin, Texas. A native of Trinidad, Bain teaches high school English in Florida. He is the godson of Nobel Prize–winning poet Derek Walcott.

K BRADFORD

K Bradford is a poet, filmmaker, and performance artist. She directs and teaches It's a She-Shoot, a feminist film program for women and girls, and is a former editor of *Borderlands: Texas Poetry Review*. Upon receiving a Fulbright scholarship, Bradford directed *White-Out* (1996), a documentary about whiteness and racism in southern Africa and the United States. In 1999 Bradford received a master's degree in creative writing from the University of Texas at Austin. She tours nationally with her one-woman show, "The Tales of a Gypsy Cowboy."

RUSTY BURKE

Rusty Burke has been studying the life and work of Robert E. Howard for almost thirty years. He has edited Howard publications for Necronomicon Press and founded the journal of Howard studies, *The Dark Man*. Currently the series editor for Wandering Star's *Robert E. Howard Library of Classics*, he is working to produce authoritative texts of Howard's stories. He has written extensively on Howard, and his *REH: A Short Biography of Robert E. Howard* (Cross Plains Comics, 1999) is the precursor to a longer biography. It is on the Internet at http://www.rehupa.com/short_bio.htm but not published as a book.

RAMONA CEARLEY

Ramona Cearley is a freelance photographer whose work has been featured in humanities-related exhibits and publications. In collaboration with Russell Scoggin, she produced a grant-funded community history program and exhibit based on the Sanderson, Texas, flood of 1965, which occurred in her hometown. After touring the Trans-Pecos region of the state, the exhibit became a part of the collection at the Center for American History at the University of Texas. Cearley has a master's degree in photojournalism from the University of Texas at Austin.

SUSAN DANIELS

A fourth-generation Texan, Susan Daniels is a member of the Writers' League of Texas and regularly helps produce shows and conduct interviews for *Writing on the Air*, which airs on KOOP radio (91.7FM). She is also an on-the-air personality for a reading service sponsored by the Austin Council of the Blind. She works in the fields of criminal defense and family law and on issues affecting the elderly, blind, deaf, and hearing-impaired communities.

KYRA EDEKER

Kyra Edeker is a freelance Web site developer and writer living in Austin.

LINDA EVANS

Linda Evans is a native Texan who grew up in Oklahoma and the Colorado Rockies. In Colorado, not content to merely gaze up at the peaks or into the canyons, she climbed Pikes Peak and Mt. Evans, both "fourteeners," and she descended into—and out of—Black Canyon on the Gunnison River. Linda has made her home in Austin since 1998 and has researched her Texas family back to the years of the Texas Republic. She received her master's degree from the University of Oklahoma and is an editor at the University of Texas.

MARK FINN

Mark Finn is a freelance author living in Austin, Texas. When he is not selling books for the largest independent bookstore in Texas, he is writing them. Finn is the author of *Gods New and Used*, *Year of the Hare*, and *Empty Hearts*. Finn's nonfiction work can be found at such places as revolutionsf.com and playboy.com. He credits his writing career to his parents and to Robert E. Howard.

LIZ GOLD

Liz Gold is a freelance writer and a former editor at the University of Texas. She lives in Chimayo, New Mexico.

PEGGY HAILEY

Peggy Hailey graduated from Southwestern University and holds a master's degree in English literature from Rutgers University. She is the head buyer at Book People bookstore in Austin, Texas. She is also the books editor for *RevolutionSF* (http://revolutionsf.com). Bailey researched and compiled the majority of the writers' bibliographies that appear at the end of this book.

JOE HOLLEY

Native Texan Joe Holley is former *Insight* editor for the *San Antonio Express-News* and now writes for the *Washington Post*. He has degrees from Abilene Christian University, the University of Texas at Austin, and Columbia University and is founding editor of the *Texas Humanist* (later the *Texas Journal of Ideas, History and Culture*) and a former editor of the *Texas Observer*. He also has been editorial page editor and a syndicated columnist at the *San Antonio Light* and the *San Diego Tribune* and a regular contributor to *Texas Monthly* and *Columbia Journalism Review*. He is coauthor with his wife, Tara Elgin Holley, of *My Mother's Keeper* (William Morrow, 1997) and is currently working on a book about race for Algonquin Press.

GARY KENT

Gary Kent is a screenwriter, filmmaker, director, actor, special-effects wizard, and stuntman with more than one hundred films to his credit. Five of his seven screenplays have been produced. Over a forty-year period in Los Angeles, he directed action sequences and provided special effects for notable directors Richard Rush, Monte Hellman, Al Adamson, Brian De Palma, Ray Dennis Steckler, and Peter Bogdanovich. During his directing career, Kent worked with well-known Hollywood stars and won numerous awards. In 2002 he completed stunt and action direction for *Groom Lake*, directed by William Shatner, and Don Coscarelli's tongue-in-cheek horror film *Bubba Ho-Tep*, starring Bruce Campbell and Ossie Davis.

RICK KLAW

Rick Klaw is a regular columnist for *SF Site* and the fiction editor for *RevolutionSF*. A former book buyer, managing editor, and bookstore manager, Klaw has experienced most aspects of the book business.

JULIE KOPPENHEFFER

Julie B. Adler Koppenheffer is producer and host of the radio program *Life Shapes: Constructing a Life You Love*. Koppenheffer took many paths as a lawyer, including being a partner in a law firm in San Antonio, Texas. It wasn't until she and her husband took a five-month sabbatical to Hong Kong that her focus changed from being a lawyer to being a person who loved the law. Koppenheffer, who had always written poetry, wrote two novels and a travelogue. After returning to Texas, she served as coordinator of the Writers' League of Texas Radio Collective and interviewed writers about the craft of writing for the radio program *Writing on the Air*.

FRANCES LEONARD

Frances Leonard has served as director of the Humanities Texas Resource Center since July 1978. In this capacity she has organized, or directed the organization of, numerous photo-panel exhibits, including "Texas Writers," the genesis of this volume of interviews. These exhibits have circulated to more than four thousand cultural programs throughout Texas and neighboring states, serving some nine million citizens of all ages. A frequent contributor of essays to the *Texas Journal*, she has published essays on medieval comedy in literary journals and is the author of *Laughter in the Courts of Love*, a book-length study of comedy and the comic vision in Middle English allegory. She holds a Ph.D. in English literature from the University of Kansas.

BRYCE MILLIGAN

Bryce Milligan first met Angela De Hoyos in the early 1980s when he was the book critic for the *San Antonio Express-News*, where he was able to review many small-press books, especially those by Chicano authors. At the same time, he was the editor of *Pax: A Journal for Peace through Culture*, one of the country's first literary magazines devoted to multicultural literature. In 1985 he founded the Annual Texas Small Press Book Fair, which grew into the Inter-American Bookfair and Literary Festival, sponsored by the Guadalupe Cultural Arts Center, where Milligan served from time to time as the director of the Chicano literature program. The author of a dozen books of fiction and poetry himself, Milligan has edited and coedited several important anthologies of Latina writing. Since 1995 he has been the publisher/editor of Wings Press, which focuses on multicultural literature.

HENRY P. MILLS

Henry P. Mills is resource coordinator for the Humanities Texas Resource Center. Besides assisting with development of this book, Mills is director and editor of the Walker Percy Project, an online literary resource. His work with the project has been featured in the *Southern Quarterly, Texas Monthly, New Orleans Magazine,* and the *Austin American-Statesman.* Mills holds an M.A. in literature from Louisiana State University.

LESLIE NAIL

Leslie Nail is associate director of the Association of Texas Colleges and Universities. She holds graduate degrees in English and creative writing. She has also provided editorial services to clients, including her mother, author Frances Nail. Each of Frances Nail's three books uses one of Leslie's poems as the foreword.

GRAHAM SHELBY

Graham Shelby was born in Lexington, Kentucky, and had early experience as a rock DJ. After graduating from the University of Kentucky, he taught English in a small Japanese town, where he learned Japanese. Shelby is a professional storyteller and has performed at the Texas Storytelling Festival, the Institute for Texas Cultures, and the Lady Bird Johnson Wildflower Center.

BRUCE SNIDER

Bruce Snider was a James A. Michener Fellow and earned his M.F.A. in poetry and playwriting at the University of Texas Michener Center for Writers, where he served as the center's academic coordinator and taught creative writing workshops for the University Extension Program. Snider's first book, *The Year We Studied Women,* won the 2003 Felix Pollax Poetry Prize from the University of Wisconsin. The same year Snider was awarded the Stegner Fellowship to study at Stanford. A resident of Austin for several years, Snider is originally from rural Indiana.

GRAHAM STEWART

Graham Stewart received a B.A. in English from the University of Illinois at Chicago. He has written technical manuals and software content, including high-tech and language arts, for several employers. Since 1999 he has been a volunteer with *Borderlands: Texas Poetry Review*. He produced the *Borderlands* Web Audio Project that features more than two hours of recorded readings by poets and interviews with them. Stewart produces and occasionally hosts the Writers' League of Texas program *Writing on the Air*, which airs on KOOP (91.7FM), Austin, Texas.

TERESA TAYLOR

Teresa Taylor resides in Austin, Texas, where she is active in community radio (KOOP 91.7FM). She cofounded the Women's Collective, helped organize the station's first year of broadcast, and has served on the station's board of directors. She has interviewed numerous artists and human rights activists and produced various radio shows over a period of years. She is also a photographer. She is an information developer for the high-tech industry.

DON WEBB

Don Webb has published one book of poetry, five books of short stories, three novels, and two nonfiction books, on Internet security and on Egyptian magic. His work has been translated into nine languages, and he has been a teacher of fiction writing for the Writers' League of Texas and UCLA. Webb's work will be included in the *Norton Book of Modern Texas Writing*. He has won awards for his poetry, fiction, and Internet journalism, including the Fiction Collective Award in 1989. He has also written for films (e.g., *The Outsider Club*), television commercials, comic books, and cookbooks and has done game design.

RIC WILLIAMS

Ric Williams is a poet and editor who has written for the *Austin Chronicle* and other newspapers and periodicals since the mid-1980s. He has a master's degree in mythology and depth psychology from Pacifica Graduate Institute. He is married to an artist and is the father of two daughters.

Bibliography of Authors' Works

Barker, Wendy. *Lunacy of Light: Emily Dickinson and the Experience of Metaphor.* Carbondale: Southern Illinois University Press, 1987.

———. *Winter Chickens.* San Antonio: Corona Publishing, 1990.

———. *Let the Ice Speak: Poems.* Greenfield Center, N.Y.: Greenfield Review Press, 1991.

———. *Eve Remembers.* London: Aark Arts Press, 1996.

———(coeditor, with Sandra M. Gilbert and Ruth Stone). *The House Is Made of Poetry: The Art of Ruth Stone.* Carbondale: Southern Illinois University Press, 1996.

———. *Way of Whiteness.* San Antonio: Wings Press, 2000.

———. *Poems' Progress.* Spring, Tex.: Absey, 2002.

Bird, Sarah (as Tory Cates). *Silhouette Special Edition, No. 65, Handful of Sky.* New York: Harlequin, 1982.

———. *Silhouette Special Edition, No. 125, Where Aspens Quake.* New York: Harlequin, 1983.

———(McCabe). *Do Evil Cheerfully.* New York: Avon, 1983.

———(as Tory Cates). *Silhouette Special Edition, No. 196, Cloud Waltzer.* New York: Harlequin, 1984.

———. *Silhouette Special Edition, No. 236, Different Dreams.* New York: Harlequin, 1985.

———. *Silhouette Special Edition, No. 310, A Passionate Illusion.* New York: Harlequin, 1986.

———. *Alamo House: Women without Men, Men without Brains.* New York: Norton, 1986.

———. *The Boyfriend School.* New York: Doubleday, 1989.

———. *The Mommy Club.* New York: Doubleday, 1991.

———. *Virgin of the Rodeo.* New York: Doubleday, 1993.

———. *The Yokota Officers Club.* New York: Knopf, 2001.

Brandon, Jay. *Deadbolt*. New York: Pocket, 1985.

———. *Tripwire*. New York: Pocket, 1987.

———. *Predator's Waltz*. New York: Pocket, 1989.

———. *Fade the Heat*. New York: Pocket, 1990.

———. *Rules of Evidence*. New York: Pocket, 1992.

———. *Loose among the Lambs*. New York: Pocket, 1993.

———. *Local Rules*. New York: Pocket, 1995.

———. *Defiance County*. New York: Pocket, 1996.

———. *Law and Liberty: A History of Practicing Law in San Antonio*. San Antonio: Taylor Publishing and San Antonio Bar Association, 1997.

———. *Angel of Death*. New York: Forge, 1998.

———. *La última oportunidad*. Barcelona: Ediciones B, 1999.

———. *AfterImage*. New York: Forge, 2000.

———. *Executive Privilege*. New York: Forge, 2001.

———. *Sliver Moon*. New York: Forge, 2003.

———. *Grudge Match: A Chris Sinclair Novel*. New York: Forge, 2004.

Byrd, Bobby. *Places and Memphis Poems*. Lincoln, Eng.: Grosseteste Press, 1971.

———. *Here: Poems*. Berkeley, Calif.: North Atlantic Books, 1975.

———. *The Bright Sun*. New Brunswick, Me.: Blackberry Press, 1976.

———. *Pomegranates*. Philadelphia: Tamarisk Press, 1984; El Paso: Cinco Puntos Press, 1986.

———. *Get Some Fuses for the House: Householder Poems, El Paso, Texas*. Berkeley, Calif.: North Atlantic Books, 1987.

———. *On the Transmigration of Souls in El Paso: Poems*. El Paso: Cinco Puntos Press, 1992.

———(coeditor, with Susanna Mississippi Byrd). *The Late Great Mexican Border: Reports from a Disappearing Line*. El Paso: Cinco Puntos Press, 1996.

———. *The Price of Doing Business in Mexico: And Other Poems*. El Paso: Cinco Puntos Press, 1998.

———(coeditor with John William Byrd and Luis Humberto Crosthwaite). *Puro Border: Dispatches, Snapshots, and Graffiti from La Frontera*. El Paso: Cinco Puntos Press, 2003.

Byrd, Lee. *My Sister Disappears: Stories and a Novella*. Dallas: Southern Methodist University Press, 1993.

———. *The Treasure on Gold Street/El tesoro en la Calle Oro: A Neighborhood Story in Spanish and English*. El Paso: Cinco Puntos Press, 2003.

Canales, Viola. *Orange Candy Slices and Other Secret Tales*. Houston: Arte Público, 2001.

———. *Angels with Mexican Faces.* Houston: Arte Público, forthcoming.
Cartwright, Gary. *The Hundred-Yard War.* Garden City, N.Y.: Doubleday, 1968.
———. *Thin Ice.* Greenwich, Conn.: Fawcett Publications, 1975.
———. *Blood Will Tell: The Murder Trials of T. Cullen Davis.* New York: Harcourt Brace Jovanovich, 1979; Pocket Books, 1980, 1984.
———. *Confessions of a Washed-Up Sportswriter (Including Various Digressions about Sex, Crime, and Other Hobbies).* Austin: Texas Monthly Press, 1982.
———. *Dirty Dealing: A True Story of Smuggling, Murder, and the FBI's Biggest Investigation.* New York: Atheneum, 1984; El Paso: Cinco Puntos Press, 1998.
———. *Galveston: A History of the Island.* New York: Atheneum, 1991; Fort Worth: Texas Christian University Press, 1998.
———(and Ann Richards). *HeartWiseGuy: How to Live the Good Life after a Heart Attack.* New York: St. Martin's, 1998.
———. *Turn Out the Lights: Chronicles of Texas during the 80s and 90s.* Austin: University of Texas Press, 2000.
Christensen, Paul. *Charles Olson, Call Him Ishmael.* Austin: University of Texas Press, 1979.
———. *Signs of the Whelming.* Mansfield, Tex.: Latitudes Press, 1983.
———. *Weights and Measures: Selected Poems.* Huntington, Vt.: University Editions, 1985.
———. *In Love, in Sorrow: The Complete Correspondence of Charles Olson and Edward Dahlberg.* New York: Paragon House, 1990.
———. *Minding the Underworld: Clayton Eshleman and Late Postmodernism.* Santa Rosa, Calif.: Black Sparrow, 1991.
———. *Where Three Roads Meet.* Bryan, Tex.: Cedarshouse/Open Theater, 1996.
———. *West of the American Dream: An Encounter with Texas.* College Station: Texas A&M University Press, 2001.
———. *Blue Alleys: Prose Poetry.* Houston: Stone River Press; Page One Publication, 2001.
———. *Hard Country* (poetry). Austin, Tex.: Tharp Springs Press, 2001.
———. *The Mottled Air.* Spring, Tex.: Panther Creek Press, 2003.
Cooper, J. California. *A Piece of Mine: Short Stories.* Navarro, Calif.: Wild Trees Press, 1984.
———. *Homemade Love.* New York: St. Martin's, 1986.
———. *Some Soul to Keep.* New York: St. Martin's, 1987.
———. *Family.* New York: Doubleday, 1991.
———. *The Matter Is Life.* New York: Doubleday, 1991.

————. *In Search of Satisfaction*. New York: Doubleday, 1994.

————. *Some Love, Some Pain, Sometime: Stories*. New York: Doubleday, 1995.

————. *The Wake of the Wind*. New York: Doubleday, 1998.

————. *The Future Has a Past: Stories*. New York: Doubleday, 2000.

————. *Some People, Some Other Places*. New York: Doubleday, 2004.

Crook, Elizabeth. *The Raven's Bride: A Novel of Eliza Allen and Sam Houston*. New York: Doubleday, 1991; Dallas: Southern Methodist University Press, 1993.

————. *Promised Lands: A Novel of the Texas Rebellion*. New York: Doubleday, 1994; Dallas: Southern Methodist University Press, 1995.

De Hoyos, Angela. *Arise Chicano and Other Poems*. Bloomington, Ind.: Backstage Books, 1975.

————. *Chicano Poems for the Barrio*. Bloomington, Ind.: Backstage Books, 1975.

————. *Selecciones: Selected Poems*. Houston: Arte Público, 1976.

————(coeditor, with Bryce Milligan and Mary Guerrero-Milligan). *Daughters of the Fifth Sun: A Collection of Latina Fiction and Poetry*. New York: Riverhead Books, 1996.

————. *Woman, Woman*. Houston: Arte Público, 1985; 2d ed., 1996.

————(coeditor, with Bryce Milligan and Mary Guerrero-Milligan). *¡Floricanto Sí!: A Collection of Latina Fiction and Poetry*. New York: Penguin USA, 1998.

Dressler, Mylène. *The Medusa Tree*. Denver: MacMurray and Beck, 1997.

————. *The Deadwood Beetle*. New York: Blue Hen Books, 2001.

————. *The Floodmakers*. New York: Putnam, 2004.

Foote, Horton. *"The Trip to Bountiful": A Play in Three Acts*. New York: Dramatists Play Service, 1954.

————. *The Chase* (novel). New York: Rinehart, 1956.

————. *Harrison, Texas: Eight Television Plays*. New York: Harcourt, Brace, 1956.

————. *Three Plays*. New York: Harcourt and World, 1962.

————. *"1918": A Play in Two Acts*. New York: Dramatists Play Service, 1987.

————. *"Courtship," "Valentine's Day," "1918": Three Plays from the Orphans' Home Cycle*. New York: Grove Press, 1987.

————. *"Roots in a Parched Ground," "Convicts," "Lily Dale," "The Widow Claire": The First Four Plays in the Orphans' Home Cycle*. New York: Grove Press, 1988.

————. *"Cousins" and "The Death of Papa": Two Plays from the Orphans' Home Cycle*. New York: Grove Press, 1989.

————. *The Death of Papa*. New York: Dramatists Play Service, 1989.

———. "To Kill a Mockingbird," "Tender Mercies," and "The Trip to Bountiful": Three Screenplays. New York: Grove Press, 1989.

———. Horton Foote: Four New Plays—1988–1993. Lyme, N.H.: Smith and Krause Books, 1993.

———. The Young Man from Atlanta. New York: Dutton, 1995.

———. Laura Dennis. New York: Dramatists Play Service, 1996.

———. "Getting Frankie Married—and Afterwards" and Other Plays. Lyme, N.H.: Smith and Krause Books, 1998.

———. Farewell: A Memoir of a Texas Childhood. New York: Scribner, 1999.

———. "The Last of the Thorntons": A Play. New York: Overlook Press, 2000.

———. Beginnings: A Memoir. New York: Scribner, 2001.

———(and Mark Dawidziak, composer). Horton Foote's "The Shape of the River": The Lost Teleplay about Mark Twain, with History and Analysis by Mark Dawidziak. New York: Applause Books, 2003.

———(and Marion Castleberry, ed.). Genesis of an American Playwright. Waco: Baylor University Press, 2004.

———. Plays, by year produced:

Texas Town, 1941

Only the Heart, 1942

Only the Heart, 1944 (Broadway)

Celebration, 1950

The Chase, 1952

The Trip to Bountiful, 1953

The Traveling Lady, 1954

John Turner Davis, 1956

The Midnight Caller, 1956

Tomorrow, 1968

A Young Lady of Property, 1976

Night Seasons, 1977

Courtship, 1978

Nineteen-Eighteen, 1979

Valentine's Day, 1980

In a Coffin in Egypt, 1980

Blind Date, 1981

The Man Who Climbed the Pecan Tree, 1981

The Old Friends, 1982

The Roads to Home (three one-act plays: "Nightingale," "The Dearest of Friends," and "Spring Dance"), 1982

Cousins, 1983

Courtship, 1984

Road to the Graveyard (one-act play), 1985

Lily Dale, 1986

The Widow Claire, 1986

The Habitation of Dragons, 1988

Dividing the Estate, 1989

Talking Pictures, 1990

*Four Plays at the Signature Theater: "Talking Pictures," "Night Seasons,"
"The Young Man from Atlanta," "Laura Dennis,"* 1994–1995

Old Man (teleplay based on the Faulkner novel), 1996

The Young Man from Atlanta, 1997

The Death of Papa, 1997

Vernon Early, 1998

The Last of the Thorntons, 2000

The Carpetbagger's Children, 2001

The Actor, 2002

Friedman, Kinky. *Greenwich Killing Time.* New York: Beech Tree, 1986; Bantam, 1987.

———. *A Case of Lone Star.* New York: Beech Tree, 1987; Berkley, 1988.

———. *When the Cat's Away.* New York: Beech Tree, 1988; Berkley, 1989.

———. *Frequent Flyer.* New York: William Morrow, 1989; Berkley, 1990.

———. *Musical Chairs.* New York: William Morrow, 1991.

———. *Kinky Friedman's Crime Club: "Greenwich Killing Time," "A Case of Lone Star," and "When the Cat's Away."* London: Faber and Faber, 1993.

———. *Elvis, Jesus, and Coca-Cola.* New York: Simon and Schuster, 1993; London: Faber and Faber, 1994; New York: Bantam, 1996.

———. *More Kinky Friedman: "Musical Chairs," "Frequent Flyer," and "Elvis, Jesus, and Coca-Cola."* London: Faber and Faber, 1993.

———. *Three Complete Mysteries.* New York: Wings Books, 1993.

———. *Armadillos and Old Lace.* New York: Simon and Schuster, 1994; Bantam, 1995.

———. *God Bless John Wayne.* New York: Simon and Schuster, 1995; London: Faber and Faber, 1995; New York: Bantam, 1996.

———. *The Love Song of J. Edgar Hoover.* New York: Simon and Schuster, 1996; Rockland, Me.: Wheeler, 1996; New York: Ballantine, 1997.

———. *Roadkill.* New York: Simon and Schuster, 1997; Ballantine, 1998.

———. *Blast from the Past.* New York: Simon and Schuster, 1998.

———. *Spanking Watson.* New York: Simon and Schuster, 1999.

———. *Mile High Club.* New York: Simon and Schuster, 2000.

———. *Kinky Friedman's Guide to Texas Etiquette: Or How to Get to Heaven or Hell without Going through Dallas–Fort Worth.* New York: William Morrow, 2001.

———. *Steppin' on a Rainbow.* New York: Simon and Schuster, 2001.

———. *Meanwhile, Back at the Ranch.* New York: Simon and Schuster, 2002; Pocket Star Books, 2003.

———. *Kill Two Birds and Get Stoned.* New York: William Morrow, 2003.

———. *Ohrensausen.* Munich: Heyne, 2003.

———. *Threebies: Kinky Friedman.* London: Faber and Faber, 2003.

———. *The Great Psychedelic Armadillo Picnic: A "Walk" in Austin.* New York: Crown, 2004.

———. *The Prisoner of Vandam Street.* New York: Simon and Schuster, 2004.

———. *'Scuse Me While I Whip This Out: Reflections on Country Singers, Presidents, and Other Troublemakers.* New York: William Morrow, 2004.

Furman, Laura. *The Glass House: A Novella and Stories.* New York: Viking, 1980.

———. *The Shadow Line.* New York: Viking, 1982.

———. *Watch Time Fly: Stories.* New York: Viking, 1983.

———. *Tuxedo Park.* New York: Summit Books, 1986.

———. *Ordinary Paradise: A Memoir.* Houston: Winedale Publishing, 1998.

———. *Drinking with the Cook: Stories.* Houston: Winedale Publishing, 2000.

———, ed. *The O. Henry Prize Stories 2003.* New York: Anchor, 2003.

Gilb, Dagoberto. *Winners on the Pass Line.* El Paso: Cinco Puntos Press, 1985.

———. *The Magic of Blood.* Albuquerque: University of New Mexico Press, 1994; New York: Grove Press, 1994.

———. *The Last Known Residence of Mickey Acuña.* Boston: Atlantic Monthly Press, 1984; New York: Grove Press, 1995.

———. *Woodcuts of Women.* New York: Grove Press, 2001.

———. *Gritos: Essays.* New York: Grove/Atlantic, 2003.

Goetzmann, William H. *Army Exploration in the American West, 1803–1863.* New Haven: Yale University Press, 1959. Republished with new introduction by Texas State Historical Association, 1991.

———. *Exploration and Empire: The Explorer and Scientist in the Winning of the American West.* New York: Knopf, 1966.

———. *When the Eagle Screamed: The Romantic Horizon in American Diplomacy, 1800–1860.* New York: John Wiley and Sons, 1966. Rev. ed., Norman: University of Oklahoma Press, 2000.

————. *The Mountain Man.* Cody, Wyo.: Buffalo Bill Historical Center; Lincoln: University of Nebraska Press, 1978.

————. *New Lands, New Men: America and the Second Great Age of Discovery.* New York: Viking Press, 1986. Reprinted by Texas State Historical Association, 1995.

————(and William N. Goetzmann). *The West of the Imagination.* New York: Norton, 1986. This book accompanies a six-part television series for PBS of the same name which Dr. Goetzmann created and wrote for KERA, Dallas, and which aired nationwide beginning September 22, 1986.

————. *Looking at the Land of Promise: Pioneer Images of the Pacific Northwest.* Pullman: Washington State University Press, 1988.

————. *The First Americans: Photographs from the Library of Congress,* Number 1 in the Library of Congress Classics Series. Washington, D.C.: Starwood Publishing, 1991.

————. *Sam Chamberlain's Mexican War: The San Jacinto Museum of History Paintings.* Austin: Texas State Historical Association, 1993.

————. *Les premiers Americains,* French translation of *The First Americans: Photographs from the Library of Congress.* Paris: Bibliothèque de L'Image, 1995.

————. *Les Indiens: Aqualles de Karl Bodmer.* Paris: Bibliothèque de L'Image, 1996.

————(and Glyndwr Williams). *The Atlas of North American Exploration: From the Norse Voyages to the Race to the Pole.* Norman: University of Oklahoma Press, 1998.

————(coeditor, with Tom D. Crouch). *World Explorers of Distant Frontiers.* New York: Chelsea House: 1999.

————, ed. (and Jared Stallones). *Zebulon Pike and the Explorers of the American Southwest.* New York: Chelsea House: 1999.

————(coeditor, with Nathan Glazer and Martin E. Marty). *Estados Unidos.* Barcelona: Editorial Labor, 2001.

Graves, John. *Goodbye to a River.* New York: Knopf, 1960.

————. *Hard Scrabble: Observations on a Patch of Land.* New York: Knopf, 1974.

————(text; photographs by Jim Bones). *Texas Heartland: A Hill Country Year.* College Station: Texas A&M University Press, 1975.

————. *From a Limestone Ledge: Some Essays and Other Ruminations about Country Life in Texas.* New York: Knopf, 1980.

————. (John Groth, illustrator). *The Last Running.* New York: Lyons and Burford, 1990.

———. *Self-Portrait, with Birds: Some Semi-Ornithological Recollections*. Dallas: Chama Press, 1991, and SourceCenter, Inc., 1991 (John Depol, wood engravings; limited edition).

———. *A John Graves Reader*. Austin: University of Texas Press, 1996.

———(essay, "Self Portrait, with Birds"; commentary and art by Scott Gentling and Stuart Gentling). *Of Birds and Texas*. Austin: University of Texas Press, 2001.

———(essay; photographs by Wyman Meinzer). *Texas Rivers*. Reprint, Austin: Texas Parks and Wildlife Press, 2002.

———(essay; photographs by Wyman Meinzer). *Texas Hill Country*. Austin: University of Texas Press, 2003.

———. *Myself and Strangers: A Memoir of Apprenticeship*. New York: Knopf, 2004.

Haley, James L. *The Buffalo War: The History of the Red River Indian Uprising of 1874*. New York: Doubleday, 1976; trade paperback reprint, Norman: University of Oklahoma Press, 1986; commemorative reprint, Abilene, Tex.: State House Press, 1998; Italian edition, Edizione Piemme, SpA, Sasale Monferrato, 2001.

———. *Apaches: A History and Culture Portrait*. New York: Doubleday, 1981; Italian edition, Ugo Mursia Editore, SpA, Milan, 1986; trade paperback reprint, Norman: University of Oklahoma Press, 1997.

———. *Texas: An Album of History*. New York: Doubleday, 1985; St. Martin's, 1991.

———. *The Kings of San Carlos*. New York: Doubleday, 1987.

———. *The Lions of Tsavo*. New York: Bantam, 1989; Italian edition, Marco Polillo SpA, Milan, 1996.

———. *Texas: From Spindletop through World War II*. New York: St. Martin's, 1993.

———. *Final Refuge: A Novel of Eco-Terrorism*. New York: St. Martin's, 1994.

———. *Stephen F. Austin and the Founding of Texas*. New York: PowerPlus Books, 2002.

———. *Sam Houston*. Norman: University of Oklahoma Press, 2002.

———. *The Epic History of Texas*. New York: Free Press/Simon and Schuster, forthcoming.

Harrigan, Stephen. *Aransas*. New York: Random House, 1980.

———. *Jacob's Well: A Novel*. New York: Simon and Schuster, 1984.

———. *A Natural State: Essays on Texas*. Austin: Texas Monthly Press, 1988; University of Texas Press, 1994.

————. *Water and Light: A Diver's Journey to a Coral Reef.* Boston: Houghton Mifflin, 1992; Austin: University of Texas Press, 1999.

————. *Comanche Midnight.* Austin: University of Texas Press, 1995.

————. *The Gates of the Alamo.* New York: Knopf, 2000.

————(and Thomas Ricks Lindley). *Alamo Traces: New Evidence and Conclusions.* San Antonio: Republic of Texas Press, 2003.

Hightower, Jim. *Hard Tomatoes, Hard Times: The Hightower Report.* New York: Hippocrene, 1973.

————. *Eat Your Heart Out: Food Profiteering in America.* New York: Crown, 1975.

————. *Hard Tomatoes, Hard Times: The Original Hightower Report, Unexpurgated, of the Agribusiness Accountability Project on the Failure of America's Land Grant College Complex.* New York: Hippocrene, 1978.

————. *Hard Tomatoes, Hard Times: A Report of the Agribusiness Accountability Project on the Failure of America's Land Grant College Complex.* Rochester, Vt.: Schenkman Books, 1978.

————. *There's Nothing in the Middle of the Road but Yellow Stripes and Dead Armadillos: A Work of Political Subversion.* New York: Harper, 1997.

————. *If the Gods Had Meant Us to Vote, They Would Have Given Us Candidates: More Political Subversion from Jim Hightower.* New York: Harper, 2000.

————. *Thieves in High Places: They've Stolen Our Country and It's Time to Take It Back.* New York: Viking, 2003.

————. *Let's Stop Beating around the Bush.* New York: Viking, 2004.

Hinojosa-Smith, Rolando (English translation by Rosaura Sanchez). *Generaciones y semblanzas.* Berkeley: Editorial Justa Publications, 1977.

————(English translation by Gustavo Valdez and Jose Reyna). *Estampas del valle y otras obras/Sketches of the Valley and Other Works.* Berkeley: Editorial Justa Publications, 1977.

————. *Mi querido Rafa/Dear Rafe.* Houston: Arte Público, 1981.

————. *Rites and Witnesses.* Houston: Arte Público, 1982.

————. *The Valley: A Re-creation in Narrative Prose of a Portfolio of Etchings, Engravings, Sketches, and Silhouettes by Various Artists in Various Styles, Plus a Set of Photographs from a Family Album.* Ypsilanti, Mich.: Bilingual Press, 1983.

————. *Partners in Crime: A Rafe Buenrostro Mystery.* Houston: Arte Público, 1985.

————. (English translation by Julia Cruz). *Claros Varones de Belken/Fair Gentlemen of Belken County.* Tempe, Ariz.: Bilingue, 1986.

————. *This Migrant Earth* (Hinojosa-Smith's English rendition of Tomás Rivera's *Y no se lo tragó la tierra*). Houston: Arte Público, 1987.

————. *Klail City: A Novel.* Houston: Arte Público, 1987.

————. *Becky and Her Friends.* Houston: Arte Público, 1990.

————. *The Useless Servants.* Houston: Arte Público, 1993.

————. *Ask a Policeman: A Rafe Buenrostro Mystery.* Houston: Arte Público, 1998.

Hirsch, Edward. *For the Sleepwalkers.* New York: Knopf, 1981.

————. *Wild Gratitude: Poems.* New York: Knopf, 1986, reprint, 2003.

————. *The Night Parade: Poems.* New York: Knopf, 1989.

————. *Earthly Measures: Poems.* New York: Knopf, 1994, 2d ed., 2003.

————. *On Love: Poems.* New York: Knopf, 1998.

————. *Responsive Reading: Essays.* Ann Arbor: University of Michigan Press, 1999.

————. *How to Read a Poem: And Fall in Love with Poetry.* New York: Harcourt, 1999.

————. *The Demon and the Angel: Searching for the Source of Artistic Inspiration.* New York: Harcourt, 2002.

————. *Lay Back the Darkness: Poems.* New York: Knopf, 2003.

Howard, Robert E. *Conan the Conqueror: The Hyborean Age.* New York: Gnome Press, 1950.

————. *Sword of Conan.* New York: Gnome Press, 1952.

————. *The Coming of Conan.* New York: Gnome Press, 1953.

————. *King Conan.* New York: Gnome Press, 1953.

————. *Conan the Barbarian.* New York: Gnome Press, 1955.

————. *Almuric.* New York: Ace Books, 1964.

————. *Red Shadows.* Hampton Falls, N.H.: Donald M. Grant, 1968.

————. *Wolfshead.* New York: Lancer Books, 1968.

————. *The Moon of Skulls.* New York: Centaur Press, 1969.

————. *Solomon Kane.* New York: Centaur Books, 1970.

————. *The Hand of Kane.* New York: Centaur Books, 1970.

————. *Marchers of Valhalla.* Hampton Falls, N.H.: Donald M. Grant, 1972.

————. *The Sowers of the Thunder.* Hampton Falls, N.H.: Donald M. Grant, 1973.

————(as Patrick Ervin). *The Incredible Adventures of Dennis Dorgan.* New York: Zebra, 1974.

————. *Worms of the Earth.* Hampton Falls, N.H.: Donald M. Grant, 1974.

———. *Pigeons from Hell.* New York: Zebra, 1976.

———. *The Second Book of Robert E. Howard.* New York: Zebra, 1976.

———. *Swords of Shahrazar.* London: Futura, 1976.

———. *Tigers of the Sea.* New York: Ace Books, 1976.

———. *The People of the Black Circle.* New York: Berkley Medallion, 1977.

———. *Red Nails.* New York: Berkley Medallion, 1977.

———. *Sword Woman.* New York: Zebra, 1977.

———. *Black Canaan.* New York: Berkley, 1978.

———. *Son of the White Wolf.* New York: Berkley, 1978.

———. *The Road of Azrael.* Hampton Falls, N.H.: Donald M. Grant, 1979.

———(with L. Sprague de Camp). *Conan: The Treasure of Tranicos.* New York: Ace Books, 1980.

———. *Jewels of Gwahlur.* Hampton Falls, N.H.: Donald M. Grant, 1985.

———. *Black Vulmea's Vengeance.* New York: Ace Books, 1987.

———. *Three-Bladed Doom.* New York: Ace Books, 1987.

———(with Glenn Lord, Rusty Burke, and S. T. Joshi, reviews). *Robert E. Howard: Selected Letters 1923–1930.* Warwick, R.I.: Necronomicon Press, 1989.

———. *Post Oaks and Sand Roughs.* Hampton Falls, N.H.: Donald M. Grant, 1990.

———. *Bran Mak Morn.* Riverdale, N.Y.: Baen Books, 1994.

———. *Nameless Cults.* Oakland, Calif.: Chaosium, 1998.

Ivins, Molly. *Molly Ivins Can't Say That, Can She?* New York: Random House, 1991.

———. *Nothin' But Good Times Ahead.* New York: Random House, 1993.

———. *You've Got to Dance with Them What Brung You: Politics in the Clinton Years.* New York: Random House, 1998.

———(and Lou Dubose). *Shrub: The Short but Happy Political Life of George W. Bush.* New York: Random House, 2000.

———(and Lou Dubose). *Bushwhacked: Life in George W. Bush's America.* New York: Random House, 2003.

———. *Who Let the Dogs In? Incredible Political Animals I Have Known.* New York: Random House, 2004.

Karr, Mary. *Abacus.* Middletown, Conn.: Wesleyan University Press, 1987.

———. *The Devil's Tour.* New York: New Directions, 1994.

———. *The Liar's Club: A Memoir.* New York: Viking, 1995; Penguin, 1996; Longman, 1997.

———. *Viper Rum.* New York: New Directions, 1998; Penguin, 2001.

———. *Cherry: A Memoir.* New York: Viking, 2000; Penguin (abridged), 2001.

Kelton, Elmer. *Hot Iron.* New York: Ballantine, 1956; Forge, 1998.

———. *Buffalo Wagons.* New York: Ballantine, 1957; Forge, 1997.

———. *Barbed Wire.* New York: Ballantine, 1957; Ace Books, 1986.

———. *The Shadow of a Star.* New York: Ballantine, 1959; Forge, 2004.

———. *The Texas Rifles.* New York: Ballantine, 1960; Forge, 1998.

———. *Donovan.* New York: Ballantine, 1961; Forge, 2003.

———. *Bitter Trail.* New York: Ballantine, 1962; Forge, 1997.

———. *Horsehead Crossing.* New York: Ballantine, 1963; Bantam, 1988.

———. *Massacre at Goliad.* New York: Ballantine, 1965; Forge, 1999.

———. *Llano River.* New York: Ballantine, 1966; Thorndike, Me.: Thorndike Press, 2000.

———. *After the Bugles.* New York: Ballantine, 1967; Forge, 2004.

———. *Captain's Rangers.* New York: Ballantine, 1968; Bantam, 1981; Forge, 1999.

———(as Alex Hawk). *Shotgun Settlement.* New York: Paperback Library, 1969.

———. *Hanging Judge.* New York: Ballantine, 1969; Forge, 2002.

———. *Bowie's Mine.* New York: Ballantine, 1971; Forge, 2003.

———. *The Day the Cowboys Quit.* New York: Doubleday, 1971; Fort Worth: Texas Christian University Press, 1986; New York: Forge, 1999.

———. *Looking Back West* (collection of nonfiction historical articles). San Angelo, Tex.: Talley Press, 1972.

———. *Wagontongue.* New York: Ballantine, 1972; Fort Worth: Texas Christian University Press, 1994.

———. *The Time It Never Rained.* New York: Doubleday, 1973; Fort Worth: Texas Christian University Press, 1984; New York: Bantam 1993; Forge, 1999.

———. *Manhunters.* New York: Ballantine, 1974; Fort Worth: Texas Christian University Press, 1994; New York: Bantam, 1995.

———(as Lee McElroy). *Joe Pepper.* New York: Doubleday, 1975; Forge, 2002.

———(as Lee McElroy). *Long Way to Texas.* New York: Doubleday, 1976; Forge, 2002.

———. *The Good Old Boys.* New York: Doubleday, 1978; Fort Worth: Texas Christian University Press, 1985; New York: Forge, 1999.

———. *The Wolf and the Buffalo.* New York: Doubleday, 1980; Fort Worth: Texas Christian University Press, 1986.

———(as Lee McElroy). *Eyes of the Hawk.* Garden City, N.Y.: Doubleday, 1981; New York: Forge, 2001.

———(text, art of Frank C. McCarthy). *Frank C. McCarthy: The Old West.* Trumbull, Conn.: Greenwich Press, 1981; New York and Trumbull, Conn.: Morrow-Greenwich Workshop, 1992.

———. *Stand Proud: A Texas Saga.* New York: Doubleday, 1984; Fort Worth: Texas Christian University Press, 1990; New York: Forge, 2001.

———. *Dark Thicket.* New York: Doubleday, 1985; Fort Worth: Texas Christian University Press, 1999; New York: Forge, 2001.

———(text, art of Tom Lovell). *Permian: A Continuing Saga.* Midland, Tex.: Permian Basin Petroleum Museum, 1985.

———. *The Big Brand* (short stories). New York: Bantam, 1986.

———. *There's Always Another Chance* (short stories). San Angelo, Tex.: Fort Concho Museum Press, 1986.

———. *The Man Who Rode Midnight.* New York: Doubleday, 1987; Fort Worth: Texas Christian University Press, 1990.

———(as Tom Early). *Sons of Texas, Book One.* New York: Berkley Books, 1989.

———(as Tom Early). *Sons of Texas, Book Two. The Raiders.* New York: Berkley Books, 1989.

———(as Tom Early). *Sons of Texas, Book Three. The Rebels.* New York: Berkley Books, 1990.

———. *Honor at Daybreak.* New York: Doubleday, 1991; Fort Worth: Texas Christian University Press, 2002.

———. *Slaughter.* New York: Doubleday, 1992; New York: Bantam, 1994.

———(text). *The Art of James Bama.* New York and Trumbull, Conn.: Bantam-Greenwich Workshop, 1993.

———. *The Far Canyon.* New York: Doubleday, 1994; New York: Bantam, 1994.

———. *The Pumpkin Rollers.* New York: Forge, 1996.

———. *Cloudy in the West.* New York: Forge, 1997.

———. *Smiling Country.* New York: Forge, 1998.

———. *The Buckskin Line.* New York: Forge, 1999.

———(text, photographs by Kathleen Jo Ryan). *Texas Cattle Barons: Their Families, Land, and Legacy.* Fort Worth: CF Ranch; Berkeley, Calif.: Ten Speed Press, 1999.

———. *Legend.* New York: Leisure Books, 1999.

———. *Badger Boy.* New York: Forge, 2001.

———. *Way of the Coyote.* New York: Forge, 2001.

———. *Ranger's Trail.* New York: Forge, 2003.

———. *Christmas at the Ranch.* Abilene, Tex.: McWhiney Foundation Press, 2003.

———. *Lone Star Rising: The Texas Ranger Trilogy* (includes *The Buckskin Line, Badger Boy, Way of the Coyote*). New York: Forge, 2003.

———. *Texas Vendetta*. New York: Forge, 2004.

Lansdale, Joe R. *Act of Love*. New York: Kensington, 1981.

———(as Ray Slater). *Texas Night Riders*. New York: Leisure Books, 1983.

———. *Dead in the West*. New York: Space and Time, 1986; Fish Creek, Wis.: Cross Roads Press, 1994.

———. *The Magic Wagon*. New York: Doubleday, 1986.

———. *The Nightrunners*. Arlington Heights, Ill.: Dark Harvest, 1987.

———. *The Drive-In*. New York: Bantam, 1988.

———. *By Bizarre Hands*. New York: Avon, 1989.

———. *Cold in July*. New York: Bantam, 1989.

———. *The Drive-In II*. New York: Bantam, 1989.

———. *Savage Season*. New York: Bantam, 1990.

———. *Batman: Captured by the Engines*. New York: Warner Books, 1991.

———. *Stories by Mama Lansdale's Youngest Boy*. Eugene, Ore.: Pulphouse Press, 1991.

———. *Batman in Terror on the High Skies*. New York: Little, Brown, 1992.

———. *Bestsellers Guaranteed*. New York, Avon, 1993.

———. *Electric Gumbo*. New York: Quality Paperback Book Club, 1994.

———(with Tim Truman, illustrator). *Jonah Hex: Two-Gun Mojo*. New York: DC Comics, 1994.

———. *Mucho Mojo*. New York: Mysterious Press, 1994.

———(and Richard Klaw). *Weird Business*. Austin: Mojo Press, 1994.

———(and Thomas Knowles). *The West That Was*. New York: Wings Books, 1994.

———. *Wild West Show*. New York: Random House, 1994.

———. *My Dead Dog, Bobby*. Sacramento, Calif.: Cobblestone Books, 1995.

———. *The Two-Bear Mambo*. New York: Mysterious Press, 1995.

———(and Edgar Rice Burroughs). *Tarzan: The Lost Adventure*. Portland, Ore.: Dark Horse Comics, 1996.

———. *A Fist Full of Stories (and Articles)*. Baltimore: Cemetery Dance Publications, 1996.

———. *Atomic Chili*. Austin: Mojo Press, 1997.

———. *Bad Chili*. New York: Mysterious Press, 1997.

———. *The Good, the Bad, and the Indifferent*. Burton, Mich.: Subterranean Press, 1997.

———. *Writer of the Purple Rage*. New York: Carroll and Graf, 1997.

———. *The Boar*. Burton, Mich.: Subterranean Press, 1998.

———(and Lewis Shiner). *Private Eye Action As You Like It.* Boston: Crossroads
    Press, 1998.
———. *Rumble Tumble.* New York: Mysterious Press, 1998.
———. *Freezer Burn.* New York: Mysterious Press, 1999.
———(with Sam Glanzman, illustrator). *Red Range.* Austin: Mojo Press, 1999.
———. *Something Lumber This Way Comes.* Burton, Mich.: Subterranean
    Press, 1999.
———. *Triple Feature.* Burton, Mich.: Subterranean Press, 1999.
———. *Veil's Visit.* Burton, Mich.: Subterranean Press, 1999.
———. *Waltz of Shadows.* Burton, Mich.: Subterranean Press, 1999.
———. *The Big Blow.* Burton, Mich.: Subterranean Press, 2000.
———. *Blood Dance.* Burton, Mich.: Subterranean Press, 2000.
———. *The Bottoms.* New York: Mysterious Press, 2000.
———. *High Cotton.* Urbana, Ill.: Golden Gryphon, 2000.
———. *Captains Outrageous.* New York: Mysterious Press, 2001.
———. *Zeppelins West.* Burton, Mich.: Subterranean Press, 2001.
———. *For a Few Stories More.* Burton, Mich.: Subterranean Press, 2002.
———. *A Fine Dark Line.* New York: Mysterious Press, 2003.
———. *Flaming London.* Burton, Mich.: Subterranean Press, 2003.
———. *Bubba Ho-Tep.* San Francisco: Night Shade Books, 2004.
———. *Bumper Crop.* Urbana, Ill.: Golden Gryphon Press, 2004.
———. *The Drive-In 3: Bus Tour.* Burton, Mich.: Subterranean Press, 2004.
———. *Sunset and Sawdust.* New York: Knopf, 2004.
Lindsey, David. *Black Gold, Red Death.* New York: Fawcett, 1983.
———. *A Cold Mind.* New York: Harper and Row, 1983.
———. *Heat from Another Sun.* New York: Harper and Row, 1984; New York:
    Crime Line, 1996.
———. *Spiral.* New York: Atheneum, 1986.
———. *In the Lake of the Moon.* New York: Atheneum, 1988.
———. *Mercy.* New York: Doubleday, 1990.
———. *Body of Truth.* New York: Doubleday, 1992.
———. *Absence of Light.* New York: Doubleday, 1994.
———. *Requiem for a Glass Heart.* New York: Doubleday, 1996.
———. *The Color of Night.* New York: Warner Books, 1999.
———. *Animosity.* New York: Warner Books, 2001.
———. *The Rules of Silence.* New York: Warner Books, 2003.
———. *The Face of the Assassin.* New York: Warner Books, 2004.

Longoria, Arturo. *Adios to the Brushlands.* College Station: Texas A&M University Press, 1997.

———. *Keepers of the Wilderness.* College Station: Texas A&M University Press, 2000.

Lopate, Phillip. *The Eyes Don't Always Want to Stay Open: Poems and a Japanese Fairy Tale.* New York: Sun, 1972.

———. *Being with Children.* Garden City, N.Y.: Doubleday, 1975.

———. *The Daily Round: New Poems.* New York: Sun, 1976.

———. *Confessions of a Summer.* Garden City, N.Y.: Doubleday, 1979.

———. *Bachelorhood: Tales of the Metropolis.* Boston: Little, Brown, 1981; New York: Morrow/Avon, 1985; Simon and Schuster, 1989.

———. *The Rug Merchant.* New York: Viking Penguin, 1987.

———. *Against Joie de Vivre: Personal Essays.* New York: Poseidon Press, 1989.

———. *The Art of the Personal Essay: An Anthology from the Classical Era to the Present.* New York: Anchor Books, 1994.

———. *Portrait of My Body: Personal Essays.* New York: Anchor Books, 1996.

———. *Totally, Tenderly, Tragically: Essays and Criticism from a Lifelong Love Affair with the Movies.* New York: Anchor Books, 1998.

———. *The Art of the Essay: The Best of 1999.* New York: Anchor Books, 1999.

———(and Burhan Dogancay, photographer). *Bridge of Dreams: The Rebirth of the Brooklyn Bridge.* New York: Hudson Hills Press, 1999.

———. *Waterfront: A Journey around Manhattan.* New York: Crown, 2004.

Magnuson, James. *No Snakes in This Grass: A Play in One Act.* New York: Samuel French, 1968.

———. *Without Barbarians.* New York: McGraw-Hill, 1974.

———. *Open Season.* New York: Doubleday, 1982.

———. *Money Mountain.* New York: Doubleday, 1984.

———. *The Rundown.* New York: Dial Press, 1987.

———. *Ghost Dancing.* New York: Doubleday, 1989.

———. *Windfall.* New York: Random House, 1999.

McMurtry, Larry. *Horseman, Pass By.* New York: Harper, 1961.

———. *Leaving Cheyenne.* New York: Harper and Row, 1963.

———. *The Last Picture Show.* New York: Dial Press, 1966.

———. *In a Narrow Grave.* Austin: Encino Press, 1968.

———. *Moving On.* New York: Simon and Schuster, 1970.

———. *All My Friends Are Going to Be Strangers.* New York: Simon and Schuster, 1972.

———. *It's Always We Rambled*. New York: Frank Hallman, 1974.

———. *Terms of Endearment*. New York: Simon and Schuster, 1975, 1989.

———. *Somebody's Darling*. New York: Simon and Schuster, 1978.

———. *Cadillac Jack*. New York: Simon and Schuster, 1982.

———. *Desert Rose*. New York: Simon and Schuster, 1983.

———. *Lonesome Dove*. New York: Simon and Schuster, 1985.

———. *Film Flam*. New York: Simon and Schuster, 1987.

———. *Texasville*. New York: Simon and Schuster, 1987.

———. *Anything for Billy*. New York: Simon and Schuster, 1988.

———. *Some Can Whistle*. New York: Simon and Schuster, 1989.

———. *Buffalo Girls*. New York: Simon and Schuster, 1990.

———. *The Evening Star*. New York: Simon and Schuster, 1992.

———. *Streets of Laredo*. New York: Simon and Schuster, 1993.

———. *Dead Man's Walk*. New York: Simon and Schuster, 1995.

———. *The Late Child*. New York: Simon and Schuster, 1995.

———. *Comanche Moon*. New York: Simon and Schuster, 1997.

———. *Zeke and Ned*. New York: Simon and Schuster, 1997.

———. *Crazy Horse*. New York: Viking, 1999.

———. *Duane's Depressed*. New York: Simon and Schuster, 1999.

———. *Walter Benjamin at the Dairy Queen: Reflections at Sixty and Beyond*. New York: Simon and Schuster, 1999.

———. *Boone's Lick*. New York: Simon and Schuster, 2000.

———. *Roads: Driving America's Great Highways*. New York: Simon and Schuster, 2000.

———. *Paradise*. New York: Simon and Schuster, 2001.

———. *Sacagawea's Nickname: Essays on the American West*. New York: Simon and Schuster, 2001.

———. *Sin Killer: The Berrybender Narratives, Book 1*. New York: Simon and Schuster, 2002.

———. *The Wandering Hill: The Berrybender Narratives, Book 2*. New York: Simon and Schuster, 2003.

———. *By Sorrow's River: The Berrybender Narratives, Book 3*. New York: Simon and Schuster, 2003.

———. *Folly and Glory: The Berrybender Narratives, Book 4*. New York: Simon and Schuster, 2004.

Mora, Pat. *Chants*. Houston: Arte Público, 1984.

———. *Borders*. Houston: Arte Público, 1986.

———. *Communion*. Houston: Arte Público, 1991.

———. *A Birthday Basket for Tia*. New York: Simon and Schuster, 1992.

———. *Nepantla: Essays from the Land in the Middle*. Albuquerque: University of New Mexico Press, 1993.

———. *Agua, agua, agua*. Glenview, Ill.: Goodyear Books, 1994.

———. *The Desert Is My Mother/El desierto es mi madre*. Houston: Piñata Books, 1994.

———. *Listen to the Desert/Oye al desierto*. New York: Clarion, 1994.

———. *Pablo's Tree*. New York: Simon and Schuster, 1994.

———. *Agua santa/Holy Water*. Boston: Beacon, 1995.

———. *The Gift of the Poinsettia/El regalo de la flor de nochebuena*. Houston: Piñata Books, 1995.

———. *The Race of Toad and Deer*. New York: Orchard Books, 1995.

———. *Confetti: Poems for Children*. New York: Lee and Low, 1996.

———. *Uno, dos, tres/One, Two, Three*. New York: Clarion Books, 1996.

———. *Aunt Carmen's Book of Practical Saints*. Boston: Beacon, 1997.

———. *House of Houses*. Boston: Beacon, 1997.

———. *Tomás and the Library Lady*. New York: Knopf, 1997.

———. *Delicious Hullabaloo/Pachanga deliciosa*. Houston: Piñata Books, 1998.

———. *This Big Sky*. New York: Scholastic, 1998.

———. *The Rainbow Tulip*. New York: Viking, 1999.

———. *My Own True Name: New and Selected Poems for Young Adults, 1984–1999*. Houston: Piñata Books, 2000.

———. *The Night the Moon Fell*. Toronto: Groundwood Books, 2000.

———. *The Bakery Lady/La señora de la panadería*. Houston: Piñata Books, 2001.

———. *A Library for Juana: The World of Sor Juana Inés*. New York: Knopf, 2002.

———. *Maria Paints the Hills*. Sante Fe: Museum of New Mexico Press, 2002.

———. *Una biblioteca para Juana*. New York: Knopf, 2002.

Nail, Frances. *Crow in the House, Wolf at the Door*. Austin: City Desk Press, 1995.

———. *When Pears and Lilacs Bloomed*. Austin: Coming of Age Press, 1995.

———. *God, Cars, and Souvenirs*. Austin: City Desk Press, 1998.

———. *I Am Not the Woman I Was*. Austin: Eakin Press, 2003.

Nye, Naomi Shihab. *Different Ways to Pray*. Portland, Ore.: Far Corner Books, 1980.

———. *Hugging the Jukebox*. New York: Dutton, 1982.

———. *Yellow Glove*. Portland, Ore.: Far Corner Books, 1986.

———. *Invisible*. Denton, Tex.: Trilobite Press, 1987.

———. *Mint.* Brockport, N.Y.: State Street Press, 1991.

———, ed. *This Same Sky: A Collection of Poems from around the World.* New York: Simon and Schuster, 1992.

———. *Travel Alarm.* Houston: Wings Press, 1992.

———. *Red Suitcase: Poems.* Brockport, N.Y.: BOA Editions, 1994.

———. *Sitti's Secrets.* New York: Scott Foresman, 1994.

———(with Yu Cha Pak, illustrator). *Benito's Dream Bottle.* New York: Simon and Schuster, 1995.

———. *Words under the Words: Selected Poems.* Portland, Ore.: Eighth Mountain Press, 1995.

———. *Habibi.* New York: Simon and Schuster, 1996.

———(coeditor, with Paul B. Janeczko). *I Feel a Little Jumpy around You: A Book of Her Poems and His Poems Collected in Pairs.* New York: Simon and Schuster, 1996.

———. *Never in a Hurry: Essays on People and Places.* Columbia: University of South Carolina Press, 1996.

———, ed. *The Tree Is Older Than You Are: A Bilingual Gathering of Poems and Stories from Mexico.* New York: Macmillan, 1996.

———(with Vivienne Flesher, illustrator). *Lullaby Raft.* New York: Simon and Schuster, 1997.

———. *Fuel: Poems.* Rochester, N.Y.: BOA Editions, 1998.

———, ed. *The Space between Our Footsteps: Poems and Paintings from the Middle East.* New York: Simon and Schuster, 1998.

———, ed. *What Have You Lost?* New York: Greenwillow, 1999; New York: Harper-Tempest, 2001.

———, ed. (with Dan Yaccarino, illustrator). *Come with Me: Poems for a Journey.* New York: Greenwillow, 2000.

———, ed. (with Ashley Bryan, illustrator). *Salting the Ocean: 100 Poems by Young People.* New York: Greenwillow, 2000.

———. *Mint Snowball.* Tallahassee, Fla.: Anhinga Press, 2001.

———. *19 Varieties of Gazelle: Poems of the Middle East.* New York: Greenwillow, 2002.

———, ed. *The Flag of Childhood: Poems of the Middle East.* New York: Aladdin, 2002.

———. (with pictures by Nancy Carpenter). *Baby Radar.* New York: Greenwillow, 2003.

———, ed. *Is This Forever, or What? Poems and Paintings from Texas.* New York: Greenwillow, 2004.

Sachar, Louis. *Sideways Stories from Wayside School*. New York: Avon, 1978.

———. *Johnny's in the Basement*. New York: Avon, 1981.

———. *Someday Angeline*. New York: Turtleback, 1983.

———. *Sixth Grade Secrets*. New York: Scholastic, 1987.

———. *There's a Boy in the Girls' Bathroom*. New York: Knopf, 1987.

———. *The Boy Who Lost His Face*. New York: Random House, 1989.

———. *Sideways Arithmetic from Wayside School*. New York: Scholastic, 1989.

———. *Wayside School Is Falling Down*. New York: Avon, 1989.

———. *Dogs Don't Tell Jokes*. New York: Random House, 1991.

———. *Marvin Redpost: Kidnapped at Birth?* New York: Random House, 1992.

———. *Monkey Soup*. New York: Knopf, 1992.

———. *Marvin Redpost: Is He a Girl?* New York: Random House, 1993.

———. *Marvin Redpost: Why Pick on Me?* New York: Random House, 1993.

———. *Marvin Redpost: Alone in His Teacher's House*. New York: Random House, 1994.

———. *More Sideways Arithmetic from Wayside School*. New York: Scholastic, 1994.

———. *Wayside School Gets a Little Stranger*. New York: Avon, 1995.

———. *Holes*. New York: Farrar, Straus, and Giroux, 1998; New York: Yearling Books, 2000, 2003.

———. *Marvin Redpost: Class President*. New York: Random House, 1999.

———. *Marvin Redpost: Super Fast, Out of Control*. New York: Random House, 1999.

———. *Marvin Redpost: A Flying Birthday Cake?* New York: Random House, 1999.

———. *Marvin Redpost: A Magic Crystal*. New York: Random House, 2000.

Shrake, Edwin "Bud." *Blood Reckoning*. New York: Bantam, 1962.

———. *But Not for Love*. Garden City, N.Y.: Doubleday, 1964.

———. *Blessed McGill*. New York: Doubleday, 1968.

———(with Barbara M. Whitehead, illustrator). *Peter Arbiter*. Austin: Encino Press, 1973.

———. *Strange Peaches*. New York: Harper's Magazine Press, 1973.

———. *Night Never Falls*. New York: Random House, 1987.

———. *The Borderland: A Novel of Texas*. New York: Hyperion, 2000.

———. *Billy Boy*. New York: Simon and Schuster, 2001.

———. As coauthor:

Nelson, Willie. *Willie: An Autobiography*. New York: Simon and Schuster, 1992.

Penick, Harvey. *Harvey Penick's Little Red Book: Lessons and Teachings from a Lifetime in Golf.* New York: Simon and Schuster, 1992.

———. *And If You Play Golf, You're My Friend: Further Reflections of a Grown Caddie.* New York: Simon and Schuster, 1993.

———. *For All Who Love the Game: Lessons and Teachings for Women.* New York: Simon and Schuster, 1995.

———. *The Game for a Lifetime: More Lessons and Teachings.* New York: Simon and Schuster, 1996.

———. *The Wisdom of Harvey Penick: Lessons and Thoughts from the Collected Writings of Golf's Best-Loved Teacher.* New York: Simon and Schuster, 1997.

Switzer, Barry. *The Bootlegger's Boy.* New York: William Morrow, 1990.

(with Bud Jennings). Jerry Jeff Walker. *Gypsy Songman.* San Francisco: Woodford, 1999.

Sterling, Bruce. *Involution Ocean.* New York: Jove, 1977.

———. *The Artificial Kid.* New York: Harper and Row, 1980.

———. *Schismatrix.* New York: Arbor House, 1985.

———, ed. *Mirrorshades: The Cyberpunk Anthology.* Westminster, Md.: Arbor House, 1986; New York: Ace Books, 1988.

———. *Islands in the Net.* New York: Arbor House, 1988.

———. *Crystal Express.* Sauk City, Wis.: Arkham House, 1989.

———(and William Gibson). *The Difference Engine.* New York: Bantam, 1991.

———. *Globalhead: Stories.* Shingletown, Calif.: Mark V. Zeising, 1992.

———. *The Hacker Crackdown: Law and Disorder on the Electronic Frontier.* New York: Bantam, 1992.

———. *Heavy Weather.* New York: Bantam, 1994.

———. *Holy Fire.* New York: Bantam, 1996.

———. *Schismatrix Plus.* New York: Ace Books, 1996.

———. *Distraction: A Novel.* New York: Bantam, 1998.

———. *A Good Old-fashioned Future: Stories.* New York: Bantam, 1999.

———. *Zeitgeist: A Novel of Metamorphosis.* New York: Bantam, 2000.

———. *Tomorrow Now: Envisioning the Next Fifty Years.* New York: Random House Trade, 2003.

———. *The Zenith Angle.* New York: Del Ray, 2004.

Tanney, Katherine. *Carousel of Progress.* New York: Villard, 2001.

Thomas, Lorenzo. *Fit Music: California Songs.* New York: Angel Hair Books (now United Artists Books), 1972.

———. *Dracula.* New York: Angel Hair Books (now United Artists Books), 1973.

———. *Framing the Sunrise.* N.p.: Sun Be/Am Associates, 1975.

———. *The Bathers: Selected Poems.* New York: Reed, Cannon (now Reed, Cannon, and Johnson), 1978.

———. *Chances Are Few.* Berkeley: Blue Wind Press, 1979.

———. *Sing the Sun Up: Creative Writing Ideas from African American Literature.* New York: Teachers and Writers Collaborative, 1988.

———. *Es gibt Zeugen/There Are Witnesses.* Eggingen: Isele, 1996.

———. *Extraordinary Measures: Afrocentric Modernism and Twentieth-Century American Poetry.* Tuscaloosa: University of Alabama Press, 2000.

Williams, Lori Aurelia. *When Kambia Elaine Flew In from Neptune.* New York: Simon and Schuster, 2000.

———. *Shayla's Double Brown Baby Blues.* New York: Simon and Schuster, 2001.

———. *Broken China, Falling Cherubs, and Aliens.* New York: Simon and Schuster, forthcoming.

Willis Walker, Mary. *Zero at the Bone.* New York: St. Martin's, 1991.

———. *The Red Scream.* New York: Doubleday, 1994; Bantam, 1995.

———. *Under the Beetle's Cellar.* New York: Doubleday, 1995; Bantam, 1996.

———. *All the Dead Lie Down.* New York: Doubleday, 1998; Bantam, 2002.

Wittliff, Bill. Screenplays and teleplays by script date and production release date:

———. *Barbarosa* (screenplay), 1973 (1982 release).

———. *Thaddeus Rose and Eddie* (screenplay), 1973 (1978 release).

———. *Raggedy Man* (screenplay), 1973 (1981 release).

———. *Redheaded Stranger* (screenplay), 1979 (1986 release).

———. *Country* (screenplay), 1984 (1984 release).

———. *The Cowboy Way* (screenplay), 1986 (1994 release).

———. *Lonesome Dove* (teleplay), 1985–1990 (1989 release). The screenplay originated as a script for John Wayne, Henry Fonda, and James Stewart, with the script written by Larry McMurtry in conjunction with Peter Bogdanovich in 1972. The project was not produced, and McMurtry instead chose to write an expansive novel about Texas's past. In 1985 McMurtry's book was published and received the 1985 Pulitzer Prize, among other notable awards. That same year, Motown Productions and CBS Television contracted to broadcast the miniseries. Bill Wittliff, whose Western scripts included "Barbarosa" and "Redheaded Stranger," signed on to write the script for the "Lonesome Dove" teleplay.

———. *Ned Blessing* (teleplay, pilot), 1991–1992 (1991 release).

———. *Ned Blessing* (teleplay, six-part series), 1992–1993 (1993 release).

————. *Legends of the Fall* (screenplay), 1990 (1994 release).

————. *The Perfect Storm* (screenplay adaptation of Sebastian Junger book), 2000 release.

————. *Vaquero: Genesis of the Texas Cowboy.* Austin: University of Texas Press, 2004.

Wright, Bill. *The Tiguas: Pueblo Indians of Texas.* El Paso: Texas Western Press, 1993.

————. *The Texas Kickapoo: Keepers of Tradition.* El Paso: Texas Western Press, 1996.

————. *Portraits from the Desert: Bill Wright's Big Bend.* Austin: University of Texas Press, 1998.

————. *People's Lives: A Photographic Celebration of the Human Spirit.* Austin: University of Texas Press, 2001.

Wright, Lawrence. *City Children, Country Summer: A Story of Ghetto Children among the Amish.* New York: Scribner, 1979.

————. *In the New World: Growing Up with America, 1960–1984.* New York: Vintage, 1989.

————. *Saints and Sinners.* New York: Knopf, 1993.

————. *Remembering Satan: A Case of Recovered Memory and the Shattering of an American Family.* New York: Knopf, 1994.

————. *Twins: And What They Tell Us about Who We Are.* New York: John Wiley and Sons, 1998.

————. *The Siege* (screenplay), 1998 release.

————. *God's Favorite.* New York: Simon and Schuster, 2000.

Wyse, Sharon. *The Box Children.* New York: Riverhead Books, 2002.

Zeder, Suzan. *Step on a Crack.* Louisville: Anchorage, 1976.

————. *Wiley and the Hairy Man.* Louisville: Anchorage, 1978.

————. *Ozma of Oz.* Louisville: Anchorage, 1980.

————. *The Play Called Noah's Flood.* Louisville: Anchorage, 1984.

————. *Doors.* Louisville: Anchorage, 1986.

————. *Mother Hicks.* Louisville: Anchorage, 1987.

————. *In a Room Somewhere* (Musical). Louisville: Anchorage, 1988.

————. *An Evening at Versailles: Featuring the Miser by J. B. P. Moliere.* Louisville: Anchorage, 1989.

————. *Wish in One Hand, Spit in the Other: A Collection of Plays by Suzan Zeder.* Louisville: Anchorage, 1990.

————. *The Death and Life of Sherlock Holmes.* Louisville: Anchorage, 1994.

———. *Do Not Go Gentle*. Woodstock, Ill.: Dramatic Publishing Company, 1996.

———. *The Taste of Sunrise*. Louisville: Anchorage, 2000.

———. *Time Again in Oz*. Produced at the University of Texas at Austin, April 2000.

Index